CRACKING THE BIBLE CODE

CRACKING THE BIBLE CODE

Jeffrey Satinover, M.D.

Quill
WILLIAM MORROW
NEW YORK

Library of Congress Cataloging-in-Publication Data
Satinover, Jeffrey, 1947-
Cracking the Bible code / Jeffrey Satinover.
p.   cm.
Includes bibliographical references and index.
ISBN 0-688-15994-X
1. Ciphers in the Bible.   2. Bible. O. T. Pentateuch—Data
processing.   3. Bible. O. T. Pentateuch—Inspiration.
4. Satinover, Jeffrey, 1947-   .   5. Witztum, Doron.   6. Rips,
Eliyahu.   I. Title.
BS1225.5.S28   1997
222'.106—dc21   97-25280
CIP

Printed in the United States of America

First Quill Edition 1998

1   2   3   4   5   6   7   8   9   10

BOOK DESIGN BY OKSANA KUSHNIR

For Julie, Sarah, Anne, and Jenny:

ME SKB PB PS . . . my four shining hearts

ACKNOWLEDGMENTS

I owe a tremendous debt of gratitude to the many people who have helped make this book a reality. Jack and Esther Freedman not only opened many doors in the Orthodox community, they opened their house to me and to my wife for a Sabbath weekend that we will long remember and cherish. Rabbi Yoel Weissmandl graciously took time from his busy schedule to speak with me at length about his illustrious grandfather, Rabbi Michael Ber Weissmandl, זצ״ל. If I have succeeded in honoring this great, unsung sage of the twentieth century with even a small fraction of what he deserves, it will be counted a great merit. Mr. and Mrs. Romi Cohn likewise opened their home, full of charm and wit and beauty, and Mr. Cohn opened his heart as well, to tell of some of his harrowing experiences during the Holocaust, as a student of Rabbi Weissmandl. From Siegmund Forst, I learned some of the most heartrending tales of the great sage, from both before the Holocaust when they lived and worked together in Slovakia, and after, in America. I am deeply indebted to him for his courtesy and assistance. Thank you, too, Yisroel Stern, for sharing with me in such moving detail your own extraordinary experiences with Rabbi Weissmandl during the Holocaust.

Rabbi Pinchas Kasnett has been a devoted teacher of Torah from whom I, my wife, and my children have learned much over the years. He has been a great help in matters of interpretation. Rabbi Daniel Lapin and his close associate at Toward Tradition, Yarden Weidenfeld, have been a consistent source of guidance and support. Rabbi Lapin's nose for some of the hidden "landmines" in the subject of this book has been especially keen. He was one of the first supporters of the scientific research herein documented. I also spent a wonderful Sabbath weekend with Rabbi Moshe Zeldman and his lovely family in the community of Neve Yaakov, outside Jerusalem. I greatly appreciate the many efforts he made on my behalf. I owe a similar thank you to Rabbi Eric Coopersmith, also in Jerusalem. Both are instrumental in the well-deserved success of the Aish HaTorah outreach program, Discovery. Rabbi Yehoshua Hecht of the Beth Israel Synagogue in Norwalk, Connecticut, has not only been a wonderful teacher to me, my wife, and my children, he has been a wonderful example as well. He carefully read through the entire manuscript and made many helpful suggestions and corrections. My warm thanks to him and his wife, Freida, for their open door and enthusiastic support.

The codes material in the United States is presented to the public by the Jerusalem-headquartered Aish HaTorah in the context of their Discovery Seminars. I owe to this organization a note of personal gratitude for how much they taught me about my own heritage. To Rabbi Daniel Mechanic, senior codes lecturer for the American Discovery programs: my very special thanks. I suppose there are few people in the world who understand as well as I do now how much of his heart, soul, and energy are devoted to love of Torah—and to the well-being of the Jewish people. Not only are you a superb teacher, you have the rare gift of making complex and difficult subjects come alive. There are many sections of this book that have benefited greatly because of your enthusiastic assistance.

I want to offer an especially warm thanks to Professor Robert Kass of the Department of Statistics at Carnegie-Mellon University in Pittsburgh for his many helpful comments—and for his admirable degree of professionalism; to Professor Steven Portnoy, also at the University of Illinois, for his keen insights; and in particular, to Eliyahu Rips of the Einstein Institute of Mathematics at the Hebrew University of Jerusalem, for his openness, fairmindedness, and courage—in addition to his many helpful explanations. Professors Bob Szcarba and Frank Firk at Yale: your teaching has been a genuine inspiration to me, and in subtle ways has influenced this book. I do hope you will forgive my abrupt appearances and disappearances as I flew off hither and yon to compete the project on a tight deadline. Thank you, too, to Yochanan Spielberg, for your assistance in clarifying some of the material when I first learned of the codes; to Matthew Berke at First Things for forwarding an early draft of an article on the Bible Code to *Bible Review;* to

Herschel Shanks and Molly Dewsnap at the Biblical Archaeology Society for editing and publishing it. What we all owe to Doron Witztum will become ever clearer.

From those scientists and mathematicians who struggle—as do I—to unite the noblest aims of the Judeo-Christian traditions to the dispassionate rigor of science, I have learned much, and offer a heartfelt salute. I have in mind, in particular, Dr. John Taylor of the Department of Mathematics at McGill University—an outstanding mathematician, a devout Christian, a severe critic, and a valued friend. Though Harold Gans of the National Security Agency (now retired) was operating under severe constraints because of his sensitive position, I also owe thanks—and offer my admiration, as well. Throughout the long process of writing he has been an invaluable source of inspiration to me as he has been to many others: Harold is not only a superb cryptologist (he is, in fact, a Meritorious Civilian Service honoree of the NSA), he is a man of great warmth, faith, integrity, and patriotism. That this book has opened the possibility of a friendship with him I count as a great and unexpected personal bonus.

Janis Vallely and Martha Kaplan have been superb literary agents. I learned more from them than I could possibly say at reasonable length. Thank you both for your encouragement, instruction, support, and guidance. To Joyce Ashley, longtime friend, professional colleague, fellow author, and (for the past fifteen years) mother-in-law and devoted grandmother to my children: a heartfelt hug for setting the process in motion. My assistant, Shirley Ciotti, cannot possibly hear often enough how grateful I am to her for her superb organizational skills, devotion, and excellence with people.

My editor at William Morrow, Toni Sciarra, has been an absolute delight to work with. Her clarity, consistency, grasp of the whole, and sensitivity to nuance have been key to this book—as has her willingness to tackle so complex a project under tight time constraints. Katharine Cluverius, Sharyn Rosenblum, Karen Auerbach, and Jennifer Brawer: your enthusiasm was infectious, and most gratefully received. Brad Foltz: a special thanks for the extra effort you put in—and my genuine pleasure at your artistic gifts. Tom Nau: thank you for so graciously managing the unusually large number of technical details.

Authors seem routinely to thank their families as well. There is nothing routine about it at all, and after this book in particular, I will read every other such acknowledgment with a far keener appreciation for what lies behind them. The truth is that writing this book *has* required tremendous support—and sacrifice—from my wife, Julie, and my three wonderful daughters, Sarah (10), Anne (9), and Jenny (6). (Jenny put it directly: "Are you still working on that stupid book, Dad?") I promised them all that I would make it up to them and I am herewith putting that promise in writing, in public. In addition to their general support, all four gave explicit, extensive assistance to me in editing early drafts of every chapter, and in assembling the complex "arrays"—yes, even Jenny. Finally, I herewith relinquish all seeming territorial claims to the "brownie kitchen" and the breakfast table.

There are many other people—scientists, people of faith, both Jewish and Christian, seekers, skeptics—who have spoken to me only on condition of anonymity. To them, I offer a heartfelt "thank you" as well. I only hope the time will come when I may offer my gratitude openly.

The subject matter of the following story is multilayered, and each layer represents a different discipline, complex and subtle in its own right. There are many opportunities for error to creep in. I have done whatever I could to prevent these—many of the above people have been extraordinarily helpful in that regard. But I bear sole responsibility for any mistakes that may yet be hiding in the pages that follow.

CONTENTS

Our referees were baffled: their prior beliefs made them
think the Book of Genesis could not possibly contain meaningful
references to modern-day individuals, yet when the authors carried
out additional analyses and checks the effect persisted. The paper is
thus offered to *Statistical Science* readers as a challenging puzzle.

—*Robert Kass, Ph.D., Editor*
Chairman of the Department of Statistics
Carnegie-Mellon University

April 1989, Washington, D.C.
Offices of the National Security Agency

Harold Gans paced the floor, stroking his neatly clipped beard in concentration. He glanced upward at the government-issue clock and cupped his hand against the back of his head. Five more minutes, he thought, or ten, and the computer run at home would be finished. The many projects he juggled here at work all sat on a back burner. No matter that—as his starchy colleagues at Foggy Bottom were fond of putting it at every occasion—"upon our work hangs the fate of men and nations." He only hoped that none of the usual crises would arise in the next half hour or so to pull him away from the conclusion of his private—and in his view, far more consequential—project.

Gans was a senior cryptologic mathematician with the United States Department of Defense, part of the long tradition of brilliant backroom technical types that began with the Manhattan Project. Today, however, he was not awaiting an analysis churned out by one of many parallel-linked Cray supercomputers owned by the agency in abundance. He was waiting for a phone call from his wife, in which she would simply read him a number—possibly, but not likely, a very small number—the end product of a nonstop, nineteen-day-long calculation he had programmed into a modest 386 desktop clone he kept at home. If the number was in fact small enough, it would confirm the outrageous claim: that between the mid to late 1980s a team of Israeli scientists had found encoded in the ancient Hebrew text of Genesis details from the lives of modern-day individuals. In short, he, and the Israelis before him, would have demonstrated—using the hardest and most rigorous of scientific methods—that there was indeed a God, and that it was He who had authored the Bible. There would simply be no other explanation. But this outcome would not happen, of course; the claim was the stuff of, well, fairy tales at best, more likely simple error, as his carefully constructed replication was about to demonstrate.

The assertions of the Israeli scientists were ridiculous—"off the wall," as he once put it to a reporter from some kind of religiously oriented magazine. Uniquely qualified to do so, he had designed this experiment for the express purpose of confirming to his own and everyone else's satisfaction the absurdity of the original results. These purported to show that highly specific information from the contemporary era—far in the future of the Bible's composition even by skeptics' reckoning—was encoded in Genesis. In spite of their ludicrousness, the "findings" had been roiling the scholarly waters of the highest circle of mathematicians and statisticians the world over, for the research methods seemed of the highest caliber. After six years, Persi Diaconis, a prominent and highly respected statistician in the Department of Mathematics at Harvard who had reviewed the work, was as yet unable to find the flaw he was certain must be there. Indeed, he had himself devised an extraordinarily elegant method to reanalyze the Israelis' data in place of more conventional methods. But the expected flaw remained undetected.

So, here, at the heart of the most daunting intelligence apparatus ever assembled by a world power stood Gans: another eminently qualified skeptic determined to restore the academic waters of his chosen field to their usual calm, by definitively proving that the complex research was flawed.

Gans had set up his replication entirely independently, using his own equipment and programs, and applying to the data set a range of additional analytic methods to cross-check each other. Negative results were, in his mind, a foregone conclusion, and the matter would once and for all be laid to rest. Nonetheless, as the minutes passed, he found himself considerably more nervous than he thought reasonable.

The phone rang. He picked it up quickly. "Gans here." It was his wife. Gans said nothing. The clock ticked away the seconds, audible in the stillness as he listened. An observer would have seen no particular reaction, but inside, the wheels were turning with a precision that had become second nature in his intelligence duties. After a moment, having said no more than to bid his wife an especially tender good-bye, he replaced the handset in its cradle. He walked over to one of the windows that looked out toward Washington, D.C. The brilliant white marble of the Capitol had always struck him as unusually solid, epitomizing its claim to power, grandeur, and permanence. As with so many other bright, ambitious young men—and now women—before him, such scenes invariably mesmerized and taunted him, the promise of heightened importance they offered always seemed just beyond one's level of achievement. What he saw, as he looked at it this time, was that it had changed; or rather he had. The implacably tangible had slid away, barely real. It was as though a curtain had been lifted, and he now saw the ropes and pulleys that had maintained an exquisite theatrical illusion. In its place, the intangible—the invisible but divinely ordained stage that he had never really noticed before—shone forth in its resplendent reality and permanence. A feeling—quite unanticipated—was rising up within him, too, one so long forgotten that only now, with its reappearance, did he remember its loss. But he couldn't yet name it.

The number was much, much smaller than he had ever imagined it could be. It was but a cipher, a minute fraction. And this meant that the likelihood of the Israeli findings being false—mere chance curiosities—was utterly insignificant. In all his years of study, research, and professional effort Gans had *almost never* seen a "p-value" so small, and he knew that no other serious researcher had either. Certainty like that was usually reserved for the uninteresting and merely obvious, predictions in no need of sophisticated confirmation, that no one would bother formalizing—such as "the sun is *likelihood* likely to rise tomorrow." As for new or unexpected findings in scientific research, these were considered sufficiently "true" if they generated p-values of say, one in twenty. But *less than one in sixty-two-thousand five hundred?* Yes; the feeling rising up in him, surprising him, was quite simply *joy*.

CRACKING THE BIBLE CODE

And for Your sake, O Living God,
inscribe us in the Book of Life.

וכתבנו בספר החיים
למענך אלהים חיים

~

CHAPTER ONE

THE ANCIENT LEGEND

This book is the story of what may turn out to be the most important scientific research ever undertaken. The research began long ago as the speculations of mystics, but ended as science of the highest caliber. The reality it hints at encompasses both.

The story begins with an ancient and mysterious tradition among the Jews concerning the Torah—the first five books of the Bible, which form the core of Judaism, and are sacred to Christians and Muslims as well. This tradition claims that, unlike all other books of Scripture—and unlike any other sacred text from anywhere else in the world, at any time—the Torah alone was not merely inspired, it was dictated directly by God to Moses in a precise *letter-by-letter sequence.*

Entirely forgotten by the larger world, this strange tradition is not widely known nowadays even among Jews. Yet for many of those learned in Judaism and faithful to its tenets, the strict veracity of such claims is not in doubt. They maintain, to this day, that the legend of letter-by-letter transmission of the Torah was passed down by word of mouth for millennia, from the time of the actual event, precisely fifty days after the Exodus from Egypt. Only much later was the claim committed to writing.

And there is more. It is also said that into the precise sequence of letters, there is encrypted information of a sort that only a divine hand could have placed there. That is why so unusual a method of transmission was required.

However quaint or absurd it must surely seem, this tradition has an illustrious and surprising "provenance." One of the greatest leaders and thinkers in all of Jewish history was a prominent eighteenth-century Lithuanian rabbi, Elijah Solomon (in Hebrew, Eliyahu ben Shlomo) known reverently as "the Great One of Vilna"—the *Vilna Gaon.* As has often been the case with the great leaders of the Jews ever since the Roman exile, the Gaon was a child prodigy in Talmud, having memorized every one of its millions of words. But he was equally accomplished in mathematics. Furthermore, he was a rationalist par excellence and implacably hostile to unrestrained mystical enthusiasms of every sort.

Nonetheless, in a cryptic aside in one of his many brilliant books, he made the following startling claim: "All that was, is, and will be unto the end of time is included in the Torah, the first five books of the Bible." Nor by this claim was the Gaon merely indulging in poetic hyperbole of the sort commonplace in religious writing. This greatest of Jewish rationalists meant it absolutely literally—and he took pains to make his point unmistakably clear: ". . . and not merely in a general sense, but including the details of every person individually, and the most minute details of everything that happened to him from the day of his birth until his death; likewise of every kind of animal and beast and living thing that exists, and of herbage, and of all that grows or is inert."[1]

That these claims were taken seriously in the tradition can be understood from the following, probably apocryphal, tales. One day a scholar who had heard of the Gaon's assertion was visiting Vilna. He sought an audience with the sage, intending to put him to the test. Knowing that the Gaon would not know ahead of time what question the visitor intended to pose (he would present the Gaon, that is to say, with *an a priori challenge*—an important concept we will discuss in detail later), he asked him: "If, as you say, the details of *everyone's* lives are encoded in the Torah, then show me where I can find the *Rambam.*"

Rambam is the acronym for *Rabbi Moses ben Maimon*—Maimonides—perhaps the greatest of all the Jewish sages of the postbiblical era. In addition to being the rabbinical leader of his generation, Maimonides was a twelfth-century astronomer, mathematician, Aristotelian philosopher, codifier of all of Jewish law, and physician to the court of Egypt. Richard the Lion-hearted sought his services while fighting in the Crusades. Two phrases are always linked to his name in Jewish lore, and to his name alone: "From Moses to Moses there is no one like Moses." And, "the wonder of the generation."

Immediately the Gaon bade his visitor turn to Exodus 11:9: "Now the

LORD had said to Moses, 'Pharaoh will not hearken unto you, that *My wonders may be multiplied in the land of Egypt.*' " In Hebrew, the first letters of this very phrase are precisely, *R*abot (may be multipled) *M*oftai (my wonders) *B*'eretz (in the land of) *M*itzraim (Egypt), shown circled below:* Moses, Egypt, wonders; in biblical Egypt and in medieval Egypt.

ויאמר יהוה אל משה לא ישמע אליכם פרעה למען

רבת מפתי בארץ מצרים:

A similar tale is told of the *Ramban*—Rabbi *Moses b*en Nachman, also called Nachmanides—another outstanding sage of the same era. One day Nachmanides was teaching about the "Song of Moses" found in Deuteronomy 32. He made the startling claim that *all* of Israel's history can be found in these passages. A brilliant but arrogant young scholar by the name of Rabbi Abner challenged him, but the Ramban refused to withdraw or even temper his extravagant assertion. Rabbi Abner retorted, "Unless you can prove to me your statement that all of Israel's history is in the 'Song of Moses,' I will never listen to anything that you have to say again. Furthermore, I will reject the Torah as nonsense and all of Judaism with it. To prove my seriousness, I have slaughtered a pig and eaten it on the very day of Yom Kippur."

"I still maintain that all of history is hinted at in the 'Song of Moses.' Test me if you will," the Ramban replied.

"Very well, where is my own fate spoken of in that passage?"

The Ramban turned his face to the wall and prayed quietly for a moment. Then he turned to face Abner. "Go to Deuteronomy chapter 32, verse 26 and look at the third letter of each word. There you will find your answer."

Confidently turning to the Torah, Abner followed the Ramban's directions. But a chill entered his soul as he read the words of the prophecy: "I thought I would make an end of them, I would make their memory cease from among men." For he discovered that his own name was to be found

---

*Hebrew is read from right to left. Biblical citations are from the 1955 Jewish Publication Society translation unless otherwise noted.

encoded in the third letter of each of these very words, *amaRti afAyhem ash-Byta mayeNosh zikRam*: "R. Abner." (Transliterated from Hebrew, his name is properly spelled as shown, "R. ABNR." There are no vowels in Hebrew; א is a letter, but silent, taking on any vowel sound.)

אמרתי אפאהם אשבתה מאנש זכרם:

His arrogance crumbled. "Is there no cure for my condition?" he cried.

"At last you understand," said the Ramban. In one version of the tale, Abner became a devoted disciple of the Ramban and a diligent scholar of Torah; in another, he set out upon the sea with neither oarsman nor oar and was never seen again.[2]

Needless to say, these simple examples are hardly impressive statistically: Anyone with sufficient motivation could surely find occasional instances of a meaningful-seeming connection between a snippet of text and the first (or third) letters of a handful of its words—merely by happenstance. But they give an initial sense of the method behind the decryption of the codes—and of its place in Jewish lore.

In fact, Bible scholars have long been aware that over the millennia, the Torah has been preserved with an amazingly small number of letter-level variations. Though not 100 percent perfect, this precision of transmission is of such a high order (especially by contrast with other ancient texts, including others within the Hebrew Scriptures) that it has long been a puzzle to scholars.

The puzzle lies not in the method that allows such precision—that is well-known—but in the reason for such attention. To this very day, every Torah scroll of the kind that may be found in any synagogue the world over is copied by hand from its predecessor, written out according to unchanging rules, by scribes who undergo an exacting course of training and preparation. To each of them, the following warning has been passed down through the ages—we should hear it as more than a poetic metaphor: "Should you perchance omit or add one single letter from the Torah, you would thereby destroy all the universe."

In this light, even one of the most often quoted passages from the Christian Scriptures takes on a new significance: "I tell you the truth, until heaven and earth disappear, not the smallest letter, not the least stroke of a pen, will by any means disappear from the Law of Moses [the Torah] until everything is accomplished."*

Shortly after the Vilna Gaon made his startling claim in the mid-eighteenth century, the scientific revolution erupted. Never widely known anyway, the tradition of the codes all but vanished from Jewish lore.

Not entirely, however. In the early years of the twentieth century, another great Jewish mind appeared, in Slovakia, at one of the great centers of Jewish culture destined for destruction in the Holocaust that lay a few years in the future. Like the Vilna Gaon, Michael Ber Weissmandl was a childhood Talmudic prodigy. Also like the Gaon, he was a mathematical prodigy as well. While still a youth, Weissmandl stumbled upon a reference to the codes in a commentary by yet another sage, Rabbenu Bachya, who lived and died in the thirteenth century. Following the clues left by Bachya, Weissmandl undertook his own investigation of the phenomenon and became convinced it was genuine. Becoming a prominent rabbi himself, he maintained a lifelong interest in the codes, writing out the entire 304,805-letter sequence of the Torah on 10-by-10 grids. (In this way, words that occur at equally spaced letter intervals would stand out more easily.)

Rabbi Weissmandl also set into motion a process that was eventually to bring the codes fully into the light, sixty years later. By the late 1980s, Israeli researchers had discovered encryptions that went far beyond what Rabbi Weissmandl or any of his predecessors had ever discovered: references to the events and circumstances surrounding the revolt of the Maccabees celebrated in the Jewish holiday, Hanukkah; details of the storming of the Bastille during the French Revolution; key features of the discovery, pathophysiology, consequences, and treatment of diabetes; a similarly detailed description of AIDS; even specifics of current history as it unfolded.

For example, on October 6, 1981, President Anwar Sadat of Egypt was assassinated in a conspiracy of army officers. Select audiences around the world were shown a series of decryptions from Genesis with details of the assassination: the name of the target, the date, the setting, the means, and much else besides. Even the first and last name of the assassin himself, "Chaled Islambooli," was shown spelled out exactly in Genesis in a remarkably small amount of biblical text:

---

*Matthew 5:18, New International Version.

■ "Chaled"
□ "Islambooli"

Similar arrays from Genesis with details of the Gulf War likewise appeared in Israel shortly after the outbreak of hostilities. Comparable details can be found in the Book of Exodus as well. There is even a widely circulated story that the date of the first Iraqi Scud attack was found *before* it happened—and discussed at high levels of the Israeli government.

The Israeli researchers were under growing pressure to place their findings on a solid scientific footing. So they did, submitting a large, rigorously controlled sample of similar arrays to high-level peer-reviewed journals of statistics. Their paper could easily have been dismissed out of hand, so outrageous were its implications. But a number of very highly respected professors of mathematics from Harvard, Yale, and elsewhere had already gone on public record cautioning against hasty dismissal. As a result, the work was subjected to critical scrutiny that was exceptional for this kind of subject matter—most such "amazing" findings never find their way beyond tabloid journalism and junk TV. Scientists, statisticians, and mathematicians from Harvard, Yale, and Carnegie-Mellon universities sought to find its flaws; none could. One such critic, Persi Diaconis at Harvard, an eminent statistician, was so fiercely opposed to the codes that he developed a brilliantly inventive mathematical method to refute them. He, too, failed; indeed, the Israeli team used his very method to substantiate their findings. What they claimed to have found—and seemed to have demonstrated to exacting standards—was this: that precise details not just about large-scale events, but from the lives *of a whole set of individuals* could be found encoded in the Book of Genesis. All of these individuals had lived and died between the ninth and eighteenth centuries A.D.—more than fourteen hundred years after even skeptics claim the Torah was written. Is it even remotely conceivable that the legend cited by the Gaon, and by the Ramban before him, could have been right?

The story behind the codes is also the story of the remarkable people who brought the research to light. Chief among these is Rabbi Weissmandl, famous not for his little-known work on the codes, but for his dramatic actions during the Holocaust. His rescue efforts are immortalized in the acclaimed Steven Spielberg film, *Schindler's List*—for it was Weissmandl who was the great genius behind the secret ransom schemes of those terrible years.*

When the war ended, Weissmandl emigrated to America and returned to his original love—the mysterious codes in the Torah. He surrounded himself with a small group of devoted students, and they worked to reconstruct as many of his findings as they could, as well as to find new ones. But for Weissmandl as for all his predecessors, searching out encoded information was exceedingly laborious. Besides, even when one stumbled upon something that looked important, how could one prove that it hadn't simply arisen by chance? Then, in a dramatic turn, the same events that had given rise to the Holocaust yielded up a mathematical technology that catapulted the codes research to a whole new level.

A top-secret project in London, code-named Ultra, had cracked the supposedly invulnerable Nazi war code, Enigma. Fiendishly clever, this code had completely eluded all previous attempts to decipher it. By incorporating mathematical, statistical, and machine-based computing advances that came out of the atomic bomb project in Los Alamos, the British and their allies were able to keep one step ahead of the always mutating Enigma scheme. Two of the quiet heroes of this endeavor were Alan Turing in London and John von Neumann in Los Alamos, both brilliant, world-renowned mathematicians. Our world has been immeasurably altered by their work, for out of it, Turing has come to be known as the "father of computing software," Von Neumann the "father of the computer" itself.

Working under unimaginable pressures, the Von Neumann and Turing teams developed—essentially from scratch—two things that proved critical to

---

*Rabbi Weissmandl did not personally organize the Schindler-related rescue, but it was he who initiated the process elsewhere in Europe. Eventually, his idea was to develop into the "Europa Plan," intended to rescue all of European Jewry. Though the Nazis appeared willing, the necessary funds were never made available to Weissmandl's organizing group within occupied Slovakia.

the success of Ultra, and ultimately to the success of the Allies altogether: high-speed computers and a set of highly sophisticated statistical techniques that could be applied to the decryption of complex codes. Ironically, our modern development of these three domains—cryptology, statistics, and machine computation—began in the ancient encoding techniques of Jewish mystics who had first mentioned codes in the Torah as long ago as the first century.

Thirty years after Weissmandl's death, when desktop computers had become thousands of times faster than the building-size device invented by Von Neumann and used by Turing, the Torah codes yielded to strategies similar to the Allies' cryptologic efforts. Outrageous as it must seem—as it remains to frustrated critics—should the evidence thus uncovered remain unrefuted, the results will be explainable in but one way: Men three thousand years ago couldn't possibly have written the Torah; neither could men of any age, our own included. But whoever wrote it had apparently done so in just the way that ancient Jewish tradition had long insisted God had: with excruciating attention to its precise, letter-by-letter sequence.

What would such an astounding finding mean? In the last analysis, each person must decide for himself. As Professor David Kazhdan, chairman of the Department of Mathematics at Harvard, was quoted as saying in a 1996 newspaper interview, "The phenomenon is real; what it means is up to the individual." Tales abound of individuals who have been brought back to religious conviction by exposure to the codes. (Indeed, this is one of the methods used to reach out to modern, skeptically minded Jews who have become alienated from the traditional Orthodox faith of their ancestors. It is a method that is hotly debated within the Jewish community itself.) A flood of books discussing a simplified variant of the codes from a Christian perspective have become instant best-sellers in the Evangelical community (an approach that has its own skeptics, and not only Jewish ones). Two such volumes leave the reader with the impression that the Israelis' research confirms that Jesus is the Messiah and each has sold over 100,000 copies within three months.[3,4] The consternation caused by this in Israel, in particular, may only be imagined. (The codes cannot legitimately be used to make any such claim, or other similar ones, as we will see. And the most highly qualified researchers emphasize that the codes should never be used to address the beliefs of others.)

But *will* the evidence remain unrefuted? Professor Kazhdan is in fact considerably more tentative than the quotation above suggests—though he remains open-minded, he told me that the reporter misquoted him. Indeed, even as I write, a semisecret project examining the codes is under way at one of the world's major academic centers. Involved in it are some of the world's most eminent names in mathematics, computer science, and statistics. Most of the participants in this project are skeptics grown irritated—some even angry—at the worldwide and rapidly growing interest the codes are attracting. Their aim is once and for all to lay such absurd propositions to rest by demonstrating a flaw at the heart of the research. That this flaw has not yet been found is for them serious evidence of nothing: The unreality of the codes is self-evident in principle to many, even if as yet unproved. But some of the outstanding intellects behind the project are not skeptics; and a small number of some of the very most outstanding scientists have become convinced from long study that the codes quite possibly are just what they seem.

Cracking the Bible Code is the story of the codes and of the people behind them—as much as is known to date. And it is also the story of the codes' extraordinary implications.

~

CHAPTER TWO

JOURNEY TO THE CENTER

For, as we have learnt, Jerusalem is the center of the earth and a heavenly place called Zion is above it, and from this place it is blessed, and
the two are indissolubly linked together.

—*Zohar*, Vayikra 3

Thursday, November 7, 1996
Jerusalem, Israel

The call to come to Jerusalem had been unexpectedly urgent: The news
about the codes seemed to be boiling over everywhere at once, and the tension was growing rapidly over the reactions to it. After years of deepening
involvement with what I had come to learn might well prove to be the most
momentous discovery of the twentieth century, I was on my way to confer
with the people responsible for presenting it to the world. If the research that
I was investigating continued to hold up, the consequences would be almost
unimaginable. And over the past four years of my scrutiny and investigation,
it had held up: Apparently there was encoded within the Hebrew text of the
Torah—the first five books of the Bible—information about modern times
that simply shouldn't—couldn't possibly—be there. There had been few
things in my life that had excited me more than the discovery of this emerging phenomenon. So I had dropped everything as requested, rescheduled my
patients, and booked the flight to Tel Aviv.

The jarring contrast between the modern and the archaic is nowhere sharper than in Jerusalem. How did this dusty backwater of an ancient Near Eastern town with no natural reason for prominence become the focus of so much international attention—and international *tension*—precisely as the ancient Jewish manuscripts claim to foretell? The people there involved in bringing the codes to light similarly represented an unusual confluence of the ancient and the modern, the religious and the technocratic. Among them are:

- Doron Witztum, the preeminent codes researcher, a mysterious, reclusive, ultra-Orthodox Jewish Torah scholar described as almost "saintly." Yet he had been a graduate student in physics specializing in studies of general relativity—an extraordinarily abstruse and difficult subject. Eleven years ago, having been introduced to the hidden mathematical background of the Torah, he had left physics to devote himself full-time to religious studies—and to the codes.

- Eliyahu Rips, a Lithuanian émigré and world-class mathematician who had arrived in Israel a fierce atheist (as are the vast majority of mathematicians). He held international stature as a group theorist—a field of especial importance to physicists—but after coming upon various mathematical structures in the Torah, the codes among them, he grew religious, and eventually Orthodox. He remains a full-time mathematician whose piety and involvement in the codes research are a source of consternation to his more conventional colleagues the world over.

- Gerald Schroeder, another physicist with an impressive career behind him. Long at MIT, Schroeder had subsequently worked for the United States Department of Defense, the Atomic Energy Commission, and the United Nations. He had been part of the team that developed the means for detecting clandestine underground nuclear explosions and personally owned the patent for the device used to detect and measure the intensity of airborne radioactivity. After publishing more than seventy scientific articles, he, too, left it all to come to Jerusalem where he lectures to people from all over the world about the interface of science and religion.

- Professor Daniel Michaelson, another mathematician in the circle of codes researchers (in fact, he had helped develop the field). Michaelson maintained appointments both in the Department of

Mathematics at the University of California at Los Angeles and the Hebrew University in Jerusalem. He, too, began as a severe skeptic, but eventually became convinced that the codes are real. Like Rips, he left behind his secular life to assume the ways of the ancient tradition.

And then there were the rabbis. Many were native Israelis—but an unusually large number had come from the United States ten or fifteen or twenty years ago, intending only to absorb a bit of culture in Jerusalem. Waylaid by the wonders they had no idea existed, they now form a substantial part of the "Haredi," or ultra-Orthodox community in Jerusalem.

- Eric Coopersmith, the young and charismatic "number-two man" at one of the largest and most influential of the rabbinical colleges in Jerusalem, had visited Israel a decade or so ago and stopped to hear a lecture at this yeshiva. A hockey player in his twenties with the obligatory long hair and careless American attire, Coopersmith had sat in the hot Jerusalem sun, stared at Rabbi Noah Weinberg—whose white beard and large black fedora and long woolen coat made him look like an Orthodox rabbi out of Central Casting—and was dazzled in spite of himself by what he heard. The turning point came when, without perspiring a bit in spite of his dress, Weinberg asserted that learning Torah is chiefly about *having fun*. Coopersmith realized, as he put it, "one of us is wrong."

  Eventually, Coopersmith was ordained, too, and became one of those chiefly responsible for presenting the details about the codes, among other things, to over forty thousand secularists like he once was. The impact of the codes on the lives of these people from all over the world has been enormous. They have often been a doorway—the only possible doorway for hardened modernists—to begin taking the faith of their fathers seriously.

- Another rabbi with whom I had already corresponded was Moshe Zeldman, a Canadian and a student of mathematics. Perhaps more than anyone else on the rabbinical side, he was intimately familiar with the codes and with people who had developed them and brought them to the current brink of worldwide interest. He, too, arrived in Jerusalem some ten years ago with his new wife for what was intended as a brief visit. They returned to Canada long enough to settle their accounts and bid their families good-bye. They never looked back. Their story parallels that of others who abruptly changed their life course to pursue the Torah. One mother, distraught at her son's decision to forgo his graduate studies in hard science in favor of religious pursuits, traveled to Israel to complain personally to the head of the rabbinical college where he was now enrolled. "Don't worry," he reassured her, "if he finds the studies too difficult he can always go back to nuclear physics!" Zeldman, too, had been a student of mathematics.

- In New York, I had already met with Rabbi Daniel Mechanic. Mechanic was "FFB"—slang for "*frum* from birth," meaning that he had been born and raised in an Orthodox Jewish home. Danny was the man chiefly responsible for presenting the codes to North Americans. He had more information about the subject at his fingertips than anyone else and was proud and fiercely protective of the discoveries. Perpetually in a frenzy of motion, he easily could have maintained a second—or third—career as a stand-up comic.

This striking confluence of science and religion was not alien to me. I had long devoted myself to just this intersection—though I had, and have, a keen aversion to "pop" versions of the subject. I have been fascinated by the mysteries of both God and the world ever since childhood. Indeed, I, too, had started out in pursuit of physics, then turned to the "softer" sciences and to psychiatry, and had spent years investigating religion. Whenever I could, I have immersed myself in communities of genuine piety—not only Jewish. I was certain that the link to God which the human heart seeks so fervently is real—and of inestimable value. And I recently had returned to the study of mathematics and physics, certain for my own reasons that the mysteries of God are deeply bound up with mysteries of His creation. In fact, I delayed this trip to Israel by just one day—long enough to take an important examination in mathematics at Yale. (Why a psychiatrist should be studying mathematics and physics at such a late date is part of the tale, for a bit later.)

My purpose in this trip was to learn as much as I could about the application of ultramodern computing and statistical techniques to the virtuoso decryption of codes hidden within a thirty-three-hundred-year-old manuscript, performed by a group of rabbis and pietists composed of an extraordinary proportion of mathematicians and physicists.

Back in the States, the codes were having an ever more powerful impact on an ever larger number of people. Heated controversies over them had broken out and were beginning to attract public scrutiny. I was certain that in the next year this impact would be amplified many times over—and so, too, the controversy. I had recently been informed, quietly, that a group of top mathematicians, probably centered at Harvard, were organizing to destroy the credibility of the codes. I had mixed feelings about this effort. On the one hand, I personally *want* very much for the codes to be genuine: partially out of sheer, childlike wonder and amazement, but partially, too, out of a keen belief that at this very late date our world desperately needs an unmistakable wave of the one unmistakably Royal hand. Yet the notion that modern information could actually have been encrypted in the Hebrew Scriptures strikes me, too, at times, as ludicrous for a hundred different reasons.

But there is an even more pressing concern behind my interest in the codes. The need for swift, serious scrutiny arose directly out of the stunning impact the codes had already had in changing people's lives. It would be a tragedy if such an effect were based on something false: first, because false belief always breeds tragedy; second, because of the disillusionment that would follow.

The codes had inadvertently created something of a crisis: Years of concerted effort by extraordinarily skilled critics had in fact failed to find a flaw in the best of the codes research, recently published by Witztum, Rips, and a brilliant young computer scientist, Yoav Rosenberg, in *Statistical Science,* a highly respected refereed scientific journal. In the minds of many, this kind of success in the face of high-level criticism meant but two possibilities: an inadvertent behind-the-scenes manipulation of the data to fit the method (or the reverse, or both); or a deliberate manipulation. The matter was made especially troubling—and not just to scientists, but to religious people as well—by the fact that literally thousands of lives had been profoundly affected upon learning of the codes from highly reputable instructors. Harold Gans, a cryptologic mathematician highly placed in the U.S. Department of Defense, was one widely known case in point. The codes had played a major role in deepening his commitment to Orthodox Judaism, and his widely respected teaching about them had affected many others.

For the modern world outside the scientific and religious communities, rigorous testing of the codes was essential. For if the codes were genuine, then this research was without exaggeration the most astounding scientific discovery—it sounds ridiculous to put it so bluntly, but there's no way around it—*ever*. If rigorous science, operating according to the most stringent standards of evidence, in the hands of most eminent practitioners, had truly demonstrated that facts of *current* history are encoded in the Torah according to a scheme that could be described and unlocked—just as an ancient Jewish tradition maintained—then the most basic claims about the nature of the world as described in that Torah would surely have to be taken very seriously, however outrageous they appeared. It was tantamount to proof that there is a God, that He is the God described in the Torah, and that the Jewish people were charged with exactly the mission as therein detailed (whether we Jews like it or not, and whether anybody else likes it).

And what were the implications for other religions? (Judaism's own traditional answer to this question is considerably more generous than one might assume, but it would be perfectly natural for others to worry otherwise.) What were the implications for the modern faith in tolerance and even-handedness toward differing belief systems and the belief in the moral equivalence of all points of view? What would happen to the conviction, shared by many, that there *is* nothing apart from the physical universe; that our destiny is solely ours to shape as we will? The majority of Jews had long ago jettisoned anything like a literal understanding of Scripture. For many of these, the Bible provided at best a palette of metaphors to describe the conflicts of life; it certainly didn't offer solutions usable in the modern world. Would the codes force them to reconsider? History has shown that any one of these concerns is hot enough to have blood spilled over it even in the absence of evidence one way or the other.

In just the past three months, a veritable stampede of hastily written popular books had suddenly appeared at the fringes of the publishing world, all claiming to show how the Jewish codes prove that Jesus is the Messiah. The methods being used to demonstrate this, however, bore only a superficial similarity to the rigorous method that had triggered the stampede. But the fact of these books was symptomatic of the unease that was being stirred up as word of the codes spread. Those most closely involved with the codes debated whether to respond by trying to use the codes to prove that Jesus *isn't* the Messiah. This proposition—the possibility of which is doubtful given the nature of the codes, as we will see—was properly met with horror by the rabbinical authorities consulted.

There were many wise people of every faith, or none, who found it flatly objectionable that scientific evidence of this sort should even be thought to exist. My father-in-law, Joseph Leff, a well-respected leader of the New York Jewish community and current president of the influential Ninety-second Street Y, was appalled at the prospect that mathematically rigorous evidence for God was claimed to exist. "What would *faith* mean, then?" he asked me, as I debriefed him in the Sky Club atop the former Pan Am Building following my return from Israel.

At a time when the universal phenomenon of murderous religious intolerance had only just—and only somewhat—begun to level, what would it mean if the most radically fundamentalist-seeming of propositions, apparently linked most tightly to but *one* faith, were proven valid using the most rigorous means of science? I had already heard a number of rabbis opine that if the codes were valid—*especially* if they were—it would be best to hide them. It was far too late for that.

Not that Jews in general were being more objective than the Christian pop writers: a smaller rivulet of books with exclusively Jewish and Israeli themes had likewise been thrown together by people with little familiarity with the serious research. Some of these in fact did misuse the codes to "prove" that Jesus isn't the Messiah. Such "negative proofs" were as badly done as the Christian "positive proofs." It was a legitimate concern that a tide of ersatz "codes" literature could taint the entire subject, rendering it the domain of kooks.

To be fair, I myself am not certain about the results. I admit that I *want* the codes to be what they seem to. I happen to want there to be proof of a God, because I am not at all sanguine about the alternative. I am also far less concerned about whether He conforms to my—or anyone's—expectations of who He is than I am by the prospect that He altogether isn't. It is the truth that counts, whatever that may be. I once heard a devout, influential Christian state that his faith in Jesus Christ gave him the strength to want to know the truth above all, even if that truth were to turn out to falsify Christianity. I cheered inwardly at his courage, which is rare enough. It was in this spirit that I was convinced that if the codes were false, that fact must be exposed quickly. So it was that in a followup to an article for *Bible Review*, a large, scholarly, interdenominational journal of biblical studies, I had written, "If the work is in error, it would be best for this to be demonstrated not just quickly but well."

In fact, a consensus seemed to be emerging that the time was ripe to settle the matter for good one way or the other. For a long time, David

Kazhdan, a full professor in the Department of Mathematics at Harvard University, had been a supporter of Witztum and of the codes. Along with a number of other eminent mathematicians, Kazhdan had signed a preface to one of Witztum's Hebrew publications testifying to the seriousness of the research. Just last year, Kazhdan had remarked, to a West Coast newspaper reporter, that he considered the codes phenomenon to be "real." But Kazhdan had also told me directly more than a year ago that he wanted to organize a team to scrutinize the codes more rigorously than they already had been. More recently, he told me that the reporter's quote was not quite accurate: He had been commenting only on the quality of the research, not on its conclusions. And now, he was part of a spreading effort by interested experts to get to the bottom of it.

The phenomenon had been emerging slowly and until now it would have been difficult for anyone to grasp all of its pieces. The serious work had begun eight years earlier when the Israeli team published a small part of their work in the eminent *Journal of the Royal Statistical Society*. It was in the form of an invited response to a long review essay by one of the grand old men of the statistics community debating the unusual subject of statistics and theology. The piece was brief—a progress report more than anything else—and it would have been difficult to assess the method based on this alone. But the codes stirred up such excitement and fascination that inevitably the response to them went beyond what the dry evidence could support. An additional concern was the fact that although the field had been developed by many researchers, it was at present being driven forward largely by one person—Doron Witztum—and Witztum was convinced that no one else fully understood his variation of the decoding method.

Rabbi Coopersmith himself would ask me my opinion about Witztum's claim that he alone could properly conduct code searches. It was not that he was skeptical—on the contrary, after testing him thoroughly Coopersmith had become a solid admirer of Witztum, both of his person and his work. But Coopersmith's position was one of leadership, and his responsibilities included the spiritual well-being of the many souls who had been affected by the Aish HaTorah outreach program which he directed. (Aish HaTorah is a rabbinical college in the Old City of Jerusalem. It also sponsors a widely respected international educational program meant to inform secularized Jews about traditional Judaism.) Though he never spoke of it directly, Coopersmith consistently left me with an impression of his strong sense of due diligence with respect to these high responsibilities. A famous passage came to mind from the Book of Jeremiah: "The heart is deceitful above all things." It is a wise man who coolly keeps that in mind, especially when his preferences are strong.

In fact, I understood a certain feature of the decoding process that would explain Witztum's claim to exclusivity without it implying something amiss. I also thought I could do a good job of explaining how and why to people who were understandably suspicious and skeptical. There are indeed certain subtleties to the codes that would make it quite difficult for just anyone to succeed in replicating them even if they have the technical aspect down pat. This elusiveness is part of what will unfold in this book; it should serve as caution to both hasty skeptics and hasty enthusiasts. The codes are powerful, but they are also subtle, and not so easy to verify.

I arrived in Jerusalem late at night after the long and tiring flight. The rabbis at Aish HaTorah welcomed me warmly and put me up in a lovely private flat in the very heart of the Jewish quarter within the walls of the Old City of Jerusalem. It had been cold and dreary in Connecticut; here in Jerusalem it was only comfortably cool in spite of the late hour, and the air still carried some of the perfume of Israel's sunny November days.

Friday, November 8, 1996

The last time I had been in Jerusalem was almost thirty years before, shortly after the Six-Day War, when I was nineteen. I recalled those days fondly, and also my Israeli girlfriend, Hava. That summer was magical for me. Israel seemed a huge and mysterious place, and I had fallen into a wonderful situation—landing a job doing physics research at the nuclear accelerator lab of the Weizmann Institute in Rehovoth. On weekends and after hours, Hava showed me her country, and made it mine, too. I remembered Jerusalem's chaotic, winding streets, and the sense of danger and the feel of things being so shockingly secular in the world's holiest city.

Much had changed: Jerusalem was far more modern and developed than it had been three decades before—and far more Orthodox. Spectacular communities of luxury town houses had been built around Jerusalem's ancient core, their windows opening onto the enormous stone walls of the Old City. The surrounding grounds are now graced with exquisite trees and plantings and lighted all the night through. The beauty is preternatural.

The ultra-Orthodox "Haredim" were everywhere, not just in the cramped quarters of the world-renowned Mea Shearim. Whole villages of modern apartment complexes faced in Jerusalem's ubiquitous, distinctively taupe stone have sprung up everywhere on the bare rock of the Judean hills. These are filled with thousands of bustling ultra-Orthodox families who live lives of intense piety and devotion, bursting with children, the little boys all with long *payis* by their ears, the men in long black caftans and black hats, the women in long dresses and stylish wigs, the little girls clamoring in high-pitched Israeli-accented Hebrew.

And as has been true for generation upon generation, the absolute center of their lives is study of the Torah. "Where is so-and-so?" "Oh, he's *learning*." I would hear this phrase over and over again, the distinctive use of *learning* meaning but one thing: total, fascinated absorption in the mysteries of the Five Books of Moses and the veritable ocean of Hebrew commentaries that the great sages of Israel have produced over three and a half millennia of religious devotion.

The hypnotic pull of these Torah studies may seem mysterious to anyone not absorbed in them, Jewish or otherwise. Yet many of the people I met had left behind North American lives of privilege and wealth to live in near poverty in modest flats in communities surrounded only by rocky ground and the ever present threat of warfare. Indeed, many have paid for these convictions with their lives. And not all those I met were formerly secularized Jews. Many had been gentiles. The change they had embraced was incredibly radical. A comparable analogy would be if I were to close up my household in lovely, suburban Connecticut and, with my family in tow, join a group of Amish who had settled in, say, the Afghan desert, where they not only lacked the lush Pennsylvania farmland, but also had to deal with marauding bands of combatants. The seriousness of Jerusalem's growing Orthodoxy is stunning.

It was in this setting that I began a series of meetings.

Much of what followed came as a surprise: Without quite realizing it, I had entered an arena with dimensions far beyond those I already understood. The questions concerning the scientific accuracy of the codes, and their religious implications, sat atop a volatile subterranean cache of entirely different, highly fluid concerns and interests, now suddenly mixed together: a major international business intrigue, risk to personal reputations, even, indirectly,

Mideast terrorism and counterterrorism—not to mention large sums of money. The only element of a classic thriller not hinted at was sexual scandal. I remembered that I had been warned—laughingly—by Yehoshua Hecht, a friend in Connecticut who is himself an Orthodox rabbi with close ties to Israeli circles, that in Israel, as elsewhere in the Middle East, *everything* takes on a Byzantine quality: There were always wheels within wheels. He could not have been more correct.

Certain details are likely never fully to see the light of day, given the players involved. But others will in fact be presented when the time is right. Much of what I cannot say now, and have left out of this book, is very likely to see print quite soon. But what I can discuss now is astonishing enough.

Part of the picture that can be discussed is the simple fact that the scope of the imminent battles was far larger, and had swelled more rapidly than anyone had anticipated. No one could quite keep up with the press of events, and there was wide disagreement over how best to proceed. The tension was enormous. (This had been part of the urgency behind my summons to Israel.) Although I myself had been politely insisting for almost two years that such an eruption was looming on the horizon, the speed of it took even me by surprise. The codes community, almost completely cloistered within the inward life of Torah studies, was utterly unprepared, and was now in a commotion.

A major article concerning the codes was about to appear in *The Wall Street Journal*. No one knew whether it might not be a debunking attack. It hit the stands the day I returned from Israel and was rather benign, and insubstantial. Everyone heaved a sigh of relief. But the article's publication highlighted the genuine risk of a seriously negative attack from an influential but ill-informed source. I also knew that one of the most well-respected science writers at *The New York Times* had been urged by her editor—despite her own great reluctance—to do an article on the codes. Given her skill and professionalism, and her orientation toward no-nonsense science reporting, the article was bound to be scathing, and would have had a significantly greater impact than the *Journal* article. (Furthermore, she had previously written a laudatory piece about the codes' chief critic, Persi Diaconis at Harvard.) Ironically, she was talked out of it by a prominent mathematician also critical of the codes. It would be, he suggested, a total waste of her time, given their shared, skeptical, worldview.

Another more significant problem threatened. Rumor had it that, after a four-year hiatus, a man apparently hostile to Witztum and Aish HaTorah had once again turned up on the Israeli scene just three weeks before and had wrangled a private meeting with Benjamin Netanyahu's father—and was pushing for a meeting with the new Likud prime minister himself—to tell him what he had in fact already been allowed to tell the Mossad: *that the codes foretold a soon to come nuclear conflagration in the Middle East.*

The very idea that the Mossad had listened to such nonsense should have been completely beyond credibility were it not for the fact that it was widely rumored that during the Gulf War some kind of supersecret use had in fact been made of the codes by the Mossad. Not surprisingly, this man was seen as a time bomb ticking in the background, and he had everyone nervous.

But of most immediate concern was the newly organized effort by a growing body of intellectually superbly armed academic critics to destroy the credibility of the codes—and inevitably, therefore, the reputation of the researchers. In fact, an unnamed group or individual had placed a large sum of money at the disposal of this team of mathematicians and statisticians for the sole purpose of proving once and for all not just that the codes were meaningless, but that possibly the entire scheme was concocted by presenting research only on carefully crafted data sets selected over many years from a mountain of concealed failures.

The people I have spoken to on the *anti* side (many of whom wish to remain off-the-record until their own investigations are completed and published) acknowledge that it's possible for such hidden failures to have accumulated unintentionally—the result more of wishful thinking and selective attention than deliberate concealment. But below the professional restraint, one sometimes detects a note of suspicion.

After completing my rounds of meetings over a couple of days, and feeling somewhat dazed by these complexities, I went over to the Aish HaTorah yeshiva and sent off a few faxes—I was hoping to learn the results of my recent, tough examination in linear algebra and vector calculus at Yale—and walked outside to take in the sun. I was startled to see that the Aish yeshiva occupied one of the most coveted sites in the world: It looked out directly on the Western Wall of the Temple Mount.

The plaza below was teeming with people of every imaginable color and nationality. Both Jews and non-Jews stood before the Wall, offering prayers: "It shall be a house of worship for all the nations," in the words of the Hebrew Scriptures. I heard a distinctively Jewish voice, speaking loudly in

English, to a group of tourists he was guiding: "We will go down to the Wall where you may offer your prayers to God. This is *your* place to pray as well as ours," he emphasized. I turned to look. He was addressing a group of black Christians, most dressed in African garb. My heart leaped a bit, and I decided to follow his instructions myself.

I headed down to the broad plaza in front of the Wall, past the numerous checkpoints manned by the relaxed boys and girls of the Israeli Army, all carrying loaded Uzi assault rifles, and stopped a meter or two away from it. The Wall stood before me, ancient and massive, the huge cubic stones from which it was built long since worn smooth at eye level by the generations of my people who had likewise stood before it, pouring their hearts out, touching and kissing the stone tenderly—first for the horrendous destruction of our nation that occurred nearly two thousand years ago under the Romans; then continually over the centuries for all manner of suffering, personal and national, that followed ever since. I walked up to it and reached my hand out, comforting it, as it comforted me: *Comfort ye, comfort ye, my people.*

As I stood facing the wall and musing, tears flowed unbidden from my eyes, blending into the vast river of history. I quietly recited the eighteen ancient benedictions of the Shemoneh Esrai or Amidah, the lengthy prayer always said standing that forms the core of almost every worship service. Before my eyes, I could see literally thousands of scraps of paper upon which were written the hopes and dreams and griefs of people from all over the world. I had prepared mine, too, to place between the stones, but waited until the end of my prayer to do so. Then I, too, gently kissed the stone before me, found a place for my folded prayer, and turned to go.

I thought about the many similarities among those whose lives had been touched by the codes, myself included. I, too, have long sought a nonfanciful, diamantine, intersection of science and religion. I thanked God for the strange twists and turns my own life had taken, however painful and disappointing they may have been at the time. For like Witztum and many others who have entered this strange domain, I, too, had been profoundly gripped by physics, specifically by relativity, even as a child. When I was as young as four years old, I was convinced that it was my destiny to become a physicist. Einstein had become my hero as early as the third grade, and even then I knew I would go to MIT (and did). In the fourth and fifth grades, my teachers were having me give lectures on the atom to my class, and design and grade exams on the material. (Kindly Mrs. Cassiopeia wanted to do something to make up for the rejection I suffered as a classically unathletic nerd who could get nowhere with his all too frequent crushes on the girls. Giving exams to my classmates didn't exactly endear me to them—or help with girls—but it definitely got their attention.) By the seventh grade, I would baffle and irritate my friends by discussing special relativity with them on the street corners. My parents didn't know what to make of my preoccupation, and finally, when I was fourteen, they arranged to have my understanding of physics assessed by the great Cal Tech physicist, Richard Feynman.

I remember everything about the day we drove down to Pasadena from the San Fernando Valley, especially my conversation with Feynman as my parents waited outside. We discussed the relativistic dynamics of rotating bodies (concerning which I had written him a preliminary letter), and he explained where I had gotten it wrong, but in ways that echoed the speculations of the physicist Ernst Mach. And we discussed some of the astounding implications of relativity—"frames of reference" in particular. How strange that these very subjects would prove central, more than three decades later, to my investigation of the codes in the Torah.

Feynman told my parents that of all the youngsters he met in this way, he was most certain I would in fact go on to become a physicist. I treasured that prediction, as also our written correspondence (which I still have). Later, as the 1960s came and went, and I, much affected by the age, went off instead to study psychoanalysis and medicine and psychiatry—and religion, which Feynman found incomprehensible—I acknowledged that Feynman wasn't right about everything. Or maybe he was: For indeed, now, after a very long hiatus, I am at last immersed in the formal study of physics, having returned to the path I left so long ago. He would surely have been amused to find out how the decision, and the freedom to make such a decision, had at last come to me: during an extraordinarily intense period of prayer.

I thanked God for the fact that, even though my long wanderings outside of the hardest of sciences had cost me much in terms of what I might ever contribute to it at this late time of my life (late for physics, widely considered "a young man's game"), I had gained tremendously. I would surely have remained far too one-dimensional had I simply followed the straight and narrow path. (It is inconceivable to me that the superb woman who is my wife would ever have been interested in a mere large-scale version of the boy I was then.)

I was comforted, too, to experience afresh during my prayers the truth that what counted was not the peccadilloes and frailties of a person: In truth, these are the least interesting dimensions of every human being. What counted here and now, what brought me to Israel, was the extraordinary possibility that a long line of sages and scientists reaching back into ancient history had actually unlocked the secret that our dying world was more desperately in need of than ever before. If so, I would present it in the most accurate, sensitive way possible. But if not, I wanted very much to know that, too—and quickly.

As to the parts that so far must remain secret: So be it. What can be told now, what had already been released in bits and pieces here and there, in private at quiet gatherings and in public at yeshivas and universities the world over, was more than amazing enough.

I spent a wonderful, quiet Sabbath weekend with Moshe Zeldman and his wife and their two little girls, then departed Israel to return gratefully to my wife and my own three little ones. Thanking *HaShem*—the Name—I prepared myself to tell the astounding tale of the Bible Code.

Like the fabled river Erethusa, which appears in one place then dives underground to appear again far away, so the mysterious Bible Code appears and disappears throughout more than three thousand years of history. It starts in the desert at the foot of Mount Sinai long ago, then disappears from view. It doesn't reappear again for thirteen hundred years, and then only briefly, in shrouded hints from the mysterious era when the Jews began their two-thousand-year-long exile and Christianity was born. A thousand years later, in the Middle Ages of Europe, we see it appear once again in tantalizing glimpses as the European powers turn to Jewish Kabbalists to learn the "secret art" of cryptology—the making and breaking of codes. Then it disappears again for another near millennium—until the Holocaust, when, as in no prior era, the fate of civilization itself hung in a balance tipped by the art of code cracking. After the Holocaust, the Bible Code would not disappear again, at least not entirely. Its modern debut—a powerful glimpse of what was to come—took place in Israel in the early 1980s, among the surprisingly religious scientific community in Jerusalem. The reborn Jewish nation was then not yet forty years old. It is to that debut we first turn.

~

CHAPTER THREE

PIERCING THE VEIL

If the letters of the Ten Utterances by which the earth was created during the Six Days of Creation were to depart from it even for an instant,
G-d forbid, it would revert to naught and absolute nothingness, exactly
as before the Six Days of Creation.

    —*Rabbi Shneur Zalman of Liadi (1745–1812), the* Alter Rebbe,
    The Gate to the Understanding of G-d's Unity

Israel, the Early 1980s

The indirect effects of the science that emerged from the Holocaust years of
World War II are impossible to grasp fully. The transformation of matter into
energy—the atom bomb—was gigantic, and visible. It is no wonder it named
our age. Yet the "atomic era" is a misnomer. *The transformation of knowledge
itself* accomplished in those years, subtler and invisible, making the bomb possible, was far more potent. In creating the computer, these war-related efforts
transformed not simply a specific domain of knowledge or expertise, or some
domains, but the very foundation of human knowledge acquisition itself:
therefore every possible domain. The advance was universal. That *cryptology*—
the science of making and breaking codes—was the unifying principle in
this transformation is not widely known simply because of its intrinsically
secret nature, and the added secrecy with which it became increasingly

shrouded as it grew in importance and power. But the simple truth is that it was out of the "secret art" that the modern age emerged, in all its horror and wonder.

That which emerged to accomplish the Nazi defeat, and which preserved the Jews against their planned destruction, also made possible, providentially, the unveiling of some of the deepest mysteries contained within that people's foremost gift to the world: the Torah. Here is how it happened.

After the founding of the State of Israel, Torah scholars began to assemble there in growing numbers. Orthodoxy itself suddenly began to grow, as well, recovering swiftly from its near extinction just a few years before. But these Orthodox were of an unusual breed. Though some lived in cloistered worlds avoided by secularists as "medieval," a surprisingly large number were anything but. They were chemists, physicists, mathematicians, physicians. From all that the Jews had absorbed over the years in exile, they were intimately familiar with the scientific method. Yet a surprisingly large number of them clung to the Torah nonetheless, and deemed the pursuit of its mysterious depths their highest endeavor.

It was only a matter of time before someone would attempt to apply scientific technique to the ancient codes whose memory had been preserved by the great Holocaust hero Rabbi Weissmandl. The process began in 1982 with one Abraham Oren, a teacher of computer programming residing at Kibbutz Sde Eliyahu. Like Rabbi Weissmandl before him, years of immersion in the Torah and its traditions had left Oren with an intuitive sense of its patterns. When something expected didn't appear, that stood out as much as when something unexpected did. Both because of his scientific training, and because it is so old a principle in Jewish interpretation of Scripture, Oren was primed to pay close attention to these seeming anomalies—and to assume first that they were hints, not mistakes or meaningless "literary" fluctuations.

Based on his prior experience, Oren anticipated (let us call this thought an a priori hypothesis, a guess made *before* the evidence is checked) that the opening passages of Leviticus—which concern the rules for the priesthood and the sacrificial system (the passage in question is a so-called open *parsha*, which forms a natural division that is not exactly identical to the passage divisions of translations)—would mention "Aaron," the brother of Moses, in some significant way, or perhaps a significant number of times, highlighting his importance. Aaron, after all, was the progenitor of the priestly line; priests—Cohanim—must be his direct patrilineal descendants.*

Oren was therefore surprised when he discovered that Aaron himself was *not* mentioned in these passages even once. His *name* was mentioned, to be sure, but oddly, it was always used to reference someone else: the "sons of Aaron," for example—even though he himself was quite alive and active in the events being described. Was it possible that even so slight a variation in the expected might be *remez*, a hint of something deeper, and not merely a fluke, or statistical variation? Oren pursued this line of thought as though saying to himself, "Here is a passage where Aaron ought to be mentioned a number of times in some unusual way. He is not mentioned openly in the text at all. Therefore, there is reason to think that he might be mentioned in a *hidden* way. His complete absence otherwise is a hint of this possibility." Rabbi Weissmandl, and others before him, thought they had seen similarly hidden structures elsewhere in the Torah.

How might Oren look for such a thing? Let's take a quick look at a simple example found in Genesis by Rabbi Weissmandl.

The Name of Abraham and the Name of God in Genesis 1:22–26

Genesis 1:22–26 describes the creation of man and the animals, and contains the blessing to the fishes and then the birds to "be fruitful and multiply." The sages traditionally viewed the like blessing of Abraham as identical to this first commandment in the Torah—hence the very first commandment given specifically to the Jewish people as a whole, and to the other Near Eastern nations descended from him. For this reason in particular, Abraham is described as "the father of many nations."[1]

Before the "mission" is given him to "be fruitful and to multiply," Abraham was known as Abram. It is at the moment that Abram receives God's blessing (which takes place when, as an adult, he is circumcised) God changes Abram to Abra*ha*m— inserting the divine name into the human one. This God does by inserting the letter ה (H), the second letter of the tetra-

---

*In a recent issue of *Nature* (Vol. 385, No. 6611 [January 1997]), one of the world's premier scientific research publications, scientists showed a persisting genetic difference between Cohanim and all other Jews. The results suggest that today's Cohanim are indeed all descended from one individual.

grammaton, יהוה (YHWH, or "Yahweh," God's name) between the letters of Abram's name. (Note the "creative" significance, or power, of *letters.*) "You will be the father of many nations," God commands. "Neither shall thy name any more be called Abram; but thy name shall be *Abraham*" (Genesis 17:5). Thus אברם (ABRM) becomes אברהם (ABRHM).

Many ancient texts amplify this subject, and because of his prodigious learning, Rabbi Weissmandl was intimately familiar with them all. One simple example is found in the *Midrash Rabbah* on Genesis (a commentary on the books of the Torah in the form of parables). It notes, "R. Nehemiah said: 'The Holy One, blessed be He, united His name with Abraham.' " (The Zohar—the sourcebook of kabbalah whose roots go back to the first century of the common era—has a much more detailed explanation of exactly how God accomplished this, explaining the sequence of complex letter permutations via an ancient method called Atbash. We'll save some of these details for later.) Based on this ancient clue handed down in the oral tradition (and on its more detailed elaborations), Rabbi Weissmandl expected there to be some hint of this insertion hidden within the written text of Genesis itself. (It is another rule that everything in the genuine oral tradition is hinted at in the written Torah.*)

This is what he found: In that very section of Genesis, Abraham's name was spelled out with forty-nine intervening letters (an interval specifically referred to in the more elaborate descriptions of the naming traditions).† And between each letter of Abraham's name, there was one occurrence of *"Elohim,"* one of the names of God. Thus, by this arrangement, God's name was quite literally inserted into Abraham. The Torah thereby provides a hint that confirms the oral tradition.

Laying out the Hebrew text in a regular grid, and eliminating spaces or punctuation, what Rabbi Weissmandl discovered in Genesis 1:22–26 looks like this:

---

*Traditional Judaism maintains that when Moses was given the Torah, it came in two parts: a "written Torah" (the Five Books of Moses), and an "oral Torah" to be transmitted by word of mouth alone. The oral Torah was to be committed to writing only *in extremis:* if ever the Jewish people should find themselves so fragmented as to be in imminent danger of losing a comprehensive and unified knowledge of its content. This was deemed to be the case in A.D. 190, forty-five years after the final razing of Jerusalem by the Romans.

†This produces an equidistant letter-to-letter interval of 50.

ו ו ב ר ו ר פ ר מ א ל מ י ה ל <u>א</u> מ ת א כ ר ב י ו

א ב ב ר י פ ו ע ה מ י מ ב י מ ה ת א ו ל מ

י ש י מ ח מ ו ב י ר ק ב י ה י ו <u>ב</u> ר ע י ה י ו צ ר

מ ל ה י ח ש פ נ ר צ א ה א ו ת מ י ה ל א ר מ א י

ו ה נ י מ ל צ ר א ו ת י ח ו ש מ <u>ר</u> ה מ ה ב נ י

מ ל צ ר א ת ה ח ת א ה י ח ת א ה ל א ע י ו נ כ י ה י

ה ש מ ר ל כ ה ל מ י נ ה א ו א ת ה ב <u>ה</u> ת א ו ה נ י

ו ב ו ט י כ מ י ה ל א ר י ו ה נ י מ ל ה ד א

מ ד כ ו נ ל צ ב מ ד ה ש ע נ <u>מ</u> י ק ל א ר מ א י

י מ ש פ ו ע ב מ י ה ת נ ד ב ר ד י ו נ ת ו

Transliterating the Hebrew for "Abraham," and for "God" ("Elohim"), and remembering that Hebrew reads right to left and includes only consonants (and silent letters):

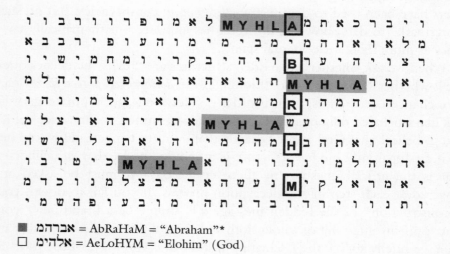

■ אברהמ = AbRaHaM = "Abraham"*

□ אלהימ = AeLoHYM = "Elohim" (God)

---

*For consistency, final forms of Hebrew letters are not used. These forms have no bearing on the meaning of a text, but simply aid in reading word breaks when the text is read in the usual way. Thus, the final *m* sound (the letter *mem*) in both Abraham and Elohim would be written ם instead of מ. In the same way, we are not using upper-case letters at the beginning of proper English nouns or names, but only to transliterate the corresponding Hebrew letters.

But Are Such "Hidden Structures" Real?

Rabbi Weissmandl is not the only one to have found various kinds of hidden structures in the Bible, especially numerical patterns. Most of these intend to disprove the so-called documentary hypothesis, the linchpin claim of "higher critics" that biblical texts are not unified creations, but pastiches of texts by various authors, cut and pasted over the centuries by committees. Like the watermark on paper currency, a numerically consistent pattern permeating the text would suggest deliberate intent by the author. It would strongly suggest that whatever text contains the pattern comes from a single source—however discontinuous that text might seem when scrutinized on the surface. The more unlikely that the pattern could arise by chance—the more intricately ordered the design—the more likely the "mark" is deliberate.

Many nineteenth-century scholars, both Christian and Jewish, defended the unity of the Bible by seeking—and finding—such numerical patterns, mostly at the level of words (for example, a key word used seven times throughout supposedly cut and pasted sections of texts). More recently, computers have been used to demonstrate *letter*-level consistencies. But no such "watermark" to date, however intricate, has impressed mathematically savvy critics as more than an accidental stain.

When we ask whether any hidden structures are "real," the deeper question is whether "Abraham" and "Elohim" were *deliberately placed there* or are mere chance occurrences, even if orderly. (Not long ago, a potato grew to look like a beloved religious figure, and it was enshrined as a miracle, but it's hard to believe that God wanted exactly that event to happen.) How can one tell if an apparently hidden structure is a genuine code, that is, deliberate? That is the crucial question in all of cryptology—it must be asked and answered at each step in any decryption process. If you fail to do so, your "reconstruction" of the hidden message will simply be a brand-new "construction," invented out of whole cloth and wishful thinking. As we will learn when we briefly survey the fascinating history of cryptology, whose roots lie deep in kabbalah, the only way to answer the question is probabilistically; that is, via *statistics*. So, before we return to Abraham Oren's query about Aaron in Leviticus, let's lay out a few simple principles about statistics that can be of help.

The Statistical Approach to Codes

If you can determine how *unlikely* it is that a given pattern can arise by chance, you have your answer as to how likely it is that the structure is deliberate.

Here is a simple example: Suppose you find a quarter lying on the street. Without a moment's thought, you assume that someone dropped it accidentally—that it's there "by chance." You assume that because it's so commonplace an occurrence. After all, consider the alternative: that *someone placed it there deliberately.* Though it's theoretically possible, your own personal experience tells you that it's pretty unlikely. How many times in your life have you taken a coin, set it down just so on the pavement, and walked away? On the other hand, how many times have you fumbled a coin and dropped it accidentally—and noticed that you did? There were probably other times when you didn't notice.

So, based on many prior samples, you guess that the odds are very low that the quarter reflects deliberate intent. It's far more likely an accident.

Now, what if you found three quarters, all close to one another? Still, it seems more likely that someone dropped a cluster of coins by accident, than that they put them there. (Maybe you feel it's a close call.) Part of this calculation (which is less certain than the prior one) involves something else, too: a reasonable guess as to people's reasons for doing things. It's hard to think of a good reason for someone to put three quarters on the ground deliberately.

Let's take it one step further. Suppose you again find three quarters, but this time they are all touching one another, forming a triangular arrangement. Was this deliberate, or by chance? Chance certainly can't be ruled out, but it seems "suspicious." It's now likely that you'll change your mind and think that someone did it "on purpose"—even though the purpose is hard to imagine.

Finally, what if you find ten quarters stacked neatly one on top of another? Though once again you can't prove it didn't "just happen," the odds against it will seem so great ("it's so odd," you'll think) that you'll be certain the stack was placed there for some unknown reason.*

---

*My thanks to Rabbi Yehoshua Hecht for pointing out that this very example may be found in the Talmud in order to clarify the principle of ownership of found items (*Baba Mezia* 21a).

Here are from-the-hip estimates of the odds for each of the four events. (The actual numbers are unimportant; it's their relative value that we should concentrate on. Feel free to replace them with your own "gut" estimates.)

Event	Chance Odds	Deliberate Odds	p
Find a quarter	9,999/10,000	1/10,000	<0.9999
Find 3 quarters	9,950/10,000	50/10,000	<0.9950
Find 3 quarters in a triangle	5,000/10,000	5,000/10,000	<0.5000
Find 10 quarters in a neat stack	1/1,000,000	999,999/1,000,000	<0.000001

Notice the final column. It takes the odds of the event occurring by chance, calls it "p" (for "probability of the null hypothesis," the null hypothesis being statistical lingo for "it doesn't mean a thing"), and phrases it as follows: "The odds of this event happening by chance are less than . . . (the symbol < means less than)." For events that are very *likely* to have happened by chance, the statement will sound stilted: "The odds that the quarter you found fell there by chance are less than 0.9999 (9,999 in 10,000)."

When the likelihood of an event happening by chance is small, the phrasing is easier to grasp: "The odds that ten quarters stacked themselves neatly just by chance are less than 0.000001 (1 in 1,000,000)."

There is one other point we should highlight. That an event didn't happen by chance does not *always* mean that it was deliberate. Another possibility is some kind of impersonal mechanical order. The fact that there are so many *e*'s in this paragraph was not deliberate on my part: It simply reflects the "impersonal" spelling rules of English. There are 63 *e*'s out of 446 letters (a–z), a frequency of about 15 percent. The expected frequency of the letter *e* in modern English is around 13 percent. The 2 percent "deviation" is well within the range expected by chance. But how about this paragraph:

Upon this basis I am going to show you how a bunch of bright young folks did find a champion: a man with boys and girls of his own; a man of so dominating and happy individuality that Youth is drawn to him as is a fly to a sugar bowl. It is a story about a small town. It is not a gossipy yarn; nor is it a dry monotonous account, full of such customary "fill-ins" as "romantic moonlight casting murky shadows down a long, winding country road."

There is not a single *e* in this passage. The odds that this happened "by chance" are very slight indeed. Try composing your own paragraph of the same length, without *e*'s, making comparably good sense and in a decent style. You'll see that it requires a tremendous amount of effort.

Now, what if we discovered that this paragraph was taken from a *267-page novel without a single* e *in it*? What are the odds that such a thing "just happened"? In fact, we can confirm our hypothesis that this almost certainly is deliberate: The paragraph comes from a book entitled *Gadsby, A Story of Over Fifty Thousand Words Without Using the Letter E,* published in 1939 by Ernest Vincent Wright.[2]

What if the above paragraph had a few *e*'s, say 0.01 percent? How confident would you be that it was deliberate? What if it had 2 percent? Or 7 percent? Such are the questions that must be asked when you examine a text containing strange statistical patterns—and the authorship is in dispute.

Eliyahu Rips: From Religious Intuition to Statistical Analysis

Following in the footsteps of Rabbi Weissmandl, Oren began to search the passage in Leviticus for hidden appearances of the word "Aaron" spelled out in the same way as "Abraham" in the example above. He looked to see if—and how often—he could find it spelled out at various *equidistant letter intervals,* compared with other words. Sure enough, he noticed something interesting. Not only did he find "Aaron" spelled out in this way within the passage, he found it spelled out ten times. His method was simple: He wrote out the text at various line lengths, then scanned the text visually for vertical equal-interval words. Though not a statistician himself, Oren nonetheless took a scientific approach in thinking *statistically* about what he found. He knew that one "Aaron" occurrence couldn't possibly mean anything; it was bound to occur just by chance in many passages. But what about *ten* times? Was that perhaps an unexpectedly large number of occurrences?

Oren could not answer the question himself, but he knew that it was the critical one. Indeed, the very asking of it marks the watershed between the scientific and the prescientific approach to any investigation. He brought his query to a friend, Professor Eliyahu Rips at the Institute of Mathematics at the Hebrew University.

Rips is as beloved a figure in the world of mathematics as he is a highly respected one. He is a world-class group theorist (an esoteric domain at the cutting edge of both pure mathematics and theoretical physics); and is universally described as compassionate, gentle, and warm. He escaped from Soviet-dominated Lithuania in the years before the Russians were expelled, and came to Israel a strict atheist. Some of the world's most eminent mathematicians (for example, Professor Ilya Piatetski-Shapiro at Yale) hold his abilities in the highest esteem. "If Rips was involved, you may be certain that there is no problem with the mathematics," in the words of one, himself the author of a number of highly regarded texts on group theory and algebraic topology.

Rips took the passage in question and had a colleague computerize it, along with a program to search out all spellings of "Aaron" at equidistant intervals within the passage, thus ensuring that all of Oren's findings were correct and that any he might have missed were also uncovered. "Aaron" in Hebrew is spelled *Aleph-Hay-Reysh-Nun* (but right to left instead), that is, AHRN (אהרן = NRHA, or, ignoring final Hebrew letter forms, אהרנ). Starting at the very beginning of the Book of Leviticus, in the passages that lack references to Aaron, Rips set his program to search for AHRN spaced every other letter, every third, every fourth, and so on, both forward and backward, beginning with the first A (א) in the text. (A forward interval is a positive number, a backward interval is negative.) When he had identified all AHRNs that began with the first A (א), if any, he moved to the second A (א), then to the third, and so on, until he had exhausted all the possibilities. In this way, he uncovered every appearance of AHRN spelled out in an equidistant letter sequence, or ELS.

Professor Daniel Michaelson, at that time an associate professor of Mathematics at the Hebrew University and at the University of California at Los Angeles, describes the outcome of Rips's investigation:

> When Rips received the results, he was overwhelmed by the large number of total appearances [of "Aaron"]: 25.* In the 716-letter long chapter, there are 55 א's (A), 91 ה's (H), 55 ר's (R) and 47 נ's

---

*This excludes, of course, any appearances of Aaron spelled out in the text in the usual way, when referring to "the sons of Aaron," for example. The shortest equidistant interval between letters was −4; the longest was +180.

(or ן: N). In a case of random distribution of these letters in a chapter, a statistician would expect only eight appearances of Aaron . . .
the probability of finding 25 . . . is about 1/400,000.[3]

The exact expected number of occurrences of AHRN was 8.3. A few
years later, a cryptologist reviewing this early result recalculated the odds of
25 at 1/2,166,818.*

The easiest way to represent what Rips found is to line up the letters in a
rectangular grid, converting all final forms to regular forms and eliminating
spacing, following the method of Rabbi Weissmandl. (This is also a typical
procedure in cryptography and, as it turns out, it is consistent with how tradition maintains that Moses was given the Torah, as is discussed in the next
chapter. As a young man, Rabbi Weissmandl had written out the entire Torah
in 10-by-10 grids of just this kind.)

Depending on the row width of the grid (the number of columns), the
embedded "Aarons" may or may not line up neatly in a horizontal, diagonal,
or vertical row. Two examples appear on pages 36 and 37.

Suddenly, the ancient idea of hidden codes in the Torah had acquired an
entirely new dimension. Never before had findings such as these come close
to appearing statistically significant. Rips and some close associates began to
do further investigations into the strange phenomenon, taking care to
exclude accidental or mechanical "confounding variables" that might
account for the startling results.

In Michaelson's words:

> A linguist could counter that the letters of biblical Hebrew are corre-
> lated so that the language "likes" אהרן (AHRN) more than would be
> expected. [But] 12 אהרן's are going backwards and it is not clear why
> the "forward" language should like *them*. And if so, then it should like
> other combinations of ן, ר, ה, and א equally well.

---

*Brendan McKay, an Australian statistician critical of the phenomenon, has publicly accused the investiga-
tors of deliberately searching for the optimal length of text and not reporting it: "The segment 1–13 stands
out as the best for Michaelson, which is of course why he (or Avraham Owen [*sic*], whom Michaelson cred-
its with this discovery) chose it." (Posting to tcode newsgroup dated Sunday, 27 April, 1997.) The accu-
sation of unreported before-the-fact tinkering has become the favored explanation of critics unable to
otherwise explain the findings, as we will see. Rips replies, "I state as a matter of fact that no optimization
of the kind described here was performed by me or by anyone I know." (Private communication)

אהרן (AHRN) at an equidistant interval of −64 letters in Leviticus 1:1–13

This concern led to another experiment in which all 24 possible permutations of the four letters as ELSs were identified and counted (AHRN, ARHN, ANRH . . .). Once again the results were unexpected: while Aaron's name correctly spelled appeared 25 times, the incorrect permutations appeared between 5 and 11 times—well within what was expected just by chance.

אהרן (AHRN) at an equidistant interval of +78 letters in Leviticus 1:1–13

How unlikely is what occurred? Roughly speaking, if just by random searching you wanted to find another passage of comparable length to Leviticus 1:1–13, containing 25 occurrences of a word that should (statistically) only be found 8 times, you'd have to search about 400,000 pages of text (more than 2 million pages, if the lower odds estimate is correct). More exactly: Since the size of the Leviticus text in question is 714 letters, and the largest possible ELS would have an interval of 714 ÷ 3 = 238 letters (otherwise a 4-letter word would extend beyond the beginning and/or end of the passage), you would have to check for every possible appearance of both AHRN and NRHA, at every possible equidistant interval ranging from −238 to +238, on every single page of every 300-page book in a library of about 800 typical books (or perhaps 4,000 books).

But Oren didn't have to search through 400,000 pages hoping to find such a rarity. His intuitive familiarity with the Torah suggested to him where to look for one—in a passage which, to a Torah scholar, seemed subtly anomalous ("Aaron" not mentioned directly).

Rips and Michaelson then set out to devise a set of tests that were yet subtler, more complicated, more refined, and even more impressive. They took all 22 letters of the Hebrew alphabet and permuted *them* in all possible ways to form 4-letter "words." This generated 117,128 such strings, treating "forward" and "backward" versions as the same. (Most of these, of course, were not genuine 4-letter Hebrew words. For example, the four English letters O, P, S, T can be permuted to form a few genuine words, and many nonwords. The genuine words consist of OPTS, POST, POTS, SPOT, STOP, and TOPS. Nonwords include OPST, OSPT, OSTP, OTPS, OTSP, PSOT, PSTO, PTOS, PTSO, etc.) Rips then searched in the same text of Leviticus for every appearance of each such permutation, whether or not it formed a genuine word.

Of course, Rips used a computer to find all of these appearances. By now, he and others were deep into the research and developing the necessary computer programs to support it. By hand, such a task would be almost beyond human endurance except for the most extraordinary reasons: The size of the task compares with the early "numerical" calculations done by teams of assistants at Los Alamos for the building of the atom bomb, before John von Neumann—whom we will meet again later—succeeded in automating the procedure by in essence inventing the computer. Rips then computed a list of how frequently each permutation was *likely* to appear as an ELS, and compared it with a list of how often it actually *did* appear.

Different "words" (four-letter permutations, whether or not they form actual words) may be expected to be found in this passage of Leviticus in widely varying numbers, merely by chance. Some are likely to appear often because of letter-frequency considerations, for example. (Just as in English you'd expect more four-letter words with the letter *e* than with the letter *x*.) Others are not likely to appear often.

The critical measure, however, is neither how often a permutation *actually* occurs nor how often you *expect* it to occur on theoretical grounds (the "expectation value" of its occurrence, as it's called). The important measure is rather *the two of these combined*. (This is the same idea that underlies bookmaking, where what matters is not just *which* horse wins, but also how unlikely it is that he'd be the winner.) Using this same logic, a word that is expected to occur often, and does, is not particularly impressive. Neither is a word that is expected to occur rarely—and rarely does.

Not surprisingly, there were many permutations with an "expectation value" smaller than that of AHRN; and there were many permutations that actually appeared more often than AHRN. Rips's impressive finding was that *not a single permutation out of the 117,128 occurred anywhere nearly so often as did AHRN, adjusted for the likelihood of its appearing.*

AHRN didn't just win the competition, it steamrolled it like a 25-handicap golfer who shoots in the mid-sixties again and again to win the U.S. Open first time out. Or put slightly differently: The odds of a typical golfer (neither pro nor duffer) hitting a hole in one is roughly once per 8,000 tee shots (once every 444 eighteen-hole rounds). If this average golfer should be lucky enough to get to play 40 eighteen-hole rounds per year, he'll average one hole in one every 11 years. If getting a hole in one were as difficult as what Rips and Michaelson found, he'd average one every five and a half centuries, that is, not even four in the past two thousand years.

Next, Rips performed the identical experiment with all 117,128 permutations using not Leviticus, but another arbitrarily selected Hebrew text. The result with this "control text," in two parts, was equally shocking:

- The distribution of "winning" and "losing" permutations was essentially identical in this control text as in Leviticus. That is, permutations expected to occur frequently did occur frequently; permutations not expected to occur frequently didn't occur frequently. In the control text, the one permutation that happened to spell "Aaron" appeared no more or less often than expected. The results were just what you'd find merely by chance—like finding 15 percent *e*'s in a paragraph of typical English.
- No other permutation of four letters, whether a genuine "word" or not, came anywhere near achieving the ranking that "Aaron" did in the passage in Leviticus.

Finally, Rips entered the *Samaritan* version of this portion of Leviticus into the computer and repeated the experiment. The Samaritan Torah (written by a sect long ago separated from the main body of Judaism) *says* the same things as the Jewish Torah, but uses many variant spellings (as our own British versus American English).* The results were again startling: twenty-

---

*In fact, this section of the Samaritan Torah contains an extra phrase, but this was deleted for the purposes of this test.

two of the twenty-five "Aarons" found in the Jewish Torah disappeared; seven new ones took their place for a total of ten. This number is within one "standard deviation" of the mean expected number. That is to say, random happenstance. The "code" had disappeared.

The Research Takes Off

Rips was becoming increasingly convinced that something was afoot. Professor Joseph Rotman from the University of Illinois is a close friend who visits Rips every year when in Israel with his wife. Close as they are, Rips wasn't pushing the issue, just dropping hints here and there to his friend—with a bit of a smile, not seeming to take it too seriously, given how many "flaky" misuses of statistics there are, especially with regard to religious matters. He mentioned to Rotman just the fact that "certain words seem to appear more often than they should."[4] But he had quietly begun to pursue the phenomenon in systematic fashion, as a scientist would.

Unlike Rabbi Weissmandl and his ancient predecessors, Rips had available to him high-powered, easy-to-use statistical methods, fast computers, and, eventually, a number of error-free electronic texts, the culmination of generations of scientific advance—and of the Holocaust years. It was apparent that if the phenomenon was as real as it seemed to be—and he was beginning to stake his world-class reputation on it—it could only have been intuited in earlier years by geniuses of staggering mental capacities; and never could it have been proven. Now, that possibility was in reach. The search for the Bible Code began in earnest.

And ancient legends that most scientists would never have taken seriously, suddenly began to make sense. Among these was the long-held belief that God had dictated the Torah to Moses in what began to sound like a cryptographic string: letter by letter, and without spaces.

~

CHAPTER FOUR

BLUEPRINT FROM HEAVEN

The earliest attestation of the consonantal framework of the Masoretic Text . . . [at] Qumran . . . date[s] to around 250 B.C. Their resemblance to the medieval form of the Masoretic Text is striking, showing how accurate the transmission . . . was throughout the ages. . . . [But] in the ancient biblical scrolls the words presumably were not separated by spaces. . . .

  —Eldon Jay Epp, "Textual Criticism"[1]

This is a work too hard for the teeth of time, and cannot perish.

  — Thomas Browne, Religio Medici

The Jews have always felt that their existence and survival were utterly dependent upon their devotion to the Torah. "The Torah is our life and the length of our days," wrote Rabbi Akiba during the Roman occupation of Judea. "Though we are in great danger while studying Torah, we would surely disappear and be no more were we to give up its study."[2]

  For nearly a thousand years, the Jews had been a major world power, having consolidated one of the great classical empires under Kings David and Solomon. Then, in the seven centuries before the dawn of Christianity, first the Northern and then the Southern halves of the Jewish Kingdom were conquered and its populations sent into exile: Israel to Assyria, Judah to

Babylonia. At the second, Babylonian, conquest in 586 B.C., the great Temple at Jerusalem was destroyed. With neither Temple nor land, the ongoing coherence of the Jewish way of life would require a far stronger grounding in its literature instead, and in its ideas. Like all ancient religions, Judaism had been rooted in its native soil; now it became transplanted not so much to alien soil as to the transcendent soil of mind. More than ever before, the Jews were "the people of the Book."

But it is not only the *words* of the Torah that contain this preserving power: The very letters themselves seem also to have held an odd fascination for those who were immersed in its contemplation.

Six hundred years later, after returning from exile in Babylonia and rising to a second height of prominence—this time, however, as an entity within a larger empire, that of Rome—the Jews were sent into exile yet again. That is where another historical oddity occurred: Unlike any other nation that has suffered such massive destruction and dispersion—and in spite of the enormous pressure upon them to do so—the Jews did not assimilate into the surrounding cultures. Across nearly two thousand years of exile, persecution, cajoling, attack, and expulsion, the Jews maintained an astonishing degree of self-consciousness, self-possession, and sense of mission.

During that time, what held the Jews together was the Torah—the first five books of the Bible—into which they poured all of their energy and concentration, granting the highest honors not to those who climbed highest by the world's standards but to those who penetrated deepest into its mystery.

Many scholars, both gentile and Jewish, have remarked upon the amazing phenomenon of Jewish existence. But a far less frequently asked question is: "What could there be about the Torah itself"—a mere five books of text, not half a million letters, much of it historical, with large chunks of census data and implausible genealogies, and the largest part of it consisting of laws the majority of which cannot even be carried out in the absence of the Temple—"that could generate such astonishing commitment, millennium upon millennium?"

Consider, as well, the many tales from the Holocaust of wizened rabbis flinging themselves upon the Torah as though to protect the very scrolls from Nazi contempt and vandalism—and paying with their lives. Stories of this devotion can be found as far back as the Roman destruction:

Centurions burst in upon Rabbi Hanina ben Teradion and found him studying Torah as always. They grabbed the prohibited scrolls and bound him over as well. As they took him, his daughter began to weep, and he questioned her why. She answered, "I weep, for you will surely be burned along with the Torah!" He responded, "The Torah is fire, and no fire can burn fire itself." When they arrived at the pyre, they seized him roughly, heaped faggots around him, wrapped him in a scroll of the Torah and lit the pyre—after placing tufts of wool soaked in water about his heart, to ensure that he would not expire too quickly. In the midst of his agony, his disciples saw him look upward. They cried out to him, "Rabbi, Rabbi, what do you see?" He replied, *"I see the parchment consumed by the fire, but the letters of the sacred Scriptures are flying toward Heaven!"* [My emphasis][3]

What is it about the Torah that could inspire such extraordinary devotion? Suspend your rational disbelief for a moment and listen to the claims about the Torah that have echoed down through the centuries. Later, we will take them up more concretely:

The Torah is the preexistent blueprint of creation.[4]

The Torah was created before the world, as it is written, *"The LORD made me as the beginning of His way."* [My emphasis][5]

The Torah was given to Moses on Sinai, but was it not created before the creation of the world?[6]

When the Holy One, blessed be He, created the world, He created it by means of the letters of the Torah, all the letters of the alphabet having presented themselves before Him until finally the letter Beth was chosen for the starting point. Moreover *the various combinations of the letters in all their permutations* presented themselves to participate in the Creation. [My emphasis][7]

When the Holy One, blessed be He, created the world, He did so by means of the secret power of letters.[8]

It is written, "I have seen an end to every purpose, but thy commandments are exceedingly broad." This statement was made by

David, but he did not explain it;* Job made a similar statement and did not explain it, namely, "its measure is longer than the earth and broader than the sea"; Ezekiel also made a similar statement and did not explain it. Indeed, the precise breadth of the commandments remained unknown until Zechariah the son of Iddo came and explained that *the entire universe is equal to one thirty-two hundredths part of the Torah.* [My emphasis][9]

The Torah has always been viewed by Jews as a map of all existence through space and time, standing outside and above it. The physical world is the Torah's derivative, not the other way around. And it is, in particular, the *letters* of the Torah that, in some mysterious way, are God's agency for the world's creation. Thus, in its mission to preserve the Torah as exactly as it can, by treasuring and preserving every letter, Israel's historical purpose is also to preserve and care for the blueprint of all existence.

Even Philo, the Hellenized Jewish philosopher who lived between 20 B.C. and A.D. 50, identified the Torah with the Logos, and with the "Word of God." Christians will of course recognize this formulation, taking more concretely than do Jews the ancient midrash (teaching) that the Messiah would most perfectly *embody* the commandments of the Torah. Thus, in the opening words of the Gospel of John in the New Testament, one may hear echoes of this matrix of Jewish mysticism whence arose Judaism's severely estranged daughter faith, Christianity: "In the beginning was the Word [the Logos], and the Word was with God, and the Word was God. The same was in the beginning with God. All things were made by it [King James Version: *him*]; and without it was not anything made that was made." (John 1:1, King James Version)

But aren't these all merely poetic metaphors expressing an intensity of devotion and admiration? In fact, the tradition goes well beyond metaphor to exacting specificity. In Chapter One, I quoted the claim of the eighteenth-century rationalist, the Vilna Gaon: "All that was, is, and will be unto the end of time is included in the Torah, the first five books of the Bible."

Two hundred years before the Gaon, there lived another of the great names of Jewish history, Rabbi Moses Cordevaro, then head of the world's highest rabbinical court, and to this day a man of towering reputation. He,

*Psalm 119.

too, made a similar claim, with an interesting added detail that the mystics had already hinted at:

> For the number of things that one can discover in the Torah via certain methods is without limit—infinite. Such matters are enormously powerful, and very deeply hidden. Because of how they are hidden, it is not possible to comprehend them fully, but only in part. Indeed, of this capacity, the Holy Scriptures themselves proclaim, "*its measure is longer than the earth and broader than the sea.*"* The secrets of the Torah are revealed . . . *in the skipping of letters.*" [My emphasis]

Letter-skip codes are well-known to the art of cryptography. And they are a form of encoding that requires a text to preserve as intactly as possible not only its "surface," word-by-word structure, but the precise sequence of underlying letters. Change "color" to "colour," and everything that follows is shifted one letter out of sequence.

The Scribal Tradition: A Passion for Perfection

In our modern era of printing presses, xerography, facsimile machines, tape drives, and magneto-optical CD storage, it is easy to lose sight of the enormous difficulties faced by ancient peoples in making and preserving accurate copies of manuscripts. For a people to hang its very existence and purpose upon its stewardship of a book—as the Jews did—is to place everything of value at risk of mere copying errors: thus the honored role of "scribe" in Jewish history.

Surprisingly little has changed in this ancient spiritual profession. Anywhere in the world where there are pious Jews, there are scribes. Even in small rural communities—for example, in the hills and mountains north of New York City, among farmers and shepherds—you can to this day find a handful of men who support their typically large families not in one of the trades that are still common to small-town America, but in a sacred religious activity that dates back some thirty-three hundred years to Mount Sinai.

Like the Amish, these men and their families usually keep their beards untrimmed; they wear dark suits even in the heat of summer; and hats at all

---

*Job, cited above and alluded to in the Talmud and elsewhere.

times—even indoors (where they wear yarmulkes); they dress and live modestly, devoting themselves above all else to the Word of God. Six days a week, they may be found indoors at their benches and desks, working at their task intently, and with infinite patience. On the seventh day, of course, they rest with their families, exulting in the goodness of the Lord, for to them the Sabbath is inviolable.

The Torah scrolls they copy out by hand may be found within the ark at the front of every synagogue, anywhere in the world. These are more than simply copies of Scripture of the sort found in every home and study hall; they are in some mysterious way living documents. Indeed, all parts of a Torah scroll must come from living creatures: from the lambskin parchment* of every page, to the ritually prescribed and sanctified sinews that hold the pages together, to the plants that may provide the ink. The transmission of one scroll from another—copied, in every case, letter by letter by these scribes—is itself a sacred ritual, much like the transmission of authority that occurs when a man is ordained as rabbi. In the same way that a chain of unbroken spiritual leadership thus goes back from man to man, all the way to Moses, so too, is each Torah scroll the spiritual child of a particular forebear—also dating back to Moses. (The apostolic succession in Roman Catholic, Eastern Orthodox, and Anglican Christianity is likewise based upon this earlier model.)

There are over twenty strict conditions that the scribe must adhere to in his work to ensure that a new Torah scroll is identical in every particular to all its predecessors. It may take years for a scribe to complete a single scroll. If so much as a single letter is misplaced or is improperly made, the layer of ink must be carefully sliced off the surface of the parchment. If it cannot be removed and properly corrected, the entire section of parchment on which it is written is no longer valid and must be unsewn and replaced.

Some of the other rules are: Only certain untanned animal skins may be used as parchment, and of those only one side; the ink must be indelible; not a single letter may touch another, or be smudged. Even the state of mind of the scribe is strictly delineated: Should he deviate even a hairsbreadth from the proper *kavanah*, that is, "intention," any portion of the scroll written thus improperly is considered invalid. It would need to be unsewn, and a newly written one inserted in its place. (How can one tell whether a scribe's

---

*The hide of certain other, kosher animals is also acceptable.

intention was proper? One can't. But stories abound of scribes who, having recalled after the fact a lapse in proper concentration, were unable to locate the "affected" passage—and started over again, even though no one could tell the difference.)

In the words of Rabbi Yishmael the scribe, to his son, "Be careful in your work as a scribe, for it is a sacred task. Perhaps you will delete one single letter or add one single letter and thereby destroy the entire world."[10]

Rabbi Shlomo Yitzhaki (Rashi: Solomon ben Isaac), the great thirteenth-century commentator warned, "The Lord your God is Emet, the 'true reality.' If you write Emet without the first letter, you destroy the world." Rashi also stated, " 'And God *spoke* [singular].' If you write, 'And God *spoke* [plural],' you destroy the world."

Are these cautions mere poetic hyperbole, meant to impress upon the scribe the seriousness with which he must take his work?

The answer is that in Judaism, the Five Books of Moses are considered different from the other books of the Hebrew Scriptures. This is so not only in terms of its centrality to the Bible (as is well known and accepted by both Jewish and Christian believers), but *especially in terms of the precision of its prophetic inspiration.* The unique status of God's revelation to Moses (and concurrently to all Israel) reflects the fact that there was never in all Israel a prophet as great as Moses. In part, this uniqueness is reflected in the claim that to Moses alone did God speak so precisely as to specify the very letters of his message.

It is easy for us moderns to miss the significance of the scribal tradition. For us, it is a simple matter to copy a text literally millions of times without a single error; to preserve that text indefinitely in multiple media; to ensure that future generations perhaps thousands of years from now will have access to exactly the same words and letters. We bury time capsules that will preserve such documents for as long as ten thousand years; the golden plaques released into space a few years ago that describe human beings for the hypothetical denizens of far-distant civilizations on other planets will remain legible for over fifteen million years.

But it is only very recently in the history of our race that such has become the case. For most of our history, written records—the very essence of a civilization—were highly perishable, unless laboriously carved into stone. (One of the great miracles of twentieth-century archaeology was the finding of the Dead Sea Scrolls: animal skin parchment writings that had survived for a nearly unheard-of two thousand years. It was the unique environment of the caves in the Judean desert, their highly inaccessible locations, and the abandonment of most habitation in that area following the Roman exile of the Jews that allowed the manuscripts to survive, undisturbed by typical use.)

Before the advent of modern techniques, if an important text needed to be preserved from one generation to the next, it had to be recopied many times. If it was needed in any other location, it likewise had to be copied by hand. This practice changed only with Gutenberg's invention of movable type in the sixteenth century, and so few of his Bibles have survived that each is now priceless. This fact may give us an appreciation of the extraordinary importance of libraries in the ancient world, especially of those few libraries that managed to amass hundreds of thousands of texts. We may likewise better appreciate the scope of the disaster when the library at Alexandria was destroyed by fire in the late third century A.D.

During the heyday of the Roman Empire, whole academies of Roman scribes turned out the popular books of the era, sometimes by the thousands. Consider for a moment how many individual errors would therefore inevitably creep into the body of texts, given the laboriousness of the copying task, and that there was no special care taken to ensure perfect accuracy.

Ancient secular documents exist in hundreds of variants. It is clear that it was common for the scribe to see his job mainly as transmitting meaning—variation in the actual form of expression was considered less important. More precise transcriptions might repeat a literal word order, but were quite casual about variants in spelling. (As mentioned earlier, "color" versus "colour" is a modern English example of such a variant.) Even copies of Shakespeare that were produced using a printing process routinely show these kinds of variations. All of these imprecisions were taken for granted in the ancient world and made feasible what would otherwise be a nearly impossible task.

Not so among the Jews, however. To them, the ancient books of what would come to be canonized as "the Bible" were far and away the most important texts. Making scriptural texts available in precisely accurate form was therefore an enormously important—and enormous—undertaking. Moreover, the Jews understood the Torah not only to be divinely inspired in its intended meaning, *but that the very letters were dictated by God for a reason.* All the hedges that bounded the Jewish scribes' activities can be seen as a set of "fail-safe" techniques meant to ensure absolute accuracy at the letter-to-letter level. The Jewish tradition in regard to letter-level accuracy is so ancient that its origins go back to a time preceding the earliest scholarly evidence.

There are two historical examples that illustrate the degree of this precision in the scribal tradition. The first is a counterexample that will play an even more important role in our later discussion.

The Samaritan Torah

It was the typical practice of conquerors in the ancient Near East to scatter a subjugated enemy to far-flung locations (whence they would no longer pose a threat) and resettle the conquered land either with their own people, or with other conquered peoples. The Assyrians conquered the Northern Kingdom of Israel some seven hundred years before Jesus and sent most of the northern tribes into an exile from which few apparently returned (giving rise to the famous legend of the "Lost Ten Tribes of Israel").

In the place of the Israelites, the Assyrians resettled in the north a mixed group of peoples from farther east. Most of these were adherents of the ancient Babylonian sexual "mystery religion" who over the centuries had also learned how to syncretize—that is, to join their own practices and beliefs to those of other religions. (For that reason, the allusions in the Bible to the sexual rites of the Canaanites, the Gnostic practices condemned by Irenaeus in around A.D. 190, and the tracts of Tantric Yoga sects extant in India to this day all sound strikingly similar in their use of "sexual magic" to attain what a modern might call an "altered state of consciousness.")

Over the years that they lived in Israel, the newcomers slowly began to intermarry with the few remaining Israelites and to adopt certain aspects of Jewish* practice. Though they insisted on calling themselves Jews, they maintained their various Babylonian forms of worship, merely syncretizing them with those secondary aspects of Judaism that would not constrain them in their accustomed practices. In fact, their rituals were largely derived from the Baal and Ashtoreth worship against which the prophets so strongly inveighed. To the observant Jew trying to remain true to the Torah, nothing could be worse than a Babylonian-style pagan passing himself off as Jewish.[11]

---

*For convenience, I am referring to all ancient Israelites as "Jews." Technically, the term "Jew" is derivative of Judea or Judah, the tribe that comprised that vast majority of the remaining, Southern Kingdom, later sent into exile by the Romans.

However, the Samaritans did accept the Torah. To this day, there exist Samaritans in Israel (in Samaria on the West Bank of the Jordan) and they have kept a Torah of their own. (Most have long since converted to a variant of Christianity.)

But in the Hebrew of the Samaritan Torah there are innumerable differences—extra words here or there, words missing, alternate spellings—few of which affect the meaning of the text. Thus, the Samaritan Torah translated into English reads almost identically to the Torah of Moses. These differences crept into the text because the Samaritans lack a scribal tradition as rigorous as the Jews'. Separated as they were from the core of Judaism, they soon reverted to the quite reasonable proposition that the exact "letters of the Law (the Torah)" were of little importance compared to its "spirit," or meaning. Here is a small sample:

ויקרא אל משה וידבר יהוה אליו מאהל מועד לאמר: דבר אל בני ישראל
ואמרת אליהם אדם כי יקריב מכם קרבן ליהוה מן הבהמה מן הבקר ומן
הצאן תקריבו את קרבניכם: אם עלה קרבנו מן הבקר זכר תמים יקריבנו
אל פתח אהל מועד יקריב אתו לרצונו לפני יהוה: וסמך את ידו על ראש
העלה ונרצה לו לכפר עליו: ושחט את בן הבקר לפני יהוה והקריבו בני
אהרן הכהנים את הדם וזרקו את הדם על המזבח סביב אשר פתח אהל
מועד: והפשיטו את העלה ונתחו אתה לנתחיה:

—Leviticus 1:1–8 in the Samaritan Torah

ויקרא אל משה וידבר יהוה אליו מאהל מועד לאמר: דבר אל בני ישראל
ואמרת אלהם אדם כי יקריב מכם קרבן ליהוה מן הבהמה מן הבקר ומן
הצאן תקריבו את קרבנם: אם עלה קרבנו מן הבקר זכר תמים יקריבנו
אל פתח אהל מועד יקריב אתו לרצנו לפני יהוה: וסמך ידו על ראש
העלה ונרצה לו לכפר עליו: ושחט את בן הבקר לפני יהוה והקריבו בני
אהרן הכהנים את הדם וזרקו את הדם על המזבח סביב אשר פתח אהל
מועד: והפשיט את העלה ונתח אתה לנתחיה:

—Leviticus 1:1–8 in the Jewish Torah

The following chart gives a summary of the differences:

Samaritan		Jewish		Missing
אליהם	ALYHM	אלהם	AL◯HM	Y
קרבניכם	KRBNYHM	קרבנכם	KRBN◯HM	Y
לרצונו	LRTZONO	לרצנו	LRTZ◯NO	O
את	(ET)	—	◯	(ET)
והפשיטו	VHFSHTO	והפשיט	VHFSHT◯	O
ונתחו	VNTHO	ונתח	VNTH◯	O

The following points are telling:

1. There are 244 characters in this snippet of text. Between the Jewish and Samaritan versions there are 7 letter-level variations involving 6 words. These variations all represent alternate spellings that have no effect on the meaning. (The 2-letter word ET itself *has* no meaning. It is used in certain instances before any direct object.) Slightly less than 3 percent of the letters in this passage are different. Overall, there are about 6,000 letter differences between the entire Samaritan and Jewish Torahs. (The New Testament is known to have roughly 15,000–20,000 letter-level variations among all its books.)

2. The text contains 85 words. Six have different spellings. That is, 7 percent of the words are spelled differently with no effect on the meaning.

3. The third point is not directly pertinent at the moment, but will become so later. Store it away for later consideration:

Among the three Torahs in use worldwide among the Jews—the Ashkenazi (in northern and Eastern European countries), Sephardi (in Latin European and some North African countries), and Yemenite (in Muslim countries)—there are only 9 letter-level variations *total* in the *entire* 300,000-letter text—in other words, a variation of .002 percent. The dispersions of these three groups go back at least to the Romans and most likely further, since before the destruction of Jerusalem Jewish communities existed all around the Mediterranean Basin.

The small fragment of the Samaritan counterexample provides a striking indication of how easy it is for the letters of a text to drift, and highlights the great care taken with Torah scrolls throughout the ages. Let's turn now to our second example.

The Book of Isaiah

Jewish canonical books outside of the Torah proper are also copied by scribes, but the process, although rigorous, is less strict than for Torah scrolls. A happy accident of history offers a glimpse of just how precise even this process is—and therefore a sense of how much more precise must be the transmission of the Torah.

Until recently, the oldest physical manuscript copy of the Book of Isaiah in Hebrew dated from around A.D. 600. But among the Dead Sea discoveries were two complete Isaiah scrolls. They date from approximately 100 B.C., that is, about seven hundred years earlier. (Some scholars would place them as much as one thousand years earlier.) With the usual methods of copying prevalent in the ancient world, one would expect there to be innumerable differences between the two scrolls, including large numbers of entirely variant or missing passages from one to the other.

Why would this be expected? Again, for comparison, consider the New Testament (which has never claimed its inspired nature to be evident at the letter level; neither does Judaism claim such inspiration for texts in the Hebrew Scriptures outside the Torah). There exist about two thousand *significant* differences among ancient texts of the Gospels alone, and a much larger number of insignificant variations that have no effect on the meaning. Some much-beloved Gospel passages are recognized today by even devout Christians to be later insertions: the famous story in John where Jesus confronts a crowd eager to stone a prostitute, for example. ("Let he among you who is without sin cast the first stone.")

But between the 100 B.C. Isaiah texts and the A.D. 600 text, a mere handful of minor single-letter or punctuation differences were found! And remember, this involved a copying process that is less rigorous than for Torah scrolls, over a period of close to seven hundred years—almost a millennium.

The King James Bible

Finally, consider one of the most famed and beloved translations of the Bible: the King James Version. It has remained unchanged—at the word level—for nearly five hundred years. (Recently there have been a spate of King James–based alternate translations, but this is a very new phenomenon.) Notice how many letter-level differences have arisen during that time in just this one typical passage:

> Comfort ye, comfort ye my people, sayth your God. Speake ye comfortably to *I*erusalem, and cry *v*nto her, that her war*r*fare is accomplished, that her iniquit*ie* is pardoned: for she*e* hath recei*u*ed of the LORDs hand double for all her sin*ne*s. [Isaiah 40:1-2, King James Version, first edition, 1611]

> Comfort ye, comfort ye my people, sa*i*th your God. Speak ye comfortably to *I*erusalem, and cry *u*nto her, that her warfare is accomplished, that her iniquit*y* is pardoned: for she hath recei*v*ed of the LORD*'s* hand double for all her sins. [Isaiah 40:1–2, King James Version, 1912]

The statistics are telling. Both versions contain precisely the same 41 words. But the original contains 199 letters, the newer 195: a 2 percent decrease in letter-count. Between the two versions there are 12 letter-level variations (additions and replacements), which represent a full 6 percent of the letters. These vary the spelling of 10 words, fully one quarter (25 percent) of the passage. A remarkably large number of letter-level changes have been allowed—but none that has any bearing whatsoever on the meaning of the passage. The two texts are treated as "identical" in all the commonsense ways that ought to count. The reason for this commonsense flexibility is easy to understand: If the word "color" and "colour" convey *exactly the same meaning*, there really is no serious reason rigidly to insist on one as opposed to the other.

This being so, we may ask our question once again of the Torah: *why* such obsession with letter-level perfection? It is not sufficient to explain it on the basis that this is not just any book, but God's word, since as we've seen, a religious message need not be fixed at the letter level in order to retain its accuracy. As the Samaritan example illustrates, such precision also represents a great exception to the prevailing standards for transmission of religious texts of that age and even of later ages (witness the many variants within the Gospels).

The late Rabbi Aryeh Kaplan, a physicist who left the world of secular studies to become one of the most highly honored of modern rabbis, summarized the Jewish approach to the Torah as follows:

> Because the Torah reveals God's will to man, it was given letter by letter. . . . [E]ven the most seemingly trivial . . . variations . . . can teach many lessons to the person who is willing to explore its depths. . . .
>
> God wrote the Torah in a complex manner so that it would be a never-ending source of inspiration and study. Just as new scientific concepts are derived from apparent contradictions in nature, so can knowledge of God's purpose and law be derived from the apparent . . . contradictions in the Torah. . . .
>
> It is taught that when King Solomon, the greatest genius of all time, considered certain commandments irrelevant, God said, "A thousand like Solomon will pass away, but not a single jot of the Torah will be changed."[12]

Given all of the foregoing, we may now better appreciate just how much attention was given to precision and accuracy in the copying of Torah scrolls—and how unusual and inexplicable such attention really is.

Finally, we should make mention of one other puzzling feature of certain very ancient Hebrew text fragments: the use of so-called *scripta continua*—a continuous sequence of letters with no breaks for punctuation or spaces between words.[13] Ancient tradition maintains that this was the form in which Moses received the Torah and archaeologists have discovered parchments written in this way. (The significance of this will become clear shortly.) The correct word breaks, which in a language lacking vowels are not at all obvious,[14] were part of the oral transmission. Oddly, a set of sixty-four marble and granite tablets with the entire Book of Ezekiel carved in *raised* letters, laid out in a square grid, and also written in *scripta continua*, was discovered in Iraq during Israel's War for Independence. The tablets remained in the possession of Izhak ben Zvi, the second president of Israel, until just before his death. Today, they are on display in a little-known facility in Jerusalem. No one is quite sure who went through the extraordinary trouble to make them in just this way or why. But one investigator unfamiliar with the Bible Code commented that the curator of the tablets told him there were "hidden messages within the stones by the manner in which the letters are arranged on the stones."

Can we say that the text of the Torah used universally in Jewish practice is *the* original text? No, we cannot. Whatever the tradition may claim, the evidence is that variations have crept into the text over the years. No process of transmission carried out by humans can possibly be perfect. But the minuteness of the errors that are known to have crept into the text is striking. Of all texts, the Torah is indeed the best candidate to contain information that goes beyond the simple meaning of its words, embedded in its letter-to-letter sequence. But would it be possible to retrieve that information?

Rabbi Michael Ber Weissmandl of the small town of Nitra in Slovakia, not far from Bratislava, had become convinced it *was* possible to do so, and he devoted what time he could to figuring out how. But then the Nazis arrived.

~

CHAPTER FIVE

THE BLACK FIRE OF HOLOCAUST

> Who has heard of such tragedy? Who has seen such events? Once, the whole world was overturned by the single sacrifice of Isaac; here in one day was he sacrificed a thousand times. Angels then shouted and the holy heavenly hosts then wept. But now the sky still glistens by day and the stars illumine the night. Must not the light grow dim when infants and innocent children—yea, thousands at a stroke—the poor and the meek are wantonly destroyed? Even now, O God, you hold your peace?
>
> —*Rabbi Eleazar ben Nosson of Ravan (1090–1170),*
> *"Elegy on the First Crusade"*

October 1944
Somewhere Near Zlate Moravcé, Slovakia

Most of the eighteen hundred men, women, and children herded aboard the cattle car bore heavy bundles and suitcases—as many of their possessions as they could carry, in anticipation of their "resettlement" far from home. Many spoke fearfully of the many Jewish exiles that had preceded this one, starting with the resettlement of the northern tribes of their people, the Kingdom of Israel, so many centuries ago. But Rabbi Michael Ber Weissmandl carried almost nothing; just a loaf of bread and three books: a treasured Torah commentary by a thirteenth-century sage given him at his bar mitzvah, and two selected volumes of the Talmud.

The Torah commentary contained a mysterious passage that had ignited in his soul a burning passion: It spoke of mysterious codes hidden within the letters of the Torah; ancient codes of the most extraordinary import that he had confirmed himself; new ones that he himself had uncovered. But the descent of Nazism had torn him away from his beloved studies: His life had become one long agonizing effort to save as many of his people as he could. That effort, too, was now being systematically ravished. If the Nazis had their way, his beloved Torah and all the secrets it concealed—the codes were but one face of a dazzlingly multifaceted jewel with depths beyond understanding—would be lost forever along with the Jewish people themselves. Weissmandl and a few others knew, in excruciating detail, that there would be no "resettlement" and no need of possessions; that the cattle train was hurtling toward the Kingdom of Death; that if the Nazi monsters succeeded, there would not even be a legend remaining.

No one observing Rabbi Weissmandl for the first time could possibly form an accurate impression of him. A colleague of his who survived those terrible days recalled him as follows:

> His face was not handsome, his black beard was not groomed and his clothes were not neat and tidy. . . . His obviously Jewish appearance alone acted like a magnet on the instinct of brutality. . . . [He] was physically attacked and insulted many times, yet could never be persuaded to change his appearance or to withdraw from open danger. Nothing in his appearance indicated his genuine humility and bashfulness, his ardent soul, his sharp intellect, the wisdom and practical philosophy of his sparkling mind, and basically serene and cheerful temperament.[1]

He was, in fact, the very embodiment of the suffering servant of God described in the Book of Isaiah: "And to whom hath the arm of the LORD been revealed? He had no form nor comeliness that we should look upon him; nor beauty that we should delight in him. He was despised and forsaken of men. . . . He was oppressed, but he humbled himself and opened not his mouth." (Isaiah 53:2–7)

But Weissmandl had the heart of a lion: During the dreadful years of the swelling Holocaust, he had been the genius behind an audacious ransom scheme that had saved the lives of thousands—and had come close to saving nearly two million more. For more than two years, with unimaginable self-control, he had negotiated face-to-face and through intermediaries with the butchers themselves; juggling and balancing—for whatever slight advantage he could detect—the often competing, invariably self-centered, interests of Dieter Wisliceny and Alois Brunner, the two overseers of the "Jewish Problem" in Eastern Europe, and their bosses: Adolf Eichmann, chief of operations for the extermination scheme; Heinrich Himmler, creator and director of the concentration and death camp network; Hitler himself. For two years, this humble Slovakian rabbi had succeeded in preventing the deportation of Slovak Jewry to the death camps; others soon followed his lead and set into motion a series of ransoms that kept the surviving remnant of Polish Jewry at work in factories owned by sympathetic gentiles, one Oskar Schindler among them.

Seeing that the Nazis were everywhere bribable, even Himmler, Weissmandl had then launched a plan of breathtaking daring to save the entire body of European Jewry—the Europa Plan. But in the end, his great ransom scheme failed for lack of funding: No one would supply the American dollars that might have saved two million lives—a mere two dollars a head out of the trillions poured into a decade of warfare. How much of this refusal was skepticism that such a plan could succeed; how much was due to simple indifference is a debate that rages to this day. Whatever the rationale, the Nazi jaws into and out of which Weissmandl had been walking in fear and trembling finally closed around him, too—and around his wife, son, and four young daughters. All now sat huddled in despair as the train sped toward Himmler and Eichmann's master creation: the death camp at Auschwitz.

Rabbi Weissmandl was in agony. The situation in Slovakia had reached a critical juncture soon after a two-year respite created by Weissmandl's negotiations was ended. With lightning speed, the majority of Jews were being deported to the camps—the Nazis were determined to make up for the slowdown created by Weissmandl's bribes. The Jews who yet remained lived in terror of the Damoclean sword that could fall upon their necks at any moment. Among his other activities during the two-year hiatus, Rabbi Weissmandl continually pressed everyone he came into contact with to prepare for escape. He knew the fate that awaited them all. He encouraged people to learn to jump off moving trams to gain skill in leaping from the moving trains they would soon be packed into. To fool their victims into false hope and acquiescence, the Nazis encouraged the terrified Jewish deportees to bring food and clothing—after all, they were just being "resettled" to a labor community; Rabbi Weissmandl encouraged them to bake hacksaws into their challahs and loaves of bread and to saw through the padlocked cattle-car doors. His underground network having tracked the train lines to their final destination, Rabbi Weissmandl distributed blueprints of the route to anyone who would take one.[2] He knew that even so slight a chance at freedom was far more certain than to step into the Nazis' iron trap.

A few did have the courage to follow his advice. Romi Cohn, now living in Borough Park, Brooklyn, was a young man and a student at the Nitra yeshiva, whose beloved head was Rabbi Weissmandl's father-in-law, Rabbi Samuel David Ungar. Cohn's mother was one of those who understood exactly what was coming and stared at it directly. "And now we are all going to die," she told her son. "But one of us must survive to say Kaddish."* Cohn was the eldest and he was chosen to carry the flame.

"I practiced jumping off of streetcars in Pressburg [Bratislava, the largest town in that area of Slovakia]," Cohn recalls, "as Rabbi Weissmandl instructed us to do. There is a technique. When we jumped off, we had to fall completely backward at the same time, but run forward at full speed the moment we hit the ground. Otherwise we would fall flat on our faces.

"Once, a Gestapo man was following me. I ran away from him and he ran after me. So I jumped onto a streetcar in Pressburg and the Nazi got on, too. Once the car got going, I jumped off—he was unable to follow. Another time I was not so lucky . . ."[3]

Cohn is a man of great vigor. Fifty years after the war ended, he lives in America with his lovely wife in a warm and beautiful home surrounded by friends and admirers. He has become a successful businessman, highly honored by the community for his kindness and philanthropy. He flies anywhere in the world, at his own expense, to perform the Brit Milah, the rite of circumcision. In spite of his terrible experiences, he is a man of enormous good humor and hospitality; he is not only an author and a scholar but an avid skier and sportsman, with the athlete's down-to-earth good spirits and bonhomie. Still, as he remembers how he was "not so lucky," that other time, his eyes fill briefly with tears. But for his father, he lost his entire family.

---

*Kaddish is the great prayer for the deceased, one of the holiest traditions in Judaism. It expresses not only unfailing faith in Divine Providence, however mysterious to our fallible human minds and hearts, but the unbroken continuity of the family through the generations. To die without someone to say Kaddish is to suffer the piercing agony of knowing that *this* branch in the living tree of one's people has perished. If there is someone to say Kaddish, then though the individual has passed on, the branch remains living.

As part of the escape plan that Cohn's family put together, he was provided with false papers that identified him as a Christian. But he couldn't bring himself to part with his *tallis katan*, an undergarment with specially braided *tzitzit*, the long fringes that the Torah commands Jewish men to wear on any four-cornered garment. To this day, Orthodox men wear them, commonly on a simple undergarment, sometimes allowing the fringes to hang out. The *tzitzit* are meant as a reminder of the commandments that produce a holy life: one committed to more than simply the wayward "desires of one's heart."

One day, Rabbi Weissmandl thought he detected that the young student was still wearing his *tallis katan*, even though the *tzitzit* were tucked away out of sight. He rushed over to him and pulled open the front of his shirt. There it was. "Are you absolutely out of your mind?" he shouted, and ripped it off. There is, of course, no higher commandment than the saving of life.

Cohn followed Rabbi Weissmandl's, and his mother's, advice and survived. Most did not. The reality that Weissmandl knew, and Romi Cohn's mother accepted, was beyond the emotional capacity of most to grasp. Who could possibly fathom such notions? Massive chambers disguised as showers, into which some of Europe's most cultured citizens would herd without scruple women and little children, all naked, all noncombatants, there to perish en masse in collective agony by cyanide gas? Trainload after trainload, night and day, month after month. Surely such were the imaginings of a mind pushed beyond endurance by the stresses of war. Most people simply did not believe the stories, ignored the maps, and brought no hacksaws with them. There were some who did, but who lacked the daring of a Cohn or a Weissmandl; some had the daring but not the athleticism: Many of those who did leap from the train died in the attempt, or broke their legs and became easy pickings for mopping-up operations.

But the reality was precisely as Rabbi Weissmandl depicted it. On board the death train were colleagues of his, who had seen the original documents from two Auschwitz escapees. The escapees had earlier made their way to Rabbi Weissmandl's "working group" headquartered at his father-in-law's yeshiva in Nitra. Once the true purpose of Auschwitz was known—it was not a forced labor camp at all; it was a death camp—Rabbi Weissmandl and his colleagues labored ceaselessly to get the word out to the West. Literally thousands of letters and cables were sent out from Nitra day after day. (Everyone working with Weissmandl in those days could read in the trickle of evasive responses that came back to them at length, the signs of acknowledgment—even of prior knowledge: There was no question but that the Allies knew exactly what was going on at Auschwitz. Their later protestations of ignorance were lies, a fact finally confirmed only in 1996.) These colleagues now sat in the railroad car with the rabbi and his family, urging him to do what he himself knew he must do, what he would be driven to do. Of all the people on board the train, it was he, they repeated, especially he, who must flee. No one else could be of help as he had been.

But there was no way that he could escape successfully with his family in tow. Were he to leave the train, his wife and five children would travel on without him to Auschwitz. The agony was nearly mortal. Weissmandl had already suffered one heart attack; he could feel his chest tightening, his heart threatening to cease altogether. How could he abandon his beloved family? But Weissmandl knew too much to listen to the desperate cries of his breaking heart. He knew that immediately upon arrival at the camp, the men would be separated from the women and children anyway; that he and they would be kept alive only to be worked to death, or to be tortured to death by Josef Mengele—"the Angel of Death"; or else they would be selected by Mengele on the spot for execution in the gas chambers within hours, his children without question. He would never see them again.

Alois Brunner was one of the most brutal and sadistic of the Nazi overlords. He took immense personal pleasure in the "Final Solution," the details of which he had learned directly from his immediate superior, Adolf Eichmann. Brunner was a relative newcomer to the Slovakian operation, having been called in to replace Dieter Wisliceny, a "soft" man in the Nazi perspective who had been successfully manipulated by Weissmandl for years. The results had been disastrous for the Nazis: A public relations fiasco had erupted just that summer in Hungary that would make escape triply difficult for all former Nazis when the war ended; and precious little of the promised "ransom" money had ever made its way into anyone's pockets.

And far worse, a "partisan revolt" had broken out in Slovakia, the native Slavic population no doubt emboldened by the failure of the Nazis to follow through in that area with the Jews, whom the Slavs sometimes seemed to hate almost as much as the Germans did. The Nazis' failure was the direct result of Rabbi Weissmandl's effect on Wisliceny. Himmler and Eichmann had flown into a rage when they learned of the uprising. There were to be no more negotiations, no more ransom schemes. Deportations from Bratislava and the surrounding territory—which Rabbi Weissmandl had succeeded in halting for nearly two years—were to be resumed at once and the entire Jewish population promptly exterminated.

The day came when Romi Cohn knew that deportation was imminent:

> The [working] group around Rabbi Weissmandl would meet every afternoon at my father's house. We would gather and wait until about three p.m., when Rabbi Weissmandl would return from his discussions with the Nazis. Then he would tell us, "No, it won't be tonight," and we knew that we could spend one more evening in our homes. One day three o'clock came and there was no Rabbi Weissmandl. We knew that the time had come.[4]

On September 7, 1944, along with thousands of others, Rabbi Weissmandl and his family were sent to a holding camp at Sered where Brunner headquartered. From there, they would be transported to Auschwitz.

While in the camp at Sered, Rabbi Weissmandl had had the temerity to attempt negotiations with Brunner, too. He argued that the war was soon to end with a German defeat, as Brunner himself surely could see; that Brunner could prepare an alibi for himself, a humanitarian "cover" by resisting the expulsion of Slovakian Jewry; that "Ferdinand Roth," Rabbi Weissmandl's fictitious, fictitiously wealthy "representative of world Jewry," supposedly living in a luxury hotel in Switzerland, would see to it that huge sums of money would be placed at his disposal in a numbered Swiss account. So impassioned had Rabbi Weissmandl become in his zeal to save his fellows at any cost that he even slammed his fist on Brunner's table.[5]

Brunner did not visibly react. But he had no intention of being duped by the same arguments the Jew had successfully used to twist Wisliceny around his finger—even if he was sincere in his willingness to pay for Jewish lives.* It was a bargain that Eichmann, and even Himmler himself, had previously seen no reason not to make: If the war ended with a Nazi defeat, they would be better off for having shown "mercy"; if it ended with a Nazi victory, they would just clean up the escaped vermin elsewhere. But the situation had now

---

*Himmler was informed of these events and apparently agreed with Weissmandl's assessment. Shortly afterward he declared the "Jewish Problem" solved, and began dismantling the gas chambers in an attempt to hide the Holocaust—and his role in it—from the world's eyes.

clarified itself to the point of unequivocal certainty: Rabbi Weissmandl obviously could not raise the money, however paltry the sums involved. Whoever this "Ferdinand Roth" was, it was evident that he spoke for no one. No one would pay even a pittance for Jewish lives.

So the opportunity for deals was finished, *schluss*. Brunner immediately ordered the rabbi and his family onto the daily transport to Auschwitz. Before they boarded, he had pictures taken of the miserable Jew in twenty-two different poses so that he could be immediately identified in the remote event he were to attempt escape. And Brunner gave special instructions concerning how Rabbi Weissmandl was to be treated upon arrival at the death camp. Let the arrogant fool try banging on Eichmann's table.

The death train rattled eastward past the Weissmandl home in Nitra, toward the rail line that ran from Budapest in the south toward Zvolen and Zilina in the middle of Slovakia, thence into Poland and to Auschwitz, not far from Crakow. Bratislava, the great center of Jewish life in Central Europe, grew farther and farther distant. With mind-numbing efficiency, and in spite of the extraordinary cost to their faltering war effort, the Nazis were making up for the years they had left the Bratislava Jews alone. Winning the war was of secondary importance; to the dark, mad, ancient spirituality of Adolf Hitler, echoed in almost every Gnostic cult that had emerged from the so-called Aryan basin of Mesopotamia, the complete elimination of the Jews took priority as it always had.

Rabbi Weissmandl was above all a sage, a man of profound learning and spiritual depth. He was keenly aware of the dire prophetic history now playing itself out. In 1931, his teacher and future father-in-law, Rabbi Samuel David Ungar, had told him a strange tale. Rabbi Ungar had been invited to assume leadership of the Nitra yeshiva. Rabbi Weissmandl tried to talk him out of it, as the older man was certain to be offered another opportunity to head a far more prestigious school elsewhere. Nonetheless, Rabbi Ungar insisted on accepting the post at Nitra. He explained why: "My heart tells me that there will come a time when there will not be a yeshiva in any other place but Nitra—and I want to be there."[6]

Such an explanation could easily have seemed absurd. However little known to the world at large, the network of Jewish learning in Central and Eastern Europe was vast and ancient, dating back hundreds of years before even such institutions as Oxford. That they could all suddenly disappear—and all within half of one man's lifetime, as Rabbi Ungar's comment suggested—was inconceivable. But as the 1930s unfolded, Rabbi Ungar's vision swiftly loomed as reality. Both he and his now-son-in-law understood that in the rapid and implausible rearrangement of historical events that produced the Holocaust—so implausible that to this day many doubt the very reality of them—there lay a deeper stratum of meaning. The vision that the older man had been vouchsafed was more than a premonition. For two years, the yeshiva at Nitra *would* be the only remaining light in the great and ancient basin of Jewish life and culture in Eastern Europe that had begun when the Romans first settled the Danube. Then it, too, was extinguished.

In the middle of the night, in that dark cattle car, Weissmandl made his decision. His sorrow piercing heaven itself, he removed the saw from inside the loaf of bread he carried. He cut through the lock on one of the cattle car's high windows, the noise of his efforts drowned out by the clatter of the wheels on the iron rails and by the ceaseless weeping of his children. In an agony from which no one could ever fully recover, Rabbi Weissmandl bid his family good-bye forever. When the train slowed, he leaped to the ground, falling backward as he had instructed others.

But Rabbi Weissmandl was not so agile as the younger Romi Cohn. He stumbled hard, struck his head, and fell into unconsciousness. He lay by the railside in a coma; for how long, no one knows for sure.

The events that followed remain mysterious. He was apparently found by a gentile who cared for him and hid him from the authorities. Miraculously, in spite of Alois Brunner's most concentrated efforts, Weissmandl made it back to a village near Bratislava without being identified. There, by the use of prearranged codes, he contacted another righteous gentile by the name of Natali who had been assisting Jews throughout the war, concealing them in his printing shop. Of German extraction, Natali had a son serving in the Gestapo, whose ruthless fanaticism was the greatest source of danger—to Natali himself as much as to the Jews Natali aided.[7] Nonetheless, immediately upon confirming that the man who had contacted him was indeed Rabbi Weissmandl—and that the encoded message he received was not a ruse—Natali hurried to the rabbi personally and accompanied him to a secret bunker in Bratislava.

Those who recall Rabbi Weissmandl's arrival at the cramped hideout in Bratislava have no words for the pain he was in. He wept without stop day and night, for days on end. His wife, his children, his friends and teachers and students and neighbors—all had been consumed in the flames. Beyond his personal tragedy, the thought of abandoning his efforts at rescue was perhaps the worst of all for him. "His stormy soul would give him no rest, for he could not bear to remain inactive while Jews were being expelled to their death."[8]

While in the bunker, Weissmandl attempted to persuade Natali to help him cross the entire breadth of Austria to Switzerland, where he could resume his rescue efforts. But such a journey would have been insanely dangerous and he was finally convinced of its impossibility. Only the arrival in the bunker, shortly before Yom Kippur, of a renowned Hasidic rabbi, Menachem Mendel Halberstam, the Rebbe of Stropkov, saved Rabbi Weissmandl from collapsing in complete despair:

> When [the inhabitants of the bunker] witnessed the Rebbe's saintly behavior they became filled with a sense of security and fervor, and they willingly accepted everything he said. Rabbi Halberstam never complained and accepted all their suffering because of his intense love of God and trust in Him. He devoted all his time to Divine service and encouraging the others. On *Yom Kippur* he gave a sermon in the bunker with as much enthusiasm as if he were addressing a congregation of thousands. . . . The Rebbe's presence in the bunker and his daily words of comfort inspired his companions with hope for their release and salvation. Rabbi Weissmandl treated the Rebbe with enormous respect; he readily accepted any advice he offered and behaved like a student in the presence of his teacher.[9]

Rabbi Weissmandl was forced to return all his attention to the one thing that transcended the horror and the helplessness: the eternal Torah and its mysterious secrets.

~

CHAPTER SIX

THE WHITE FIRE OF DESTINY

See, I have taught you rules and laws as the LORD God has commanded me, so that you will be able to keep them in the land to which you
are coming. . . . Safeguard and keep them, since this is your wisdom
and understanding in the eyes of the nations. They will hear all these
rules and say, "This great nation is certainly a wise and understanding
people." [Deuteronomy 4:5–6]

The only possessions Rabbi Weissmandl had with him in the bunker were
his three books: two volumes from the Talmud; the third, a commentary on
the Torah. One of the two Talmudic volumes—titled *Makkoth*—says much
about the state of Weissmandl's tormented soul: It is devoted to finely
nuanced discussions of the punishments to be meted out for various crimes.
This volume he studied intently, weeping, for he considered himself personally at fault for his failure to have done more to save his people—and his family. He was a man of complete honesty and integrity, yet he had poured out
his lifeblood negotiating with thieves and murderers, lying to them without
scruple if only he could save but one life more.

Yet at the end, his great rescue schemes had crumbled into nothingness.
He had been unable even to save his own wife and children. When he missed
a deadline with a Nazi official by a single day, the man sought out the rabbi's
brother-in-law, wrapped him in his prayer shawl, and shot him.

There was, however, a remnant of joy to be found in the one thing Rabbi

Weissmandl knew to be eternal: the Torah—the "Torah of Delight" as he would later title a collection of his own commentaries, assembled by his devoted students after his death. Perhaps this other possession—the only other one he chose to bring with him on his own personal exile—an analysis of the Torah written in 1291, says even more about him, and about the fire that illumined his soul.

Like most Jewish boys, the young Michael Ber Weissmandl participated in his first reading of the Torah in synagogue at age thirteen, at his bar mitzvah. In preparation for it, he wrote an original lecture to be delivered to the congregation, as is customary still. But just before the event, his grandfather from Bratislava, Rabbi Menachem Meir Berthauer, stopped him with a striking offer: If the boy would refrain from delivering the lecture, his grandfather would give him ten gold crowns.

As a young boy, Rabbi Weissmandl had already established a reputation as a prodigy, not only in sacred studies, but in mathematics and astronomy as well. His grandfather had had a chance to read his bar mitzvah lecture, leading to the strange offer. There was nothing wrong with it. In fact, the talk was brilliant. Rabbi Berthauer feared that the adulation that would surely follow would have a dangerous effect on the boy's character. (Thirty-six years later, the nearly fifty-year-old Rabbi Weissmandl would deliver that same lecture publicly for the first time to students at the yeshiva he founded in America following the war. Even then, "the audience was deeply impressed by his brilliance and erudition."[1])

The boy agreed to his grandfather's offer, and with the money he purchased the volume of Torah commentary that would remain with him his entire life.[2] It was to exert a profound effect on him, especially given the boy's love of mathematics and astronomy. The book was written by a thirteenth-century sage, Rabbenu ("Our Rabbi"*) Bachya ben Asher of Saragossa, in Spain.

Rabbenu Bachya's more general writings are widely taught today, especially because of the clarity and simplicity of his style. His teachings in kabbalah—the Jewish mystical tradition, combining contemplative prayer with a variety of mathematically influenced methods for studying Torah—were highly respected at the time, and continue to be until today. Yet his commentaries contain some unusual and cryptic asides.

For example, at the very beginning of his major work (the one

---

*The term is usually reserved for an especially beloved teacher.

Weissmandl purchased with the money given him by his grandfather), Bachya makes a remark that clearly must have electrified the young Weissmandl when he first came upon it. Indeed, he would return again and again throughout his life to the principles therein hinted at, especially during the dreadful days in the bunker. Bachya introduced the subject as follows:

> You should know that a decryption [literally, *kabbalah*] of this second section in Genesis has been passed down to us, beginning from the verse "In the beginning . . ." up to the letter ב [*beyt*, the forty-second letter in Genesis] which contains a name of 42 letters that hints at God's activities before the creation—but only by means of "many permutations."

Bachya was referring to a little-known observation made two centuries earlier by another sage, Rabbenu Tam (and even earlier by one Nechunya ben HaKanah, discussed below). Tam had observed that encoded into the opening passages of Genesis was a forty-two-letter name of God.[3] But more than that, Bachya claimed, there lay within its compass the necessary information for calculating the unfolding of the "days and seasons," starting with the moment of the creation of the sun and moon and *ever after*, according to the ancient tradition that "the luminaries were created on the fourth day, and by them we count the years of the world."[4] Tam did not commit the details of this calculation to writing, however.

Two centuries later, Rabbenu Bachya did so, by describing in one of his books what he called "the date which is the true starting point of all calculations of the astronomers" (hence the date to be used for "prophetic" calculations as well). He explained:

> If the eyes of your heart will be illumined, you will find this date encoded in the text, such that *between each of its numbers** lies as well 42 letters. The wise will understand that this is not by chance, but a clear sign involving the very birth of the world. [My emphasis]

The calculations Bachya was talking about are extremely complicated. But even as a boy, Rabbi Weissmandl had mastered them and confirmed for

---

*Numbers in the Torah are written as letter equivalents:

א	ב	ג	ד	ה	ו	ז	ח	ט	י	כ	ל	מ	נ	ס	ע	פ	צ	ק	ר	ש	ת
1	2	3	4	5	6	7	8	9	10	20	30	40	50	60	70	80	90	100	200	300	400

himself that the critical number was indeed encoded precisely as Bachya said it was. Later, while still a student, Rabbi Weissmandl became an expert in the equally complicated rules that govern the construction of the mikveh, or ritual bath (from which, incidentally, the tradition of baptism evolved). And in 1931, he published his first book, a volume that hearkened back to his earliest discoveries in Bachya's text: *Hilchot HaChodesh* (*The Laws for Fixing the New Moon*).

Throughout his life, Rabbi Weissmandl remained certain that there was embedded within the Torah, *via Bachya's description of the skipping of equal intervals of letters*, divinely ordained information. Bachya was not the first to point to the existence of encrypted information in the Torah. Hints were scattered throughout the vast store of Jewish literature. Indeed, the ancient belief that God had created the world via combinations of letters was directly linked to the mysterious ideas concerning the various "names of God." It was said, for example, that the Torah consists *entirely* of permutations of the names of God.[5] And of Bezalel, the craftsman who constructed in the desert the movable Tabernacle that housed the Ark—containing within it the Tablets of the Law and the original Torah scrolls (following the escape from Egypt)—it was said, "He knew how to combine the letters of the Divine Names with which heaven and earth were created."[6]

His imagination fired, Weissmandl took an extraordinary step as a youth: He wrote out on white cards, in 10-by-10 arrays, the entire 304,805-letter text of the Torah. This formalized the method hinted at by Bachya's statement; and it facilitated the discovery of at least those codes encrypted at intervals and multiples of ten letters, of which Weissmandl believed there were many. Thus began Weissmandl's lifelong quest to retrieve from the depths of history and dispersion another long-lost stream of Jewish understanding.[7]

Rabbi Weissmandl was aware that certain more recent luminaries—Rabbi Moses Cordevaro and Rabbi Elijah Solomon (the Vilna Gaon, mentioned in earlier chapters)—knew of the codes and had alluded to them. But the heyday of such speculations seemed to have been during the great flowering of Spanish kabbalah that took place in the Middle Ages, during an era of mounting persecution. Rabbenu Bachya's main teacher, Rabbi Solomon ben Abraham Adret (1235–1310), was one such rabbi in Spain. He was reputed to have in his possession manuscripts dating from as far back as the Babylonian captivity hundreds of years B.C. Because of Adret's great learning and massive library, students flocked to him in Spain from all over Europe.

The most mysterious of these insights were written down deliberately only as hints, however, because of a reluctance on the part of authors to discuss kabbalistic matters. Their rediscovery was made even more difficult by the fact that manuscript troves were periodically ravaged in the harassment and open attacks that Jewish communities repeatedly suffered; and by the ever present danger of expulsion. (Between 1182 and 1495, there were sixteen major expulsions of Jews from their chief centers of settlement on European soil.) Adret's library no longer exists. But the young Weissmandl was determined to search out as much as he could of the mysterious links among these tantalizing hints.

The Golden Thread of Sages

The codes in the Torah have a long and mysterious provenance. Hints that they were searched for—and found—go as far back as we have written records. Rabbi Weissmandl would have been among the very few moderns to see these manuscripts and the hints (or more) they contained. For the largest collection of them had made their way to the famed Bodleian Library at Oxford University. Before the war, Weissmandl made many trips there specifically to search them out. Quite a few existed in but one handwritten copy; many had been lost for centuries. Though most of the codes' history associated with these manuscripts remains hidden (either deliberately or lost), the tales of some of the great names associated with the codes are told below. In a striking example of the spiral of history's seemingly recurring pattern, Weissmandl's predecessors seem also to have been forced to carry out their studies in the teeth of relentless persecution.

Rabbi Eleazar ben Judah

The sage Eleazar ben Judah of Worms, who lived between 1165 and 1230, was one of the first rabbis in the Middle Ages whose works pointed in the direction that Rabbi Weissmandl was later to pursue. His major extant work, *Sodei Razayya* (*Secrets of Secrets*), discusses the creation of the world, in particular the heavenly luminaries, through the operation of the twenty-two letters of the Hebrew alphabet. His analysis reflects an understanding quite at odds with the typical claims of the many creation accounts found in cultures the world over.

First, in rather modern fashion, Jewish sages have long maintained that only children, and others capable of no more than simple understanding, should be encouraged to take the account of the creation in Genesis with absolute literalism: six 24-hour days, and so on. The wise may instead come to understand that the account expresses the deep structure of a mysterious, divinely ordered *process*. That process is indeed reflected by patterns in physical reality, but not so simply as the literalists take it to be.

For example, the creation via divine agency of "man" (Hebrew *adam;* * whose life principle is found in the blood—Hebrew *dam*, from "the dust of the earth," *adamah*) has long been understood in Jewish tradition to reflect an agency that exerted its influence *within* or *via* the processes of nature (the dust of the earth) not by some abrupt, magical transformation of a particular pile of silica particles into a single, specific individual. The challenge to those of us seeking a deeper understanding is to grasp—even if only through intuition or metaphor—something of the nature of an intricate physical process. Should we succeed, we may discover a startling correspondence between the patterns assumed by the physical world and the ideas that inform the creation.[8] In grasping these forms, we begin to understand (a small part of) the nature of the divine mind itself. This understanding inspires us to bring our ephemeral and time-limited mind, personality, and actions ever more into conformance with the standards of their immortal source.[9] Prophecy and moral education—profound "understanding" in this distinctive, divinely informed sense and the shaping of character in conformance to God's standard of holiness—are in this view inextricably intertwined. There is no true wisdom apart from sanctity.

Moreover—and here is where the accounts of the Jewish mystics depart radically from both literal and symbolic understandings—the creation of the world and everything in it actually occurred *via* the specific actions of the words of the creation account itself, in particular via the very letters of that account. Genesis, in short, is not simply a *description*; it is the very instrument of the act of creation itself, a blueprint in the mind of God[10] made manifest in physical form.

---

*In Hebrew, אדם = *adam*, which means at the same time "man," "mankind," "a man," and the proper name of the first (or more precisely, primordial) man, "Adam."

Hellenized variations on this theme would find their way into Christian theology where, wedded to certain conceptions of the Messiah, they would eventually find expression in the notion of the Trinity: God as Father made flesh in the Son/Messiah by the power of the Holy Spirit/the Word made flesh.

In Judaism, "the Word becomes flesh" preeminently in the transforming effect that God's word—the Torah—exerts upon human character. Where that effect is absent, because resisted, God is not. There is no greater meaning; there need not and cannot be any loftier or more important understanding of "incarnation" than this. Although the formal shapes of the letters in the Torah may (and did) change, what they represent, and their precise sequence, must not—it is their sequence that gives them meaning. Hence, the ancient midrash (homiletic interpretation) that every person present at the giving of the Torah was one of its letters.

Part of the reason that Rabbi Eleazar, and others, wrote of these kabbalistic "secrets" hesitatingly, and often in secret, was for fear that they would be taken up by zealous missionaries and used against the Jews because of the analogies that could be, and often were, made to Christian theology. (The Jews were in no position to force the reverse interpretation on their persecutors.) As we will see in the next chapter, the Middle Ages and early Renaissance produced a curious phenomenon as a matter of course: the so-called Christian kabbalist. Mostly these were people who were simply interested in learning what they could from Jewish mysticism; but from time to time the purpose was not so benign.

Into the Depths

At the end of the twelfth and beginning of the thirteenth century, a new wave of persecution by the Crusaders broke out against the Jewish communities of Central Europe. Rabbi Eleazar ben Judah was severely injured and his wife, daughter, and son were murdered before his eyes. In poems and stories he poured out his grief, both at his personal loss and at the decimation of the Jewish community in Germany and central Europe. He grieved equally for what he felt must surely be the coming loss of the Torah itself in these lands of exile, convinced that the death of so many sages would soon extinguish the oral tradition there. And so he committed many of his secrets to writing, in the hope that some of it, at least, would survive.

Most of Rabbi Eleazar's works have in fact been lost; the few that remain exist in manuscript form only and are stored at libraries in Vienna and Oxford. Before the Nazis put an end to Europe's Jewish community some 650 years later, Rabbi Weissmandl would travel to Oxford personally to read these and other similar rarities. The scope of his scholarship was impressive:

> On one occasion an ancient manuscript was brought to the library while he was there and the resident scholars identified its author mistakenly. Rabbi Weissmandl revealed the true author to the chief librarian and from then on he was treated with great regard. He was given the rare privilege of using the library's facilities even when they were closed to the public.[11]

There is more to the story. The head librarian was in fact quite ashamed by his mistake, being a distinguished historian and scholar himself. Rabbi Weissmandl was pained for the man and went out of his way to assure him that he meant to cause no embarrassment; and he surely had no need to claim the credit for himself. Being interested solely in the truth, he told the man that he would be perfectly happy for the correct attribution simply to be made from the librarian's office without mention of his involvement. It was this humility, more than anything else, that led the librarian to treat Rabbi Weissmandl with the highest respect.

From then on, when the library closed for the night, the rabbi was trusted to remain inside where he would study the whole night through. His ability to absorb material was astonishing. He actually memorized in their entirety many of the manuscripts, and copied out by hand at least one of the most important ones—just as the ancient scribes did (this was in the days before xerography, of course). It was part of a project he had conceived: to retrieve from exile all the lost treasures. The project was ended when the Holocaust broke out and he, too, became subject to a determined effort to end Judaism and the oral tradition in Europe once and for all.

The Template: Abulafia

A generation after Rabbi Eleazar of Worms, there arose one of the greatest and most mysterious of the medieval Jewish mystics, Rabbi Abraham ben Samuel Abulafia, born in 1240. Rabbi Abulafia expanded the teachings of

Rabbi Eleazar, specifically focusing on combinations and permutations of letters and on the relationship between the letters that comprise words and the first letters of every word in a correlated sentence (as in the example of RMBM—the Rambam—cited in Chapter One). He saw this method as a gateway to prophesy that allowed man to commune with God, accessing and bending to the Creator's divine and immortal intelligence. He called this approach "the way of the divine name" and "the science of permutation." One of his treatises expounds chiefly upon the seventy-two-lettered name of God. However abstruse his formulations seem to the modern, skeptical mind, Abulafia was in fact strenuously opposed to the wild imaginings and unfettered abuses to which kabbalah inevitably lent itself. In the end, his aim was not mere "enlightenment," but to uncover the ineffable mystery of *character*—that it might be taught.

In the summer of 1280, overcome by the never-ending suffering of his people, Abulafia traveled to Rome. There he intended to confront Pope Nicholas III and "to call him to account"[12] for the persecution of the Jews. It is something of a mystery that Abulafia thought such a mission feasible. Just two years before, Nicholas issued a bull ordering regular sermons promoting conversion to Christianity to be delivered at all synagogues. Attendance was compulsory, and "excitators" were assigned to inspect the listeners' ears for stuffed cotton, and "to keep them awake throughout expositions on the truth of Christianity and the falsity of Judaism that sometimes lasted two hours."[13]

The pope immediately threw Abulafia in prison and condemned him to burn at the stake. Providence, however, decreed otherwise. On August 22, 1280, Pope Nicholas himself suddenly died, before the sentence could be executed. His successor, Martin IV, was of a different temper, and had been placed in the papacy through the efforts of King Charles of Sicily, of the House of Anjou, the mortal enemy of Nicholas's patron, Rudolf of the House of Habsburg. After a month's incarceration, Abulafia was released. The persecutions he had sought to end, however, would only intensify over the next three decades.

History would later frame itself around a similar template. During the Nazi expulsions of Jewry from Slovakia in 1942, Rabbi Weissmandl and his father-in-law Rabbi Ungar would contact Bishop Karl Kmetko, then residing in Nitra, to see if he would be willing to intercede on behalf of the tormented

Jews. Kmetko had already written Berlin to protest at least *some* of the expulsions—of those Jews who had accepted baptism in a desperate attempt to protect themselves and their families.

But their appeal to twentieth-century rationality was as futile as Rabbi Abulafia's appeal in the midst of medieval superstition. Bishop Kmetko's response was unequivocating:

> This is not an expulsion! There [in the German camps] you will not die from hunger or the plague; there they will slaughter all of you together, from the aged to the infants and the women on one day! And you deserve this punishment. The only piece of advice I have for you is to come over to our religion, and then I will do what I can to annul the decree.[14]

Two years later, during Weissmandl's internment in the camp at Sered, he was granted a brief leave by Alois Brunner. (His late return from this leave resulted in the execution by Brunner of his brother-in-law.) During that leave, he begged Monsignor Giuseppe Burzio, the papal nuncio in Bratislava, to intervene on behalf of twenty thousand Jews already concentrated at Sered alone, awaiting transport to their deaths.

Burzio at first responded laconically that, the day being Sunday, he was of course unable to deal with secular matters. Stunned, Weissmandl pleaded that the "innocent blood of thousands of children" was at stake. The nuncio grew indignant:

> There is no such thing as "the innocent blood" of Jewish children! All Jewish blood is guilty, and the Jews must die because that is their punishment for that sin.[15]

Having learned of these accounts a few years later, it is surely no wonder that better men, for example, the archbishop of Crakow, Karol Wojtyla, later Pope John Paul II, would instead humbly refer to the Jews, in a public book, in a print run exceeding two million, as "our elder brothers in *the* faith." The papal nuncio in Istanbul during those same years, Angelo Roncalli, later Pope John XXIII, who transmitted to the Vatican without fail each and every Jewish appeal that reached him during those years, would write, in anguish:

We realize now that many, many centuries of blindness have dimmed our eyes, so that we no longer see the beauty of Thy chosen people and no longer recognize in their faces the features of our firstborn Brother. We realize that our brows are branded with the mark of Cain. Centuries long has Abel lain in blood and tears, because we had forgotten Thy love. Forgive us the curse which we unjustly laid on the name of the Jews. Forgive us that, with our curse, we crucified Thee a second time.

The increasing savagery directed toward the Jews during these centuries was like a refining flame, driving Jewish learning and the Jewish spirit ever more inward, away from the harsh physical realities they were forced to endure, concentrating it around the inner core of absolute truth itself.

Rabbi Gikatilla: *Verses on the Forty-two-Lettered Divine Name*

The line of sages that would eventually lead to Weissmandl continued under Abulafia's most outstanding student, Joseph ben Abraham Gikatilla of Castile and Segovia. Even though Abulafia honored him as his most successful student, Gikatilla's temperament inclined less to the ecstatic than that of his mentor, and more to the rational. He published his first book in 1274 at age twenty-six, a compilation of methods for seeking out hidden insights in the Torah via "gematria" (the numeric value of letters), "*notarikon*" (initial letters of sentences, as mentioned above), and "*temurah*" (permutation of letters). Another book of his—*Verses on the Forty-two-Lettered Divine Name*—points at the encoded information discussed by Bachya. As did Abulafia before him, Gikatilla claimed that many of his methods derived from a more hidden side of the teachings of Maimonides (the Rambam) himself. Along with those of Eleazar of Worms, many of Gikatilla's original manuscripts were available to Rabbi Weissmandl at Oxford.

Rabbi Moses ben Nachman: The Great Defender

Towering behind all of these, however, was one of the greatest Jewish sages of all time, second only perhaps to Maimonides: Rabbi Moses ben Nachman of Gerona (Nachmanides), in Catalonia. Born in 1194, the Ram*ban,* as he is known (RMBN), was a philosopher, poet, biblical scholar, physician, and kabbalist. For centuries, his work was held in as high, or higher, esteem as the Zohar itself, the compilation of Jewish mystical thought whose roots reach deep into the same matrix that fed early Christianity.

Yet the Ramban, too, shrouded his mystical interpretations in ambiguity. For an early version of his widely respected Commentary on the Torah, Nachmanides seems to have been prepared to discuss his kabbalistic insights in detail. But "he fell ill and was informed in a dream that he should desist."[16] But at least some of his orally transmitted ideas were written down by his students. Among such attributions were those by Bachya concerning the skipping of letters in the Torah.

Nachmanides' vision of the Torah is a lofty one, and he is beloved for the great clarity and beauty with which he expressed it. For the Ramban, the Torah is the quintessential expression of God's immeasurable knowledge. The historical accounts therein are not the mere records of past events, but portraits of the forms to which all of history would conform. The stories of the Patriarchs foreshadow the entire future of the Jewish people; the account of the creation in Genesis establishes the large-scale unfolding of the next six thousand years, and these would draw to a close at the dawn of the seventh, Sabbath, millennium—the Day of the Lord—about a thousand years following his own era.[17]

The Helix of Time

Nachmanides said it most directly: If the stories told in the Torah are indeed templates upon which history repeatedly plays itself out, then the advance of time is not so much the sharp linear flight of an arrow, but a series of repeating loci on a rising helix. Over and over, the same events recur. The shell changes but the kernel remains the same. The details vary: Never again does a precise configuration recur. There is no such thing as a single fixed reality—all phenomena and experience are unpredictable, "fuzzy," subject to—what? Will? Fate? Chance? Yet the forms are eternal. A lazy hawk circles ever upward on the warm updrafts of desert air, yet never moves; its eye fixed always upon the unchanging center. To learn the template is to make present both past and future; to study sacred history is to see the eternal in the mundane. What happened then will happen yet again, but you must *look* to see it. What Weissmandl confronted had happened many times before. What happened long ago at the end of an era would lay the groundwork for the next turn of the helix.

Thus, Nachmanides, too, was the target of persecution, though not of physical violence. In 1263, after more than thirty years of accepting the Ramban in the royal confidence, King James I of Aragon ordered Nachmanides to public debate on the contrasting claims of Judaism and Christianity. The debate was proposed to the king by a Jewish convert to Christianity, now a Dominican friar, who had assumed the name Pablo Christiani ("Paul the Christian"). Nachmanides was loathe to accept, since such debates were almost always a lose-lose proposition for the Jews. He acceded under royal pressure, but only after extracting from the king a guarantee that he would be allowed full freedom of speech.

The disputation took place in Barcelona on July 20, 23, 26, and 27, 1263. The king himself presided over most of the sessions and participated as well, mostly on the Christian side. Along with Pablo Christiani, Christianity was officially represented by the general of the Franciscan Order of Aragon, Peter de Janua, and the prominent Dominicans, Arnold de Segarra, Raymond de Penaforte, and Raymond Martini. Nachmanides was the sole representative of the Jews.

A Church historian later summarized the outcome as follows:

> Nachman was considered by some to have won the debate and actually received a prize from the King. He later suffered exile of two years for publishing an account of the disputation. At all events, Christiani denounced the Talmud to Clement IV (1265–68) and succeeded in having all Jewish books searched for anti-Christian passages.[18]

James I afterward remarked to Nachmanides, "I have never seen a man defend a wrong cause so well." The king himself attended the Barcelona synagogue, in state, on the Sabbath following, and personally addressed the congregation with that day's missionizing sermon—an unheard-of action in those days. Moreover, he allowed Nachmanides to respond to him: an equally unheard of liberty on such occasions. Nachmanides returned home the next day with three hundred golden sólidos that the king awarded him for his yeshiva in Gerona.

Nonetheless, the aftermath of the dispute was not so gentlemanly. Raymond Martini and the bishop of Gerona initiated proceedings against Nachmanides before the court of the Inquisition in 1265. Fearing for his friend's life, King James proposed instead to banish Nachmanides for two years and to burn his account of the disputation along with the *Mishne Torah*, the most outstanding work of Maimonides (since the chapter on the Jewish laws of kingship include a critical aside concerning Jesus' qualifications in this regard).

The Dominicans were not satisfied, however. James therefore pressed to try the case personally, intending to suspend it "until the fanaticism abated." Before he could do so, however, the Dominicans and the Franciscans pressured Clement IV to issue the papal bull *Turbato Corde*. That bull formed the basis for the Inquisition's subsequent mass persecution and burning of Spanish converts to Christianity suspected of harboring persistent Jewish loyalties (known as Marranos): a direct consequence, in other words, of the Barcelona dispute. Upon learning of the bull, in 1267 Nachmanides and his family fled to Israel, where he died.

The fury against the Jews would continue to grow for more than two hundred years. It culminated on March 31, 1492. On that day, King Ferdinand of Iberia proclaimed that after the deadline of August 2, the sun should not rise upon any Jew in Spain, upon pain of death. By the last day they were allowed in the country, the entire community in Spain went into exile, somewhere between 150,000 and 800,000 souls.*

By the Hebrew calendar, this last day was Tishah-b'Ab, the ninth day of the month of Ab: the same day, that is, as the destruction of the first Temple in 586 B.C., beginning the Babylonian exile, and the second Temple in A.D. 70, beginning the Roman exile, more than five centuries apart. It was likewise the date of the massive expulsion from England in 1290 (July 18). The helix had turned again; fate had ratcheted itself up another line, different yet always the same.

For Rabbi Weissmandl, it was almost as though the ninth of Ab was permanent. Yisroel Stern was on the next train to Auschwitz following Rabbi Weissmandl's. He survived the death camp and spoke with the great man after the war, who described his leap out of the cattle car:

" 'Why didn't I try to take at least *one* of my children with me?' He knew they would all be killed; there was nothing to lose. 'Even if I were simply to *throw* one of them out of the moving train and he, or she, died—still, it

---

*With his Jewish secretary, Luis Torres, on board, Christopher Columbus set sail to the New World one half hour before the deadline. The form of his name he used in all his writing is "Colón," a typical name among the Marranos of Genoa, his native city. These and other details have given rise to speculations that Columbus might have been a Marrano himself. Columbus's writings include prophetic speculations linking the end of the Jews' exile to the founding of a new world.

would be no worse than what I knew would happen anyway. And maybe, maybe he would live! O my God, why didn't I? Why!' "

Weissmandl's torment, the torment of the living, unlike that of the dead, would never end. Siegmund Forst, a friend from those days who also survived the flames, and who, like Weissmandl, came to America after the war, describes a call he received from Weissmandl one day in 1952:

"Rabbi Weissmandl was in New York. He had rented a small hotel room and had stayed in it for days. I could barely understand what he was saying through his cries of anguish. So I went to him. For an entire day, morning to evening, he cried out and wept and threw himself upon the floor and banged his fists upon the walls and furniture. I truly thought he would die, for he had already suffered many heart attacks. His agony was beyond belief, over one thing in particular. 'Why did I not try to save at least *one* of my children,' he shouted, over and over. It was all I could do not to break down utterly myself. To this day the unending pain of his soul haunts me. He insisted that no one but those who lived through it could possibly understand the Holocaust, or learn its lessons, for it was, *au fond*, a *spiritual* event. What he learned of the human soul—and of the astounding magnitude of mankind's ignorance of its own nature—created an unbridgeable gulf between him and almost everyone else. Even I cannot bear to see what he saw." Forst is now ninety-six years old.[19]

The Hebrew word for hell is *Gehinnom*, whose anglicized form is Gehenna. In Judaism, Gehenna is not a place where an immortal soul goes in the afterlife for all eternity; it is that place where the soul goes in *this* life: an eternity locked in time. Here, in the bunker, Weissmandl sank into his Gehenna. But after many months of this living hell, he forced himself to set aside the book of punishments and once more took up Bachya's commentary. He would go on, though heaven and hell would ever after coexist beside one another for the rest of his life. His fellows in the bunker describe him:

> Most of the time, Rabbi Weissmandl sat alone, deep in thought, with a Bible in his hand. He spent a great deal of time making complicated calculations based on the letters of various Biblical chapters and verses, looking for hidden meanings. He wrote his notes in the margins.[20]

The original inspiration in Bachya's commentary was the reference to the dating of the new moon, about which Weissmandl had written his first book twenty-three years earlier. The encoding that Bachya had written about seemed simple enough on the surface, but it had astounding implications as to the kind of details that might be found in the Torah through "the skipping of letters." The code that Bachya described was composed of four letters, forty-two letters apart, starting with the first letter of the opening passage of Genesis: "In the beginning, God created the Heaven and the earth. . . ." Ancient kabbalistic tradition maintained that these passages not only described the creation in overview, but properly "decoded," revealed explicit details about the creation, in particular the exact duration of critical astronomical events and cycles.

This passage was said to contain the "forty-two-lettered name of God," in code, and the tradition claimed that this name referred specifically to God's activity during—and even before—the creation in establishing the "times and the seasons."

The specific code that Bachya cited was thus four letters: ב (B), ה (H), ר (R), and ד (D), one each at intervals of forty-two letters. (Furthermore, the first forty-two letters of Genesis were convertible by "multiple permutations," a coding process we will explore in a later chapter, into the forty-two-letter name itself.)

■ בהרד = BHRD at a skip of forty-two letters, yields the lunar cycle.
□ the first forty-two letters of Genesis permutable into the forty-two-letter name.

These four letters represented a number, and from that number one could calculate the length of the lunar month, critical to the age-old monthly religious rites still celebrated by Orthodox Jews. The length of the lunar month consistent with this encryption, and used for millennia by the Jews, differs slightly from all the astronomy-based calculations of surrounding cultures dating back to the Babylonian exile (as the table on page 82 shows).

Nor is there evidence of competing astronomical methods in Jewish history. So where did the Jews obtain their number and why did they cling to it?*

DURATION OF LUNAR MONTHS[21]					
Source	*Century*	*Days*	*Hours*	*Minutes*	*Seconds*	*Total in Days*
Meton (Greece)	5th B.C.	29	12	42	45.22	29.52969
Kidinnu (Babylon)	4th B.C.	29	12	44	05.05	29.53061 (14)
Hipparchus (Greece)	2nd B.C.	29	12	43	56.06	29.53051
Al-buruni (Arabia)	11th	29	12	44	02.29	29.53058 (82)
Rambam (Jewish)	12th	29	12	44	02.69	29.53059 (86)
Copernicus (Europe)	16th	29	12	44	03.17	29.53059 (92)

Jewish tradition holds that when God gave the written Torah, He also gave Moses additional information, not to be written down, which would be needed to fulfill the commandments properly. That additional information forms the kernel of the oral tradition. God also explained that within the written Torah could always be found confirmatory hints for anything given orally. The length of the lunar cycle was part of this additional information:

> The LORD said to Moses and to Aaron: ". . . this month shall be for you the beginning of the months. . . ." And at the moment when Moses our teacher received this command, the Holy One, blessed be He, transmitted to him the precise rules for intercalating the New Moon. Thus He made known to Moses the method for establishing the times and the seasons. [*Midrash Sod HaIbbur*: On the Mystery of the New Moon]

---

*"In the fourth century, however, when oppression and persecution threatened the continued existence of the Sanhedrin, the patriarch Hillel II took an extraordinary step to preserve the unity of Israel. In order to prevent the Jews scattered all over the surface of the earth from celebrating their new moons, festivals, and holidays at different times, he made public the system of calendar calculation, which up to then had been a closely guarded secret. It had been used in the past only to check the observations and testimonies of witnesses, and to determine the beginnings of the spring season." (Arthur Spier, *The Comprehensive Hebrew Calendar, Twentieth to Twenty-second Century, 5660–5860, 1900–2100*, 3d rev. ed. Jerusalem; New York: Feldheim, 1989)

The encryption of BHRD that yielded the ancient length of the lunar cycle was to the kabbalist the promised encoded confirmation.

Of course, that this "confirmatory" number happens to be encoded in Genesis at just that point, at just that interval, could easily be coincidental. What makes it eerie is that while this length of the lunar cycle differs slightly from other ancient calculations, *it is identical to modern scientific estimates and within two parts in 1 million to values obtainable only by satellite:*

Lunar Month: Method	Length of One Month (Days)	Difference in Days from NASA Figure
Satellite (as of 1996)	29.530588	—
Numerical pre-Satellite (as of 1968)	29.53059	0.000000–0.000002
Jewish Month	29.53059	0.000000–0.000002

Just as Weissmandl was inspired by Bachya, Bachya himself attributed much of what he had learned from an even earlier kabbalist, Nechunya ben HaKanah, who lived in first-century Judea, just after the destruction of Israel by the Romans. In addition to being an expert in many subjects, Nechunya (his name will come up again in our review of cryptology in the next chapter) specifically asserted that if you properly understand how to use the forty-two-lettered name as a key to "the times and seasons," Genesis also reveals a lengthy period of time between the origin of the universe and the creation of man.[22] In his view, the universe is thus not a mere few thousand years old as the text seems to claim on the surface, but *is 15.3 billion years old,* the very age arrived at only recently by the estimates of modern astrophysical theories of the "big bang."

Like the length of the lunar cycle hinted at in Genesis, this result from nearly two thousand years ago, utterly at odds with the beliefs of both scientists and religious scholars until our own era, raises the questions: Did Nechunya obtain this number from some other source and then retrofit the information into complicated "permutations" of Genesis? Since he lived in the first century, where could this information have come from? And: Could it really have somehow been embedded in Genesis by an author who had access to such information?

Out of the Flames

With the mysteries of the tradition to strengthen his anguished soul, Weissmandl clung to life as the days in the bunker wore into weeks. He began the laborious process of reconstructing the many codes—"boxes and boxes" of which, according to a friend from those days,[23] had been lost to the great conflagration that was consuming the remains of European Jewry.

When the war was over, Weissmandl's spirit was nearly broken. He had lost his entire family; Europe had been stripped almost bare of its enormous and ancient depths of Jewish culture; fully one third of the world's population of Jews had been slaughtered—an unheard-of catastrophe. With a few close friends, Weissmandl made his way to America, there to attempt to put together once again the shattered pieces of his life. The yeshiva in Nitra was gone forever in the destruction—as his father-in-law had foretold. Europe was a gigantic Jewish graveyard; the most important task would be to start a new school yet farther west, in the United States, to replace the one destroyed at Nitra. Weissmandl's great dream of retrieving from exile the ancient manuscripts would have to wait, perhaps to be carried on by others.

Slowly gathering a core of dedicated students around him, Weissmandl resumed again the sacred task of studying and teaching Torah. He had little time to spare, and would have few years left him. Most of his free time in those early postwar years he spent establishing the new yeshiva—and battling the bedroom community of Mount Kisco, just north and east of New York City.

Someone who understood fully the stature of the rabbi had bought the estate of a prominent Westchester County industrialist and bequeathed it to Weissmandl for his yeshiva. The recently revealed Holocaust notwithstanding, many of the well-bred residents of the area—gentile and Jewish alike—were furious that a yeshiva filled with impoverished Eastern European Jewish orphans—black hats, beards, sidelocks, accents, and all—had been planted in the heart of their community. The man who had negotiated face-to-face with the Nazi overlords of Europe was now forced to defend himself and his students—almost all of whom were sole survivors of large, exterminated families, like Weissmandl himself—to the overlords of planning and zoning committees whose objections were always in polite code. The yeshiva was saved by an unexpected ally: a well-to-do lady of gentile society. "She couldn't understand the depth of hatred displayed toward pious Jews," Weissmandl would later explain to his closest friend in America. "Of course she couldn't understand it—it is a spiritual phenomenon, not psychological or social."[24]

The reconstruction of the lost codes could be no more than a sideline. From time to time, he would speak of one or two, alluding to them in the context of his lessons. On one occasion, Rabbi Weissmandl quietly showed one of his discoveries to a most illustrious rabbinic scholar. The man was dazed, and began to cry. Many other highly esteemed rabbis begged Weissmandl to commit his findings to writing and to publicize them. But always he refused, out of modesty, and because no matter how striking his code discoveries seemed, he could not place them before the needs of his yeshiva. He left their redaction to his students, if they wished. A few would later be collected in a book that was published posthumously; but none in English. Some of the students' versions have errors, and most of Rabbi Weissmandl's original findings were lost.

Among the few that survived was an extension of the ancient one located by the Vilna Gaon (see Chapter One), concerning Maimonides (Rambam). The Gaon had discovered the name "Rambam" encoded as the first letters of the words of a phrase in Genesis that seemed directly related to the highlights of Maimonides' life and reputation. Weissmandl discovered more: At an equidistant letter-skip encoding (the type described by Bachya in Genesis) in that same passage was encoded the title of the Rambam's most significant work, his *Mishne Torah*. As mentioned earlier, that is the work that codified and firmly established in Jewish law the precise list of 613 commandments that obligate observant Jews to this day. The passage in question also happens to be the one that opens with the "first command given to all Israel" on the eve of the Passover, to mark the beginning of the months. With 613 letters between the beginning of the two words, both "Mishne" and "Torah" were encoded at intervals of 50 letters. (Between the giving of this first commandment in Egypt and the 613th given at Sinai transpired exactly fifty days, an interval commemorated in the festival named Weeks, or Pentecost, by both Jews and Christians).[25]

Many of the other codes Weissmandl found and discussed with students (some of which they tried to record) were subtler and more complex, and far more dependent upon the nuances and details of Jewish lore, than this one. The linkages that made them meaningful were obscure and intricate and often mathematical—like the connections that Bachya presumed would be familiar to his readers. As difficult as it is even with simple codes to tell whether they aren't merely coincidences—commonplaces to be found any-where if you devote enough time to looking—it is far more difficult to assess the "statistics" of these others. But among the boxes lost to the Nazis, Weissmandl told a friend, had been his collection of relatively straightforward codes similar to that of the Rambam and the Rambam's *Mishne Torah*. This collection contained codes for literally *hundreds of the great sages of Israel's history*. Astonishingly, he had been able to find encodings for *all* the most important ones. Though the codes themselves were now lost, the claim itself was a clue that in time would prove extraordinarily important.

But this clue could not be pursued until three streams of intellectual history would come together to create an entirely new set of instruments that would greatly magnify the power of the human intellect: Kabbalah would have to merge with mathematical cryptology, and cryptology with machine computation. It was the Holocaust that brought about the final consolidation, but the results of the union would not appear before the final years of Weissmandl's life had passed away—he died in 1957. It would take thirty years more for his beloved codes to reemerge, dramatically transformed. When they did, it would be with an intellectual force behind them that had taken at least two millennia to build, beginning in the first century A.D.—or earlier. Only hints of it occur in the Bible, in passages that discuss Israel's fight with its first—or perhaps more accurately—*primordial* adversary: Babylon.

~

CHAPTER SEVEN

FROM ENIGMA TO ATBASH AND BACK

It is sad to observe that a war seems to be essential to encourage and stimulate developments such as the computer. The example is not unique—nuclear energy is another instance; moreover, there was a synergistic relationship between the two disciplines. We shall try to describe this development as seen from Los Alamos.

> —*Norman Metropolis, "disciple" of Richard Feynman and John von Neumann on the Manhattan and Differential Computation projects at Los Alamos. Currently senior faculty there.*

War is the Father of all things.

> —*Heraclitus, ca. 500 B.C.*

1946: *The Secret Victory*

Within months of the Axis's final surrender, the Allies raced to return their budgets to a peacetime footing. Thousands of top-secret projects were declassified en masse, deemed by Congress of no further value. One unusually high-tech project seemed especially ripe for defunding: the cracking of codes via something called a computer. The oversight committee anticipated a quick, routine termination.

It was not to be. To legislators knowledgeable in the more traditional forms of military prowess, Congressman Clarence B. Hancock's assessment came as a surprise: "Cryptanalysts did as much to bring that war to a successful and early conclusion as any other group of men." The final congressional report stated:

> The success achieved . . . merits the highest commendation and all witnesses familiar with [it] have testified that it contributed enormously to the defeat of the enemy, greatly shortened the war and saved many thousands of lives.[1]

Intimately familiar with many of the still-secret details, Vice Admiral Walter S. Anderson put it more bluntly: "It won the war." His testimonial was seconded by no less a soldier's soldier than General George C. Marshall, in writing.[2]

The immense value of cryptology was nowhere more dramatically in evidence than with regard to General Erwin Rommel. Possessed of an uncanny ability to anticipate the Allies' every move, Rommel's strategic genius became the stuff of legend. In fact, he owed his success almost entirely to the fact that the British war codes had been cracked by German cryptologists. He was simply informed ahead of time of every Allied move—until the fall of 1942, when the cracking was discovered.

Under the harsh desert moonlight of October 23 of that year, all his brilliance—and half the strength of his vaunted Afrika Korps—vanished in a surprise British assault at El Alamein. Within three months, Rommel was driven back more than 1,250 miles in an uninterrupted retreat. By mid-1943, the Korps was ready to surrender.

The abrupt vanquishing of the Nazi North Atlantic submarine wolfpacks, the amazing in-air interception and killing of Japan's Admiral Yamamoto—who had devised the attack on Pearl Harbor—in April of 1943, the destruction of the core Japanese carrier fleet and the cream of its naval aviators at the Battle of Midway in June, all these miracles had been wrought by cryptology. Even the deceptive feint that masked the site of the D-Day invasion was accomplished through the making and breaking of codes—and the hiding of that fact. "Before Alamein," said Winston Churchill, "we never had a victory; after Alamein, we never had a defeat." What Churchill really meant when he called 1942 the "hinge of fate" would become clear only many years after Rommel's forced suicide and the Axis's final surrender.

Given these assessments, the cryptology project was immediately reclassified and resumed—larger than ever. At the outbreak of World War II, the then SIS—Signal Intelligence Service—employed 231 officers, enlisted men, and civilians at their headquarters in Washington, D.C. and in the field. Their chief had warned the United States about the Japanese plans for Pearl Harbor—to the day and hour—and his warnings had been dismissed. Congress would see to it that the mistake would not be repeated with the Russians.[3] During World War II, the service had grown to 10,609. By 1968, its peacetime successor, the National Security Agency (NSA), employed more than 20,000 people, twice as many as the CIA. (The exact number is classified, and that last figure is now thirty years out of date.) The "cold war" was not so much cold as *calculated* and covert.

With the veil of secrecy around cryptology operations being drawn ever tighter, a huge explosion in knowledge was being hidden from view. Cracking codes was no longer the domain of gentlemen and generals: It brought together the most brilliant of mathematicians, statisticians, linguists, and machine computationalists—in fact, it created the very domain of computer science that now dominates our world. The NSA itself swiftly became the world's largest employer of mathematicians. But the general public—even academia—was allowed to see, and to use, only a fraction of what the NSA was accomplishing in-house.

The Ancient Source

The thread of secret knowledge that ended with the victory of the Allies in World War II begins long ago in the history of the Jews, closely allied to their distinctive, seemingly puzzling, approach to Scripture. For as far back as records exist, "decryptions" and multiple interpenetrating meanings at the letter level were crucial teachings in the oral tradition. Among observant Jews, the same methods are taught today, beginning in childhood, moving from the easiest to the most difficult, in four steps.

To ascend those four steps is compared to entering a secret *garden*. The word for "garden" in Hebrew is *pardes* (PaRDeS), and each of its letters represents one of the four steps: P for *p'shat*, the simple surface meaning of the text; R for *remez*, hints provided by variations in vowelization or word breaks; D for *d'rasha*, parables that are at once true, yet not to be taken literally (as in the surface Genesis account of the age of the creation, according to Nechunya); and S for the most mysterious layer of all, *sod*, or hidden.

Sod, the fourth level of interpretation, was most highly developed among the kabbalists. From them, there quite organically sprung the earliest arts of encoding and decoding. Eventually, cryptology took on a life of its own as one of the arts of statecraft, growing increasingly distant from its religious origins. But the same conflagration that produced the Holocaust also produced the sophisticated methods needed to scrutinize—rigorously, for the first time—the codes in the Torah from which cryptology had long before grown and separated.

The Language of Secrets

The earliest explicit use of a *second* layer of meaning (known in cryptology as "plaintext") deliberately embedded in a text that reads properly on the surface (called "ciphertext") seems to have been by the ancient Israelites. At least that is where the earliest written references are found. They occur, for example, in Jeremiah 25:26 and 51:42, where the peculiar word "Sheshach" is openly substituted for "Babylon." "How is Sheshach taken! And the praise of the whole earth seized! How is Babylon become an astonishment among the nations!"

This is an example of a letter-substitution code called *atbash* (אתבש = ATBaSh in which the first letter of the Hebrew alphabet, *aleph* (A = א), is replaced by the last, *tav* (T = ת); the second, *bet* (B = ב), is replaced by the second-to-last, *shin* (Sh = ש), and so on. Kabbalistic sages of the Middle Ages referred to this substitution as the "permutation" of letters.*

Couriers of the Secret Art in Europe

Writing about the earliest Hebrew ciphers, David Kahn, the noted cryptologist, points out:

> Three substitutes are used here and there throughout Hebrew writing, particularly Atbash, which is the most common. Their importance consists, however, in that the use of Atbash in the Bible sensi-

---

*An echo of this Jewish crytpography practice may be found in the synoptic Gospels, applied parabolically to individuals: e.g., "And, behold, there are last which shall be first, and there are first which shall be last." (Luke 13:30)

tized the monks and scribes of the Middle-Ages to the idea of letter-substitution. And from them flowed the modern use of ciphers . . . as a means of secret communication.[4]

A variety of codes were used by many nations in ancient times, and most of them were relatively simple: the single-step replacement of one letter by another. Such "substitution ciphers" were relatively easy to decode, as would have been the Atbash permutation—if that was all there was to it. Not until the early Renaissance did cryptology begin a steep development into a complex art, and science. It did so because, at that time, the monks began quietly to investigate ancient kabbalistic ideas—part of the oral tradition rejected by official Church theology—that lay hidden behind the simple Atbash ciphers in the Scriptures proper. The influence of Atbash on cryptology was far more profound than even Kahn realized, because the hidden kabbalistic understanding and use of cryptology was far more extensive than the examples in Jeremiah suggest.

A prime instance of ancient cryptologic sophistication—and of its intimate connection to kabbalah—is the work of Nechunya ben HaKanah of Emmaus in Judea, discussed in the last chapter. He was one of the most prominent students of Simeon ben Yochai, the mysterious originator of the Zohar, the very font of kabbalah.[5] Nechunya lived in the second half of the first century A.D., just after the destruction of the second Temple by the Romans. It was he, recall, who had found in the forty-two-lettered name of God the length of the lunar cycle and the age of the universe. He claims to have done so specifically via Atbash (suggesting that this method must be more complex than a simple single-step substitution cipher), though how he did so he reveals only partially.

Nechunya's book, *Sefer HaBahir*, was one of the major sources for the medieval kabbalists, and many wrote commentaries upon it. Rabbenu Bachya cited Nechunya extensively. In theory, anyone could have learned Nechunya's methods at the time he lived, and probably earlier, since it's unlikely he invented them. But he lived at the beginning of the Jews' great two-thousand-year exile. Buried as his methods were in the mystical core of a religious tradition condemned as fatally flawed by the rising dominant culture, and written in a language that would soon be considered "dead," his methods were as invisible to the world at large as the scrolls that were buried in caves around the Dead Sea at about the same time. Though from time to time, learned churchmen of the Middle Ages would consult contemporary rabbis (and extrabiblical Hebrew texts), it was not until the Renaissance that the treasure trove of Jewish learning, and its independent line of scholarship, began to be taken seriously by non-Jews. Only then did cryptology of sophistication comparable to that of the ancient kabbalists begin to appear in the courts of Western powers.*

As the Renaissance grew ever more fascinated by ancient "classical" ideas from pre-Christian Europe (and elsewhere), the trickle of kabbalistic ideas slowly became a major stream of influence. Because it rarely translated well, and was often misused, this influence was not something most rabbis were interested in cultivating. The contemplative and theological system of the "Ten Sefiroth" (a distinct set of ideas complementary to kabbalistic encoding systems), for example, quickly became corrupted into the occult method of tarot cards. In the Jewish matrix whence the ideas arose, attempts to "foretell the future" by any such means were and remain strictly forbidden.

The influence of kabbalah in Western culture was transmitted chiefly via the arcane and deliberately mystifying concepts of *alchemy*, which served as a repository for a broad spectrum of semiheretical speculations about both spirit and matter. But remarkably often, and invariably overlooked by historians, the *great cryptologists of the Renaissance also happened to be the prominent alchemists*. The point is this: The Renaissance received from the ancient kabbalists not the secret of making gold out of lead in the world of matter, but of making sense out of nonsense, in the world of mind.

Wheels Within Wheels

Simple, single-step substitution ciphers prevailed in European cryptology from the Roman era until the fifteenth century. There then quickly appeared a series of advances that not only transformed cryptology, but laid the groundwork for the development of both statistics and the computer. All those advances were based upon the sudden appearance of the "cipher disk," attributed to the first of the great "Renaissance men," Leon Battista Alberti (1404–1472), known

---

*There may be a hint of a similar process having occurred during the Babylonian exile, when Daniel was called upon to decipher the mysterious "handwriting on the wall" that suddenly appeared at the royal court. Ancient tradition maintains that the reason it needed deciphering was because it appeared in Atbash. The literal text of the Bible is puzzling otherwise, since the text as reported seems to need no decryption.

therefore as "the father of cryptology." "With this invention," writes Kahn, "the West, which up to this point had equaled but had never surpassed the East in cryptology, took the lead that it has never lost."[6]

An architect, athlete, mathematician, moralist, musician, poet, painter, sculptor, satirist, and much else besides, Alberti was a monk whose writings were nonetheless remarkably devoid of theological content. "I make two disks out of copper plates," he wrote. "One, the larger, is stationary, the smaller is movable." Upon each disk, Alberti inscribed one of two different circular sequences of twenty-four letters and numbers. These sequences can be lined up facing each other in any one of twenty-four different ways. One pair of opposing letters (an "index") is conveyed to the recipient who can then properly align his own identical set of cipher disks. The result at this point is nothing more than a simple *substitution* cipher, a convenient way of scrambling ("permuting") the alphabet sequence, as it were, and creating a cipher by assigning each letter the significance of its new position. The cipher disk was mechanically clever, but still created a simple one-step substitution. Alberti took it a crucial step further: "After writing three or four words, I shall change the position of the index in our formula, by turning the circle . . . and all the other stationary letters . . . will receive new meanings."[7]

By permuting the letters of the alphabet not once, but many times, the result was a modern "polyalphabetic" cipher vastly more complex than those previously in use. The word "the" could read "yjr" on first occurrence, "ukt" on second, "ily" on third, and so on.* Alberti's wheel within a wheel looked like this:

---

*The letters *t*, *h*, and *e* were first permuted one step to the right on the standard keyboard, then two, then three.

Interestingly, Alberti explained clearly how he arrived at his many other inventions. But about the thought process behind the cipher disk and multiple substitutions he remained silent.

The Renaissance Men

Alberti was but the first in a rapid succession of brilliant, polymath Renaissance scholars who forged the abrupt advance in cryptology. One of the most prodigious who followed was Trithemius of Spannheim, Germany, who lived in the late fifteenth and early sixteenth centuries. Trithemius entered the Benedictine Abbey of Saint Martin and almost immediately was elected abbot—at age twenty-two. He wrote widely on every imaginable subject, both reputable and shady. Though an influential churchman, he was the teacher of two of the most prominent heretical occultists and alchemists: Cornelius Agrippa and Paracelsus. Reuchlin, the originator of "Christian kabbalism," got his start in Trithemius's renowned library. Eventually, Trithemius's works were placed on the index of banned writings.

In 1499, Trithemius began to publish his cryptographic treatises. Like Alberti, he was evasive as to his sources, claiming that he was taught the art of codes in a dream. Following kabbalistic methods, with which his writings demonstrate he was familiar, he described methods involving the skipping of letters—for example highlighting the second letter of every second word starting with the second word to create (or decode) a cipher. He adapted the kabbalistic method of computing numerical values for names (gematria) to compose a hierarchy of the angels. Like other alchemists and occultists, he considered Moses to have been not so much a prophet as a particularly accomplished magician. This idea was a hallmark of non-Jewish "kabbalists," and as with the tarot, was completely alien to their Jewish sources.

Trithemius's best-known work is his variation on the great prayer, the Ave Maria, which he reworded and cleverly "modularized" so that by varying its phrases, it would serve as a code. According to Kahn:

Each word represents the plaintext letter that stands opposite it. Trithemius so selected the words that, as the equivalents for the letters are taken from consecutive tables, they will make connected sense and will appear to be an innocent prayer.[8]

Trithemius's method is based directly upon a prayer composed by none other than Nechunya ben HaKanah entitled the Ana BeKoach (אנא בכח) found in the Orthodox prayer book to this day. Composed of forty-two words, the first letter of each word forms the sacred "forty-two-lettered name of God." As noted before, this name is itself derived from the first forty-two letters of Genesis via Atbash—but requiring what is called "many permutations." As we will see, "many permutations" is none other than Alberti's "polyalphabetic" cipher—wheels within wheels included.

Another colorful figure of the sixteenth century was Girolamo Cardano of Pavia. Like Trithemius before him, Cardano's exposure to kabbalistic ideas seems to have come via their adoption by non-Jewish circles, most probably in the school of scientist-occultists close to Leonardo da Vinci. (Cardano's father Fazio was a close friend of Leonardo.) Cardano was a breathtakingly iconoclastic and flamboyant physician. In 1522, he traveled to Scotland to treat Archbishop John Hamilton for asthma, a risky, high-profile undertaking in an era when good outcomes were few and far between. His success led to wealth and worldwide fame. He was also the first physician ever to give an accurate clinical description of typhus; he devised somewhat effective treatments for syphilis; and he invented a Braillelike system to teach the blind how to read by touch.

Cardano was even more outstanding as a mathematician, publishing the earliest solutions for cubic and quartic equations. A century before Pascal and Fermat, he published the first systematic (though often inaccurate) computations of probabilities and devised an integrated theory of statistical outcomes in the form of a treatise on games of chance.

But Cardano has achieved immortality for his outstanding contributions to cryptography. Building upon Alberti's "cipher disks," his first invention was the so-called autokey, in which the first few letters of the plaintext itself (the hidden, intended message) provide the rule that tells the recipient of a polyalphabetic cipher how far and how often the inner wheel should be turned against the outer.

From Alberti's "cipher disks" and Cardano's "autokey" were eventually derived all the sophisticated encoding machines used by the Axis in World

War II. Instead of two disks to permute one letter into another, three nested disks, or more, could be used. Mechanically, the only additional modification was to place the disks side by side instead of within each other. (With the addition of electrical motors, the prototypes of what would eventually become the Enigma machines used by the Nazis were born.)

These devices did something else, too: They mechanically "mapped" multiple arithmetic inputs onto a single output. But it took nearly a century after Cardano for cryptologists to realize that, in effect, these mechanical cipher disks *computed*.

Cardano's second contribution to cryptology reflects another form of kabbalistic encoding and decoding: skipping letters within an otherwise plausible ciphertext. His method would later form a key component in mechanical and electronic data and instruction processing. It consists of a stiff sheet of paper or cardboard into which has been cut a set of holes. They may be of uniform size and spacing, or one or both may vary. The encoder writes his intended message in the openings, removes the grille, and fills in the remaining space with blind text (nulls), preferably meaning-ful-seeming.

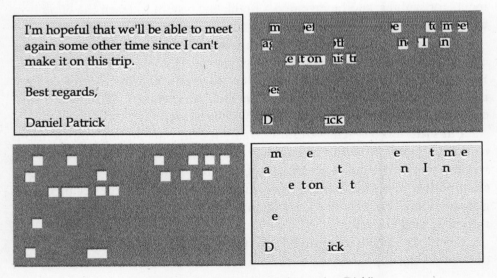

Cardano Grille: "Meet me at nine tonite. Dick"

To decipher a message, the recipient must either have a grille identical to the sender's, or must know the spacing rule that created it, if it conforms to a rule. An equidistant letter cipher, like the Bible Code, is the equivalent of a "simple" Cardano Grille. Note that although the *rule* is simple, the encryption process is more difficult since the encoder must devise a sensible-sounding message that accommodates encrypted letters at fixed positions: for a complex message, an exceedingly challenging problem in "combinatorics."

Kahn rightly notes that "the method's chief defect, of course, is that awkwardness in phrasing may betray the very secret that the phrasing should guard: the existence of a hidden message."[9] For the kabbalists, such "awkwardness in phrasing," and other seeming "defects" or inconsistencies may be hints that there is more to the text than meets the eye. Often enough, "The stone which the builders refuse is the keystone of the arch" (Psalm 118:22).*

Even today, training in cryptology begins with the study of tabularized cipher disks whose resulting encryptions are crackable only via statistical methods. These are universally known as Vigenère tables, after the French diplomat who devised them. But Blaise Vigenère (1523–1596) was also an alchemist profoundly influenced by kabbalah. In his alchemical treatises, he quotes directly from the Zohar to echo the ancient understanding of the Torah as the "blueprint" used by God to create the world: "The world is fashioned after the likeness of its archetype," he wrote ("*Ad archetypi sui similitudinem factus*"),[10] the "archetype" being the configuration of letters—the "key," or in alchemical language, the "philosophers' stone" ultimately derived from the very names of God Himself—that gives each element of the world its essential nature.

Full Circle

Once Alberti introduced the method of polyalphabetic substitution and the cipher disks to mechanize the process, cryptology never abandoned them, as the illustration on page 98 shows:

---

*Freely translated.

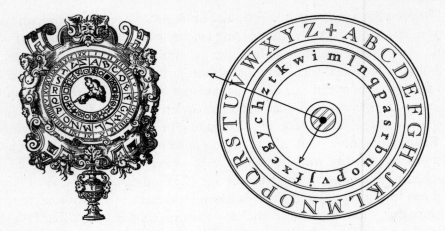

Cryptographic encoding wheels after Alberti: (*left*) Giovanni Battista Porta (sixteenth century); (*right*) Charles Wheatstone (nineteenth century), used by the Confederacy in the U.S. Civil War

The kabbalists did not often draw explicit diagrams of such ideas. But in the eighteenth century, a little-known kabbalist by the name of Rabbi Abraham ben Jechiel Michal HaKohen, published a treatise in Hebrew describing in detail the ancient method of Atbash. He also provides a diagram of what Nechunya meant by "many permutations." It looked like this in the original:[11]

Redrawn for more careful consideration and comparison are the original Hebrew version and a comparable device with English letters:

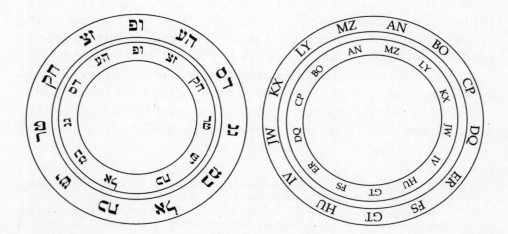

If you follow the sequence of first letters in a pair around the circumference of a disk, you'll see that it takes only half the letters to go around once; the second half of the alphabet then forms the second member of each pair. The result is a more compact device that offers two possible "indexes" (directly across in pairs or criss-crossed) for each permutation. Although the pairs on the inner wheel are the same as those on the outer, and the order within pairs is the same, the sequence of pairs around the wheel is reversed. The Hebrew wheels are shown aligned in the initial Atbash position that gives the method its name, with the outer א (A), ת (T), ב (B), and ש (Sh) at the bottom right. The outer (large) א (A) "crosses" to the inner (small) ת (T); the outer ב (B) crosses to the inner ש (Sh); the outer ל (L) crosses to the inner כ (Ch), and so on. Depending on how the wheels are aligned, the letters are permuted differently; the presence of wheels illustrates that the ancient reference to "many permutations" is identical to Alberti's method of polyalphabetics.

In the Atbash transformation of the first forty-two letters of Genesis, the first three letters of the decryption turn out to be the first three letters of the Hebrew alphabet: a strong hint that the "many permutations" use the first three letters of the forty-two-lettered name of God as an autokey (or at least part of it), the method later reinvented by Cardano.

Recall that the system of Atbash is "hinted" at—a small example is actually given—in the Bible itself, in the Book of Jeremiah. Even the most skeptical "higher critic," who denies any divine transmission or inspiration of Scripture, places the authorship of Jeremiah hundreds of years before the first century A.D. Another hint as to what the ancients were about may be found in the fact that there are *two* biblical texts that serve as foundations for the kabbalah. One is the opening passage of Genesis. The other is from the prophet Ezekiel: "Now as I beheld the living creatures . . . their appearance and their work was as it were *a wheel within a wheel*" (Ezekiel 1:15–16; my emphasis).

In short, the methods that ignited cryptology in the Renaissance not only go back fourteen hundred years earlier to the mysterious oral Jewish tradition of the first century; they appear to go back at least another four hundred to five hundred years before that—they represent a continuous body of knowledge occasionally feeding, but mostly hidden from the larger world around it.[*12]

---

*The intimate connection of kabbalistic Atbash disks to the Hebrew calendar, one of Nechunya's main concerns, is evident in this ancient mnemonic for the days of the week on which fall the festivals of any given year: *Alef, bet, gimmel, dalet, hay, vav* (א ב ג ד ה ו) represent the first six days of Passover for that year, whatever they happen to be. Via Atbash, *alef* = *tav* (Tishah-b'Ab); *bet* = *shin* (**Shavuoth**); *gimmel* = *resh*

The Mathematicization of Cryptology

Once the wheels-within-wheels methods of Atbash made their way out of the closely guarded world of kabbalah and into the surrounding culture, there followed a direct and rapid line of development to the modern computer. Cryptology slowly lost its mystical dimension and acquired instead a profoundly mathematical character.

Sir John Wallis was England's preeminent cryptologist and until Isaac Newton, its greatest mathematician. Like many of the great cryptanalysts, both religious and secular, Wallis was a man of wide-ranging interests and prodigious talent. He was an accomplished logician and musician; he mastered French, Latin, Greek, and Hebrew. He was ordained in the Church of England in 1642 and achieved fame that same year by decrypting a crucial cipher during the conflict between Cromwell and the Royalists. In his *Arithmetica Infinitorum*, Wallis laid the foundations of the calculus and of the binomial theorem, a crucial element of statistics. He was driven to it because with the advent of polyalphabetic ciphers, the cracking of codes had become a quintessentially *statistical* process, requiring a sophisticated application of theories of chance, probability, and combinatorics. (Cardano, too, had been driven to develop primitive statistical methods as a consequence of his cryptologic pursuits.)

Though mathematics and statistics are intimately related, a gift in one does not necessarily mean a comparable gift in the other; and many more people are comfortable with mathematics than with statistics. For this reason, the development of solid statistical theories and methods took place well after mathematics had become quite sophisticated. The person chiefly responsible for placing statistics on a solid footing was a French contemporary of Wallis, the religious-mathematical giant Blaise Pascal—known as well as the father of the computer.

Night of Fire

Pascal was born on the eve of June 19, 1623, in Clermont, France. His universal intelligence was evident from the earliest years of his life. By the time

---

he was twelve, he had completed the equivalent of a doctoral education in the humanities, arts, and sciences. On the side, he also worked his way through the complete geometric analyses of Euclid. By age sixteen, he was breaking ground in calculus, inventing methods for the computation of so-called conic sections that encompassed—and superseded—the nineteen-hundred-year-old and until then definitive works of Apollonius of Perga.[13] His methods in calculus are still in use today.

Pascal developed the first orderly analyses of fluid dynamics (the incredibly complex unfolding of currents and vortices in liquids and gases), and his equations have hardly been advanced upon since. The problems he only partially solved long remained among the most intractable in physics. The next major advance was not made until World War II at Los Alamos, by John von Neumann, who has become known as the father of the *modern* computer.

But as a mathematician, Pascal is best known today for having conducted the first systematic, accurate investigation of probability, laying the groundwork for the scientific method that would emerge with the European Enlightenment that erupted just after him. In his own age, he achieved universal renown for inventing a machine that could calculate: the first computer.

Frail from birth, Pascal died when he was thirty-nine. The manner of his death reveals what this great scientific and mathematical genius considered of greatest value in his brief, brilliant existence. It was neither mathematics nor mechanical computation, but man's relationship to his Creator, and thereby to his fellow man.

Born into the upper reaches of French society, lauded by royalty and the cream of the intelligentsia, as he grew more ill, Pascal gave away more and more of his possessions to the poor. In June 1662, he took in an impoverished family all of whom shortly thereafter developed smallpox—dreaded in that era as a crippling and often fatal disease. Rather than turn them out, Pascal himself left to stay in inadequate quarters elsewhere. There, his own lifelong frailty caught up with him. Two months later, on August 19, 1662, he died.

Indeed, for all his profound contributions to mathematics and science, Pascal is probably more widely known for his religious writings, especially his *Pensées* (*Musings*). They were preliminary sketches for a comprehensive defense of the Christian faith against what he considered the shallow and poorly thought through materialism and determinism of the emerging Enlightenment—which gave rise to hedonism, as well. Pascal sacrificed completion of this monumental work of theology—the sketches alone have become a classic—his dearest effort, that he might provide comfort to the last days of an unknown peasant family, and in doing so, willingly shortened his own life as well.

"Pascal's wager" is his application of statistical mathematics—not quite rigorously, but more than metaphorically—to the question of God's existence: that in the absence of certainty, the odds of His existence, and of the benefits of His existence, greatly outweigh the odds against—and the price of disbelief. It was, in effect, the first cost-benefit analysis, as applied to the most important kind of cure: that of the soul. For the scrupulously rational man, he concluded, faith is the more, not less, rational choice. "The heart has its reasons of which reason knows nothing." This famous aphorism comes from a man whose mind operated at the very pinnacle of rational clarity, precision, and brilliance.

On the night of November 23, 1654, eight years before his death, Pascal underwent a two-hour-long mystical experience, the details of which he recorded on parchment. To the end of his days, Pascal kept this parchment sewn into the tunic he wore. When one tunic wore out, he transferred it to the next. It begins:

> *Fire*
>
> *God of Abraham, God of Isaac, God of Jacob, not*
>   *of philosophers and scholars;*
>   *Certainty, certainty, heartfelt, joy, peace . . .*

How was Pascal able to reconcile the seeming contradiction between faith and reason, and to maintain such a high level of each? A careful reading of his writings on *miracles* provides the answer: Pascal understood intuitively that the material world was intrinsically *probabilistic;* that it was not, as the emerging Enlightenment philosophy implicitly presumed, deterministic, that is, a gigantic machine whose every subsequent state was wholly determined by its preceding ones. For that reason Pascal was able to attain such keen insights into statistics before so many others.

The philosophy of determinism is so much a part of our everyday worldview that we hardly notice it at work. Neither are we aware of the extent to which it is merely presumed, rather than demonstrated. When René Descartes wrenched mind apart from matter, the practical implication was this: Whatever happens in the material world—anything whatsoever, and everything—happens solely *because of some other prior material cause.* Mind or spirit add, nor can add, nothing to the result. Hence, neither mind nor spirit is *relevant* because neither can have any effect (except, perhaps on themselves and each other). This presumption produces the explicit statement (by some) or the implicit belief (of many) that the world is at bottom meaningless because it is just a machine. In a wholly determined, mechanical world, the organ of religious faith is the mind's vermiform appendix: universal, atavistic, useless, toxic when inflamed, best excised at the earliest opportunity.

It certainly seems plausible that "given sufficient knowledge," the reasons for *anything* may be known. After all, it is true that *a very great deal indeed takes place with sufficient reason.* And that which may thus be known increases inexorably. Once, long ago, it was thought that the sun moved about the earth because a god pushed it where he wanted. Should he change his mind, it would go elsewhere. Later, it was understood that the earth simply falls around the sun, and that there is no more intentionality in its orbit than in the fall of an overripe apple. So the deists—believers in a personal God—fell back to defend areas where ignorance still prevailed: "Inanimate material is a machine," they conceded, "but life is another matter."

Then living matter, too, was shown to consist of many, molecule-size machines. Once again, the deists retreated: "Yes, we were mistaken. Life, that is the body, is a machine. But the mind, the human mind, the *psyche*, the heart of man; that's another matter." Then Prozac is developed while we await other drugs to reduce aggression, increase our nurturing impulses, and raise our IQs.[14] Is the soul, then, simply a collection of neurotransmitters?

Since the current state of any material thing is wholly determined by its preceding state, the flux of all existence is likewise determined. If the God of Abraham, Isaac, and Jacob can't quite be proved nonexistent, according to determinists, He is in any event utterly impotent.

Pascal the genius, the author of modern statistics, the father of computer science, lived as all these notions were germinating. He saw clearly the bitter fruit they would one day bear and said, "No, these clever notions are probably not true." Nor was he bluffing: When a family of impoverished strangers arrived at his door and, by their suffering, wordlessly asked him to stake his own life upon his wager, he laid it down without hesitation. What transient worldly advantage could possibly be worth a permanent place of honor in the world to come? Alas, it is chiefly his scientific, computational, and statistical achievements for which he is now honored by us; not for his religious writings, spurned by moderns as the last gasp of a dying primitivism. So whence arose his nobility of character? Before he died, he left a cryptic hint: "The Old Testament is a cipher." But we moderns can no longer read the key.

The Dawn of the Modern Era

In the early to mid-nineteenth century, the Lucasian Professor of Mathematics at Cambridge University was Charles Babbage. He is known today above all for formalizing the principles of mechanical calculation, and for creating a working prototype significantly in advance of Pascal's, the "difference engine."

But because his "astonishingly advanced"[15] works on the subject were never published, Babbage's immense stature as a cryptologist is almost entirely unknown outside of professional circles. In fact, Babbage's pursuit of cryptology was the shuttle that wove mathematics, statistics, and machinery together to produce the difference engine. The use of mechanical cipher disks and Vigenère tables led naturally to his attempt to develop machines that could generate mathematical tables; those tables in turn had been the product of his fascination with *trends*, that is, probability and statistics. It was he who discovered that the "wheels within wheels" of cipher disks could be reversed to create general calculating machines. So, why was Babbage's cryptology work never published? For the same reason that most such work was not: national security.

Cryptanalysis had suddenly became serious business, upon which "the fate of men and nations" did in fact hang. "The secret art" became the organized province of governments, and more secretive than ever before. Meanwhile, methods in statistics and mechanical computation began developing with similar rapidity, the three domains feeding and refeeding each other, moving toward convergence. When that occurred during World War II, the result would be the world-transforming technology of *computer science*: software and hardware crystallizing around a hidden seed of cryptology. The shock that stimulated the final sixty-year run up to convergence came in the form of what many later historians would evaluate as *the* critical event of World War I.

The Zimmerman Telegram

"Almost alone, the unraveling of the Zimmerman telegram . . . brought America into World War I." So writes a former senior officer of the British Intelligence Service.[16] There is no question that had America *not* entered the Great War, it would have been lost to the Central Powers. But Americans were profoundly reluctant to join the fray. What changed their minds was a broken cryptogram from the German foreign minister to the German ambassador to the United States, "[t]he unraveling . . . of [which] changed the course of history as no other feat of cryptanalysis has ever done." The telegram read:

> We propose to begin on the first of February unrestricted submarine warfare. In doing so, however, we shall endeavor to keep America neutral. In the event of this not succeeding, we make Mexico a proposal in the following terms: . . . Generous financial support and an understanding on our part that Mexico is to reconquer the lost territory in Texas, New Mexico and Arizona. The settlement in detail is left to you.[17]

Less than three months later, America declared war. The director of German Intelligence wrote in his memoirs that the decryption "was a great intelligence coup and did us irreparable harm."[18]

A small United States cryptology service was established and funded. Nonetheless, a fierce resistance to the power of code cracking remained in certain circles: "Gentlemen don't read other people's mail," in the 1929 words of then U.S. Secretary of State Henry L. Stimson. And most people could barely understand the methods of the cryptanalysts. It took the intelligence disaster of Pearl Harbor for them to be taken completely seriously.

World War II

> "Midway was essentially a victory of intelligence," Nimitz has written. . . . General Marshall was even more specific. . . . The codebreakers of the Combat Intelligence Unit had engrossed the fate of a nation. They had determined the destinies of ships and men. They had turned the tide of a war.[19]

Thus wrote Kahn regarding the war in the Pacific. On the other side of the globe, the situation was no less dramatic:

> The Allies turned the tables on [German Admiral] Dönitz . . . when they had mastered the German U-boat code, and fast as Dönitz radioed orders to his submarines, direction-finders enabled their positions to be determined and they were pursued, hunted down and sunk. German losses during that period accounted for the greater part of her fleet of U-boats.[20]

But there was a larger secret, "the best-kept secret of World War II," not revealed until 1974 when Congress decided that secrecy was not all that important to cryptologic success. (The NSA was also pressured then to reveal the history of its own origins.) That secret was that in 1934, the Poles (who have given the world an astonishingly large number of the most brilliant mathematicians) had quietly broken the vaunted, supposedly indecipherable German "Enigma" encryption scheme, and that the British and Americans had continued without interruption to crack every update and improvement to it, however advanced, without the Germans ever suspecting. Indeed, they had a hard time believing it was true even in 1974. But it was.

After Pearl Harbor, the American *military* fully appreciated the value of cryptology. More than two million encrypted words per day were transmitted from Allied Supreme Headquarters; thousands of individuals worked day and night unraveling enemy transmissions. Among those thousands, three individuals stand out starkly. For in addition to their immense contribution to the Allied victory, their work produced the final convergence of software, hardware, and cryptology. The results would transform the world—and, as it happened, would provide the instruments needed to propel the ancient codes of the Torah into the fierce spotlight of modern science.

William Friedman and 97-Shiki O-bun In-ji-ki: a.k.a. *Purple*

The vast American cryptologic establishment of today, with its thousands of employees, its far flung stations, its sprawling headquarters—this gigantic enterprise . . . is a direct lineal descendant of the little

office in the War Department that Friedman started, all by himself.
. . . His life's work, as extensive as it is intensive, confers upon William
Frederick Friedman the mantle of the greatest cryptologist.[21]

Friedman was born Wolfe Friedman in Kishinev, Russia, in 1891. After
his family emigrated to the United States and changed his name to William,
Friedman went on to become a geneticist. But then he, and his fiancée,
became fascinated with then-popular tales of secret codes found in the works
of Shakespeare. Those codes, it was claimed, revealed the bard actually to be
Roger Bacon. By 1920, at the age of twenty-eight, Friedman published what
is widely considered the single most important publication in cryptology: *The
Index of Coincidence and Its Applications in Cryptography*, a work that sin-
gularly "led cryptology . . . into the broad, rich domain of statistics."[22] (As a
sideline, the Friedmans debunked the Roger Bacon/Shakespeare codes.)

By 1938, Friedman was head of a hand-picked team of brilliant cryptanalysts at the renamed Signal Intelligence Service. Whereas British
and American intelligence had secretly cracked all the most important
German war codes, including Enigma, the Japanese had recently brought on
line a new code system—nicknamed "Purple"—that really *was* frighteningly
secure.

It took Friedman and his men nearly twenty months to arrive at the first
successful cracking of a Purple cipher. So strenuous was the mental effort that
upon completion, Friedman suffered a nervous collapse and was hospitalized
for four months. He was discharged just before Pearl Harbor, only to learn
that a German official had been leaked news of the cracking of Purple, and
had passed the information on to Tokyo. Everyone heaved a sigh of relief
when the Japanese simply refused to believe it.

But the Japanese weren't the only skeptics. The United States military
itself didn't believe it when, as a result of Friedman's efforts, the Signal
Intelligence Service passed word that Admiral Yamamoto had convinced the
Japanese war cabinet to attack the U.S. fleet at Pearl Harbor on December 7.*

---

*Twenty years after the war, the Americans showed the Japanese a version of the Purple cipher machine
they had "reverse engineered" based on Friedman's decryptions. The Japanese were dumbfounded, and
insisted that the Americans must have gotten a look at an actual Purple device somewhere. But they eventually swallowed the bitter truth—and soon thereafter they placed their own fledgling machine computation industry on a top-priority crash course of development. The results speak for themselves. (Neither have
the Japanese suffered any second thoughts about the importance of keeping such developments top secret.)

War is indeed "the father of all things." By 1942, the Allies—the Americans and British in particular—had come fully to appreciate the power they had in their hands. Both wartime governments assigned top priority to the immediate, integrated development of ever more sophisticated techniques in cryptology, computation, and mathematical statistics: The Ultra Project was born. Theoretical techniques grew ever more complex, forcing the development of ever faster calculating machinery. Mathematical geniuses were aggressively courted and supported; costs ballooned. But the results were dazzling.

Turing and Von Neumann: Ultra and Manhattan

The name Los Alamos is permanently wedded in the public mind to the Manhattan Project and the development of the atomic bomb. But computerized numerical computation techniques—a direct outgrowth of computerized decryption—made the bomb possible. It was an explosion of mind, rather than of matter, that had allowed the Manhattan Project to succeed, and it changed our world forever.

A key figure in the numerical computation effort, and one of the most important people in the parallel development of the atomic bomb, was John von Neumann. Like an increasingly large number of mathematically minded young men in the early twentieth century, Von Neumann was drawn both to the most abstruse realms of higher mathematics and to the astounding world of quantum mechanics.

The results of quantum physics suggested a world that operated according to mysterious principles utterly at odds with the mechanistic model that science had espoused for so long. The mystery fascinated Von Neumann's questing spirit. Following in the footsteps of Pascal, he was the first to attempt a rigorous mathematical proof, based upon quantum mechanics, that determinism is in principle impossible and that the world, therefore, must unfold according to absolutely unknowable "causes" that are not "part" of that world itself at all.

This union of higher math and higher physics (and unsettling strangeness) has become even more in evidence today than in Von Neumann's day. And once again cryptology plays an unexpectedly large role. As I write, early in 1997, a dramatic report was published in the eminent scientific journal *Nature*, describing a direct technological implementation—the first in any domain—of the utterly mysterious foundational principles of quantum mechanics. The domain of the application is—by now it should come as no surprise—cryptology.[23] British researchers had constructed a device for *quantum key encryption and decryption*. The device allows a key to be secretly distributed in such a way that should the key become *known* to an unintended listener, both the transmitter of the key and all designated recipients of it will *instantaneously know that illicit knowledge has come into existence*, and so can immediately avoid using that key. The principles involved are such that this knowledge of illicit knowledge occurs everywhere at once—in principle, over the entire universe. Limitations of present technology severely constrain the distances over which this "transmission" is currently practicable, but based on their working prototype, the editor of *Nature*, commenting on the research, suggests that encryption among agencies within, say, the Washington, D.C., metropolitan area, is already attainable.*[24]

After fleeing Nazi Germany, Von Neumann settled at the Institute for Advanced Studies at Princeton along with Albert Einstein and other fellow refugees. There, he turned his immense abilities to foundational questions in mathematics, picking up trails followed by Pascal. He concentrated in particular on a subject that had long been intractable: the *numerical* solution of complex equations in fluid dynamics. His success would prove crucial to the war effort, with respect to both cryptology *and* the unleashing of atomic energy.

It turns out that many of the most important processes in nature are governed by equations that cannot be perfectly solved. An example is the so-called three-body problem. The equations that describe the motion of objects moving about in each others' gravitational fields can be solved exactly for two objects (say, the sun and one planet). But they cannot be solved for three objects or more. That such equations *have* answers, however, is evident by the fact that nature works; but we can only approximate them "numerically." The difficulty, of course, is in obtaining approximations sufficiently precise to be useful.

The method for doing so is straightforward in principle, complex in practice: Guess, measure how wrong you seem to be, tinker with your initial

---

*The astonishing announcement of quantum cryptography should have greatly excited the world's media—but it was overshadowed by another report in that same issue of *Nature*. Scientists had shown a genetic difference among the Jews of today between "Cohanim" (the ancient biblical "priests" from the tribe of Levi) and "Israelites" (laymen from the other eleven tribes) consistent with the oft-considered legendary claim in Scripture that all Cohanim are descended from one person: Aaron, the brother of Moses. Apparently, the orally transmitted tradition of one's tribal origin was startlingly accurate.

guess accordingly, again measure, tinker, measure, and so on—iterating over and over to whatever degree of accuracy you need, or can obtain.

It may turn out that you need thousands, or millions, or even billions of iterations, to achieve the needed precision. Even relatively simple problems could require teams of people working for months on mechanical adding machines and tabulators to get but one adequate answer. This was in fact the state of the art in 1941. There are photographs that show teams of clerks filing, sorting, collating, and refiling stacks of cards (like Cardano Grilles) according to "dumb," but megastep mechanical rules, for hours on end. The process was inelegant, intellectually unsatisfying, and boring almost beyond imagining. The results were, literally, explosive. The route to improvement, of course, is to find better ways to automate the brute calculations: Hence numerical methods forced the rapid development of computers.

Also, as soon as one tries to gain knowledge through the use of approximations, one has entered decisively into the domain of *statistics*, since statistics is, precisely, the science of guessing, *and most importantly of understanding how to estimate the likely error in a guess* (that's the science part; anybody can guess), based on large numbers of similar items.

Since without a key, decryption of an unknown message involves all of these principles, their convergence was inevitable—so, too, the tapping of John von Neumann. The direction his work would take was likewise apparent. Once the theoretical methods had been developed, the machinery to perform the iterations needed to keep up with the ever changing Nazi and Axis encodings was essential.

But that understates the matter. It was of mortal consequence that numerical analysis advance with utmost rapidity: Whoever "got there" first got the atomic bomb. "Getting there" entailed the ability to solve theretofore completely unsolvable mathematical problems in a way never tried before. That was the *only* way of tackling the differential equations that would make possible the extraction of uranium and plutonium in sufficient amount and purity to explode. Thus was Von Neumann forced by war to father the modern computer.

There was still one piece missing from a complete convergence of statistics, cryptology, and computation. The available encoding and decoding devices were, in effect, automated statistical calculators that were specialized exclusively for cryptologic purposes. To develop a general "equation solving machine," it would be necessary to have a kind of universally applicable device that was *not* specialized in its application—a kind of machine "brain." Just as Charles Babbage had "reversed" the cryptologic machines of his day to generate the first "calculators," it would be necessary to "reverse" modern cryptologic machines to produce an all-purpose computing device.

We now take the existence of "programmable" hardware for granted, but the principles underlying such a device are far from obvious: Its design must reflect the universal principles that are involved in *all* forms of knowledge.

Those principles exist. They had been lurking at the heart of pure mathematics for centuries. They were extracted by a brilliant, greatly troubled, but fiercely patriotic Englishman named Alan Turing. Turing, too, went to Princeton where he met and was offered an assistantship by Von Neumann. With the help of a logician by the name of Alonzo Church, the concept of "computable numbers" was born, and shortly thereafter the "Turing Machine." It was not a physical device, but it was the conceptual prototype for a "universal computation device" that would make possible the actual device assembled by Von Neumann.

A top-secret project aiming at the construction of a Turing-type computer began. (Its existence was not revealed until 1976.) But the war clouds on the horizon grew too menacing for Turing to remain in the United States. He returned to England and accepted a high position in the ultrasecret headquarters set up at Bletchley Park outside London. Von Neumann similarly traded in his academic comforts in order to join the team being assembled at Los Alamos.

But the interdigitation of their work continued, and code breaking was its guiding activity and its goal. Already back in 1936, Turing had noted: "We are then faced with the problem of finding suitable branches of thought for the [Turing] machine to exercise its powers in. . . . The field of cryptography will perhaps be the most rewarding."[25] Closely allied to the applications to cryptology lay large philosophical questions about the very nature of chance and reality itself. Neither Von Neumann nor Turing ever lost sight of these great issues despite the pressures on them to develop immediately useful military applications. Each time a practical obstacle occurred, their teams would develop a whole new method that after the war would become an independent field of study.

Von Neumann pushed on into game theory (first explored by Cardano) and developed the now universally used statistical methods of so-called Monte Carlo simulation (central to the Torah codes debate), in which the odds of an event could be calculated most readily not by theory, but by mimicking the system in miniature. The method reflected his old conviction that a profound and *irreducible* mystery lay concealed within the foundationally statistical nature of quantum mechanics.

Turing, meanwhile, pushed ever toward the boundaries of knowledge and of meaning itself, while almost single-handedly ensuring the great naval victories over the Nazis that helped seal their fate. He focused on the "subjective" aspect of probability, the probability of "knowing" something given imperfect information and multiple influences. (What are the odds that the coin in my hand is resting heads up? Fifty percent? Only if you don't already know that it is in fact tails up, as I know, because I put it that way. So perhaps the odds are 0 percent.) He proved something quite amazing, too: that no general (Turing) machine could physically exist that would be able, even in theory, to solve *whatever* mathematical problem given it. He showed that there exist "noncomputable problems." Yet human beings seem able simply to "see" their solutions. These are not equations with only numerical solutions, but general "truths" that we can intuit, and can sometimes prove logically after the fact. Turing showed that no machine can arrive at such a solution. (Then what exactly *is* the human brain, we might ask? And how did it come into physical existence?)

Turing was able to show that a class of problems exists (he showed some subtle ones) for which the number of machine steps involved in a proof are infinite. Yet human beings can intuit the presence of these kinds of "patterns" relatively easily. Building upon Turing's work and certain features it has in common with quantum mechanics, Roger Penrose is at the forefront of a rigorous and controversial group of highly accomplished scientists who believe that the mystery of human consciousness itself is dependent upon quantum mechanical principles that seem, in an eerie way, to mimic features of the world of spirit.* Among other projects, they are today pushing toward the development of "quantum computers" that can indeed arrive at "noncomputable" solutions—just as the mind seems to. Practical implementations (in the world of cryptology, again) are already in the works.[26]

---

*While this subject invariably runs the risk of attracting fringe enthusiasts, Penrose has shared the Wolf Prize in physics with Stephen Hawking for his own contributions to cosmology. In addition to being a superb mathematician, he has made outstanding contributions to both general relativity and to fundamental quantum mechanics.

Turing, too, was fascinated by quantum mechanics—precisely because it seems to offer a way around the limitations of the mechanical worldview. While circumspect in their professional publications, both Von Neumann and Turing were clearly driven by a fire that could only be termed "spiritual." As a young man, Turing had written:

> We have a will which is able to determine the action of the atoms probably in a small portion of the brain, or possibly all over it. The rest of the body acts so as to amplify this. There is now the question which must be answered as to how the action of the other atoms of the universe are regulated. Probably by the same law and simply by the remote effects of spirit but since they have no amplifying apparatus they seem to be regulated by pure chance. *The apparent non-predestination of physics is almost a combination of chances.* [My emphasis][27]

The italicized comment should be filed away for later reference.

In March 1954, Turing sent some postcards to a close friend, who kept three. On them Turing had written:

Messages from the Unseen World

The Universe is the interior of the light-cone of the Creation.

Science is a Differential Equation. Religion is a Boundary Condition.

> *Hyperboloids of wondrous Light*
> *Rolling for ages through Space and Time*
> *Harbour those Waves which somehow might*
> *Play out God's holy pantomime.*[28]

Whole books could be written about these terse physical/spiritual speculations. Suffice it to say that Turing was referring to the quite serious attempt by physicist David Bohm, who, startled by the implications of quantum mechanics, was attempting to understand—and give mathematical expression to—quantum mechanics' overthrow of standard determinism by appealing to waves of "active information" that permeate the universe, coordinating everything into a mysterious, willed unity. Rearrangements of atoms—even those that compose the biological basis for mind—rearrangements that generate or influence thought, that produce insight or delusion, could occur not solely because other nearby atoms exert their mechanical influence, but because it is so *willed*. Invisible, these "waves" even guide the hand that writes—with the most accurate "transcription" of the silent pantomime produced by he whose mind is most conformed to that will, perhaps?

Precisely whose will, if it is a who, is another matter altogether. Three months later, Turing died.

Weissmandl and Ultra

All the effort that goes into breaking a code is lost the moment the enemy realizes that it has been broken. (Hence the shattering security implications of the quantum cryptographic keys mentioned above.) Cracking a really difficult cipher is therefore only half the job; the other half is keeping the fact hidden. Unfortunately, one of the fastest and easiest ways to let the cat out of the bag is to give evidence of knowing something that can only be known by reading the cipher. One of the most dreaded decisions facing any military strategist is whether to refrain from acting upon a discovery—and so perhaps allowing a terrible price to be paid by others—for fear that action would result in a far higher price later.

At one time one of Turing's Enigma decryptions *had* been too directly acted upon, and as with the Americans' near disaster with the Japanese code previously, it almost reversed the course of the British victory at sea. By playing off German ignorance of the decryption, the Allies fooled many (but even so not all) of the Nazi high command into believing that a feint on D-Day was the actual invasion. Success depended almost wholly on the Allies knowing what the Germans knew (and thought); and upon the Germans knowing neither what the Allies knew nor that the Allies knew. By the time Berlin figured out what was going on, it was too late. (Rommel, sensitized to the extraordinary value of decryption, had long before figured it out—but Hitler would not listen to him.)

As Rabbi Weissmandl sat in the bunker, immersing himself in the ancient codes discovered by the kabbalists, he agonized over the Allies' failure to respond to his pleas to save his people from destruction. Why did they not bomb the rail lines to Auschwitz? It wasn't that they disbelieved his smuggled information: He had letters acknowledging it. In the years after the war, the Allies repeatedly claimed that it was simply because such bombings would have done no good in the larger scheme of things. The Germans would just rebuild immediately.

But Weissmandl knew that most of the Nazi high officials were keenly aware of the price they would pay were the world to become aware of their secret crimes. If the lines to Auschwitz—of no military significance—*had* been bombed, the message to Berlin would have been unequivocal: We know, and you shall pay. The deportations and exterminations would have ceased immediately. And Weissmandl knew the Allies knew this, too. So why did they not act?

Only in 1996 was it finally revealed that even before Rabbi Weissmandl forwarded his smuggled map of Auschwitz, British and American intelligence already knew about the Holocaust—in excruciating, bureaucratic detail—from the Ultra Project, Enigma transmissions intercepted and decoded by the Allies in London. The British Americans knew about it in June 1941, seven months before implementation of the "Final Solution" would begin; six months before the attack on Pearl Harbor, the foreknowledge of which the Americans did not believe. A calculation had been made, and agreed to by Churchill himself, long a friend of the Jews: Saving the Jews was not worth revealing to the Nazis the fact that their vaunted war-code had been penetrated. The Allies feared that the Nazis would conclude that the cracking of Enigma was the only way their dire secret could have been exposed. It would have been inconceivable to them that the deed had been done by a pathetic Slovakian rabbi.

But what seemed, and perhaps was, a heartless failure of the Allies to respond to the plight of his beloved Jewish people left Weissmandl himself a broken man. If it was true, as he believed and lived by, that "to save a single life is to save the world," what could be said about a calculation that deliberately paid out one or two million of them? That the calculation itself was carefully kept from public knowledge until November 1996, and then forced into the open, not volunteered, suggests an answer.[29]

The "hinge of fate" that won the war also closed the circle: The Jewish kabbalists had given the world cryptology and all its fruits; to keep secret the acquisition, Auschwitz would be allowed to operate until the very end. What would Weissmandl have thought had he lived to learn that there would subsequently arise a powerful movement that denies the Holocaust altogether; that points to the Allies' failure to act on what they were told as prima facie evidence that the Holocaust never happened; indeed that claims the Holocaust was *invented* by one man: Rabbi Michael Ber Weissmandl?[30] The Holocaust denial movement, or anything that could even vaguely be thought of as evidence for its claims, would never have had the opportunity to arise were it not for Allies' decision to keep secret for more than fifty years its own extensive knowledge of it.

The ancient underground stream had come full circle; the primordial serpent had bitten its own tail: What more fitting image could there be than the bite of a serpent for such a cruel intersection of time and eternity as Rabbi Weissmandl had had to live through? Could the antivenin for the toxin of ultimate meaninglessness be extracted from the bite itself?

CHAPTER EIGHT

THE BIBLE CODE EMERGES

We shall not cease from exploration
And the end of all our exploring
Will be to arrive where we started
And know the place for the first time.

—*T. S. Eliot, "Little Gidding"*

For millennia, the codes in the Torah could never have been more than a sidelight. They were simply too hard to find, and they were extraordinarily difficult to confirm. Indeed, the very idea of *statistical* confirmation is relatively new (and it remains confusing to many still). When, in the thirteenth century, Rabbenu Bachya had remarked that "if the eyes of your heart will be opened, you will see that [the encoded date of the primordial new moon] is not by chance," he was conceptually far ahead of his time in even addressing the possibility that it might be. But he did not have the mathematical tools to justify his claim. It only *seemed* to him to be true. The skeptic would—and should—try to burst the bubble: The eyes of the heart always see what they want to see. Jeremiah himself pointed out that "the heart is deceitful above all things" (Jeremiah 17:9).

What precipitated a dramatic new era in the ancient story of the codes was not simply the discovery of the never before identified "Aaron" code in Leviticus (discussed in Chapter Three); it was the application of formal statistical analyses to the codes—and the unexpected results. Therein lay the confluence of generations of intellectual, spiritual, and scientific endeavors. The claim that codes existed in the Torah lay at the very heart of kabbalah, the ancient Jewish tradition. Out of this tradition, as we have seen, developed the art of cryptology, and as the crucial element for cryptology's further development there emerged mathematical statistics. In time, success in the making and breaking of codes became a life-and-death matter for nations— and by the twentieth century, for the entire world. Such pressures force-bred the development of computers. With all these elements in place, it became possible for the first time ever to reexamine the ancient mystery. Before Eliyahu Rips's work on the "Aaron" phenomenon, no code in the Torah had ever been approached in that way—nor could have been.

At about the same time, other Israeli scientists had become aware of the phenomenon and were beginning their own investigations. Mostly the investigations were cooperative, but as in any scientific endeavor, competition began to arise as well—all to the good, since structured adversarial debate between qualified disputants is both the emotional fuel for scientific advance and the best insurance of intellectual rigor. (Your work had better be good because your highly qualified opponent has a big investment in proving it isn't.)

But this precipitated another kind of debate: between religion and science. Even at this early stage, some religious voices were beginning to express concern that in such an approach to the sacred Torah, science was treading where it ought not. It was a reaction that would arise repeatedly, among both believers and skeptics. This dichotomy is the modern form of Cartesian duality, a kind of mental and psychological "keeping kosher"—not with separate plates for meat and milk, but with separate mental repositories for science and faith, matter and spirit, head and heart. But to keep science apart from religion is to keep hope and wish uncontaminated by solid evidence. In any event, the first of Maimonides' thirteen principles of the Jewish faith states, "*Know* there is God . . . ," don't just believe it. How does one do that without evidence?

By the late 1980s, the challenge as to whether the codes research was "kosher" had been put to respected rabbinical authorities: Had an ancient gateway, theretofore tightly sealed, been opened wide to yet another level of meaning in the Torah, or was the gate an illusion? Should the gate be opened using so cold and profane a key as statistics, in principle a "skeleton key," which anyone could use on anything? Should it be opened *at all*? Assuming the work proved scientifically valid, just what *were* its religious implications?

What if the research failed? What would that prove, or seem to? What effect might be expected on the spiritual well-being of those involved in the research, not to mention those not closely involved—and unable to form an independent assessment?

These were serious concerns with potentially serious consequences. Not long ago, a young Jewish couple considering a return to Orthodoxy put off the bris of their newborn son—the ritual circumcision that brings the child into the Covenant of Abraham—pending the publication of a refereed scientific paper on the codes. When such a paper was published (see Chapter Twelve), they proceeded with the bris. This scenario had to have been a thoughtful rabbi's worst nightmare for dozens of reasons. The most obvious of these is the question, What would they do if the paper was later rebutted?

But in the eighties, these storms were as yet no more than mild crosscurrents to Eliyahu Rips's careful, dispassionate process of testing and probing the solidity of the growing number of findings. As the head began to discern the outlines of what the heart had long envisioned, specific parameters of the codes phenomenon began to take shape—parameters that could be sharply defined and measured. Accordingly, the search process was refined. The research began to grow more focused, and therefore increasingly subject to rigorous scrutiny and quantitative assessment. Unstructured exploration slowly gave way to a-priori hypothesis formation, controlled testing, and statistical analysis. The phenomenon began to look genuine, possibly, even to those with scientific—not just religious—training. It was now worth examining, even if still too imprecise for formal publication and peer review. One of the most crucial of the parameters that emerged early on was that of *clustering*.

Clustering

Rips, and others, had noticed something about the "Aaron" phenomenon that he thought might represent another clue to where significant encodings might lie. Abraham Oren had noticed the *absence* of explicit references to Aaron in a specific passage in Leviticus, but an absence of something (especially on such subtle grounds) would be very difficult to quantitate. But even though Aaron himself was not specifically referred to in the text, the *word* "Aaron" (as in "sons of Aaron") *was* present in a little "flurry" in the simple text ("ciphertext," using cryptologic terms) of the Torah itself.

Rips thus reformulated the "hypothesis" in more objective terms. It was as though he said, "Perhaps significant *encoded* words will tend to cluster around flurries of their *simple* appearance in the text." (That is, perhaps significant *plaintext* [encoded] words will cluster around their *ciphertext* [surface] equivalents. Later, Rips would conclude that the phenomenon seemed to hold up even when the ciphertext word wasn't in a flurry.) He then shaped an investigative procedure that was a little less like mere exploration and a little more like a research protocol:

1. Assume the hypothesis is true. Decide beforehand (that is, before actually checking) on some locations in the Torah likely to conceal hidden words related to the passage itself.

2. Select words to search for. Why, at the start, certain words are selected and not others will be based on the nuances, history, and religious import of certain words in Hebrew, in the Torah, and in the oral tradition. The selection may seem arbitrary to someone who has never heard these "silent overtones" to certain words. But from a scientific point of view this does not really matter. The important point is that once a passage is chosen and a word selected for investigation—on whatever grounds—both the search for hidden occurrences and the statistical testing must take place *after* the selection. Rips did not simply search for coincidental appearances of words, use statistics to identify the really impressive ones, and then throw out all the failures. Indeed, at the end, and only then, he performed a rigorous computerized analysis on *all* the words in Genesis and did a statistical analysis on the aggregate (discussed below).

3. Perform statistical analyses on the selected words (similar to the ones described in Chapter Three), and additional checks as well.

Once again the results were startling. Rips discovered an extremely large number, and proportion, of cases where, as he had surmised, *the topical theme for a given passage as represented by a single word in the surface text* (e.g., the word "Eden" in passages that discuss the Garden of Eden) *was echoed by an unusually large cluster of encoded appearances of that same word in that same passage*—more often than could reasonably be expected merely by chance. It was as though *this* paragraph had deliberately been written in such a way as to ensure that the word "cluster" could be extracted from it many times at many different equidistant letter skips. Following are two of the simpler examples that illustrate the phenomenon:

מארצושמימוכלשיצהשדהטרמיהיהבארצוכ
לעשבהשדהטרמיצמחכילאהמטיריהולאלהי
מעלהארצואדמאיעלעברהאתאתהאדמהואדיעלה
מנהארצוהשקהתכלפניהאדמהוייצריהוה
אלהימאתהאדמעפרמהאדמהויפחבאפיונש
מתחייהמויהיהאדמלנפשחיהויטעיהוהאלה
ימנגבעדנבמקדמוישממשמאתהאדמאשריצרוי
צמחיהואלהיממנהאדמהכלעצנחמדלמראה
וטובלמאכלועצהחיימבתוכהגנועצהדעת
וברעונהריצאמעדנלהשקותאתהגנומשמי
פרדוהיהלארבעהבראשימשמהאחדפישונהוא
הסבבאתכלארצהחוילהאשרשמהזהבוזהבהא
רצההואטובשמהבדלחואבנהשהמהנהרה
שנייחתונהואהסובבאתכלארצכושושמהנה
רהשלישיחדקלהואההלכקדמתאשורוהנהר
רביעיהואפרתויקחיהוהאלהימאתהאדמוי
נחהובגנעדנלעבדהולשמרהויצויהוהאלה
ימעלהאדמלאמרמכלעצהגנאכלתאכלומעצה
דעתטובורעלאתאכלממנוכיביומאצלכממנ
ומותתמו

Genesis 2:4–17 SHOWING the three appearances of "Eden" in the surface text (shaded עדן = EDeN) plus 19 hidden "Eden"s spelled out at various equidistant intervals. Many letters are used more than once.

מארצושמימוכלשיצהשדההטרמיהיהבארצוכ
לעשבהשדהטרמיצמחכילאהמטיריהולאלההי
מעלהאראצואדמאיעלעברהאתאתהאדמהואדיעלה
מנהארצוהשקהתכלפניהאדמהויייצריהוה
אלהימאתהיהאדמעפרמהאדמהויפחבאפיונש
מתחייהמויהיהאדמלנפשחיהויטעיהוהאלה
ימנגבעדנבמקדמוישממשמאתהאדמאשריצרוי
צמחיהואלהיממנהאדמהכלעצנחמדלמראה
וטובלמאכלועצהחיימבתוכהגנועצהדעתט
וברעונהריצאמעדנלהשקותאתהגנומשמי
פרדוהיהלארבעהבראשימשמהאחדפישונהוא
הסבבאתכלארצהחוילהאשרשמהזהבוזהבהא
רצההואטובשמהבדלחואבנהשהמהנהרה
שנייחתונהואהסובבאתכלארצכושושמהנה
רהשלישיחדקלהואההלכקדמתאשורוהנהר
רביעיהואפרתויקחיהוהאלהימאתהאדמוי
נחהובגנעדנלעבדהולשמרהויצויהוהאלה
ימעלהאדמלאמרמכלעצהגנאכלתאכלומעצה
דעתטובורעלאתאכלממנוכיביומאצלכממנ
ומותתמו

Genesis 2:4–17 showing three appearances of "the river" in the surface text (shaded הנהר = HaNaHoR) plus thirteen hidden "the river"s spelled out at various equidistant intervals. Many letters are used more than once.

The following table shows a small selection of the findings in the Eden story from among those that have been presented widely in a number of venues. In one publication (*B'Or HaTorah*) where they appear, the authors offer statistical assessments. I have taken the basic claims, repeated the search process, and performed my own rough estimate of the statistical value using conservative measures. These should not be taken as providing anything more than a rough approximation, however, since they are not the result of formal, controlled experiments. But the numbers should provide the reader with a feel for what was generating the intense interest, both among skeptical scientists and among the lay audiences beginning to hear about the codes. I have selected some examples that appear quite impressive; others appear less so. Note the values for the number of times a given word or phrase was expected to appear, and the approximate odds for the actual number of appearances (based on a relatively simple so-called Poisson distribution for expected versus actual occurrences).

Hidden Hebrew Word	English Meaning	Passage in Genesis	Number of Letters in Text	Expected Appearances of Hidden Word	Actual Appearances of Hidden Word	Odds
עדן	Eden	2:4–17	657	13.16	20	1/100
הנהר	The River	2:4–17	657	6.12	13	1/1,000
מקום	Location	1:6–13	407	2.05	5	1/50
מקוה	Body of Water	1:1–13	604	3.34	12	1/10,000
המועדים	The Appointed Times	1:6–19	705	0.00122	1	1/70,000,000

Here are some of the highlights of the above examples:

- Hidden "Eden"s cluster around open "Eden"s in the passages that describe the Garden of Eden. Where approximately 13–14 hidden "Eden"s are expected to occur in this text of some 657 letters, 20 actually do. The odds against this are better than 100 to 1.
- Hidden "the river"s cluster around open "the river"s in the same pas-

sages as above. They also describe the rivers that run through the garden. Since "Eden" is three letters long in Hebrew and "the river" is four letters long in Hebrew (and unlike in English is a single word), there is a measurably lower expectation of finding the latter than the former. Six to seven hidden appearances of "the river" are expected to occur in this 657-letter text; 13 actually do. The odds against this are better than 1,000 to 1.

- The next sample, "location," is a word with a quite different nuance in Hebrew than in English, conveying a sense of specialness. "Location" appears openly once in Genesis 1:1–1:13. Clustered about it are 5 hidden appearances of the same word. In text of that length, one would expect to find only 2 occurrences. The odds against this are better than 50 to 1.

- Twelve hidden "body of water"s appear in a similar section of text as "location," but fewer than 4 such appearances are expected by chance.

- The final example, "the Appointed Times," is of a different class, and it indicates a distinct line along which the research was beginning to converge. In all of Genesis, there is only 1 open appearance of the word HaMOADYM, "the Appointed Times": in the same area of Genesis discussed by Rabbenu Bachya, Rabbenu Tam, the Zohar, and by Rabbi Weissmandl. That is the part that discusses the creation and the fixing of the sun and the moon to establish the calendar. The term appears again later on, in Leviticus 23, where 70 "Appointed Times" are delineated for each of the special holy days of the calendar.* HaMOADYM is a long word, and we would therefore not expect to find it many times in a short section of text, if at all. In fact, the expectation of finding HaMOADYM hidden even once in *any* portion of Genesis 705 letters long (the length of the passage that includes its 1 open appearance) is about 1 in 1,000. It is expected to appear only 5 times in *all* of Genesis, a text of 78,064 letters. In fact, HaMOADYM appears in hidden form only once in all of Genesis. On that one occasion its equidistant letter interval is exactly 70, and centered within the span of that hidden appearance is precisely its sole open appearance in Genesis.

---

*Fifty-two Sabbaths, 7 days of Passover, 1 day of Shavuoth ("Feast of Weeks"), 1 day of Rosh Hashanah ("Feast of Trumpets"), 1 day of Yom Kippur ("Day of Atonement"), 7 days of Sukkoth ("Booths") and 1 day of Shemini Atzereth ("Eighth [Day] of Assembly") (52 + 7 + 1 + 1 + 1 + 7 + 1 = 70).

The odds against this are better than 70,000,000 to 1. Note that this phenomenon was *anticipated*, not merely discovered and reported after the fact. (Babe Ruth hit lots of home runs, but everyone remembers the game when he pointed ahead of time to where he would hit one at that moment. It would have meant nothing had he pointed to the stands after he hit the ball there—then claimed that he knew he would; or always pointed to the stands, sometimes hitting it there, usually not.)

■ המועדים = HaMOADYM* = "The Appointed Times"
□ מועדים = MOADYM = "Appointed Times"

*This appearance of HaMOADYM = "The Appointed Times" has a skip of 70 letters, which is "minimal over 100 percent of Genesis." It contains within it an appearance of "Appointed Times" (no "The") which is "minimal over 92 percent of Genesis." The meaning and significance of this further qualification will be discussed in Chapter Nine.

Understanding this "cluster" effect will help us see that what distinguishes the Bible Code from the usual kinds of codes used in intelligence work is that the *codes in the Torah do not appear to convey a hidden message.* Instead, they seem to be a purely statistical phenomena: noteworthy because they appear in situations where the odds *against* their appearance are so great.

Take a look at the assemblages of dots below. Technically, both assemblages may be called clusters, but the one on the left is too ordered for that word. Note that there *is* an orderliness to the assemblage on the right, even though that order is "fuzzy." That's what we mean by "cluster": a tendency for things to more or less hang together, to happen one way and not another, yet imperfectly. Such phenomena can be intuited with great accuracy (our minds seem specially suited for just that purpose—detecting patterns in "noisy" streams of input). But many of these can be shown to be genuine, and not illusory, only by using very sophisticated statistical methods. (The downside of our pattern-detecting powers is our tendency to invent patterns when nothing is there but noise. This is an especially common problem when the emotional investment in seeing meaning or pattern is high, and the concepts involved are slippery. Religion is the domain par excellence for this kind of distortion to creep in.)

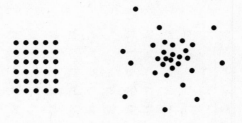

The fact that there may not be a precisely delineated rule to describe the "fuzzy" order does not mean there is no rule. The methods for arriving at these fuzzy rules are the very ones developed by cryptologists over the preceding 200 to 300 years: Don't just try to "guess" what the hidden cipher is (and then assert that your guess must be correct because it makes sense to you, and it's what you want it to be); use rigorous statistical methods *on a*

large enough sample to detect "statistically significant" deviations from what would be expected simply by chance. Those deviations point to hidden order; in the case of genuine codes and ciphers, to *intentional* order. So many phenomena turn out to be understandable only with this kind of statistical approach that a whole new area of study has arisen called "fuzzy logic," wherein "pretty much so," "almost," "not quite," and "just about all" are mathematically manipulated with the same accuracy as are simple numbers.

Following these principles, Rips focused his attention on the first two chapters of Genesis. More so than any others, these passages have long been held by Jewish tradition to embody "concealed" information that can be mined using the cryptanalytic methods first proposed by the early kabbalists and students of the Zohar. Rips looked for areas within these two chapters where a significant word appeared in the surface text as a flurry of actual occurrences, not just as a topic. He found a number of such localized clusters. He then searched the entire two chapters identifying the *hidden* appearances of those same words. Once again the same phenomena seemed to emerge. *Hidden* appearances of a word tended to cluster around localized *open* flurries of that same word in the ciphertext.

It should be emphasized right away that even though this orderliness was "fuzzy" rather than exact, it quickly became apparent that it was likely to be *intentional*, rather than, say, a peculiarity of the mechanics of the language. There are simply no mechanical processes that can plausibly give rise to that degree of clustering. Many subsequent tests were run to check this, and indeed, no mechanical cause has ever been found.

Just within these two chapters of Genesis, Rips—and a growing body of people who were becoming quite intrigued with results, other scientists among them—found an enormous number of clusters, a small sampling of which was reported in print by Professor Daniel Michaelson, a mathematician at UCLA and the Hebrew University who was now living in Israel full-time.

A skeptic would be wise to argue at this point that, apart from quarrels concerning which statistical measures are best to use for these kinds of "fuzzy" analyses, how can we be certain that good examples haven't been disproportionately selected over bad ones, which are ignored? This needn't imply any intent to deceive—it is an unconscious selection process well-known to scientists who do not trust even themselves without adequate controls.

Aware of this possibility, Rips, now working together with Michaelson, who had been drawn like a magnet to these astounding findings, pushed the analysis to the next logical step. They examined *all* of the words in these sections of Genesis—computationally a huge undertaking, on a par with serious cryptanalytic work—looking for clustering effects not unlike those found by Friedman. Michaelson describes their results:

> What about other words? Obviously, we cannot here show all the results.* However, about 40% of the words in the above three pages [of examples reproduced by Michaelson in this article] produced a strong clustering effect. Another 40% showed a moderate clustering. And the rest—no clustering.[1]

That is an extraordinary claim. Were a passage of 600 words to show only a *moderate* clustering effect for 40 percent of them, and the rest nothing, the evidence for some hidden order-creating effect would still be overwhelming. (If you flipped a coin repeatedly and got 60 percent heads and 40 percent tails, is that evidence of some hidden bias toward heads? Not if these results were based on 10 coin tosses: a 6:4 ratio is well within chance expectation for just 10 tosses. Intuitively, we know that 50:50 odds for heads or tails doesn't mean that there will always be a perfectly equal number of each. But the more times we toss the coin, the closer we expect the results to come to 50 percent. So, what if we tossed the coin 1,000 times and still got a 6:4 ratio of heads to tails? Practically speaking, 600:400 is clear proof that something's *not* even in the procedure. Las Vegas casinos make fortunes in the long run by skewing the odds in their favor far less than that—1 or 2 percentage points are more than enough.)

A growing body of scientists, rabbis, astonished secularists, and curious visitors from all over the world were beginning to peek over the shoulders of the growing number of scientific experts now seriously studying the "poetic exaggerations" of the sages. Dr. Moshe Katz, a bioengineer at the Technion in Haifa, Israel's equivalent of MIT, began to pursue the phenomenon at first in concert with Rips and later independently. Controversy began to brew, with highly qualified scientists and nonscientists, religionists and secularists, lining up on both sides of the question, Can these findings possibly be real?

---

*Over six hundred independent analyses would have been needed.

Opinions were rarely moderate. Either the material was unequivocal proof not only of divine authorship, but of any theological principle you wish (all at the same time); or else it was utter nonsense. That Eliyahu Rips was on the former side of the debate, however, was a bit disconcerting.

By now, it was the mid-1980s. A physics student in Israel who had just completed his master's thesis on general relativity had also recently left his secular life behind to become a *baal t'shuva*. The term means literally a "master of repentance" and refers to those who return to a strict observance of the ancient faith. He, too, had come to learn of the codes in the Torah, and the more he learned, the more he became convinced they were genuine. He carefully consulted with the senior rabbis who were his teachers and guides as to how he should best pursue this material—or whether he should pursue it at all. They gave him their blessing, and with that he turned his considerable intellectual gifts to the daunting task of placing the codes on a rock-solid scientific foundation. In short order, Doron Witztum would become the preeminent codes researcher in the world, ratcheting up the technique to a yet higher level of sophistication and power; generating evidence of its validity that began to reach high-level scientific publishing circles.

Occasional flurries of public interest, too, would surface here and there, but in general codes research was a fairly esoteric matter. Most "enthusiasts" lacked the mathematical skill to evaluate the findings critically and independently; they had the potential to damage the research by their excitability. On the other hand, most of those with the requisite skills considered the matter beneath consideration. That it was tainted by religion only made things worse.

In the meantime, Rips and Michaelson had traded in their casual Western dress for skullcaps and tzitzit. For Michaelson, the codes had been a secret passage back to the faith of his fathers; he soon left the codes behind to concentrate on the life of that faith: the religious, spiritual, and moral transformation commanded by God. For Rips, the codes were a sideline of a different sort, however important. His return to Orthodoxy had been influenced by other factors. But both were adept with the mathematical and statistical skills required to assess the Bible Code critically. They were amazed at what they were finding. There would soon be many others who were equally amazed, and many more astonishing findings.

~

CHAPTER NINE

THE ARCHITECTURE OF THE GARDEN

In the days of the sixth part of the sixth millennium, the gates of supernal knowledge will open above along with the wellsprings of secular wisdom below. This will begin the process whereby the world will prepare to enter the seventh, Sabbath, millennium.

—Zohar, Commentary on the destruction of
the world at the time of the flood

Some of the brightest intellectual searchlights in the world had swung to scrutinize with laserlike intensity the strange findings emanating out of Jerusalem. Though from a certain highly disciplined point of view one might insist that even if real, these odd correlations of the inner and outer layers of the Torah needn't automatically imply something "supernatural," most people felt in their guts quite otherwise. Once the possibility of divine influence was at least hypothetically allowed (and after all, the text itself made just that claim), it actually seemed *more* plausible an explanation than that, over the ages, a cadre of brilliant, obsessive-compulsive, and dishonest combinatorial geniuses had written and rewritten the text in order to encode as many weird correlations as they could, even though no one else could possibly detect their presence. The findings had reached such a degree of complexity and subtlety that inevitably, one either started to wonder about God, or dismissed the phenomenon out of hand as ridiculous on principle.

The dramatic impact the codes seemed to be having on people did not go unnoticed. Michaelson had entered a yeshiva; Rips was now fully *frum* (Torah observant, down to the last detail). A second circle of people now sprang up around the initial researchers and begun "translating" the findings for the nonspecialist. The trickle of American, Canadian, and other secularized Jews from the Western world who had once again taken up the ancient mantle of traditional Jewish devotion to Torah was turning into a flood. Not a few were scientists themselves, some quite accomplished and eminent who had spent decades of high achievement as secularists—"what intelligent person took seriously the fairy tales of religion?" said one well-known physician. He now refers to his own earlier worldview as "knee-jerk secularism."

One of the most influential "doorways" to this other world was and is the Aish HaTorah (Flame of the Torah) Yeshiva, headquartered in Jerusalem, but with branches all over the world. There was no question but that the codes research it was given access to often proved the match that lit the flame. The effect was explosive.

There seemed to be a certain kind of mental hide that grew thicker and thicker through the long decades of wandering in the desert of enlightened materialism (roughly four hundred years since the start of the so-called Enlightenment). The attitude projected by that "hide" went something like this: "I don't need religion; that's for weaklings. Not only am I smart and independent-minded enough to see through those—let's be frank, *silly*—illusions, *but I'm made of sterner stuff.*" For example, the author of the lead essay in *People of the Book: Thirty Scholars Reflect on Their Jewish Identity* calls herself a "Jewish non-Jew." Yet even this faint residue of her ancient being she feels may be "capitulating to a faddish, retrograde identity politics."[1] Noting the growing hunger among his students and colleagues for a spirituality that runs deeper than the "deconstruction of texts," another literary scholar castigates their longing as "the triumph of ritual over reason and . . . born-again fanaticism over whatever it is that links us as humans."[2] Another insists that to be Jewish "is . . . to be territorial, narrow-minded, militaristic and above all patriarchal."[3] Another summarizes it tersely: "I am Jewish precisely because I am not a believer."[4]

Furthermore, the Bible Code was no ordinary miracle, defying analysis and insisting that it be taken on faith. It sat there without protest or evasion, allowing itself to be poked and prodded any which way at all, subjecting itself day in and day out to whatever scrutiny modern science could muster. Its rev-

elations required nobody's secondhand report: anyone with sufficient determination to insert himself into the mystery could, for all practical purposes,
be "present at Sinai," as their ancestors were said to have been, witnessing en
masse the impossible as it became real.

Unwrapping the Hidden Text

In oversimplified form, the method of skipped-letter encryption is easily
grasped, and when it is used this way by inexperienced enthusiasts, it produces a great deal of nonsense. Most of the real power of the method lay in
subtleties, as they were uncovered, step by step, over years by many different
investigators. The most serious research, now spearheaded by Doron
Witztum, was finding that the encryptions had a number of complex, unexpected features. For example, equidistant intervals between letters could be
quite large—in the thousands at times. (That raised the question of how
"clustering" could mean anything in such a case. This will be explained
shortly.) It became evident that, however many relatively simple individual
examples might have been stumbled upon previously, no well-informed skeptic could possibly have been convinced of their validity on scientific
grounds—nor should have been—until the advances of our own era.

To understand the process clearly, let's follow a series of approximations,
each subtler and closer to the actual method than the one before. In doing
so, we will roughly be following in the footsteps of the codes' history. Earlier
discoveries are relatively easy to grasp—but hard, perhaps impossible, to
prove or to disprove. To comprehend fully the most recent methods and
results requires a sophisticated knowledge of statistics and computation.
Nonetheless, with care, anyone can grasp the basic principles of how the
codes can be uncovered.

What does it mean for something to be in "code"?

What exactly is a "code" and how can you tell when you've stumbled
upon one?

To answer these questions as applied to the Bible Code, let's use a real-
life analogy. Imagine a secret agent—a "mole"—who has been placed in foreign territory on a long-term mission. Over the long years in exile, our mole
depends upon instructions he receives from time to time from his faraway
"control," a man—or perhaps a woman—whose identity is completely
unknown to him. Even though the success of our agent's mission—not to

mention his safe return home—depends utterly upon these instructions, direct contact with his control is out of the question. The instructions he depends upon are cleverly written so that there is no need for them to be in code. His prior training in his home country, before he departed, gave him all he needed to make good use of these instructions. Anyone else reading them would likewise find them practical, but would miss their full significance, lacking his depth of experience with their original context. Our agent need only read and take to heart the simple meaning of the text, filtering it through his long familiarity.

One day at long last, shortly before he anticipates being called home, his luck turns: The enemy has apparently learned of his existence and has devised a cruel and clever method to foil his plans. When next he arrives at the agreed-upon drop, he discovers not one, but *ten sets of different instructions*—all plausible. He panics: Which one is genuine? *Or maybe*—since the enemy has obviously learned what's going on—*none is*.

But the panic is short-lived. Soon, he remembers a rather cryptic exchange that occurred just before his departure so many years ago: "If anything should ever happen," he was told, "remember this: *You will be able to figure out which guidelines to follow.*" Of course, he had inquired how. But almost before he had framed the question, he had been cut off with a simple raise of the hand—and a knowing smile. And then this: *"That we haven't told you precisely how, is itself a clue as to how."*

In the early years, our man had puzzled from time to time over this strange "clue." But things were going smoothly, so eventually he stopped trying. Now, in the urgency of the moment, it was all coming back to him.

In the days that follow, his mind kicked into high gear by anxiety, he thinks the matter through from the bottom up. He has certain facts at his disposal, he has been told, and if only he takes these at face value, they ought to suffice. These facts are:

- First, control had foreseen the possibility of this very problem—how to verify that a communication was genuine—and had devised some subtle means to solve it.
- Second, control has always been superbly logical and of the highest intelligence.
- Third, control's mysterious solution requires no further information than what lies at hand.

After some reflection, our agent deduces the following: There must be some method of determining—beyond any doubt—which of the sets of instructions is genuine. That method must be such as to require *no outside validation*. There is only one way this could happen: The genuine text must contain some kind of authentication within it—like the faint watermark on paper currency. The existence of such a "fail-safe" necessarily requires the following to be true:

1. There must be *at least one additional level of meaning* hidden in his instructions, a level of meaning he had never before noticed or looked for, because there was no need for it—even if its existence had in fact been hinted at long ago.

2. Any such additional level (or levels) of meaning must be *disguised*, for otherwise it could conceivably be detected, mimicked, and distorted by the enemy, just as they had mimicked and changed the surface meaning of his instructions.

3. Any further level of meaning must contain information that would validate the authenticity of the genuine instructions and no other. In other words, *it must be information of a kind available to the genuine author*—control—and to no one else.

From this, our agent reasons further: Any kind of meaningful information (plaintext) deliberately embedded in the surface text of his instructions (ciphertext) must itself be in the form of a *language*. That is, it must be a series of symbols sequenced according to a set of rules.[5] That is because it is the rules that transform an otherwise meaningless sequence of symbols into a meaningful communication. (Let's also note here for later use that the idea of a *sequence* is the most fundamental rule of all. If you didn't know which letter to consider next, there'd be no way of understanding any language. A "linear" sequence—one letter after the other in an uninterrupted series—is the simplest and most obvious "rule," so obvious, in fact, that it's easy to overlook.)

What kinds of rules must these be, then? For example, all languages have rules of *spelling*. But spelling alone is not enough. *Try run purple head forgetfulness weird yes* is a sequence of letters that all form properly spelled English words. But even so, it makes no sense. So there must also be rules of grammar and syntax that enable words to form sentences.

Even so, while rules of grammar and syntax are necessary to communicate, like spelling, they are not sufficient, either. For example, *While exploding, I ate the automobile on the fertile book* is meaningless, even though it conforms to all the rules of spelling, grammar, and syntax.

There's really only one parameter left, the subtlest and most difficult one: meaning itself. *The whole must be connected by a meaning that unites the parts.* So, for instance, unlike *While exploding, I ate the automobile on the fertile book*, the following sentence does make sense because its meaning is consistent as a whole: *While relaxing, I ate the sandwich off the china plate.*

Unlike the fairly precise rules that govern spelling, grammar, and syntax, the rules that govern meaning are especially "fuzzy" (as in the rapidly developing computer discipline of "fuzzy logic").

This fuzziness is particularly true in literary uses of language; less so in scientific use. Pubescent human females are not composed largely of compressed, enormously hot, hydrogen and helium gas—and yet nonetheless, *Juliet is the sun.*

Having worked his way down to this foundational conclusion, our agent now asks the question more pointedly: Is there a simple way of deducing whether or not there is likely to be *meaning* encoded in a sequence of letters, other than the obvious meaning of the "surface" sequence itself? This is tantamount to asking whether there's a simple way of telling whether a sequence of symbols is a language. It might seem at first that the answer is no, since meaning in language is so fluid.

But the answer to the question whether a sequence is a language is actually a qualified yes. It *is* possible to tell how *likely* it is that a sequence of letters is a language—once any fuzziness in the order can be manipulated mathematically by the use of probability and statistics. Like all probabilistic estimates, it will get more and more accurate with more and more data to examine. The method is rather obvious, once it's stated: If there is a meaningful, communicative pattern to a sequence of symbols, it's going to show itself as *a tendency for meaningfully related words to cluster more closely together than unrelated words.*

Consider the most important meaning-bearing words in the last two short sentences above, *While exploding, I ate the automobile on the fertile book*, and *While relaxing, I ate the sandwich off the china plate.* Taken in isolation, *ate, sandwich, china,* and *plate* form a cluster of words related by meaning. *Ate* and *sandwich* are very closely related to each other, as are *china* and *plate.*

These two subclusters are then linked to each other by the "fuzzier" relationship of *sandwich* and *plate*. Computer scientists are well along in the process of implanting these kinds of probabilistic connections into machines.

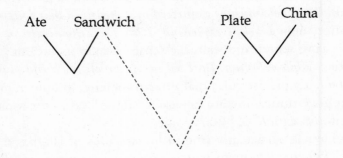

By contrast, consider the words that compose *While exploding, I ate the automobile on the fertile book*. There are almost no potentially meaningful relationships that wouldn't either be a stretch—*fertile* and *book* might conceivably form a metaphoric link in certain rare contexts; or in a relatively unique situation, one might find *exploding* and *automobiles*, say, in thrillers, for instance.

To summarize: Our agent has concluded that in the genuine message there must be some encoded information. He can detect its presence by finding words with related meanings—a fuzzy, but roughly measurable idea—*that tend to cluster relatively "close" to one another in the text*. Now he is ready to take the next step: He must figure out *what kind of encoding rule* control would have used to create these words out of the sequence of letters that form the text. Having studied the art of code making and breaking—cryptology—during his years of training, he immediately sees that only one kind of encryption scheme can be used; all others would require some kind of key, and he was deliberately *not* given one. Indeed, he was told explicitly that having no key was itself the key!

With this insight, the pieces fall together. For two other crucial points dovetail perfectly with the particular kind of encryption scheme he realizes must be present. First, this kind of scheme must involve *information that he himself already knows to be true*. Put differently, he himself will have to choose something to look for—it won't be some piece of information that is new to him. For the purpose of this code isn't to communicate with him—it is simply meant to fail-safe the validity of the surface communication. And, as he realized before, it must also be *information that only control would know.*

With this understanding, the last clue snaps into place, and he smiles to himself: He now understands why, on three separate occasions before his departure, control (whom he himself had never met in person) had ordered him to have dinner with three different dinner partners—and why nothing of particular importance had taken place during those dinners (or so he thought). The one kind of encryption scheme that fits all these parameters works as follows:

1. Control had selected an assortment of events all of which were known both to control and to himself—but only to them. (Each dinner partner, for example, would have known only of his own dinner with our agent, of course, but not necessarily of the others.)

2. Control had then created a grid as follows:

3. Control had then selected a set of likely words that referred to these key events in a variety of obvious ways—names, dates, locations, etc. For example, "Jim, July" and "Bob, June." Then control placed the words onto the grid, *with a variety of regular spacings between the letters,* but kept related words relatively close together, and unrelated words relatively far apart. (Perhaps he even used a Cardano Grille.)

4. For each word he would have chosen spacings that would be "noteworthy," and in some sense obvious, that is, the short spacings rather than long ones:

The salient information contained in the grid, the plaintext, was now a simplified form of "you had dinner with Bob in June and with Jim in July."

5. Finally—and this is the tough part, but he would have no doubt used the agency's very advanced computers to help him—control tinkered with the precise wording of the surface message so as to accommodate the embedded words . . .

A	B	E	J	O	I	N	B	E	N	J	A	M	I	N	J
A	C	K	S	U	N	C	L	E	T	O	O	I	F	I	U
P	T	H	E	I	N	T	E	R	E	S	T	A	M	A	L
I	A	W	I	L	L	E	N	T	E	R	A	L	S	O	Y

. . . which now fade away into the "surface" communication:

A	B	E	J	O	I	N	B	E	N	J	A	M	I	N	J
A	C	K	S	U	N	C	L	E	T	O	O	I	F	I	U
P	T	H	E	I	N	T	E	R	E	S	T	A	M	A	L
I	A	W	I	L	L	E	N	T	E	R	A	L	S	O	Y

(He would also have used the agency's computers to ensure that his embedded words don't accidentally appear elsewhere at shorter intervals.) The surface message is not a mere blind; it is a genuine and important statement. But it now serves as well as a ciphertext containing a hidden plaintext. Control now writes out the message in linear sequence—A B E J O I N B E N J A M I N J A C K S U N C L E T O O I F I U P T H E I N T E R E S T A M A L I A W I L L E N T E R A L S O Y—and adds capitalization, punctuation, and spacing, and sends it out in its usual form:

> Abe:
>
> Join Benjamin (Jack's uncle), too. If I
> up the interest, Amalia will enter also.
>
> Y.

Of course, our agent must reverse this process. And this requires two things if he wants to accomplish it with any certainty: First, he must have some good guesses as to the kind of shared information control was likely to have encoded (since he hasn't been told ahead of time exactly what this was); second, he needs to be able to do some kind of *statistical analysis* that will tell him whether what he found *was unlikely to have occurred just by chance*— for a certain number of such "encodings" (perhaps a large number) are bound to happen at random. (In that case, they aren't "encodings" at all, but are just accidents.)

In fact, he realizes that this means there can't be just one, or a handful, of such "embeddings" in the genuine message, since a small number *will* certainly happen by chance. In order to do the statistical analysis, he must find a large enough number of examples. In fact, even if a single encoded "cluster" *were* put there deliberately, there'd most likely be no way of telling it apart from a cluster that just happened to be there by accident. Here's how he would proceed.

The Decryption Process, Step by Step

Our agent has no idea what the skip interval is—or rather, interval*s* are— between letters (they needn't all be the same, just the same within a single word—"equidistant skips"). But he reasons that the equidistant skip intervals used by control must be small—or rather, small*ish*. Two reasons for this occur to him. One is that if the skip intervals get large, "close" might start to lose its meaning. In any case, it would be far more difficult to assess. The other reason is that in a large enough bit of text, it might be possible to find a given word many times at different intervals. The shortest interval would be the obvious way to mark one appearance as worthy of note.

So, our agent will look for words that tend to be created at equidistant skips that are relatively small, as close as possible to the minimum (which of course would be an interval of two). It will then be the proportion of pairs of related words with these smallish intervals that should show a tendency to cluster near one another—that is, nearer than would occur by chance.

He selects some likely word candidates, based on the events that he and control alone share: "Bob" and "June," "Jim" and "July" (as noted above; but also "Joan" and "May," the third special dinner). And our agent reasonably surmises further that perhaps the locations of these dinners were used by control, too: There's no reason to think that only names and dates were used. So he creates some other "overlapping," likely pairings: "Bob" and "Angus" (the name of the steakhouse they went to), "Joan" and "Burke" (the town in Virginia, not far from Langley, where he and Joan had dinner), and so on. Then he starts searching in the text as follows:

First, he eliminates all the spacing, capitalization, and punctuation in the first message, and writes it out in a grid. Thus, "Abe, join Benjamin (Jack's uncle), too. If I up the interest, Amalia will enter also. Y." becomes A B E J O I N B E N J A M I N J A C K S U N C L E T O O I F I U P T H E I N T E R E S T A M A L I A W I L L E N T E R A L S O Y, and this is entered, in sequence into the grid:

A	B	E	J	O	I	N	B	E	N	J	A	M	I	N	J
A	C	K	S	U	N	C	L	E	T	O	O	I	F	I	U
P	T	H	E	I	N	T	E	R	E	S	T	A	M	A	L
I	A	W	I	L	L	E	N	T	E	R	A	L	S	O	Y

Our agent does likewise for all ten messages (not knowing yet, of course, which is genuine). So, message number 2—"Abe, don't join Benjamin (Jack's uncle). Even if I up the interest, Amalia won't help. Y." becomes A B E D O N T J O I N B E N J A M I N J A C K S U N C L E E V E N I F I U P T H E I N T E R E S T A M A L I A W O N T H E L P Y:

A	B	E	D	O	N	T	J	O	I	N	B	E	N	J	A
M	I	N	J	A	C	K	S	U	N	C	L	E	E	V	E
N	I	F	I	U	P	T	H	E	I	N	T	E	R	E	S
T	A	M	A	L	I	A	W	O	N	T	H	E	L	P	Y

He now carries out the following decryption method on all ten samples, and for every one of the set of likely words he decided upon ahead of time. Starting with the first word, "Bob," he finds the first occurrence of its first letter, "B." (Let's use what we know is the second, "false" message above, since we already know what will happen with the "real" one):

A	B	E	D	O	N	T	J	O	I	N	B	E	N	J	A
M	I	N	J	A	C	K	S	U	N	C	L	E	E	V	E
N	I	F	I	U	P	T	H	E	I	N	T	E	R	E	S
T	A	M	A	L	I	A	W	O	N	T	H	E	L	P	Y

Now he skips *one* letter and looks to see if that letter happens to be an "O," the second letter of "Bob." It isn't (it's a "D"). If it had been an "O," he would again skip one letter and look for another "B," the final letter of "Bob." If all three letters had been found in this fashion, he would have located the first occurrence (of perhaps many) "Bob's" embedded in the text at a skip of 2 (the minimum possible). But since there is no "O" in the proper place, he begins again with the initial "B," looking for its *next* occurrence in the text:

A	B	E	D	O	N	T	J	O	I	N	B	E	N	J	A
M	I	N	J	A	C	K	S	U	N	C	L	E	E	V	E
N	I	F	I	U	P	T	H	E	I	N	T	E	R	E	S
T	A	M	A	L	I	A	W	O	N	T	H	E	L	P	Y

Again he looks for an "O" and a "B" at an equidistant skip of 1, this time starting at the second "B." Not finding even the "O," he begins again at the next "B" (if there is any) and the next.

In this case, there are only two "B's" in the entire text, and neither can form the beginning of an embedded "Bob" at an equidistant skip of 1. So, our agent starts once again at the beginning, but now he searches every "B" looking for "Bob" spelled out at an equidistant skip of 2. This time, he finds an "O" with two letters between it and the first "B":

A	B	E	D	O	N	T	J	O	I	N	B	E	N	J	A
M	I	N	J	A	C	K	S	U	N	C	L	E	E	V	E
N	I	F	I	U	P	T	H	E	I	N	T	E	R	E	S
T	A	M	A	L	I	A	W	O	N	T	H	E	L	P	Y

He skips two letters and looks for a "final" "B"—but it is not there. And neither will an equidistant skip of 2 produce an embedded "Bob" using the second "B" as the starting point.

So, again finding nothing, the agent repeats the process at skips of 3, then 4, and so on. He keeps this up until he either satisfies himself that the word is not embedded at any distance, or else he *finds it at its minimum (shortest) equidistant skip.* In the above case of our "false" example, "Bob" is not embedded at *any* equidistant skip. However, in the "real" example (created for this purpose), our agent finds "Bob" embedded at the small, equidistant skip of 2:

A	B	E	J	O	I	N	B	E	N	J	A	M	I	N	J
A	C	K	S	U	N	C	L	E	T	O	O	I	F	I	U
P	T	H	E	I	N	T	E	R	E	S	T	A	M	A	L
I	A	W	I	L	L	E	N	T	E	R	A	L	S	O	Y

In like fashion, he searches for all the words in his list, using exactly the same method for all ten messages. He finds at least some of his sample words embedded in every message (since as we've noted this is bound to happen from time to time in any text, just by chance); and in none of the messages does he find every last word (since control didn't, in fact, use *all* of them, at least not in the same way). Nor can our agent tell whether any *single* example of embedding was deliberate, or just happenstance. But what's important is that no matter how many of his sets of words he finds in the various messages, *in only one message does he find an unusually high proportion of meaningfully related word* pairs *that appear close together in the text*. It is this unusual closeness ("fuzzily" defined) of an unusually large proportion of pairs that flags the one message as genuine.

There's another clever feature of this method that dawns on our agent, and as he realizes it, he shakes his head in even more profound admiration of control's intelligence. What if he had accidentally dropped a letter or two from the real message in transcribing it; or confused it with another? Unlike other, exactly precise, nonstatistical codes, which are critically dependent upon perfect letter-level transmission, this one can accommodate a certain number of errors without being entirely garbled. It is true that the more errors, the lower the probability of discovering the encrypted words and that enough errors would destroy it entirely. But the method has a certain degree of "fault tolerance" built in—a lot like living systems. In fact, our agent remembered that the human brain itself is similar in that regard, that many of its functions are not starkly on or off, like computer hardware—one connection gone and the whole thing fails. Instead, it "degrades gracefully," in the lingo of neuroscience.

Entering the Garden

By the mid to late 1980s, all the principles contained in the above example had been identified in the Bible Code.

- Genesis (and the other four books of the Torah) could be treated both as an important text in the usual way, and as a "ciphertext" containing some kind of "plaintext."
- The plaintext was apparently constructed by utilizing successive letters in the ciphertext but selected at equidistant intervals—equidistant letter sequences, or ELSs.
- At least to date, the content of the plaintext was not an additional message, but a confirmatory mark indicating the unity and integrity of the ciphertext.
- The content appeared in the form of a statistical tendency for selected

words to appear in identified locations at greater frequency than should occur by chance.

- Early on, one such tendency was for a single word to appear as an ELS many times in a passage of related text.
- But as the research proceeded, it seemed that *two or more different but related words* could be found as ELSs, "in unusually close proximity" to one another. The relationship of the surface meaning of the text to a single decoded word receded in importance; the proximity relation of two (or more) different decoded words began to seem the more distinctive feature of the phenomenon.

The "garden" of meaning hidden within the Torah was designed upon a set of principles only hinted at in the ancient manuscripts. The researchers were now much closer to a complete description. Eliyahu Rips proceeded to test the principles arrived at so far by looking for unusual clusters of different but related words, in locations where—if the phenomenon was real—they "ought" to occur. Two convenient examples to test in Genesis consisted of lists of terms: the "seed-bearing plants" and the trees with "seed-bearing fruit" given to man for food in the Garden of Eden. Both the plants and the trees were mentioned in Genesis, but neither group was listed expressly there; all were named specifically, however, in the oral tradition, as species native to the land of Israel. As confirmation, perhaps these names were encoded in Genesis, as ELSs, close to one another, at relatively small skips between their letters—just as the length of the lunar cycle needed for religious purposes had been.

The Garden

In fact, *all seven edible species of seed-bearing fruit in the Land of Israel were found encoded in just that passage of text that alludes to them,* at a range of equidistant intervals smaller than the same list could be found encoded elsewhere in Genesis; and in a smaller amount of overall text:

- ■ (1) Barley (שערה at –28)
- ■ (2) Wheat (חטה at +5)
- □ (3) Vine (גפן at –18; "ן" is a final "נ")
- □ (4) Date (תמר at +5)
- ≡ (5) Olive (זית at –9)
- ▤ (6) Fig (תאנה at +14)
- ■ (7) Pomegranate (רמון at +8).

The seven species of seed-bearing fruit in Israel embedded in Genesis (1:29) beginning with "God said, 'Behold, I have given you every seed-bearing plant on the face of the earth, and every tree that has seed-bearing fruit . . .' " and ending with " 'You may definitely eat from every tree of the garden. But from the Tree of Knowledge of good and evil, do not eat, for on the day you eat from it, you will surely die.' "*

Partially overlapping with the end of this section of Genesis (1:29–2:16) is another portion of text describing the Garden of Eden. There, too, is a similar statement, this time about edible fruit (Genesis 2:7–3:3): "You may definitely eat from every tree of the garden. But from the Tree of Knowledge

---

*King James Version.

of Good and Evil, do not eat, for on the day you eat from it, you will definitely die."*

Rips predicted that within these passages one ought similarly to be able to find the names of the trees: all twenty-five delineated by tradition. Michaelson later described the results:

> He took all the 25 trees . . . and found them in the above chapter![†]
> Before the reader jumps out of his seat, let us explain that three- or four-letter words would normally appear at some intervals in a segment as long as ours (about 1,000 letters). What is so exceptional here is that most of the intervals (except for ערמנ [chestnut] and לבנה [poplar]) are very short. There is no other segment in Genesis of such length which contains so many trees at intervals less than twenty.[6]

The method was becoming increasingly sophisticated and the findings more and more dramatic—but the statistical assessment was becoming ever more problematic. Rips and Michaelson and others were beginning to push the limits of the kind of statistical assessment techniques available. By one method of analysis, the odds of finding the twenty-five trees were about 1/100,000. That was startling enough, but a whole range of encodings appeared to be overlapping in the same passages of Genesis all at once. The odds against *this* seemed to be astronomical.

But were they really? Wasn't it possible that such encodings could in fact happen merely by chance? Perhaps all that was occurring is that no one had previously had both the necessary computers and the inclination to search for such letter permutations. Perhaps similar kinds of clusterings at minimal distances could be found in any text.

Informally, the researchers had been performing control tests, and what could be found elsewhere happened far less frequently. On a statistical basis,

---

* King James Version.
† In order of appearance, and using no final forms, they are: חטה (wheat); גפנ (vine); ענב (grape); ערמנ (chestnut); עבת (thicket); תמר (date palm); שטה (acacia); אטד (boxthorn); ארז (cedar); בטנ (pistachio); תאנה (fig); ערבה (willow); רמונ (pomegranate); אהלימ (aloe); אשל (tamarisk); אלונ (oak); לבנה (poplar); קדה (cassia); שקד (almond); אלה (terebinth); סנה (thornbush [*Crataegus*]); לוז (hazel); זית (olive); הדר (citron); גפר ("gopherwood," the uncertain species from which Noah was commanded to build the ark. The oral tradition maintains that it was one of two species of cedar; one was especially resinous, the other "rocklike" in its density).

the codes seemed unique to the Torah; especially to Genesis, where most of the work was being done. Formal tests were as yet out of reach. The phenomenon was far better defined than ever before in history, but it still seemed elusive. The final piece would be put into place by Doron Witztum.

Transformations

The astute reader may have noticed a "missed step" in our story of the spy. Let's imagine that he received the various competing messages not on paper but electronically—perhaps as a sequence of letters in Morse code, or as E-mail. In the first case, while there would be simple punctuation (e.g., STOPs), *there would be no line breaks*. In the second case, most E-mail programs "wrap" the lines arbitrarily: at whatever width the screen "window" of the receiver can accommodate. It need not be the same width as that used by the transmitter. There is no absolute line width at all.

In fact, just as our agent removed punctuation and word breaks in order to transform the text into cryptographic form, there's nothing absolute about the line width of the message he received. Cryptologically, a *sequence* of letters is just that: a one-dimensional string of letters and nothing more. Note, too, that the surface meaning of the string, the ciphertext, does not depend at all on what line breaks are used: it derives exclusively from the one-letter-after-another sequence. Write any text out as a string (picture the letters on a long tape, for instance): You may lay it out any way you wish. You can even jumble it up in a three-dimensional ball, but so long as you don't disrupt the sequence, the message remains intact because it is fundamentally one-dimensional.

But control's method of embedding doesn't just require that the one-dimensional sequence be received intact; it also requires that the correct line length—*the dimensions of the original two-dimensional array*—be discovered. Two words that are close at one line-length might not be at another. If control had laid out the terms with a line length of 16, as follows

	B		J	O		B									J
			U												U
				N										M	L
					E										Y
													I		

and our agent searched for them at a line length of 6 (not knowing that 16 was the size of the original grid), the results would look very different:

It would now be very difficult to say whether "Jim," for example, is closer to "June" or to "July." In fact, in the original array laid out by control, the word "July" forms a neat vertical sequence precisely because the line length was equal to the interval between letters. Put slightly differently, control deliberately "wrote" out the embedded terms not only in the usual one-dimensional fashion, but simultaneously in *two* dimensions. When the correct two-dimensional array is hit upon by our spy, the pattern of related words snaps into focus.

More precisely, suppose that I had embedded a number of pairs of words *in this very paragraph*. They would appear close at certain line lengths, but not at others. What if the line length determined by the graphic artists at William Morrow was different than the line length I used when I created the embedding? The closeness—the hidden two-dimensional patterning—would disappear, even though the meaning of the text would be identical:

```
M O R E P R E C I S E L Y S U P P O S E T H A T I H A D E M
B E D D E D A N U M B E R O F P A I R S O F W O R D S I N T
H I S V E R Y P A R A G R A P H T H E Y W O U L D A P P E A
R C L O S E A T C E R T A I N L I N E L E N G T H S B U T N
O T A T O T H E R S W H A T I F T H E L I N E L E N G T H D
E T E R M I N E D B Y T H E G R A P H I C A R T I S T S A T
W I L L I A M M O R R O W W A S D I F F E R E N T T H A N T
H E L I N E L E N G T H I U S E D W H E N I C R E A T E D T
H E E M B E D D I N G T H E C L O S E N E S S T H E H I D D
E N T W O D I M E N S I O N A L P A T T E R N I N G W O U L
D D I S A P P E A R E V E N T H O U G H T H E M E A N I N G
O F T H E T E X T W O U L D B E I D E N T I C A L
```

Four words in very close proximity: "Meet me at limo"

```
M O R E P R E C I S E L Y S U P P O S
E T H A T I H A D E M B E D D E D A N
U M B E R O F P A I R S O F W O R D S
I N T H I S V E R Y P A R A G R A P H
T H E Y W O U L D A P P E A R C L O S
E A T C E R T A I N L I N E L E N G T
H S B U T N O T A T O T H E R S W H A
T I F T H E L I N E L E N G T H D E T
E R M I N E D B Y T H E G R A P H I C
A R T I S T S A T W I L L I A M M O R
R O W W A S D I F F E R E N T T H A N
T H E L I N E L E N G T H I U S E D W
H E N I C R E A T E D T H E E M B E D
D I N G T H E C L O S E N E S S T H E
H I D D E N T W O D I M E N S I O N A
L P A T T E R N I N G W O U L D D I S
A P P E A R E V E N T H O U G H T H E
M E A N I N G O F T H E T E X T W O U
L D B E I D E N T I C A L
```

Same four words not in close proximity

This observation led the codes researchers to reconsider the search process, looking not only for the appearance of embedded words at their minimum equidistant intervals, but searching for that line length of the two-dimensional array in which two or more related terms in fact formed a "compact" cluster. It was critical, of course, that the pair or cluster of words be at their *minimum* skip interval, or very close to it—otherwise the reshaping process would allow almost anything to be found close together at some line length. Rips and Witztum developed a simple measure of "how minimal" a given skip was: namely, the percentage of the text for which the ELS in question contained no other identical ELS with a smaller skip. In the example immediately above, the word "AT" is spelled out at an interval of three letters. Were there no occurrences of "AT" spelled out at an interval of two letters, we would say that this ELS for "AT" is its "100 percent minimal appearance," meaning that the skip of three is the minimum for the entire text in question.

However, "AT" appears elsewhere as an ELS with a skip of *two* letters in our sample paragraph. In fact, counting both forward and backward intervals, it appears at a skip of two in five places. Hence its appearance at an interval of three is not minimal for 100 percent of the text, only for a portion. That portion may be quantified as follows: The ELS "AT" with an equidistant skip of three letters is minimal for that portion of the text within which no other ELS for "AT" may be found with a shorter skip, shown in gray:

```
M O R E P R E C I S E L Y S U P P O S E T H A T I H A D E M
B E D D E D A N U M B E R O F P A I R S O F W O R D S I N T
H I S V E R Y P A R A G R A P H T H E Y W O U L D A P P E A
R C L O S E A T C E R T A I N L I N E L E N G T H S B U T N
O T A T O T H E R S W H A T I F T H E L I N E L E N G T H D
E T E R M I N E D B Y T H E G R A P H I C A R T I S T S A T
W I L L I A M M O R R O W W A S D I F F E R E N T T H A N T
H E L I N E L E N G T H I U S E D W H E N I C R E A T E D T
H E E M B E D D I N G T H E C L O S E N E S S T H E H I D D
E N T W O D I M E N S I O N A L P A T T E R N I N G W O U L
D D I S A P P E A R E V E N T H O U G H T H E M E A N I N G
O F T H E T E X T W O U L D B E I D E N T I C A L
```

The text is 355 letters; 155 are in gray. That equals 42 percent of the text. Hence we say that this ELS for "AT" is "minimal over 42 percent of the text."

The method for uncovering the Bible Code includes the notion of "minimal" encodings—but not perfectly so. Likewise, our agent need only detect a statistically significant *tendency* for proximal clusters of terms to be composed of ELSs at their 100 percent minimal appearances. (The exact details of this measure are described in the Technical Appendix C.)

Once these subtleties were identified and quantified by the codes researchers, the results were immediate: Closely related words of many different kinds could now be found embedded close together almost with regularity. An obvious concern was that the freedom to shape and reshape an array allowed so much manipulation that correlations were inevitable just by chance—and therefore meaningless. But early on, Rips and Witztum checked into this carefully: Correlations did happen randomly, of course, in any text, but they were far less frequent in texts outside the Torah, or with arbitrarily selected terms in the Torah.

The Hanukkah Code

One of the first arrays they discovered and visually represented widely both in their published articles and in hundreds of seminars sponsored by Aish HaTorah involved the Jewish holiday Hanukkah. Hanukkah (which literally means "the dedication") commemorates the uprising of the Jewish community against its Syro-Greek occupiers in 164 B.C. The victory occurred on the twenty-fifth of Kislev, led by Judah and his brothers, the sons of Mattathias, a Levite (that is, of the tribe of Levi) and a Cohen, a priest. The seven brothers and their followers came to be known as "the Maccabees." Their victory was wholly unexpected, and led to the establishment of the "Hasmonean" dynasty, descendants of Mattathias who ruled as kings in Israel until the Roman conquest. Upon their victory, the Maccabees rededicated the Temple, which had been desecrated by the Greek ruler Antiochus Epiphanes IV, who was one in a long line of enemies of the Jews who considered himself divine (and who therefore took special offense at Jewish refusal to worship a man). But the ritual rededication was threatened by a severe shortage of the sacred oil used to keep lit the menorah (the seven-branched candelabrum) without interruption. Although there was only a one-day's supply of oil, the menorah miraculously burned for eight days, until a new supply arrived. Those eight days are still celebrated at Hanukkah by an eight-day festival and a special, eight-branched candelabrum.

The Hebrew word for Hanukkah was found embedded at a 261-letter interval, the minimal equidistant skip for more than 80 percent of all of

Genesis. Witztum and Rips laid out the text in rows 261 letters long, such that "Hanukkah" was spelled out vertically. It was in just *this* arrangement that a closely related word was also found spelled out only one letter-step away from the vertical at its minimal equidistant skip for 100 percent of Genesis, in extraordinarily close proximity to Hanukkah. This second word was "Hasmonean," the family name of the Maccabees, the heroes of Hanukkah who led the revolt against the occupiers of Judea. The name "Judah" was also found there, in the "ciphertext," in that section of Genesis (the story of Judith and Tamar) where the name is found most frequently in the surface text of the Torah. (Note the story of Hanukkah itself is not told in Genesis, but in the much later books of the Maccabees.)

At a horizontal interval of two letters, the word "Maccabee" cut directly across "Hanukkah" in the same array. When the array was reshaped to about one eighth of 262 letters (made one eighth as wide and eight times taller) yet more words appeared in tight clusters directly related to the story of Hanukkah: "Mattathias," the father of the Maccabees; "oil" and "flask of oil," the central miracle celebrated by the lighting of candles in a Hanukkah menorah; "candles" and "menorah" itself; "eight days," the number of days the oil burned and the length, therefore, of "the celebration"; the "twenty-fifth of Kislev," the date that Hanukkah is celebrated; an alternate spelling of Hanukkah, which when broken differently reads, "on the twenty-fifth of Kislev they rested" from their enemies. Even subtleties little known outside the Orthodox community appeared: References to the fact that Judah Maccabee was of the tribe of Levi were linked to references concerning the ultimate destruction of this line of kings. Their destruction was foreordained, it is taught, because of the ancient prophecy—and an associated prohibition—that Levites (priests) should never be kings as well.

The Purim Code

A similar set of terms cluster about the key features of another holiday, Purim, which celebrates the rescue of the Jewish people from their near extermination in ancient Persia, through the intervention of Esther, who had become queen, and her heroic uncle, Mordechai. One of the many arrays found in Genesis that shows details of its events is the following, with the name "Purim," its date ("the thirteenth of Adar"), the name of "Mordecai" and the name and title of "Queen Esther":

Details of Purim in Genesis: The long phrase "13th of Adar, Purim" (בְּיוֹם אַרְבָּעָה עָשָׂר = 13 B'ADaR) anchors an array with the words for "sons of Haman" (בְּנֵי הָמָן = B'NeI HaMaN), "the judgment" (twice; הַדִּין = HaDYN), "Mordechai" (מָרְדְּכַי = MoRDeChaY), and "Esther" (אֶסְתֵּר = ESTeR) all at 100 percent minimums in Genesis. When the array is extended to the right by another 25 percent, additional terms appear including "The Queen" and two more appearances of "the judgment." There are five appearances of "the judgment" at this minimum. Four of them thus cluster within this one array.*

_____

*This array was discovered by the author after learning of the phrase "13th of Adar, Purim."

The Late 1980s: Pressing Forward

The codes work now proceeded on two fronts: general and scientific. Convinced that they had found the hidden key to the encoding process, Witztum and Rips began generating a whole series of general discoveries. Many of these were discussed before Israeli scientific audiences as well as the public; in 1989, Witztum published a book in Hebrew titled *HaMaimod HaNosaf (The Added Dimension)*, which presented nearly two hundred arrays, in which he briefly explained his concept of "two-dimensional writing." As with the example of "Hanukkah," most of these arrays were especially striking in that their terms were related by *historical* circumstance—the name of a person, for example, and the date and place of crucial events in his life; the details of major events in history—relationships, in other words, that did not even exist until long after the letters of the Torah had been written down.* A cluster of "Aarons" in a passage concerning him; or a list of plants clustered in passages concerning the Garden of Eden conceivably could have been placed there by a clever human author—like the checksums used to validate telephone credit card numbers. (A correct number must add up to a certain sum known only to the phone company.) But who could have embedded clusters of words only related by history *after the fact*?

Witztum and Rips were sensitive to the criticism that the reshaping of arrays might appear a manipulation capable of generating almost anything. They knew that they needed a rigorous test of the method. In Witztum's book, they offered a preliminary method for assessing the statistical significance of individual arrays, and arrived at probabilities of better than 1 in 1,000,000 for most of them. But even greater rigor was needed to convince serious skeptics. They began work on the experiment that would eventually see print in the high-level journal *Statistical Science* and that Harold Gans, to his own shock, would validate. This experiment is the subject of Chapter Twelve. But before we turn to it, let's examine some of the codes discovered by Witztum, Rips, Moshe Katz, and others—starting with a test example that we will develop freshly ourselves.

---

*Higher critical scholarship, which denies the tradition of transmission to Moses, dates the text of the Torah to around the end of the Babylonian exile in ca. 500 B.C.

~

CHAPTER TEN

THE HELIX OF TIME

The Sages tell us to study history carefully. For what happened to our forebears is bound to happen again to us.

—*The Ramban,*
Commentary on the Torah

Rabbi Abraham "the Angel"

Presentations of the Bible Code have electrified audiences and observers around the world. Even if the codes' statistical nature limits decryption to events that have already become part of our own past, there is ample reason for amazement—and skepticism: The codes seem to embody information about the unfolding future at a level of detail previously unimagined even by the wildest of biblical pop prophecy fanatics.

As I found myself more and more deeply immersed in the intricacies of the codes as the methods developed over the years, I decided to try to get a direct feel for them by attempting independent decryptions, also using historical data. (Especially since, as we will see, the mathematical assessments about the codes are still being debated.) The steps of one such decryption follow, pursuing clues laid down by Rabbi Weissmandl.

His close friend Siegmund Forst had told me that Rabbi Weissmandl claimed to have found a huge number of equidistant encodings of the names of the great sages. Since they were lost to the Nazis, what these arrays looked like no one will ever know. But we do know what Weissmandl found in the case of the Rambam. Recall that in the passage of text in which Nachmanides (the Ramba*n*) had found the Rambam's name, Weissmandl found the title of the Rambam's greatest work. (See Chapter Six.) It seemed likely that Weissmandl would therefore have found other sages' names coupled to various details of their lives. Of course, this is the basic data pattern used by Witztum, Rips, and Yoav Rosenberg—their various formal studies involve a total of sixty-six different individuals. I do not believe, however, that they were aware of how many more similar instances had been found by Rabbi Weissmandl. It seemed probable to me, therefore, that—for whatever reason—the names of the great sages were especially likely to be encoded. The passage recited every year at the High Holy Days came to mind, too: "Inscribe us, O LORD, in your Book of Life. . . ."

Finally, for purely personal reasons, I settled on the name of one of my own family, a great-great . . . grandfather about whom I have always been curious: Abraham "the Angel"—in Hebrew: *Avraham HaMalach.*

Rabbi Abraham was born in the Ukrainian town of Fostov, near Kiev, and became a Hasidic zaddik, one of the leaders of the great spiritual revival that swept the Eastern European Jewish community in the eighteenth and nineteenth centuries—a last great flowering before the destruction. He was unusual, possessed of a preternatural intensity of spirituality that kept him above earthly concerns—unlike most zaddikim—yet he was compassionate and exceedingly gentle. Once, on the ninth day of Ab, the date that commemorates the destruction of both Temples (and various expulsions as well), a visitor happened upon him in prayer. So agonized was Abraham's weeping, so profound both his grief and his supplication to heaven, that immediately the shaken visitor understood why he was called the Angel. "Surely, no man born of woman," he later explained, "could have uttered such unearthly prayers." Abraham wrote only one book, *Chesed L'Avraham (Kindness to Abraham)*, a pun on his own name. He died on the twelfth day of Tishri.

Using a computer, I looked through Genesis for "Abraham" spelled out at equidistant letter intervals, searching for that instance among many where his name appeared at its shortest skips. Given the actual frequencies in Genesis of Abraham's name—A (א), B (ב), R (ר), H (ה), M (מ)—one would expect roughly three thousand occurrences at all possible equidistant intervals (between 4 and 19,516). Since I was interested only in minima, I did not actually compute all of them, but as a check, I noted that for intervals between 2 and 1,000 (about 5 percent of all intervals), ABRHM could be found over three hundred times.

There was only one appearance of ABRaHaM at a minimal interval (for 100 percent of Genesis) of –4 letters. It was in Genesis 43:11 ("And their father Israel said unto them, If it be so now, do this . . ."):

ויאמר אלהם ישראל אביהם אם כן אפוא זאת

Laid out in a one-line array, with the letters of Abraham's name highlighted, the passage looks like this:

ו י א‬מ‬ר א ל‬ה‬א ל א‬ש‬ר‬א ל א‬ב‬ י ה מ‬א‬מ כ נ א פ ו א ז א ת

There is nothing of particular interest in this single occurrence.

I then searched for the twelfth of Tishri, the date of Abraham's death, in a standard Hebrew format, י"ב בתשרי (Y"B B'TiShReY). This word appears as an equidistant letter sequence (ELS) only four times in Genesis. Its minimum equidistant skip is 1,238 letters beginning in Genesis 38:20 and ending in Genesis 43:18. When both the name and date are laid out in a common two-dimensional array, we see immediately that they form a compact configuration. Indeed, both the minimum skip and the *second* most minimal skip of his name form a compact array with the date of his death. As a very rough measure of the degree of compactness, we might note that all three terms can be contained within a rectangular array composed of about 1 percent of all the text of Genesis. The odds of this occurring by chance are less than 1 in 1,000—roughly thirty times less likely than calling the exact slot on a roulette wheel:*

---

*Taking into account the ability to reshape the array. More accurate statistical measures of this probability are quite complex—and debatable. These figures are meant only to give the roughest sort of impression.

יולאמרכדברימהאלהעשהל יעבדכויחראפוויקחאד‏נ‏יךיוספאתחוית נה
קדשרהטבחטבחימאתיוספאתחמוישראתאתמויהיימיהבממשמרויחלמ וחלומש
רעהואתנאתהכוסעלכפפרעהואמרליואמרלויוספזהפתרונושלשתהשריכימ שלש
מישאפרעהאתראשמעליךותהלהאוחכעלעלהעכלהעואפאתבשרכמעליכוי
בעהפפרותיפתהתמראהוהברעיאתויוקצפרעהוישנויחלמשנית והנהשבע
דלשרהטבחימונספרלויופתרחדרלנואתחלמתמינאושכחלמופתרויהיכאש
נההפרוהתהרקויהוהרעותחאתהשבעהפרותחראשנתהברעאתחוֶתנהאלקרב
רעבהואהדברצרדברתיאלפרעהאשרהאלהימעשהראהאתפרעהנחשבע
אשרתחייינבארצמצרימולאתחכרהארצמהרעבכיטבהדברבעיניפרעהוב
בכלארצמצרימויקראפרעהשמיוסאפצפנתחפנעחויתנלואתאסנ‏ת‏בתפוטי
שיויקראאאפפרעהמכיהפרניאלהימבארצעניויחכלינהשבעאעשרה
דואחייויספעשרהלשברברממצרימואתמואבניםיינאחייויספלאשלחי
עבדיכמרגליימיואמראלהמלאכיערותהארצבאתמ וירותואמרושני
ואלייאמנונדבריכמולאתמותחתוייעשוכנויאמרואישאלאחיואבלאשמ
ווהנחהואבפ יאמתחתוויאמראלאחויהשבכספיוהנהבאמתחתיוייצ
תסחרויויהיהממרי‏ק‏מ שפ יהמ ‏ה‏נהאיש‏צ‏רורכספיו‏א‏נאישצ וירא ו
תראופניבלתיאחיכמאאתכמכמ‏יש‏כמשלחאאתאחינואתנונרדהונשברהלך
‏מ‏ראל‏ה‏מיש‏ל‏אל‏א‏ךיה‏מ‏מ‏א‏כאכלואזאתעשוקחומזמרתהארצבכליכמוהור
אישכאשראמריוספוי‏ב‏אהאישישאתההאנשימביתהיוספוייר‏כ‏נ
אאליייוצאאלהמאתשמעוניויבאהאישישאתהאנשימביתהיוספ ויתנמימו

Two most minimal occurrences of "Abraham" (אברהם = ABRaHaM) in
a compact configuration with the date of death of Rabbi Abraham the
Angel on the 12th of Tishri (יב בתשרי = 12 B'TiShRY)

If the entire grid below represents all of Genesis, the area of compactness
is smaller than the area shown in gray:

Next, I looked for Abraham's honorific name, "the Angel," spelled ה (H)
מ (M), ל (L), א (A), כ (Ch) = HaMaLaCh. It occurs twice in Genesis at a
minimum skip of −3—very close to the name and date pair:

Two most minimal occurrences of "Abraham" (אברהם = ABRaHaM) in
a compact configuration with the date of death of Rabbi Abraham on the
12th of Tishri (יב בתשרי = 12 B'TiShRY), along with his honorific name,
"the Angel" (המלאך = HaMaLaCh)

The array that includes Abraham's name, date of death, and
"HaMaLaCh" now covers slightly more text, but still less than 2.2 percent
of Genesis. The odds of *four* consecutive terms all being found by chance
within this proportion of text are roughly less than 1 in 100,000.

I next looked for the city in which Abraham HaMaLaCh was born—
Fostov, spelled פ (F), ס (S), ט (T), ו (O), ב (V) or alternately, פ (F),
א (O), ס (S), ט (T), ו (O), ב (V). Both variants were found in close proximity to the cluster of terms already found, at their minimum skips for 100 percent of Genesis. When looked at only in combination with the minimum skip
for "Abraham," the two sets of terms lay out in arrays that cover less than
0.33 percent of Genesis:

100 percent Minimal appearance of "Abraham" (אברהם = ABRaHaM) in
a compact configuration with one common spelling of "Fostov" (פאסטוב
= FOSTOV) at its 100 percent minimum

Same 100 percent minimal appearance of "Abraham" (אברהם = ABRaHaM) in a compact configuration with a second common spelling of "Fostov" (פסטוב = FoSTOV) at its 100 percent minimum

All three terms were contained in a rectangular area of text equal to about 5 percent of Genesis.

I then continued to look for the following in sequence: the title of his book, "Chesed"; the date "ninth of Ab," because of its historical significance in his life; the appearance of his name at its *next* shortest equidistant interval; the appearance of his date of death at its next shortest interval. *All* of these terms were found in highly compact arrays in relationship to each other. I did not search for any other terms.* The crude odds of all this occurring by chance appear on the order of well less than 1 in 1,000,000. At least in this one example, the Bible Code appeared genuine.

---

*There were two variants of terms that either did not appear or did not form compact arrays.

The remaining examples in this chapter come from four sources. They are marked by initials: a selection of Doron Witztum's arrays from among those presented widely by Aish HaTorah (DW); arrays found by Moshe Katz and published in his recent book *Computorah* (MK); arrays found by Eliyahu Rips (and others) also included in Katz's book (ER); arrays that I have developed myself (JS). Using Rips's and Witztum's terms, we will refer to a decrypted ("plaintext") word in an array as an equidistant letter sequence, or ELS. The count from one letter in an ELS to the next, we will call the skip. The first few examples are in tabular form only. Selected later ones are shown in detail.

Franz Joseph (DW)

Prince Franz Joseph I became emperor of Austria in 1848 and remained on the throne until 1916, the last important scion of the great Habsburg dynasty. It was his nephew, Archduke Ferdinand, whose assassination precipitated the First World War. Though his role in world history is far better known, he holds a special place in Jewish hearts as well for the extraordinary degree of friendship he displayed, creating an environment within the Austro-Hungarian Empire in which Jewish communities flourished until close to the Holocaust:

> He was especially noted for his exceptional attitude to Jewish soldiers serving in the Austrian army, concerning himself over the availability of kosher food of the highest standard, assuring them of access to the necessary religious articles and ensuring unhindered Sabbath observance. . . .
>
> Many of the world's Jews referred to him as "the King of Jerusalem"—this was actually the title conferred on him by the monarchs of Europe, ridiculing his attitude to his Jewish subjects.[1]

Franz Joseph visited Jerusalem in 1869. Because of his reputation, he was received by the Jewish community with great warmth. The occasion was marked by a special blessing said by Rabbi Meir Auerbach (pronounced "Oyerbach"):

> As soon as the royal coach neared the Jewish encampment of exuberant welcomers, the great Rav Meir Auerbach stepped forward from

the ranks and recited the blessing instituted by our Sages upon seeing the face of a monarch: "Blessed art Thou, HaShem, our God, ... Who has bestowed of His glory upon flesh and blood." A mighty "Amen" burst forth from the crowd.[2]

Arrays pertaining to Franz Joseph found by Witztum in Genesis include the simple juxtaposition of "Franz" and "Joseph" in Genesis 45:18, a passage describing the kind pharaoh who welcomed Joseph and eventually the Jews: "Come unto me, and I will give you the good of the land of Egypt." The array is constructed at an equidistant interval of 36 letters for FRNTZ, which is the minimum for about 90 percent of the Book of Genesis.

Franz Joseph Array 1: Width 36 (DW)					
	English	*Transliterated*	*Hebrew*	*Skip*	*Minimum*
Term 1	"Franz"	FRaNTz	פרנצ	36	90%
Term 2	"Joseph"	YOSeF	יוסף	1^3	NA

When the line length is divided by four, these two words (shaded) remain in close proximity, but additional elements come into focus along with them, most important, "King of Austria":

Franz Joseph Array 2: Width 36 ÷ 4 = 9 (DW)					
	English	*Transliterated*	*Hebrew*	*Skip*	*Minimum*
Term 1	"Franz"	FRaNTz	פרנצ	36	90%
Term 2	"Joseph"	YOSeF	יוסף	1	NA
Term 3	"King of Austria"	MeLeCh AUSTRY	מלך אוסטרי	10	100%
Term 4	"Vienna"	VYNA	וינא	9	NA*
Term 5	"In the City of"	B'EYR	בעיר	1	NA

When the row length of this array is decreased by three letters from 36 to 33, the array becomes defined by another word that appears vertically at a skip of 33 × 6 = 198 letters: "Jerusalem," along with "Auerbach":

---

*Not a near minimum.

Franz Joseph Array 3: Width 33 (DW)					
	English	*Transliterated*	*Hebrew*	*Skip*	*Minimum*
Term 1	"Franz"	FRaNTz	פרנצ	36	90%
Term 2	"Joseph"	YOSeF	יוספ	1	NA
Term 3	"Auerbach"	AUYRBaCH	אוירבכ	31	100%
Term 4	"Jerusalem"	YeRUShaLYiM	ירושלימ	33	100%

Diabetes (DW)

Witztum uncovered a whole series of compact arrays relating to various illnesses, among them anthrax, AIDS, and diabetes. Diabetes is a condition in which the pancreas produces too little insulin, a chemical that makes it possible for us to absorb and use sugars, the most basic food. Without adequate sugars, cells starve. Diabetes effectively causes starvation, and the body is driven to break down its own proteins, releasing as a by-product a substance called ketones. In 1917, Bernhard Naunyn first demonstrated the link between diabetes and ketones. Treatment with insulin followed in 1921.

The following array is laid out at a row length of 5,875, the minimal equidistant skip interval over all of Genesis for the word "ketones" (קטונימ = KeTONYM). Close above "ketones" is found the phrase in the text, "I have caused greatly to increase." Running through "ketones" is the word, "substances"; and horizontally at an interval of −6 (minimal over 100 percent of Genesis) is the Hebrew name for diabetes, SuKeReT (cognate to the English word "sugar"). "Naunyn," whose role in diabetes is most closely connected to ketones, is present as well.

Diabetes Array 1: Width 5,875 (DW)					
	English	*Transliterated*	*Hebrew*	*Skip*	*Minimum*
Term 1	"Diabetes"	SuKeReT	סכרת	-6	100%
Term 2	"Ketones"	KeTONYM	קטונימ	5,875	100%
Term 3	"I have caused greatly to increase"	V'HaRBYSY	והרביתי	1	NA
Term 4	"substances"	ChoMeRYM	חמרימ	1	NA
Term 5	"Naunyn"	NAUNYN	נאונינ	34	100%

The central word, "diabetes" (shaded), forms the link to related arrays. Thus, "insulin" appears as an ELS at a 100 percent minimum skip of 3,378. In an array of exactly 3,378 letters, each letter of "insulin" lies directly on top of the previous one. When the row length is changed to one third of 3,378, each letter lies vertically three letters above the previous one. When this is done for insulin, an array emerges with the same appearance of SuKeReT as in the array above, plus the Hebrew word for "pancreas," all in close proximity to one another.

Diabetes Array 2: Width 1,126 (DW)					
	English	*Transliterated*	*Hebrew*	*Skip*	*Minimum*
Term 1	"Diabetes"	SuKeReT	סכרת	-6	100%
Term 2	"Insulin"	INSULYN	אנסולין	1,126	100%
Term 3	"Pancreas"	LaVLaV	לבלב	1	NA

AIDS (DW)

Witztum's arrays pertaining to AIDS display such terms as "AIDS" (אידס = AIDS), "death" (מות = MaVeT), "in the blood" (בדם = B'DaM), "from apes" (מהכופים = MeHaKUFYM), "annihilation" (מחיה = MeChYaH), "in the form of a virus" (בדמות וירוס = B'DiMUT VYRUS), "the HIV" (ההיו = HaHIV), "the immunity" (החיסון = HaChYSUN), "destroyed" (הרוס = HaRUS), and many more.

Perhaps, more optimistically, he also found the phrase הקץ למחלות = HaKeTz L'MaChaLOT—"the end to all diseases."[4]

The Assassination of Anwar Sadat (JS)

Throughout this book, we have focused almost exclusively on Genesis, since most of the early research was done there. But tradition holds that the Code persists throughout the entire Five Books of Moses. The assassination of Egyptian President Anwar Sadat provides an opportunity for an independent exploration of the Code in the Book of Exodus. Sadat's assassination was a watershed event in the life of both Israel and of Egypt; the Book of Exodus tells of an earlier intersection of these two nations. Two of the simpler Sadat arrays will be shown in detail; three more complex arrays will be summarized in tables. All of them are anchored by a near-minimal appearance in Exodus of the name "Sadat."

After his dramatic peace overtures toward Israel, Sadat was murdered as the result of a conspiracy of military officers and religious militants during a parade on October 6, 1981—8 Tishri, 5742, by the Hebrew calendar. The organizer of the conspiracy was a man named Chaled Islambooli.

The ancient term for "assassin," one which preserves its religious connotations, is מכה נפש (MaKeH NeFeSh), a "slayer of the soul." It appears in Exodus once at its 100 percent minimum skip of 102 letters. Immediately above it is an appearance of the assassin's name, חאלד (ChALeD) at its 100 percent minimum skip of two letters:

ר	ו	ל	א	ה	ח
ו	ו	ה	ע	ר	ל	א
ע	ח	ל	ש	ת	ר	ש
י	ו	ג	ה	כ	מ	ע
נ	מ	ע	כ	ת	כ	ל
נ	י	נ	א	ר	ה	ר
א	ל	י	כ	י	נ	פ
י	א	ר	ו	י	פ	כ
ה	ו	ת	ר	ב	ש	ר

(JS)

Another array is based on the 100 percent minimal appearance of a form of Sadat's name, B'SADAT (בסאדאת) as the object of an action. The skip of 3,800 serves as the line length, revealing the 100 percent minimal appearance of both the date of Sadat's assassination, the eighth of Tishri (חתשרי = 8 TiShRY), and the word "murderer" (רוצח = ROTzeaCh):

Sadat Array 2: Width 3,800 (JS)					
	English	*Transliterated*	*Hebrew*	*Skip*	*Minimum*
Term 1	"a murderer"	ROTzeaCh	רוצח	21	100%
Term 2	"at Sadat"	B'SADAT	בסאדאת	3,800	100%
Term 3	"8 Tishri"	8 TiShRY	חתשרי	24	100%

Another appearance of the date, the eighth of Tishri, at its second minimal skip distance of 1,117 (minimal for 40 percent of Exodus), defines another line length. When the array is thus reshaped, the word for "military" appears at its 100 percent minimum skip close to the 100 percent minimum skip for "officers" (קצינים = KaTzYNYM) also at an interval of 1,117 letters:

Two somewhat more complex arrays linked by this appearance of the eighth of Tishri create a unified whole with the other arrays (linked elements are shaded):

Sadat Array 4: Width 221 (JS)					
	English	*Transliterated*	*Hebrew*	*Skip*	*Minimum*
Term 1	"the conspiracy"	HaKeSheR	הקשר	-6	100%
Term 2	"to assassinate"	HiKaH NeFeSh	הכה נפש	1,989	100%
Term 3	"Sadat"	SADAT	סאדאת	-15	100%
Term 4	"parade"	MiTzAD	מצעד	-14	76%
Term 5	"on the 8th of Tishri"	8 B'TiShRY	חבתשרי	1,117	40%
Term 6	"Chaled"	ChALeD	חאלד	-2	100%

Sadat Array 5: Width 1,002 (JS)					
	English	*Transliterated*	*Hebrew*	*Skip*	*Minimum*
Term 1	"the conspiracy"	HaKeSheR	הקשר	-6	100%
Term 2	"to assassinate"	HiKaH NeFeSh	הכה נפש	1,989	100%
Term 3	"Sadat"	SADAT	סאדאת	-15	100%
Term 4	"by the hand of"	AL YaD	על יד	-3	100%
Term 5	"a murderer"	ROTzeaCh	רוצח	21	100%

In his own investigation of codes pertaining to the Sadat assassination (in Genesis), Witztum found the following elements (among many others):

Sadat Arrays (DW)		
נשיא יירה	NaSYe YYReH	"a prince will be shot"
מצעד	MiTzAD	"a parade"
תשמב	5742	"1981"
ירצח	YiRaTzaCh	"murdered" (but not a near minimum)
בסאדאת	B'SADAT	"Sadat" as direct object
חתשרי	8 TiShRY	"eighth of Tishri"
קשר	KeSheR	"a conspiracy"
חאלד	ChALeD	"Chaled"

Witztum also found the following compact array that includes the assassin's first and last names "Chaled" (חאלד = ChALeD) "Islambooli" (אסלמבלי = ISLaMBuLI) both at their 100 percent minimal skips in Genesis. Even that day's *New York Times* had it wrong, reporting the name as "Is*tan*booli."

(DW)

The phenomenon is even more striking upon further investigation. "Islambooli" appears as an ELS twice in Genesis, once in Deuteronomy, and nowhere else. It turns out that, as with the example above of Rabbi Abraham "the Angel," the *second most minimal* appearance in Genesis for both "Islambooli" (77 percent) and "Chaled" (74 percent) form a second compact array elsewhere in Genesis; and the sole appearance of "Islambooli" in Deuteronomy (at a skip of 10,380 letters) forms yet another compact array with a 90 percent minimal occurrence of "Chaled."

It is a sad truth that much of history deals with tragedy. Certainly, the history of the Bible Code is tied all too closely to wars, especially those that aimed at the destruction of the Jews. As we've seen in earlier chapters, the very methods that have led to the discovery of the codes are ironically mostly the product of the response to such attacks: history spiraling around upon itself, telling the same story, again and again. We should anticipate therefore, that these wars should themselves appear, in detail, in the Bible Code.

~

CHAPTER ELEVEN

THE FLAMES OF AMALEK

In the history of mankind, Amalek [the descendent of Esau who was the ancestor of the Edomites, of the wicked Haman and of King Herod the Idumean] symbolizes the "foremost evil among the nations," and has always risen up to destroy Israel when the time of redemption is imminent. "But his end will be eternal annihilation," for evil and those who embody its values are destined to non-existence.[1]

In man's heart, Amalek is the power that "freezes" man, causing him to see only "absurd chance" and therefore deny an ethical conscience and the moral perfection it entails.

In physical space, Amalek is sworn to prevent Israel from dwelling in the Land.

> —*Rabbi Tzadok HaCohen (1823–1900)*

Rebecca was informed that she carried two nations in her womb—Jacob and Esau—who would represent two different forms of social government. The one state would build up its greatness on spirit and morals; the other would seek its greatness in cunning and strength. Spirit and strength, morality and violence: these oppose each other from birth onward. The whole of history is naught else but the struggle as to whether spirit or sword, Caesaria or Jerusalem, is to have the upper hand.

> —*Rabbi Samson Rafael Hirsch (1808–1888),*
> *Commentary on the birth of the twins, Jacob and Esau*

The war for world domination will be fought entirely between us and the Jews. All else is facade and illusion.

> —*Adolf Hitler*

"SheSheCh": War in the Gulf, 1991

Upon first learning of the codes, almost everyone wonders whether they could be used to predict the future. In fact, the peculiar encoding method seems to preclude it: The Code emerges only *when you find ELSs for two or more related facts that you have decided to look for* an event and a date. If you know an event, but not its date, for example, you may well find the event at some (minimum) skip, but what then? You can find innumerable arbitrarily selected dates in reasonably close proximity to any ELS. It is the fact that the *one* actual date appears surprisingly close to the event, surprisingly often, that constitutes the code. To be known to the person looking, the date must already be in *his* past.

This distinctive "boundary" on the phenomenon comports well with what the Torah itself says about fortune-telling of any sort: without claiming that it is invariably impossible, the Torah states it is strictly forbidden. (If it *were* impossible, there would hardly be any need for the prohibition. The kabbalists' reluctance to share their insights has always been based in part upon the fact that their methods were routinely misused in this way.) Nonetheless, there are stories floating in the background of the codes community that hint at something a tiny bit in that direction. These stories' greater importance, however—if the tales are true—has to do with a lesson they may teach us about the nature of time, and our own role in the unfolding of history, a subject we will return to again in later chapters. One such story is linked to a series of codes concerning the Gulf War. I have heard a number of somewhat consistent variations of the same tale, some from reputable sources, but none willing to confirm it unequivocally, let alone on the record.

Indeed, more than one of the codes investigators have close ties to the cryptology services within the renowned Israeli intelligence service, the Mossad, and other covert agencies. (Given the history you now understand of the codes, this should come as no surprise.) Perhaps the involvement of the Mossad is true, or partially true; perhaps it is merely a legend in germination. One source told me flatly that if I quoted him, he would deny the connection. But otherwise, yes, he said, in its essentials it happened as described below. The codes themselves that relate to the story, of course, are open for examination—and have already been seen by thousands of people the world over.

The Gulf War was an unusual one for Israel. Although it was precipitated by Saddam Hussein's attempt to conquer Kuwait, Israel was the ultimate target. Tectonic shifts in international alliances and local power buildups had placed Israel at the center of a highly unstable situation: Its military advantage now lay almost solely in the element of surprise. Just as Japan had gained a crucial (if short-lived) advantage over the more powerful United States by striking at Pearl Harbor, so, too, the only way Israel could prevail against the huge armies arrayed against it would be to destroy the threat preemptively (as before in 1967). Yet she was being asked by America and her allies not only to refrain from attacking, but *not to defend herself if attacked first*. That was an extraordinary request, the risk of which was almost impossible for anyone in the West to appreciate.

In the meantime, Saddam Hussein had obtained an arsenal of Russian Scud missiles and modified them to extend their range. The "Scud B" could now easily hit any target in Israel. Hussein threatened to use the Gulf War as an excuse to destroy Israel's population centers with chemical warfare payloads.

This was no idle threat. As part of my own U.S. Army training in nuclear, biological, and chemical warfare defense, I had a chance to study photographs of the effects of modern chemical agents on actual civilian populations. The populations in question were Saddam Hussein's own citizenry. He had dealt with political unrest in the Kurdish regions of Iraq by targeting whole villages, towns, and county-sized areas with a variety of chemical weapons, utterly wiping them out: men, women, and children. Having seen those photographs, and having learned of the kind and scope of death he unhesitatingly inflicted on his own people, with his own weaponry, it is difficult to imagine anything he would *not* have been willing to do to Jews, in the hated nation of Israel.

It was evident even then that Hussein was well advanced in the development of nuclear weapons. But neither those, nor the poison gas arsenal, constituted the most serious concern. The biggest danger—never even mentioned outside of military circles—was Hussein's rapid development of *biologicals.* (That he in fact had a huge biological warfare program under development—and under cover of his nuclear program—was not revealed to the public until 1994. Intelligence agencies were well aware of this fact long before.) Nonetheless, the Israelis agreed not to retaliate if—rather *when*, for it was certain to occur—Hussein launched his Scud attacks.

The tension in Israel was unimaginable. Her agreement to eschew self-defense had created an extraordinary situation. There would be no preventing injury and death caused by the simple explosive effect of Scud B detonations; there was no adequate defense against biological agents—most likely modified anthrax—and Saddam did not quite have nuclear capability. So all of Israel's civil-defense effort was necessarily directed toward chemical agents—with which Saddam had the most practice and skill in delivery.

There do exist fairly good defenses against a chemical attack: Every U.S. soldier is instructed in the use of chemical warfare garb, masks, antidotes, and decontamination procedures. Used properly and in time, the gas mask alone can prevent a large proportion of injury and death. As a result, these were issued *to every single person in Israel*.

There was only one major problem: From western Iraq to Tel Aviv is less than four hundred miles. From launch, a Scud B would fly less than twelve minutes to impact. Even if satellite detection could unfailingly identify every launch, that is far too little advance warning to process the information, confirm it, transmit it to Israeli authorities, verify the missile's intended destination in flight,[2] warn the civilian population, and allow for the population properly to protect itself—even though everyone kept a gas mask by his side twenty-four hours a day.

But the alternative was impossible: *wearing* the gas masks twenty-four hours a day. The crucial problem boiled down to this: In the weeks and months leading up to the inevitable first attack, for Israel's population to remain in a state of high readiness would be physically and psychologically devastating. The entire Israeli economy could be undermined, destroyed without a shot being fired, by having to function in such a state interminably.

In this unique set of circumstances, there was one piece of intelligence information that was of utmost practical significance: *On what day would the first missiles fall*? If it were possible to identify that date, or even a list of probable dates, then the population could be placed in the state of highest alert only then, rather than continuously.

Here, then, is the unverifiable tale. Certain unnamed codes researchers met with the Mossad to discuss the possibility of discovering the date of the first Scud attack. Codes relating to the developing situation in the Gulf had already been found. The date of the crucial attack on Israel had not been found, of course, because it had not yet taken place. The codes could only reveal a statistically significant correlation between *known* data points. If you didn't already know the date associated with a given event (or person), *you couldn't search for it*, let alone measure its statistical significance.

Was there a way around this limitation? (Bear in mind that, to save life, perhaps thousands of lives, there is almost no commandment in the Torah that may not be suspended. Indeed, it was the very commandment Rabbi Weissmandl was following in all his efforts during the Holocaust.)

The researchers came up with the following possibility, "fuzzy" though it was. They knew where the codes relating to the Gulf situation could be found. Via conventional intelligence-gathering techniques and strategic considerations, the Mossad and the Israeli military had already created a list of plausible strike dates. Three of those stood out as most likely. For lack of actual known dates, these plausible dates could stand in for consideration as "already known information." They weren't "dates of events," but they were "dates identified by the Mossad as likely."

Perhaps if *one* of those dates was destined to be "real" (in being the actual date of the attack to come), then only that date would show up in the cluster of other Gulf-related terms. And if one of the dates did show up, perhaps that fact in itself (assuming the codes were genuine) would suggest that it was the actual date.

What they found was eerie: *All three* probable dates were in fact found in a compact configuration with other Gulf-related terms, and *only* those dates. One of these three was, of course, closest. That one was the third of Shevat, 5751—Friday, January 18, 1991. It turned out to be the actual date of the first Scud attack.

The Gulf Arrays

The Western world sees Saddam Hussein chiefly as an opportunistic tyrant driven by the materialistic motives it finds in itself: the quest for dominance, power, wealth, military advantage, territory. But perhaps that it is only a partial picture of how Saddam sees himself. Just as in the waning years of World War II, the Nazis diverted a huge proportion of their rapidly dwindling resources in order to transport, concentrate, and exterminate Jews for world-historical/religious reasons (as detailed in Hitler's *Mein Kampf*); so, too, has

Saddam Hussein spent down his enormous oil revenues in order to rebuild the ancient ruins of Babylon into a habitable city once again—only he has his own visage adorning the walls in place of Nebuchadnezzar's. He apparently sees himself as the modern avatar of ancient Babylon's greatest ruler: Nebuchadnezzar, the man who conquered Jerusalem, destroyed the Temple, and expelled the Jews into their first exile. Saddam sees his role as religious in essence, world-historical in scope. His aim seems sharply focused by the eternal battle with Israel.

Recall that in Chapter Seven, we pointed out two hints in the Bible of the ancient encrypting method called Atbash (in which the first letter of the alphabet becomes the last, the second becomes the second to last, and so on). Both of those hints, and a third one, occur in the context of this same struggle between Israel and Babylon. Of the "wine of the LORD's fury" given to the nations, the prophet Jeremiah foretells, "And the King of *Sheshech* shall drink after them" (Jeremiah 25:26). And later, "How is *Sheshech* taken! And the praise of the whole earth seized! How is Babylon become an astonishment among the nations!" In another passage (51:1), the prophet exclaims, "Behold, I will raise up against Babylon, and against them that dwell in *Leb-Kamai*, a destroying wind." (My emphasis,)

One permutation via Atbash converts "Babylon" (בבל = BaBeL*) into "SheSheCh" (ששך) and "Chashdim" (כשדים = ChaShDYM)—Chaldea, the archaic name of Babylon—into the phrase above, "LeB-Kamai" (לב קמי = LeB* KaMaY) which means literally, "the heart of my enemy."

Saddam's name (in the Arabic-to-Hebrew transliteration, literally "Tzadam") appears in Genesis as an ELS at a 100 percent minimum interval of 7 letters (צדאם = TzaDAM). There are a surprisingly small number of appearances of the word "Sheshech" at its 100 percent minimum skip of 2 letters. One of these forms an extremely compact array with "Tzadam," occupying less than 1/2,500 of the text of Genesis:

---

*The letter ב may be pronounced either as "B" or as "V." In "Babylon," בבל is pronounced "BaVeL," ב taking on both pronunciations. In לב קמי, the ב is pronounced as a "V," so the word is actually LeV KaMaY.

(JS)

When the line length is changed to 37, the location of Saddam's reconstructed capital of "SheSheCh"—"in Baghdad" (בבגדד = B'BaGDaD) appears nearby at its sole 100 percent minimum skip of 75:

לואידעתממכינחשינחשואישאשרכפמני
מהנאמרלאדנימהנברומהנצמדקקהא
ונעבדיכהנלנועבדימלאדנינמאנחנ
הנביעבדיודוויאמרחלילהולימעשותז
מצאהנביעברידהואיהיהליעבדואת
לביכמוינשאליויהודהויאמרביא
בדכדברבאניאדניואליחראפבבעב
רעהאדנישאלאתהעבדריולאמרהישלכם
ראלאדנישלנויישלזקניוימק
יותרההואלבדולאמוואביראהפוותא
וורדהואליואשימהעינויעליורנאמר
כלהנערלעזבאהאביוועזבאהמיעו
בדיכאמלאירדאהחכמהחקטנאתהכמלאת
נייהיכיעלינואלעבדכאבירנדרל
יויאמראבכילינשבושברולנומעשאכל
ללרדתאמישאחינוהקטנאתנורירלהן
ראותפניהאישואחינוהקטנאינרא
דכאביאלינואתהמידעתממכישנימילה

When the line length is changed to 75, the Atbash ciphers for "heart of" (לב = LeB) and "my enemy" (קמי = KaMaY in reverse) appear in the ciphertext in close proximity to the other three terms:

שאשרכפמניויאמריהודהקהנאמרלאדנימהנברומהנצ
נמאנלחנונגמאשרנמצאהאהנביבילכבאיכמוינשאליויהודהויאמרחלילהלימע
עבדואתמעלולשלומאלאביכמוינשאליויהודהוי
פכבעבדכדכימוככפרעהאדנישאלאתהעבדריולאמריהל
נימקטנואחיומתויתרהואלפרולאמוואביראהפוות
אמראכאדניכאיוכלהנערלעזבאתהאבירוועזבאתהאביוו
אתספונלראותהפנייהיכיעליינואלעבדכאביונדרכו
לונאמרלאנוכלללרדתאמישאחינוהקטנאתנוריחנוכ
תנוויאמרעבדכאביאלינואתהמידעתמכישנימילהלי

The first Scud B attack, on Tel Aviv, took place on the third of Shevat (גבשבט = 3 B'SheVaT). There are five ELS appearances in Genesis of the Hebrew word for "missile" (טיל = TYL) at its 100 percent minimum skip of + or −2. Two of these form compact arrays with the sole 100 percent minimal appearance of both "the third of Shevat" and "on the third of Shevat" at an interval of 258. One is shown below with a shared "T" (ט), from an array of line length 256:

(MK)

When the line length is changed to 263, the same words reappear in close proximity to "Scud B" (סקאדב = SKUDB) with a skip of −15, its sole 100 percent minimal appearance in Genesis. Dr. Moshe Katz, who published a number of related arrays during the Gulf War, notes that within the compass of this appearance of "Scud B" is the adjective "Russian" (רוסי = RUSY), running backward at a "skip" of −1.[3] There are only two such skip-1 appearances of the ELS for "Russian" in Genesis; this one is unique for over 97 percent of the text:

Additional linked arrays found by Witztum in Genesis (as reported by Aish HaTorah, but not published), and by Rips and by Katz (published in his book) include various combinations of the following elements:

Gulf Arrays (DW, ER, MK)		
סקדימ	SCuDYM	"SCUDs"*
רוסי	RUSI	"Russian"
טיל	TYL	"missile"
צדאמ	TzaDAM	"Tzaddam" (Arabic)
חסינ	ChuSeYN	"Hussein"
נשבט	3 ShVaT	"3rd of Shevat" (first SCUD)
עירק	EYRaQ	"Iraq"
סאדאמ	SADAM	"Saddam" (Anglicized)
בשבט	2 ShVaT	"2nd of Shevat" (war began)
שורצקופ	ShVaRTzKOF	"Schwarzkopf"
אמריקה	AMeRYKA	"America"
בסעודיה	B'SAUDYaH	"in Saudi Arabia"

Katz even reports finding the expressions for "CNN," "Peter," and "Arnett" in astonishingly close proximity in the Book of Numbers. "CNN" here appears as a minimum for 80 percent of all Five Books of Moses; both "Peter" and "Arnett" for 57 percent. The latter two names occur literally on top of each other at skips of −4 and +2, traversing only fifteen letters total: less than 1/20,000 of the text of the Torah.

Additional related arrays in Genesis (with common elements shaded) include:

Array Width 121 (JS)					
	English	*Transliterated*	*Hebrew*	*Skip*	*Minimum*
Term 1	"missile"	TYL	טיל	2	100%
Term 2	"at Tel Aviv"	L'TeL AVYV	לתל אביב	853	100%
Term 3	"on the third of Shevat"	3 B'SheVaT	נבשבט	258	100%

When the line length is increased to the minimum skip for "at Tel Aviv":

---

*This is the more common, non-"plene" spelling, with the optional silent letter (*mater lexionis*), א, absent in the plural.

Array Width 853 (JS)					
	English	*Transliterated*	*Hebrew*	*Skip*	*Minimum*
Term 1	"at Tel Aviv"	L'TeL AVYV	לתל אביב	853	100%
Term 2	"5751" (1991)	5751	תשנא	-3	100%

And at 342:

Array Width 342 (JS)					
	English	*Transliterated*	*Hebrew*	*Skip*	*Minimum*
Term 1	"missile" (twice)	TYL	טיל	2	100%
Term 2	"on the third of Shevat"	3 B'SheVaT	נבשבט	258	100%
Term 3	"Iraq"	IRAQ	עראק	6	100%
Term 4	"Scud" (and "Scud B")*	SKUD SKUDB	סקאד סקאדב	15	100% (both)
Term 5	"Scud"	SKuDYM	סקדים	-17	100%
Term 6	"at Israel"	L'YSRAeL	לישראל	-15	100%
Term 7	"in Tel Aviv"	B'TeL AVYV	בתל אביב	1,028	100%

In addition, I found a whole series of arrays in Genesis linking the names and dates of the major figures involved in the ancient Babylonian conquest of Israel to Saddam Hussein's attempt to repeat history. (The significance of the various names, dates and spellings may be found in the accompanying chapter note 4.)

Gulf Arrays Linked to Ancient Babylon (JS)[4]	
Term	Minimum
(Nebu)chadrezzar	100%
"Chief of the Butchers"	100%
(Nebu)zaradan	100%
"Butcher"	100%
Ninth of Ab	100%
Tzadam	100%
In Baghdad	100%
1991	100%
Missile	100%

*Both "Scud" and "Scud B" are at their 100 percent minimum skip in the same location.

Although it was not for distribution or attribution, I have seen a document that states unequivocally that "that date"—the third of Shevat, the day that the first Scuds were actually launched and fell on Israel—"was found *before* the war started." The content of this document was later confirmed in an audiotaped postwar interview with one of the principals involved.

But there is a subtlety to the tale. Remember that the third of Shevat was one of *three* dates supposedly identified by Israeli intelligence as most probable for the anticipated attack by Saddam. That date was clustered tightly within the other Gulf-related codes discovered early on, when the situation in the Gulf became critical following Saddam's attack on Kuwait. But what about the other two dates? Were they simply wrong?

The other two dates were also found in close relationship to the same clusters. As it happened, the actual date of the attack was the closest. But what if (a) Israeli intelligence had failed to identify the first of the three dates; and (b) the attack had occurred on one of the other two dates that had been identified? Indeed, there is no way of knowing that that is not exactly what *did* happen. That is, there may have been yet other possible dates for the attack that were not identified and therefore could not have been looked for.

That a number of potential dates (but not necessarily *all* potential dates) were identified in close proximity to the event and that one of them turned out to be the actual date, and happened also to be the closest of the three dates to the event, suggests an entirely different way of understanding how "time and chance happeneth." We will return to this subject in the last chapter, when we discuss what the codes imply about the nature of our world. We will see there that the unexpected relationship hinted at in the codes among "chance," human choice, and predestination reflects the ancient Jewish view of "prophecy" and perhaps some modern scientific understandings as well, as these have emerged over the past century.

In the face of the mortal peril facing Israel during the Gulf conflict, did the Mossad and the Israeli government utilize the codes in any degree whatsoever? Or did they dismiss them as nonsense? Did the events described above even occur? We will probably never know for certain.

It's not wholly inconceivable for the following reasons. First, as mentioned in Chapter One, just of late, the Mossad was willing to meet with another group of people to discuss the codes as relating to current tensions in the Middle East. Second, Doron Witztum himself has given more than one presentation on the codes to the Israeli Academy of Sciences (which body has also published some of his research). Third, there is a greater willingness to entertain their significance in Israel than there would likely be elsewhere.

But fourth, and most important, Israelis might well have been willing to take the codes seriously because of how the Gulf War was experienced in Israel. It was understood there very differently indeed than in countries whose experience of the war came through television news reports and Western newspapers. This difference was in large part due to a concatenation of inexplicable events.

For example, the Scud attacks occurred as feared—yet their total effect was almost unbelievably minor. The Israeli newspapers at the time were filled with astonished commentary. In spite of the success of the American Patriot missiles in intercepting Scuds on the fly,[5] thirty-three Scuds immediately hit their deliberately selected targets in Israel, mostly densely settled civilian areas of cities such as Tel Aviv. Neither were the Scuds "minor" missiles as was somehow conveyed in the media outside Israel. (Perhaps we have grown so accustomed to worrying about nuclear-tipped ICBMs—intercontinental ballistic missiles—that the destructive capacity of a missile with a range of "only" four hundred miles seems slight.) The first one alone on 3 Shevat destroyed or damaged nearly 500 residences. In total, Israel would be struck by thirty-nine Scuds; 3,773 buildings were damaged, among them 10,992 apartments, and 1,235 private homes were completely demolished. Yet *there was not a single fatality*. Innumerable people were pulled from mounds of wreckage several meters high. The closest to mortal consequence was that one elderly man died of a heart attack in hospital after surviving a Scud explosion that destroyed his home. (The single Scud that struck a U.S. military facility in Saudi Arabia killed nineteen soldiers. Recall the number of deaths and injuries among men, women, and children caused by the terrorist bombing of a single building in Oklahoma City.)

As more and more inexplicable events built up, commentary by Israel's generally secular leadership reflected a sense of awe that was never communicated to the West. Reacting to the almost unbelievable lack of casualties from the Scud attacks, the president of Israel, Chaim Herzog, addressed the nation on February 22, 1991:

The Jewish nation witnessed many miracles in its history, from the splitting of the Red Sea to this very day. This time, as well, we were blessed with Divine intervention.[6]

HaOlam HaZeh (*This World*) is a fiercely secular weekly journal whose editorial policy has always been opposed to traditional Judaism. Nonetheless, its editor in chief wrote the following astonished lines in one of his editorials:

G-d's hands guide the Scuds, its lethal shrapnel, from people to walls. G-d's hands—it could be nothing less. You stand, shivering and shuddering, opposite a house reduced to rubble, and you are amazed that these tons of concrete and steel can tumble while the residents of the sealed rooms are barely scratched. Miraculous. Time after time, miracle after miracle, and then yet another miracle; there is no other explanation.[7]

The most senior IDF (Israeli Defense Forces) general, Moshe Bar Kochba was appointed by the IDF General Staff to direct the postwar analysis of the Gulf conflict. In addition to the expected strategic, intelligence, logistics, and tactical lessons he drew from the experience, his report included the following from his on-the-spot observations:

I speak as a military man and as a realist, and I clearly state that there is no way rationally to understand the wondrous events which we are beholding. These days even the most hardened military officers speak consistently of "miracles." Their logical explanations have run out. . . . What we have here is a series of wonders . . . layers of miracles upon miracles.

Bar Kochba continued:

I . . . am on the General Staff; I have witnessed and participated in many events. I repeat: the events in the Gulf are beyond human understanding. It is not our vast wisdom that has brought this salvation upon us. A sharp turning point in our history has been reached which can definitely be called wondrous and miraculous.[8]

The army spokesman, Brigadier General Nachman Shai, addressed a thanksgiving rally after the war with these words:

> You have called a thanksgiving rally. Do you really know why you give thanks, I wonder? Now I may reveal the secret: you have no idea how many miracles took place during the Gulf War. When the Butcher of Baghdad threatened to incinerate half of Israel he knew whereof he spoke. Some of the missiles were well-aimed and hit their targets at point-blank range. . . . There are no words to describe the tragedy that was narrowly averted.
> Understand, then, that I know why we must give thanks.[9]

The rationalist would insist that, however moving, these are anticipated expressions of feeling voiced by many accidental survivors of tragedy. Under the impact of high emotion, the human mind routinely attributes to Divine Providence what is, in fact, blind, indifferent chance.

Maybe. But there is another feature of human psychology, perhaps more irrational, and with potentially far worse consequence, than thanking a nonexistent deity for acts with which he had nothing to do: namely, ignoring a God who is actually there. In the keen words of an anonymous seventeenth-century observer of human nature:

> *Our God and the soldier we alike adore*
> *But at the brink of danger, not before:*
> *After deliverance, both alike requited,*
> *God is forgotten, the soldier slighted.*

The Holocaust

Some truly chilling codes concern the most tragic event in the thirty-three hundred years of Jewish history: the Holocaust, out of which the codes themselves emerged through a unique confluence of events. It should come as no surprise, then, that an extremely large number of arrays have been discovered that reflect this tragedy.

As we consider their presence in the ancient books of Moses, we should remember something hinted at by the codes, which we will discuss in detail later: The codes do not present a portrait of a fixedly predetermined world, though upon first consideration they may seem to. They show, rather, the crucial role of a genuinely free human agency in determining—more precisely *in participating in* determining—what *actually* happens in history from among the options laid down by Divine Providence. "Therefore choose life," said the Lord (Deuteronomy 30:19). Often we do not. Following, then, are some of the Bible Codes that refer to the horrifying events of the Holocaust, indicating the precise details of the Nazi extermination project.

"A Great People"

Genesis 46:3–4 reads: "And He said, I am God, the God of thy father: fear not to go down into Egypt; *for I will there make of thee a great people. I will go down with thee into Egypt; and I will also surely bring thee up again.*" The italicized portion, in Hebrew *scripta continua*, reads:

כילגויגדולאשימכשמאן

Within it may be found the 100 percent minimal appearance of "Eichmann" as an ELS in Genesis (shown below in black: איכמנ = EYChMaN), and of "they [or he] consumed" (boxed below: כלו = CuLO) running through "a great people" (shaded below: לנוי גדול = L'GOY GaDOL):

This dense encryption anchors a number of related arrays. One includes the following elements, with "by the hand of the SS" at the same skip as "in Auschwitz," linked to the word "consumes":

Holocaust Array 1: Width 300 (DW)					
	English	*Transliterated*	*Hebrew*	*Skip*	*Minimum*
Term 1	"Eichmann"	EYChMaN	איכמן	2	100%
Term 2	"they [or he] consumed"	CuLO	כלו	2	100%
Term 3	"a great people"	L'GOY GaDOL	לגוי גדול	1	NA
Term 4	"in Auschwitz"	B'AUShVYTz	באושויץ	300	100%
Term 5	"by the hand of the SS"	B'YaD SS	בידסס	300	100%
Term 6	"consumes"	MiCaLeH	מכלה	-1	NA

The array itself (part of a larger one) looks like this:[10]

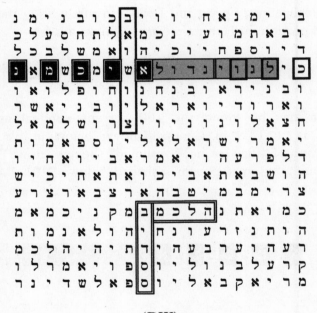

(DW)

When the line length is changed, another linked array appears:

Holocaust Array 2: Width 120 (9,180 ÷ 9) (DW)					
	English	*Transliterated*	*Hebrew*	*Skip*	*Minimum*
Term 1	"Eichmann"	EYChMaN	איכמנ	2	100%
Term 2	"they [or he] consumed"	CuLO	כלו	2	100%
Term 3	"a great people"	L'GOY GaDOL	לגוי גדול	1	NA
Term 4	"gas"	GaZ	גז	1	NA
Term 5	"Zyklon B"	TzYKLON B	ציקלונב	9,180	100%

And another:

Holocaust Array 3: Width 25 (75 ÷ 3) (DW)					
	English	*Transliterated*	*Hebrew*	*Skip*	*Minimum*
Term 1	"Eichmann"	EYChMaN	איכמנ	2	100%
Term 2	"they [or he] consumed"	CuLO	כלו	2	100%
Term 3	"a great people"	L'GOY GaDOL	לגוי גדול	1	NA
Term 4	"one third of my people"*	Sh'LYSh AMY	שליש עמי	75	100%

Finally, when the line length is changed to 367 ÷ 4 ≅ 92, the following array appears above Genesis 10:9 describing Nimrod: "He was a mighty hunter before the LORD." It also encompasses the phrase "consumes them" in the ciphertext, with the encrypted word "massacre" at its 100 percent minimum skip running through it. This array anchors a new series that includes the following elements (among others):

---

*The six million killed were one third of the Jewish population at the time.

Array Series: Width Various (DW)					
	English	*Transliterated*	*Hebrew*	*Skip*	*Minimum*
Term 1	"He was a mighty hunter before the LORD"	HU HaYaH GiBoR TzaYaD L'(YHWH)	הוא היה נבר ציד ל(יהוה)	1	NA
Term 2	"consumes them"	MiKaLeH BaHeM	מכלה בהם	1	NA
Term 3	"massacre"	MaTBeaCh	מטבח	-5	
Term 4	"Hitler"	HYTLeR	היטלר	31	100%
Term 5	"the cruel king"	HaMeLeCh HaAChZaRY	המלכ האכזרי	367	100%
Term 6	"Nazi"	NATzY	נאצי	-2	100%
Term 7	"Nazi"	NATzY	נאצי	1	NA
Term 8	"Berlin"	BeRLYN	ברלינ	-4	97%
Term 9	"in Germany"	B'GeRMaNYA	בגרמניא	-153	100%

The description of Nimrod in Genesis is not only that he was a "mighty hunter," but that he was "the first man of might" on earth following the flood, that is, the first to found and rule an empire, the primordial prototype of the "dictator."

According to Jewish tradition, because Abraham refused to worship him, Nimrod ordered Abraham thrown into a furnace. But Nimrod is an ever recurring *type*—the man whose quest for material, temporal power conceals a deeper spiritual motive: rebellion against and overthrow of God Himself. He is therefore seen again and again throughout history, as though each is "descended" from the prototype:

> Come and hear: For R. Johanan b. Zakkai said: "What answer did the Voice from Heaven give that wicked man, Nebuchadnezzar, when he asserted, 'I will ascend above the heights of the clouds; I will be like the Most High'? The Voice rebuked him: 'Thou wicked man, son of a wicked man, *descendant of the wicked Nimrod*, who incited the whole world to rebel against Me during his reign!' " [My emphasis][11]

As Nimrod's type is seen ever again, so is his necessary counterpart: the person—in us all—who unwittingly worships power, mistakenly equating strength, success, efficacy, accomplishment, with moral right. This identical spiritual motif—"might makes right"—was powerfully at work during the Holocaust. Though everyone is aware of Hitler's preoccupation with the extermination of the Jews, few people are aware that during the Third Reich, Hitler replaced the traditional Christian Lord's Prayer with:

> Adolf Hitler, you are our great leader! Thy name makes the enemy tremble! Thy Reich comes, thy will alone is law upon the earth! Let us hear daily thy voice and order us by thy leadership, for we will obey to the end even with our lives! We praise thee! Heil, Hitler!

And grace at table was replaced with:

> Führer, my Führer, sent to me from God, protect and maintain me throughout my life. Thou hast saved Germany from the deepest need, I thank thee today for my daily bread. Remain at my side and never leave me, Führer, my Führer, my faith, my light. Heil mein Führer! Heil mein Führer!

In Hitler's perverted form of Christian worship, we see a hint of something deeper of which Hitler himself was undisputed master: In whatever land and whatever age he arises, "Nimrod's" power over others lies not in the strength of his sword alone, but in the strength of his *word*—the inverted counterpoint to God's word.

The greatest of all Torah commentators was Rashi, Rabbi Solomon ben Isaac, of Troyes, in France, who lived from the middle eleventh to early twelfth century. Rashi survived the massacres of the First Crusade, but lost many relatives and friends. Nonetheless, legend maintains that with startling precision, Rashi correctly predicted not only that the bloodiest leader of the bloodiest Crusade, Godfrey of Bouillon, would ultimately be defeated, but that he would return to Bouillon with three horses—no more, no less. Understanding full well the deeper implications of someone described in the Torah as "a mighty hunter before the LORD," Rashi—as though peering ahead in time into the burned remnants of Hitler's own soul—commented about Genesis 10:9: "By his *words* Nimrod seduced the minds of the people." (My emphasis)

What Happens Again

Jacob our forefather said to G-d: "don't grant the desires of the evil man." This refers to Esau. "And don't let him draw out his bit." This refers to Germamia of Edom, for should they go forth, they would destroy the entire world.

—*Rabbi Yitzchak bar Acha (ca. A.D. 100)*
Babylonian Talmud, Megillah *6b*

Germamia: the name of a monarchy from the Kingdom of Edom (Esau).

—*Rabbi Shlomo Yitzhaki (Rashi), 1040–1105*

Does everything repeat itself, spiraling back upon the ancient template, the single divine blueprint? So the Jews claim. Eerily, their enemies seem aware of this reality as well. The Book of Esther tells the story of yet another episode when a tyrant in the mold of Nimrod, Haman in Persia, set out to destroy the Jews once and for all. (Oddly enough, Haman was not a Persian himself, but an "Agagite," hence a descendant of Esau and the Amalekites, the Jews' primordial, and eternal, enemies, according to the blueprint.)

In the end, Haman's plan to destroy all of Jewry in the Persian Empire was foiled. He and his ten sons were hanged in their stead once the king, Xerxes I,* was made fully aware of his plot against them. The joyous holiday that celebrates the occasion is "Purim." This story is told in the *Megillah*, a scroll unique in the Bible for nowhere mentioning the name of God, at least not openly.

There is another strange thing about this scroll. There is a certain page that describes the last-minute turn of the tables against Haman and his ten sons. It names all ten of Haman's sons, who, by order of the king, and in place of the Jews whose extermination Haman and his sons had plotted, were to be executed by hanging following the death of Haman himself. The writing upon this page is always done in a peculiar way. Though the sons play a minor role in the story, as told, their names are written in odd, greatly enlarged, and stretched-out script. In the names of three, however, *one* letter

---

*Known in Hebrew as "Ahasueres," and in Old Persian as Khshayarsha, Xerxes the Great (519–465 B.C.), was the son of Darius I. He is known to world history chiefly for his invasion of Greece at the Battles of Thermopylae, Salamis, and Plataea.

is written unusually small. Taken as numbers, the three letters could represent a specific year in some undesignated millennium. (Like Roman numerals, Hebrew numbers are written using letters. Modern Hebrew usage in Israel has incorporated Arabic numerals, of course.)

Nineteen forty-six was one of the six possible years represented by these numerals. October 16 of that year corresponded to Hoshana Rabbah, the day of the year when "judgment of the nations of the world is issued from the residence of the King, and executed."[12] Hitler had twelve top-echelon henchmen who stood trial at Nuremberg, accused chiefly for the Holocaust. One (Martin Bormann) fled to South America and escaped trial. The remaining eleven were sentenced to hang. Hermann Göring committed suicide the night before the scheduled execution. The remaining ten "sons" of Hitler were, in fact, hanged on Hoshana Rabbah, in the year hinted at in the Scroll of Esther, in a reenactment of the events celebrated by Jews on Purim every year for the past two and a half millennia.

Now, any thoughtful person will surely say, "This is a fascinating interpretation, but surely it is a bit far-fetched." If so, its significance seems not to have been lost on the Nazis themselves. The October 28, 1946, issue of *Newsweek* described the ten high Nazi officials as they went to their deaths:

> Only Julius Streicher went without dignity. He had to be pushed across the floor, wild-eyed and screaming, "Heil Hitler!" Mounting the steps, he cried out, "And now I go to God!" He stared at the witnesses facing the gallows ["with burning hatred in his eyes" according to the October 16, 1946 issue of the *New York Herald Tribune*] and shouted: *"Purimfest, 1946!"*[13]

But to be convinced that any of this is real, a serious critic should demand serious scientific evidence, not merely "amazing" coincidences. That evidence comes next. It also happens to be even more amazing than what has preceded it, and it has catapulted the Bible Code into the harsh spotlight of international scrutiny and debate.

CHAPTER TWELVE

~

THE GREAT SAGES

R. Judah said: It has been laid down that the term 'eth (time) is a designation of the community of Israel. Why is the community of Israel designated "time" ('eth)? Because all things with her are regulated by times and periods, when to come near the Deity, when to receive light from above, and when to commune.

R. Jose said: When the community of Israel was exiled from its home, the letters of the Divine Name flew apart. But in the sixth millennium the letter ו (V) will resurrect the letter ה (H). In the sixth part of the sixth millennium, the gates of supernal knowledge will open above along with the wellsprings of secular wisdom below. This will begin the process whereby the world will prepare to enter the seventh, Sabbath, millennium, as man makes preparations on the sixth day of the week to enter the Day of Rest, when the sun is about to set.

R. Judah replied: This is what I have learnt from my father concerning the mysteries of the letters of the Divine Name: the duration of the world as well as of the days of creation all belong to the same teaching—"the community of Israel will be raised from the dust, for the Holy One will remember her, and the lowly will be exalted."

Said R. Jose to him: All you say is right.

—*Zohar*, Bereshit *(Genesis)*

The findings emanating from Jerusalem concerning the codes soon spread around the world at increasingly well-attended Aish HaTorah "Discovery" seminars, and via reports on formal presentations by various codes researchers to the Israel Academy of Sciences and to university audiences in Israel. Eventually, the attention of high-powered skeptics was drawn to them. Among them were highly trained and accomplished scientists such as Professor Andrew Goldfinger, a senior physicist at Johns Hopkins University and number two man at the Space Computer and Technology Group there.

Like many others whose professional skills were rich in the most advanced forms of information processing theory, Goldfinger was also past chairman of the International Society for Photogrammetry and Remote Sensing. His close friend was Harold Gans, senior cryptologic mathematician at the National Security Agency. (Yoav Rosenberg, the third man on the Israeli research team, did not know Gans or Goldfinger, but he, too, had a background in advanced mathematical techniques that could be used to detect, with great accuracy, "fuzzy" signals in a sea of static. He was at work in Israel on his doctoral dissertation in that area, with specifically military applications. Though no one would say so directly, it was rumored that he, like many of Israel's brightest, had indirect ties to the Mossad.)

Almost everyone who took this work seriously, but critically, shared common background in certain mathematical techniques that lay at the heart of the cryptologic endeavor and the advances that emerged out of World War II. That the Israeli intelligence service was the world's most vaunted was likewise no coincidence: Whatever it was that drew their ancestors to such complex and abstruse subjects as kabbalah (and its ancient, mathematically based techniques of encryption) seemed to draw modern-day Jews to the current reincarnation of such pursuits.

Even though Gans had studied the Torah intensively as part of his childhood upbringing—or perhaps *because* he had—the idea of hidden codes in the Torah "sounded so off-the-wall to me, I disbelieved it immediately."[1] But he was satisfied with the credentials of the individuals developing them, and with the sophistication of the methods. (Later, but only after his mind had been changed by hard evidence, he got to know the codes researchers personally. He would be even more impressed with their honesty, integrity, humility—and high level of spirituality.)

Gans alerted Goldfinger to the findings. Together, the two of them set out to probe them for the weaknesses they were certain must be there. Gans describes it as follows:

Here's how I got involved in the whole thing. I have a cousin who is a mathematician (it apparently runs in the family) who went to Israel for a mathematics conference. There he met an old friend from college: Daniel Michaelson from UCLA—a confirmed atheist. Lo and behold, he sees that Daniel Michaelson is now wearing a yarmulke. So, my cousin goes over to him and said, "Danny, is that you? What happened to you?"

He says, "Well, they showed me the codes." Everyone in mathematics in Israel knew what "the codes" were, apparently.

But my cousin has no idea what Danny was talking about: "What codes?" he asks. So one thing leads to another and soon my cousin comes back to me and tells me that there are codes in the Torah that speak about current events, recent things.

I say, "Nonsense," and don't give the subject a moment's thought for about a year.

Then one day my wife hears about the codes and thinks I might be interested. I tell her that I already heard all about them and they're a bunch of nonsense. So she asks me just how it is that I *know* they're nonsense. Now I'm in trouble. Because I don't really have the kind of rigorous answer she's asking for. It's just that the whole idea is so . . . off the wall. "So," she says, "why don't you check it out?"

Now when your cousin says "check it out," that's one thing; when your wife says "check it out," it's something else. So I call up a very close friend of mine by the name of Andrew Goldfinger, a physicist, one of the best in the country—a very smart guy. "Andy, why don't you come with me to a lecture and we'll find out what this whole business is about." He says, "You're on."

So we drive up to New York together and sit in on one of these "Discovery" seminars, just like anybody else. Except I have my trusty computer. Every time the guy giving the "codes" presentation, shows some "amazing" finding, we do a quick computation of the probabilities.

Needless to say, the poor guy is a bit rattled. Every time he says,

"Look: diabetes!" or "Look: Hanukkah!" Andy and I look at each other—nope, that doesn't convince us. It isn't long before the audience realizes what's going on. So now every time he says, "Look at this!" everyone turns around and looks at us.

This stuff is clearly not cutting it. Eventually we tell him, "Come on, let's see something *real*." The guy is really shaken now—until he shows us a controlled, scientific experiment on the codes. This time Andy and I look at each other differently. This was something we could sink our teeth into.

After the seminar ends, I ask the guy for a draft of the paper, and I'm prepared to finish the whole business off once and for all. But instead it's my turn to get a bit rattled. It takes me a few hours to go through all the math. I can't find a single flaw. I call up my very smart friend Andy. "Andy, can you find the mistake?" No, he can't find the mistake either.

Next, I go back to the Discovery program and say, "I want the data." If they give me the data at least I know they're on the level about all this, because with the data I can check the whole thing out for myself. And if it's not on the level, boy is everyone going to hear about it.

Three months later I get a call, that a guy is coming in from Israel with a disk for me. I try it in my computer. I get the same results.

I felt a chill go up my spine. I didn't believe it until I saw it myself. That's how I got involved.[2]

Not long afterward, I myself learned about the existence of the codes research, and began to hear about a number of outstanding people who had left high-powered careers in the United States after visiting Jerusalem. (One of them was my wife's cousin, a brilliant young economist at MIT who had been Martin Feldstein's assistant at the White House. No one could quite understand why a young man of such extraordinary promise could "disappear" into the world of Torah studies. And then his younger brother, an equally talented pianist, followed him, and is now Chief Rabbi of Slovakia, reestablishing Rabbi Weissmandl's community, devastated by the Nazis.)

I decided that it was time to attend a Discovery seminar sponsored by Aish HaTorah. There I met Rabbi Daniel Mechanic, a truly outstanding teacher, whose presentation on the codes was fascinating—but also professional, objective, and fair. He made it clear that Aish HaTorah had been scrupulous in obtaining outside verification for the results they were presenting, and that they were prepared to drop the codes altogether if ever they should be substantively refuted. (Media reports often made it seem as though the entire program was structured around codes—this distortion seemed to reflect the desire of reporters to come up with a "story.")

But I was most impressed by the fact that the codes were clearly not being used to drive the seminar or "convert" the participants: mostly secularized Jews and a handful of curious Christians. The codes were offered as but one potential piece of evidence for the value of the Torah among many others—at most 6 or 7 percent of the total information offered by the seminar. The relevance of the Torah to everyday life was the main focus of Discovery, and was always highlighted as the matter of most serious interest—the codes were secondary. Furthermore, the beliefs of others, whether religious or skeptical, were always respected.

One feature of the codes phenomenon stood out for me especially starkly. Without it I would have surely dropped them as a mere titillation on a par with Amazing Discoveries on TV, or UFO abduction stories. That was the fact that a high-level peer-reviewed and refereed journal of mathematical statistics (meaning the paper would be critiqued by highly qualified outside statistical experts) was supposedly about to publish a full-length paper on the codes. (I first learned of its pending publication in late 1992, and Rabbi Mechanic was unhesitating in sharing the scientific material in preprint form as soon as it became available, just as Harold Gans had discovered himself.) The content of the experiment was a large data set of names and dates of birth and/or death of people who had lived long after the Torah was composed (even if by committee, long after Jewish tradition maintains).

That such a paper would be published in such a venue was a signal that only a scientist could fully appreciate. It did *not* mean that the findings were necessarily valid—many controversial findings in science were ultimately disproved after a long publication history, pro and con. But it did mean something quite unique in the history of science: that a hypothesis of the most outrageous or foolish-seeming sort—on a par, indeed, with UFO abductions or alien crop circles—had met a very high standard of care, intelligence, integrity, and critical scrutiny by trained outside experts. The fact is that UFO abductions or crop circles or any one of innumerable such amazing stories *never* come even remotely close to meeting such standards. The promoters of such stories rarely have even the barest appreciation what those standards are and why they are so important and powerful as "truth detectors"; perhaps not even one author in a thousand would even try to submit their claims to proper scrutiny. The life history of those few that are tested is usually painfully brief: It rarely takes more than cursory examination to uncover the flaw. (This same principle is now at work among untrained enthusiasts foolishly promoting rudimentary Torah codes "research" and tarnishing the subject altogether.) The tour de force demolition job done by William Friedman and his wife (see Chapter Seven) on the supposed Roger Bacon codes in Shakespeare has become the prototype for the debunking efforts that are almost always successful whenever findings such as these arise.

But no one had yet succeeded in debunking Witztum's and Rips's findings—not in six years of review, so the rumor went. It would therefore end up being published. If it in fact saw print, I knew, something was afoot at an unheard-of scientific level for a finding of this nature. Was this the genuine "divine fingerprint" that I and so many others had been seeking for so long?

About a year later, the paper had still not been published. But I was given an English translation of the earlier version that Witztum, Rips, and Rosenberg had published in Hebrew. It was indeed astounding. I also saw a handwritten reanalysis of these results that Harold Gans had performed and signed while at the Defense Department. And he had gone public in supporting the quality of the work. That, too, raised my eyebrows: As someone with a security clearance myself, I knew that people in sensitive, behind-the-scenes positions are usually quite circumspect and not at all eager to become associated with projects that could be tarred as fringe. Finally, I saw a statement that had been published in the preface to Witztum's book, referring specifically to the formal research, but also implying that the larger body of work had to be taken seriously. The statement was lengthy and carefully worded, but one key section leaped out at me. It read as follows:

> The present work represents serious research carried out by serious investigators. Since the interpretation of the phenomenon in question is enigmatic and controversial, one may want to demand a level of statistical significance beyond what would be demanded for more routine conclusions. . . . The results obtained are sufficiently striking to deserve a wider audience and to encourage further study.

The statement was signed, "H. Furstenberg, the Hebrew University; I. Piatetski-Shapiro, Yale University; D. Kazhdan, Harvard University; and J. Bernstein, Harvard University."

I took some time to look into who they were. I already knew of Ilya Piatetski-Shapiro from Yale: Like Rips, whom he knows well, he is a refugee from the Soviets, and is widely considered one of the world's most outstanding mathematicians. All the signatories were full professors in major departments of mathematics. Most possessed international stature and were recipients of high awards; Kazhdan would later win an appointment at the Institute for Advanced Study at Princeton, Einstein's renowned academic home in America. These credentials did not mean they couldn't be wrong (and they didn't endorse the truth of the findings, simply the high quality of the research, and by implication, the bona fides of the researchers as well), but these respected individuals were clearly going out of their way, and onto a limb, to say, "Don't dismiss this work as quickly as will surely seem reasonable. It deserves, and requires, careful examination and serious consideration."

Witztum and Rips had already worked out a tentative method for assessing the statistical significance of these arrays, and it was that method that had attracted the approbation of serious scientists. In his 1989 book, Witztum presented an assessment method that he claimed showed that most of the arrays he had discovered (those with several terms or linked in a series) were statistically significant with chance odds of well less than 1 in 1,000,000.*[3]

But the thoughtful skeptic, considering the large distances between encoded letters, the complex arranging and rearranging of arrays at various line lengths, the various spellings, is sure to conclude that there is simply too much freedom to pick and choose and "manipulate." Given a large enough text of *any* sort, the necessary motivation, and lots of time, "any damn fool with a computer" can find anything he likes,[4] the skeptic would insist.

The fact is that the methodology *is* so subtle that a valid statistical assessment—of the kind that would meet the standards of the toughest and most sophisticated critics—lay somewhat beyond even the high-level scientific skills of both Witztum (in theoretical physics) and Rips (in pure mathematics). It barely fell well within the capabilities of the most specialized and

---

*This is roughly the same level of significance I worked out myself for the test case of Rabbi Abraham discussed in Chapter Ten.

advanced statistical theory. (As we will discuss later, many of the highest-powered critics acknowledge that their own skills may be insufficient to perform the necessary analysis.)

As it turns out, the method allows for considerably less freedom to select good findings and discard bad ones ("cherry picking" as it's called in statistics) than it seems at first—but this is hard to get a feel for without hands-on experience. And this intuitive "feel" is far from sufficient as evidence. Clearly what was needed was some variant of the findings, using the same method, but designed specifically so as to be subject to rigorous statistical assessment.

Part of the difficulty lay in the fact that most of Witztum's findings, and those of Rips and others before him, consisted of a large number of varying array *types,* each with a different number of terms, all in various grammatical forms, the terms relating to one another in various ways. For example, one array might consist of four terms of which two were names, one the name of an object or event, and the fourth a date (for example, "Saddam," "Hussein," "Scuds," and "third of Shevat"). A second array might consist of two terms: one name and one place ("Saddam" and "Bagdad").

This amount of variability in the data leaves open the possibility that one has simply selected the groupings that seem to work—while ignoring everything that doesn't. ("Why a date in array number two, but none in array number one?" the skeptic should ask. "Perhaps because it doesn't work with a date in the first one?") To perform a valid mathematical assessment, it would be necessary to test the method on a large number of *uniform* arrays, each with the same number of terms—the first step of course would examine only two terms—containing a uniform set of grammatical forms, with the two terms in each pair relating in the same way to each other. Convenient "structured pairs" might each consist of one name and one place, or one event and one date. (Of course, what constitutes "sufficiently uniform" is itself subject to debate. Should the terms each be the same number of letters, too?)

Two Experiments

Six years would elapse between when Witztum, Rips, and Rosenberg submitted their work for formal consideration and a final, fully fledged publication. In effect, their research occurred in two distinct stages—and involved two distinct but similar sets of data. (Outside the Hebrew-speaking world this fact, the reasons for it, and its implications were not made clear. The resulting confusion has served to increase skepticism, but as we will see, it speaks powerfully to the reality of the phenomenon.) A sketchy report on their first experiment first saw print in English in 1988, around the same time that Witztum described the results in detail in *The Added Dimension* (in Hebrew).

The Great Sages I

In 1988, one of the prominent "elder statesmen" of statistics, D. J. Bartholomew, was invited to publish a paper in the eminent *Journal of the Royal Statistical Society*. Bartholomew's article was entitled, "Probability, Statistics and Theology."

This understated paper itself was something of a landmark. Over the preceding decades, an increasingly large number of highly respected mathematicians, neuroscientists, biologists, computer specialists, and physicists were beginning to suspect that there might be more to the universe than met the enlightened materialist eye. Propositions that fifty years ago would have been considered "fringe" were now being taken quite seriously. (For example, as I write, in January 1997, the eminent scientific journal *Nature* published comments examining the hypothesis that the physical universe in its entirety might be a living, information-processing organism.*) Bartholomew reviewed a number of these ideas, offering a sympathetic perspective on how statistics might actually help support certain theological propositions—rather than undermine them as it does routinely.

Not every such speculation was accepted by Bartholomew and the discussants as correct, needless to say, but it was not so long ago that such notions would simply have been dismissed as beneath contempt. Witztum, Rips, and Rosenberg were invited to respond to this paper. They did so by tersely reporting on their research to date. Their brief piece fit neatly into the discussion, which, among other things, looked at yet other evidence that the Bible might not be the pastiche it has long been considered to be.

---

*A surprisingly high percentage of the scientists are British who are now reconsidering propositions that were once considered too "religious" to be entertained seriously. I believe this reflects the influence of Alan Turing on the next two generations of mathematicians and physicists.

Their presentation was sketchy at best. They simply reported that when pairs of related words were found in Genesis as ELSs, at minimal skips, they appeared in close proximity too often to be accounted for by chance—"tending to zero," in their own phrasing.[5]

They offered one small array to illustrate the method and offered an extremely small p-value to quantitate their findings, using a relatively standard statistical method. The sample array merely showed the two Hebrew words for "hammer" and "anvil" in close proximity, leaving the reader with the impression that the word pairs they were reporting on were related on quite general grounds.[6]

But Witzum, Rips, and Rosenberg also published a paper in Hebrew that explained the details of what they reported on so tersely in *Journal of the Royal Statistical Society*. And in seminars that were being held quietly by friends and colleagues around the world, they explained exactly what they were doing, demonstrating some quite astonishing arrays (of the sort presented in the last two chapters) and detailing the nature of the statistical confirmation. Slowly, copies of these—and new discoveries by others—made their way around the world.

It turns out that the data set they were reporting on was *not* simply general pairs of words; it consisted of a set of the names of thirty-four individuals and their dates of death (or birth), all of whom lived between the ninth and the eighteenth century A.D. It was *those* pairings that they claimed were found in close proximity in Genesis—not a single example, but a large, relatively uniform set of pairs, but still, involving information that had not come into existence until long after anyone would claim the Torah to have been written down.

Earlier, Rabbi Weissmandl had found references not only to the Rambam (Maimonides) encoded in the Torah, but references to *all* the so-called Gedolim—"great ones," or Great Sages in Jewish history. (Recall that, according to his closest friend in the United States, Siegmund Forst, Rabbi Weissmandl told him that he had left behind "boxes and boxes" of findings when he fled Slovakia, specifically mentioning the "Gedolim" in particular.) This category of "Great Sages" is a distinct one. An analogy might be found in the culture of China (the world's *second* oldest civilization), where reverence for one's ancestors is as strong as in traditional Judaism, and where there is a somewhat similar sense that the "great ones" of one's people have a kind of continuing, almost living impact in the present.

The "great souls" clustered in the family tree of one's people *are* the living structure of the tree itself. The blessings we recite with our hands upon our children's heads, every Sabbath eve, say, "May God bless you [to be] like Ephraim and Manasseh [or Sarah and Rebecca, Rachel and Leah . . .]," and it is often added, "*who carried forth the life of our people*" (my emphasis). If anyone's name is to be inscribed in the Book of Life, as the Torah is called, surely it is the names of those whose lives were lived so as to carry forth that life in a veritable torrent. (Not that others weren't there as well, but the "great ones" ought to stand out in some way.)

Following in Rabbi Weissmandl's footsteps, Witztum, too, had therefore expected to find, and had in fact discovered, a very large number of references to the Great Sages. Often, those references included a name, and a place of residence or birth, for example, and a date of birth or a date of death, honorific names, and an assortment of other details from the person's life—just as we found in Chapter Ten with respect to my ancestor, Rabbi Abraham "the Angel." Working closely with Rips to ensure that the process was in fact mathematically sound, Witztum settled on the following data structure:

1. Names of Great Sages would be selected according to some arbitrary criterion that would limit the data set, but could in no way influence the outcome. The first criterion would simply be that the names were all of those "Gedolim" with text entries three columns long or longer from a scholarly Hebrew-language biographical reference, *Encyclopedia of Great Men in Israel.*[7]

2. Then, only those names were used for which a date of death or a date of birth or both were given.

3. From this smaller subset, only names within a certain size range were used because of technical limitations.[8] (This additional selection process would not affect the outcome, because it favored neither positive nor negative results. It also provided a convenient avenue for further testing of the phenomenon as better resources became available. That is now happening.)

4. Each date (whether of birth or death or both) was written in three standardized Hebrew-language formats, e.g., י״ט תשרי (19 Tishri); בי״ט תשרי (on the 19th of Tishri); and י״ט בתשרי (19th of Tishri). (These would be somewhat equivalent to searching in English for August 12, twelfth of August, 8/12, and so on.)

Then:

1. The maximum degree of "compactness" was measured between every pair of *related* terms decoded from Genesis at their respective minimum equidistant skip intervals.

2. The overall degree of compactness of the entire data set was calculated—very roughly speaking, a kind of "average." Compactness, and the precise nature of this aggregate measure, are explained in detail in Technical Appendix C. Some arrays were very compact (more compact than the theoretical average); others were not compact at all (less compact than the theoretical average). Substantiation of the codes would not require that *every* pair be compact, but the more pairs that are—and the more compact each one is—the more likely it is that the codes are real. This also implies that statistically, it isn't possible to tell the difference between a "real" single finding and an accidental single finding. (If you don't know that a coin has two heads, and when you flip it, it lands heads up, you won't be able to tell the difference between its being a "chance" or a "deliberate" event. If you flip it ten times, the ten heads in a row will surely make you wonder; a few more and you will be certain to inspect it closely.)

3. The actual average compactness for the set was compared with a theoretical average (and with a large number of controls) by using a variant of the Monte Carlo simulation method developed by John von Neumann at Los Alamos.[9] (In brief, this was done to see whether it is true that, with a computer, "any damn fool can find whatever he likes" in any text.)*

Although the purpose of the experiment was to "pare down" the unwieldy mass of varying kinds of "amazing" findings, and homogenize them, the result was actually a testable hypothesis that was even *more* amazing than what had preceded it: that, "on average," properly matched names and dates belonging to any one individual will be found as ELSs in Genesis in closer proximity to one another ("more compactly") than improperly

---

*The theoretically expected "average" turns out to be harder to calculate than it might seem, so *actual* chance results were used. The process is not unlike measuring a thousand coin flips to come up with an actual chance average of 50-50, rather than simply deducing this must be the outcome. Very few sets of 1,000 flips will turn out exactly 500:500, but most will be close.

matched names and dates; or than in control texts; or than would be expected merely by chance.

It is the implication of all this that is so astounding: that the names and dates of Great Sages will be found encoded in Genesis in such a way that *the text displays an extraordinarily high degree of foreknowledge as to details of their lives.* That knowledge was embedded in the text many hundreds, perhaps thousands, of years before those people ever existed: all had lived and died, it turned out, between the ninth and the eighteenth century A.D.

The positive results astonished even the Israelis themselves. The odds of what they found having occurred merely by chance were astronomically small.

It was as though they had been guided by the very words of the Vilna Gaon himself: "the details of every person . . . of everything that happened to him *from the day of his birth until his death.*" Perhaps it was no wonder that, when reporting on their findings in the *Journal of the Royal Statistical Society*, they cautiously avoided detailing the precise nature of the "word pairs." (In that informal format they were not obliged to; nor did their work require prior review by outside experts.) Had they revealed the prophetic implications of their data set then, they almost certainly would have been dismissed as beyond the pale, however sterling Rips's reputation was among mathematicians.

Proceeding cautiously, they soon after sought full publication, submitting their work in precise detail through the proper channels to refereed journals for peer critique. An intense, behind-the-scenes debate began that would last for six years.

The Great Sages II

At the end of those six years, the rumors I had heard concerning a forthcoming high-quality publication on the codes proved accurate. In August of 1994, the review journal *Statistical Science*, published and refereed by the Institute for Mathematical Statistics, published the full article by Witztum, Rips, and Rosenberg, "Equidistant Letter Sequences in the Book of Genesis." The abstract at the top, in the dry language of science, barely gave a hint as to the data and findings therein:

Abstract: It has been noted that when the Book of Genesis is written as two-dimensional arrays, equidistant letter sequences spelling words with related meanings often appear in close proximity. Quantitative tools for measuring this phenomenon are developed. Randomization analysis shows that the effect is significant at the level of 0.00002.

The "significance level" of 0.00002 meant that the odds were less than 1 in 50,000 that what had happened did so merely by chance. (In the body of the paper itself, these odds were reported more precisely as < 1/62,500.) Furthermore, the conservative statistical method for measuring those odds was developed by the referees themselves.* The vast majority of scientific journals accept for publication papers whose hypotheses are validated at a significance level of 0.05 (1 chance in 20 that the results happened just by chance). Life-and-death medical decisions may require odds of 1 in 50. Because the ELS phenomenon was so strange—and its implications so vast, were it accurate—the editor and referees at *Statistical Science* raised the bar to publication to 1 in 1,000 (in line with the suggestions of Professors Kazhdan, Piatetski-Shapiro, Bernstein, and Furstenberg, quoted earlier). The results bettered even that by more than sixty times.

Robert Kass, then editor of *Statistical Science,* and currently chairman of the Department of Statistics at Carnegie-Mellon University in Pittsburgh, commented on the piece in the same issue:

> Our referees were baffled: their prior beliefs made them think the Book of Genesis could not possibly contain meaningful references to modern day individuals, yet when the authors carried out additional analyses and checks the effect persisted. The paper is thus offered to *Statistical Science* readers as a challenging puzzle.

What made these results even more startling was the fact that the data set on which Witztum, Rips, and Rosenberg performed this experiment for *Statistical Science* was a list of 32 *new* individuals and their dates of death or birth. The p-value of < 0.000016 did not even take into account the results on the 34 other individuals reported on previously.[10] Altogether, there were 298 name-date pairs in the new experiment, constructed from every possible

---

*These methods were not the same as those used by the researchers in their report in the *Journal of the Royal Statistical Society* on the "Great Sages I" list.

combination of one name variant and one date variant obtained from standard reference sources.*

Some of the Great Sages Encoded in Genesis

NAME	YEAR	COMMENTS
Rabbi Shlomo Yitzhaki	1105	Rashi, greatest biblical and Talmudic commentary
Rabbi Avraham Ibn-Ezra	1164	The Raviyeh, illustrious poet and liturgist
Rabbi Moshe ben Maimon (Maimonides)	1204	The Rambam, physician; most illustrious figure in postbiblical Judaism
Rabbi Avraham, son of the Rambam	1287	Son of Maimonides, head of Egyptian Jewry
Rabbi Yosef Caro	1575	Mahariyeh Caro, authoritative codifier of Orthodox Jewish law
Rabbi David Ganz	1613	Tzemach David, astronomer, mathematician, historian
Rabbi Moshe Chaim Luzzatto	1746	Ramchal; childhood genius, prodigious kabbalist, and synthesizer of all of Jewish thought
Rabbi Yisrael ben Eleazar	1760	The Besht, or Baal Shem Tov, founder of Hasidism
Rabbi Eliyahu ben Shlomo	1797	The Vilna Gaon

Some of the first set of 34 Great Sages found encoded in Genesis with the years of their birth or death. (In the actual research, only months and days were used—even though years were often found encoded as well.) Technical Appendix C contains a complete list of the 32 Great Sages in the second experiment.

The paper went through a number of rounds of critical scrutiny with, as Robert Kass states, "additional analyses and checks." The identical procedure, for every pair in the sample, was carried out on:

---

*The data represent plausible variations of available birth and/or death dates for, and plausible variations of the names of, 32 individuals. The complete listing of their names and dates is in Technical Appendix C.

1. A Hebrew-language translation of a selection from the start of *War and Peace* equal in length to Genesis.

2. The Book of Isaiah.

3. The Book of Genesis randomized by scrambling all of its letters over the entire text.

4. The Book of Genesis randomized by scrambling all of its words within verses, but leaving the structure of the verses intact, and the letters of each word intact.

5. The Book of Genesis randomized by scrambling all of its verses, leaving the word sequence within each verse intact.

6. Other early Hebrew texts. (In the first version of their paper, the authors checked for the phenomenon in the Samaritan version of Genesis. This was apparently not done for the second sample.)

In none of these control texts was there any evidence whatever of a relationship between names and their appropriate dates; the results were indistinguishable from what would occur simply by chance. Only in Genesis did the name-date pairs show an overall compactness that deviated from chance expectation—by odds of 62,500 to 1. This value was arrived at by testing the actual name-date pairs against 999,999 different pseudopairs (a name matched to an incorrect date) and rank-ordering the results. The correct name-date pairs ranked far to the top, but only when tested in Genesis.

Could the phenomenon be real, then? Did the author of the Torah know the future in such detail? This was clearly not a Jewish version of the Bacon-codes-in-Shakespeare embarrassment. With publication in *Statistical Science*, the debate over the codes was raised to a wholly new level and engaged in earnest. It would soon draw in individuals who surely would never have imagined themselves discussing such a thing seriously.

CHAPTER THIRTEEN

~

ARE THEY REAL? THE DEBATE IGNITES

Faced with having to change our views or prove that there is no need
to do so, most of us immediately get busy on the proof.

—*John Kenneth Galbraith*

How has research on the Bible Code been received? Eliyahu Rips notes
with disappointment, but not surprise, that responses so far have mostly
fallen into two categories: immediate acceptance or immediate rejection. The
former, by believers and enthusiasts (especially those without mathematical
training), is indeed not surprising. But the latter is—or should be. Since to
date no one has discovered a fatal flaw in the authors' work, despite vigorous
efforts to do so by some of the world's most skilled critics, it is reasonable to
ask of scientifically trained, a priori skeptics (who are certain these results
must be a fluke), "What standard of proof would you accept as an indication
that the phenomenon might be genuine?" The most frequent answer by far
is "There is no standard. I will not believe it regardless."

One is reminded of the persistent (but after eighty years at last weaken-
ing) skepticism that greeted certain results in quantum mechanics research:
for example, that instantaneously—or even backward in time—events in
every part of the universe are correlated statistically, in measurable degree,
with events everywhere else. (Recent experiments demonstrate this occurring
right in the laboratory.) Should the codes phenomenon remain unrefuted,

perhaps in the light of such astonishing findings in modern science it, too, will one day seem not so preposterous.

On the scientific side, criticisms in the year or two following publication of the *Statistical Science* article tended to be hasty and reflected basic misunderstandings of the research methods and claims. Those were relatively easy to refute. But as word has spread, the situation has changed. Scrutiny has become more intense and more sophisticated. Refutation has required that the research itself be fine-tuned and, in some cases, extended beyond its original parameters. In short, after years of relative quiet, the debate over the Bible Code has taken on the character of an intense scientific dispute.

The debate on the religious side is even more intense, with divisions of opinion over the merit and implications of the codes having arisen between secularists and religionists; Jews and Christians; liberal and traditionalist Jews; among different Christian communities and even among Orthodox Jews. Among scientists, criticism of the Bible Code comes from a variety of quarters. Some is quite sophisticated—at the very edge of mathematical statistics' power—and needs to be taken seriously. On the religious side, the criticism can be quite harsh, perhaps because intensity of feeling in that domain is unmitigated by the objective standards of scientific testing. (When you can simply *prove* that something is false, mathematically, there's no need to shout. Alas, some scientists critical of the phenomenon have taken to shouting, too, calling others names, accusing them of deliberate deception, and so on—just as on the religious side.)

In fact, both sides seem too ready to conclude that the reality of the codes, or their nonreality, is an open-and-shut question—already settled. Why? The answer is simple: what the Bible Code implies. About "the crisis of spirit at the century's end," Marty Kaplan, a speechwriter for former Vice President Walter Mondale, recently wrote in *The New York Times*, in a piece aptly entitled "Maybe Reason Isn't Enough":

> Upward of 90% of all Americans say they believe in God. But I bet a lot more than one of 10 also believe that science has got it basically right.
>
> This is the sadness at the heart of our secular lives. No one wants to live in a pointless, chaotic cosmos, but this is the one science has given us, and that our culture has largely championed.[1]

Most people immediately understand that if science were conclusively to demonstrate that the Bible Code is valid, the most profound debate since the Enlightenment—the fracture line between faith and reason—would be settled once and for all: in favor of faith. It would utterly overthrow the premises upon which the modern (and postmodern) world has been constructed. Hence the readiness of supporters to insist the codes are real; of detractors to insist they couldn't possibly be.

What does science actually say about the Bible Code? That is the topic of this chapter.

Some Common Misunderstandings About the Codes

Certain questions concerning the Bible Code appear repeatedly. With brief responses, they are:

> 1. What's so amazing about finding words at equidistant intervals? It must be possible to concoct thousands of such "codes."

An individual cluster taken by itself—however compact—has no evidential value. But the Bible Code consists of systematically (rule-determined) *sets of related ELSs*, at minimal equidistant intervals in such quantity that *in the aggregate, so many sets of compact pairs or clusters would be very unlikely to occur just by chance.*

> 2. But if you have so much freedom to choose skips, it makes it easy to find whatever you want.

This would be true but for one crucial parameter: the skips *must be minimal (or near-minimal) intervals for that word.*

> 3. But some words *aren't* at their absolute minimum equidistant interval. Doesn't this provide lots of opportunity for random occurrences to appear meaningful when they aren't?

Once the importance of the minimum interval is grasped, it then becomes possible to make the constraint somewhat "fuzzy"—*without* losing any of its rigor. Furthermore, as detailed in Technical Appendix C, Witztum, Rips, and Rosenberg actually look at pairwise proximity over the *ten* most minimal occurrences, not just one. That means dealing with mathematics and statistics that most people find baffling—but done properly it neither hides nor distorts anything. (This is one of the reasons that it takes very highly qualified critics to address properly the pros and cons of the research.)

4. Can't you treat just about anything as "related"?

There are a number of ways of systematizing the relationship between words so as to shape the data into a format that is analyzable statistically, and not just by "gut feel." The method used by Witztum, Rips, and Rosenberg emerged out of less formal arrays (of the kind shown in Chapters Ten and Eleven) and is quite solid: historical fact subject to no interpretation. Furthermore, their experiment even accounted for variations in spelling.

5. How about a statistical effect from the structure of Hebrew? Maybe that's what causes the results.

If the effect were due to some incidental feature of Hebrew spelling, grammar, or syntax, then comparable results should have appeared when, in the same text of Genesis, *names were matched with incorrect dates*. But when the historical link was broken, the phenomenon vanished.

6. Perhaps there are mistakes in the original data itself. For example, how do we know that the dates of birth and death are accurate?"

It would be a most strange outcome, indeed, if a divinely transmitted Torah contained deliberately encoded mistaken data! (With what higher equivalent of the Office of Research Integrity should one file a scientific misconduct complaint? And who would conduct the investigation?)

In fact, there *are* certain errors and uncertainties in the data. Some of those mistakes are at the source (in the reference encyclopedia, *Great Men in Israel*) and corrected data were used in their stead.* After publication,

---

*See the complete list of the Great Sages in Technical Appendix C for the details of these corrections.

questions have been raised as to whether a small number of names or dates remain in error. The critical issue, however, is not whether a given date is correct, but whether a small proportion of corrections could have a large effect on the results. This was tested, and they do not. (In fact, most of the minor data corrections suggested by critics after publication have led to somewhat *improved* results.)

Moreover, if the phenomenon is due to errors in the second set of Great Sages' names and dates, they would have to be just the errors needed to make everything work—and only in Genesis. The odds of that are, once again, 1/62,500. And you'd have to say that a similar set of errors "just happened" in the first set of Great Sages as well. Since those kinds of coincidences just don't happen often enough to take seriously, this line of thinking will inevitably lead the skeptic to wonder, "Well, maybe it didn't 'just happen.' Maybe it was deliberate—or at least subliminal."

For all practical purposes, careful scientific scrutiny of the codes leaves this as the only likely and hidden flaw: the possibility that the data set was in some way inadvertently skewed. It is discussed in detail below (see "Tuning and Snooping: Robert Kass").

The Bible Code and the Transmission of the Torah

The Bible Code implies a degree of unity and integrity to the text of the Torah that is no longer credible to Bible scholars. Dr. Rupert Chapman, executive secretary of the Palestine Exploration Fund, expresses well the scholarly consensus as applied to the codes, in response to an article I wrote on them for *Bible Review:*

> Satinover implies, though he does not state, that the Masoretic text has been transmitted correctly, that is, without scribal errors, since its composition. This is not correct. . . . Professor Sir Godfrey Driver . . . says:
>
> > . . . this [Masoretic] text incorporated the mistakes of generations of copyists, and . . . many errors of later copyists also found their way into it. The earliest surviving manuscripts of this text date from the ninth to eleventh centuries A.D.; and it is this text, as printed in R. Kittle's *Biblia Hebraica* (3rd Edition, 1937 [the BHS text]), which has been used for the present translation."

. . . Variants in the text would clearly change the analysis of the [codes]. . . . Hence, a single variant letter, let alone a variant word, destroys all such combinations.

Of course, mysticism of this sort does have its place, but it is important that it should not masquerade as science.[2]

I have quoted Dr. Chapman at length because of his scholarly credentials and because he expresses particularly well an interrelated set of misunderstandings common among those critics of the Bible Code with a strong background in and preference for "higher" textual criticism.*

In fact, one of the features of the scholarly consensus concerning the Bible that would *not* have to be abandoned should the codes prove valid is the conviction that the text of the present Torah is not 100 percent error-free. That is because the evidence for the codes is as yet only *statistical* in nature. (I suspect more than this: that the Bible Code is *inherently* statistical; that there is no additional "plaintext" message. But the researchers themselves claim only that we as yet have an insufficient understanding of the Code to detect such a message.[3])

It is the *overall* degree of compact clustering of related words at equidistant intervals—not of individual samples—that tends, in the aggregate, to occur at the relatively minimal skips. If the text does get changed, but not too much, the codes will *not* disappear. The more errors that creep in, the more the Bible Code loses its robustness, not being entirely effaced until a critical number of mistakes has occurred. If one wanted to preserve a code against the inevitable ravages of time, this built-in resistance to error would be just the way to do it.

The "graceful degradation" of the Bible Code has been tested and quantified. On the first set of Great Sages, Witztum, Rips, and Rosenberg ran a control study in which they deleted the first ה (H), counted 1,000 letters, deleted the next ה (H), counted 1,000 letters, and so on (a total of 77 letters were deleted). This is an orderly "destruction" that concentrates on a single letter, so its effect is likely to be greater than a random "destruction."

---

*I am not being entirely fair to him, for he states that he did not read Witztum, Rips, and Rosenberg's actual paper, merely my simplified summary of it. I trust he will take with British good cheer my using him here as a foil.

Furthermore, as the change consisted exclusively of deletions, each deletion "shifted the frame" of the subsequent text, progressively causing the count for every successive code to be farther off. As in the aging of DNA, a deletion causes worse damage to a code (on average) than does a substitution. (A substitution affects the local sequence but leaves everything "downstream" unaffected.) On average, random errors—mixed deletions, substitutions, and additions—will cause as much *local* damage as a deletion, but will leave a long string of symbols relatively un-frame-shifted. Substitutions will cause no frame shift; every addition will cancel out the frame-shifting effects of one deletion.

In sum, the presence of a limited number of transmission errors will not erase the Bible Code if it's really there. It goes without saying that the presence of a uniform code that cuts across the various documents purportedly stitched together to make up Torah violates the fundamental premises of "higher criticism," which presumes multiple authors. Nonetheless, the only way of determining whether the codes are really there is cryptologically, which is to say mathematically.

Different versions of the Torah may therefore be looked at in another way. The BHS (*Biblia Hebraica Stuttgartensis*) text mentioned by Mr. Chapman and used by non-Jewish Hebraists is not identical to the traditional Jewish (Koren) text used by Jews the world over.* There are some 130-plus differences between them in the entire Five Books of Moses—not all that much on a proportional basis, but still significant.[4]

The Jewish sages contend that, over the millennia, they have done an unusually good job of preserving the text. They do not claim perfection, however. In fact, an ongoing record of known and suspected errors has been incorporated directly into the text itself. The act of preserving the Torah has always been, for them, not merely a scholarly endeavor, but a sacred one.

That being said, 130-plus differences is not a huge number. Knowing that it requires roughly 77 deletions to erase the Bible Code entirely, one would hypothesize that it *should* be present in the BHS text—but not so robustly as in the Koren. That is precisely what later results have shown.

---

*The Koren edition of the Masoretic text incorporates the best understanding of the Jewish scholarly tradition of textual transmission.

Replications and Variations

Alexander Pruss, Ph.D., a mathematician and probabilist formerly at the University of British Columbia, now at the University of Pittsburgh, performed his own informal replications of the Witztum, Rips, and Rosenberg study and reported on them to the scholarly Hebrew-language Internet discussion list "B-Hebrew" moderated at the University of Virginia.

Pruss's approach and assessment are especially instructive because he addresses the codes from the point of view of a critic who has concluded they are *not* real. He independently repeated the experiment reported on in *Statistical Science* (the second set of Great Sages), writing his own software on a different computing system. He reports finding no errors and considers the experimental design "a very pretty self-controlling study which, strictly speaking, does not even require control texts for the statistics to be valid."

His criticism is that when he reran the experiment on the BHS text, the p-value increased from roughly < 0.00002 to < 0.002, a factor of 100. "The extreme sensitivity of the analysis to the precise text used . . . suggests that the results are not meaningful." Nonetheless, he also notes that the result on the BHS text "*isn't all that bad on an absolute scale*" (my emphasis).

Note that one critic, whose expertise is in biblical texts but not mathematics, probability, or statistics (Dr. Chapman), expects that if the codes were genuine, they would have to be so *sensitive* to slight variations that even a handful of differences between texts would destroy them utterly. But a different critic, whose expertise is in mathematics and probability theory (and at least to a substantial degree in biblical texts as well) expects that if the codes were genuine, they would surely be so *robust* that 130-plus differences between texts will have little effect; so little, that a change in "statistical significance" from $p < 0.00002$ to $p < 0.002$ would be "extreme." But recall that a $p < 0.05$ is sufficient in most scientific studies. This difference in statistical significance of the Bible Code between the Koren and BHS text could fairly be considered a change from a "very highly significant result" (in the words of the nonetheless skeptical editor of *Statistical Science*) to what perhaps should be called a "highly significant result," some fifty times better than the usual minimum requirement for publication.

In fact, even these informal analyses* are quite consistent with one hypothesis that ties them all together: the BHS text of Hebraic scholars is pretty accurate; the rabbinical text is more accurate; neither is perfect. That is precisely what the Jewish tradition has claimed from the start.

The Peer Review Process

For anyone not closely connected to the codes and able to form an independent opinion concerning them, the fact of their publication in *Statistical Science* is potentially a crucial fact—a threshold that, as I've noted before, no similar findings have ever crossed. How much does this fact actually mean? Those "in favor" of the codes tend to say, "Almost everything." Detractors say, "Almost nothing." The truth lies somewhere in between.

Witztum, Rips, and Rosenberg were well aware of the need to formalize their findings. Without that, skeptics had every good reason to consider the phenomenon a fantasy. The researchers thus initially prepared a paper on the (first) set of thirty-four Great Sages' names and dates and it was published in the Hebrew-language journal of the Israel Academy of Sciences. (It was this work which was then reported on briefly in the *Journal of the Royal Statistical Society*.)

The next step was submission to an upper-echelon journal of statistics in a widely accessible language, where their findings would undergo both a full-fledged review by highly qualified referees and exposure to a wide professional readership.

This particular refereeing process stands out in certain ways. For example, it was exceedingly long: approximately six years from submission to print. Most papers take well under two years. Furthermore, the journal in which it was finally published, *Statistical Science,* was not the one to which it had been originally submitted, *Proceedings of the American Mathematical Society.*

In a lengthy process such as this, what typically occurs is this: The paper is submitted to the editor of a publication selected by the authors. If it

---

*Another statistician, Brendan McKay, performed the same comparison using a slightly different method than Witztum, Rips, and Rosenberg and found essentially the same thing: The Code was still present in the BHS but at a $p < 0.005$. Because they are informal, these studies should not carry the weight of refereed publications. The debate will not really become fully engaged until critical pieces are published, which will then open the door for further rebuttal by the original authors, replications by others, and new extensions of the method. This is all brewing at the moment.

appears potentially publishable, that is, the study appears competently conducted, it is then assigned to two, three, or even more, referees. They will be selected, highly qualified and respected professionals, in the same or in a field of study closely related to that of the paper. It is their task to function anonymously as part devil's advocate, part coach, looking aggressively for flaws and proposing additional checks or tests that will raise the paper to publishable level. The referees then return the paper to the authors for revision, often asking for additional procedures to strengthen the results; they may insist on them as a condition for publication.

A paper may go back and forth this way a number of times. If the review process continues without the referees being perfectly satisfied but without the paper ever having failed a critical test, a decision must be reached either to publish the paper or not, based on its merits to that point. This kind of a situation arises *very* commonly in science when highly controversial or abstruse subjects are at issue, especially when the review process is long. (It is not fair to authors to keep them coming back again and again, seemingly endlessly and raising the bar, as it were, higher each time.) Even so, there is never a guarantee that a paper accepted for review will in fact be published.

The Witztum, Rips, and Rosenberg paper seems to have gone through a process similar to this, for an unusually long time—clearly a reflection of how far outside the mainstream of statistical and mathematical science its findings and implications lay. But however complex the process may have been, Eliyahu Rips expressed to me clearly his appreciation that it was published at all.

> The number of iterations [back and forth between referees and authors] seems to be more than usual, but . . . most of all, I'm satisfied with the very fact that our paper was published. I had serious doubts whether this could at all happen. Therefore I'm grateful to Rob Kass and to the reviewers for the decision to publish the paper despite their personal convictions. I hope there will also be other people with the same amount of (inter)cultural tolerance.[5]

The paper did, in fact, seem to put the early reviewers in something of a bind, in two ways. First, as noted before, Rips is internationally renowned in mathematics, and it was inconceivable that he would lend his name to a project with easily detectable flaws. Second, the review process did not turn up the kinds of weaknesses that a secular skeptic could reasonably have expected to find.

In the end, their exacting standards were met. Yet the implications of the results were simply too extreme to credit at face value. The conclusions were fundamentally inconsistent with the most deeply held personal convictions of the referees—and more important, with the editorial policy of the journal to which the paper was initially submitted.

So the referees and editors were faced with a situation they perhaps hadn't anticipated: The paper had met the standards they had set, but they had absolutely no confidence in the results. ("I don't think anyone ended up believing in it," noted Kass a few years later. "Something weird seems to be happening. It's just not clear what that weird thing is.") Furthermore, the subject matter itself fell rather far outside the editorial parameters of the journal.

The result was a compromise, especially honorable given the personal feelings of one of the most highly respected of the referees—Persi Diaconis of Harvard, who was, and is, both intellectually and viscerally opposed to the subject: Diaconis himself helped the paper see publication in a different journal—*Statistical Science*—whose editorial policy allowed for excursions into unusual territory now and then. *Statistical Science* was edited by Robert Kass, now chairman of the Department of Statistics at Carnegie-Mellon University in Pittsburgh.

Tuning and Snooping: Robert Kass

"You have to understand, in some ways statisticians are professional skeptics." I had asked Professor Kass about the basic attitude that the typical statistician would be likely to have toward the Bible Code. "We see a very large number of experiments with seemingly solid claims that turn out not to be true. This happens most typically in clinical trials of various new medications, or other medical treatments. Most of them achieve statistical significance at first, and they're published—that's how they come to our attention—but then after increasingly rigorous scrutiny over a long enough period of time, they eventually fail. So we're accustomed to taking initial trials with a grain of salt, no matter how successful they are—especially ones with highly unexpected results."

Why does it often take so long for errors in scientific work to be discovered? Because of human nature, which is inevitably prone to "tuning" and "snooping."

Tuning is statisticians' lingo for the inadvertent process of subtly reshaping one's measuring devices to better fit the data, and thereby produce a better result. For example, suppose someone has devised a new medical treatment for cancer and has come up with a scale to measure improvement. The global measure of posttreatment outcome includes a great many objective parameters (weight, tumor size, exercise tolerance, etc.) but subjective ones as well ("feels better"). The researcher has invested a great many years of his life in his new treatment, but the results are iffy. Somewhere along the line he changes his outcome scale to give more weight to "feels better." He does so for perfectly plausible reasons, and is completely sincere, but the statisticians who review his work for publication note that by changing the weighting after the fact he improved his results. It turns out that his treatment makes people feel better—but that's all. In the case of the Bible Code, "tuning" would have come in the form of subtle tinkerings with the compactness measure, selecting from among numerous plausible alternatives one that gives the best results for the given data set.

"Snooping" is a related error, needed for "tuning." It involves peeking at the data so as to tune the method to it. This was the reason that the editors and referees insisted the experiment be rerun on a second set of newly selected Great Sages, and that results be reported officially *only* on these. But the question inevitably remains: Over the years, had not at least *some* of the individuals on the second list been previously identified as producing good results? When a result is too astounding to be taken at face value, it is easier to assume that behind-the-scenes snooping has in fact occurred. In Kass's words:

"These are very common problems, and it is extremely rare for them to happen deliberately. It's simply a fact of human nature, and we all do it to some extent even when we're trying most sincerely not to. As I say, we're so accustomed to these kinds of errors that whenever we see genuinely implausible results, we immediately assume that some kind of snooping or tuning has taken place—unwittingly. There was lots of time for that to happen. It's a good puzzle and the paper had no glaringly obvious problems. But nobody considered for a moment that the results might be valid, and none of the referees changed their minds in the course of the review. It has been my hope that someone would rise to the occasion and definitively solve the mystery."

Persi Diaconis: The Skeptics' Skeptic

Persi Diaconis is not only eminent in the field of probability theory; he is a man whose interests and point of view seem almost perfectly opposed to the point of view and implications of the Bible Code. As he is himself currently looking into the codes professionally, he will not speak to anyone about them. Presumably, his statement concerning them, if any, will come in the form of a similarly refereed publication. Nonetheless, he made his overall attitude toward the codes clear to me: "The subject is absolutely of no interest whatsoever. None. Every second I spend on this I could spend better doing my own research, or teaching my graduate students. People who find things in the Bible—it's ridiculous."[6]

There is a powerful debunking current that runs through *all* of science. And not without reason—the damage caused by religious enthusiasms run amok are all too evident: Witness the recent mass suicide of the pseudoscientific religious cult in San Diego, whose members were convinced that the Hale-Bopp Comet harbored a UFO arriving to take them to another level of existence. Nonetheless, debunking sometimes takes on a coloring that is oddly similar to religious enthusiasm itself: a reflection of the fact that under the surface, the clash of ideas is often a clash of entire worldviews as well.

Nonetheless, it is easy to see how a debunking spirit develops. Once someone becomes sufficiently skilled in scientific principles and statistical methods, it becomes apparent how powerful an instrument these really are for separating reality from wishful fantasy.

It is not so much that the skeptical scientist dismisses the possibility of anything new and revolutionary and astounding *ever; or* that he is inevitably opposed to religion. Indeed, a recent survey conducted for the prominent scientific journal *Nature* discovered that 39 percent of scientists (biologists, mathematicians, physicists, astronomers) believed in a personal God and 38 percent in human immortality[7]—figures little changed from a similar survey conducted in 1916.* But the attentive scientist sees time and again the huge numbers of enthusiasms that promise so much, make great claims as to their scientific validity, and then sooner or later dissolve in the solvent of really rigorous scrutiny: Having done their damage, they fade away and are soon forgotten, something new always ready to take their place.

---

*The desire for immortality among scientists, however, dropped from 43 percent in 1916 to only 10 percent today. Among psychiatrists, incidentally, only 6 percent believe in God.

For some, the elimination of nonsense thus becomes almost an expression of service, a voluntary police action, aimed at improving mankind's lot by extirpating the cuckoos from the nests where genuine intellectual progress is being hatched and nurtured. In fact, there exists an aptly named organization devoted to this end: CSICOP—the Committee for the Scientific Investigation of Claims of the Paranormal. It is supported by a roster of eminent scientific members, including Francis Crick, Murray Gell-Mann (Nobel Prize, Physics), Stephen Jay Gould, and before their deaths, B. F. Skinner and Carl Sagan—and a great many others.

Some of the topics they have tackled and debunked were listed by Carl Sagan.[8] The following is but a handful of the forty subjects he named, all characterized by CSICOP's executive director as "utterly screwball . . .": "The Bermuda Triangle, 'Big Foot' and the Loch Ness monster, 'crashed' flying saucers, the 'hundredth monkey' confusion, numerology, miracles, Atlantis . . ."[9]

CSICOP is noteworthy, too, for the high proportion of prominent stage magicians who belong to it. Indeed, one of its founders was the Amazing Randi. That is not surprising, for who knows better the many illusions that fool people than someone who has learned all the tricks of the trade and uses them routinely?

Both of these skeptical strains come together in Professor Diaconis: Not only is he an eminent statistician; he is an eminent stage magician as well, listed in the *Encyclopedia of Magic and Magicians*, and ranked among the world's top six card manipulators. In a series of published scientific papers reported on in *The New York Times*, Diaconis and a colleague showed for the first time that seven properly executed "dovetail" shuffles will maximally randomize a deck of cards.[10] Most gamblers and gaming establishments fail to do so, and therein lies a potential source of what looks like "luck"—at least for those clever enough to keep track of which cards are going where: "There are people who go to casinos and make money on this. I know people who are out there doing that now," observes Diaconis, himself a member of CSICOP. (Physicist Jack Sarfatti has specifically called for a CSICOP investigation of the Bible Code.)

But behind the sheer drama of an almost set-piece matchup between Witztum, Rips, and Rosenberg on one side and Diaconis, professional skeptics, and high-powered statisticians on the other, there lie profound issues that cut to the very heart of the spiritual dilemma facing the modern world:

Is the universe a gigantic machine, or is there something else at work in the world, though not necessarily of it, influencing the course of events? Diaconis has published over 110 professional papers. Most are in subjects that surely seem far from having direct cultural, let alone spiritual, implications (five of them deal with the mathematics of card shuffling). But a surprisingly large number, however technical in content, do point to larger philosophical considerations. We will mention some of them here, because they raise topics that go directly to the heart of what a real Bible Code would imply about our world.

In 1978, Diaconis published a paper in *Science* critically examining the flaws in ESP research;[11] in 1981, for *Behavior and Brain Science*, a journal outside his usual purview, he wrote briefly on "The Persistence of Cognitive Illusions."[12] For *Statistical Science*, he wrote "A Subjective Guide to Objective Chance."[13] Most pointedly, he wrote a long article for the *Journal of the American Statistical Association*—perhaps the premiere journal of mathematical statistics in the world—entitled "Methods for Studying Coincidences."[14] This last work, in particular, is considered something of a classic, tackling as it does the whole question of how and why people so routinely place their faith in falsehoods.

For example, the "Chance" course at Dartmouth College is designed to train students to be suspicious of what look like "meaningful coincidences" when careful statistical analysis will show they are not meaningful at all.*[15]

Professor Diaconis has given seminars demonstrating just this principle at work in C. G. Jung's popular notion of "synchronicity" ("meaningful coincidences"), in particular as applied to the ancient Chinese book of oracles, the *I Ching*. And, more subtly, Diaconis has presented seminars at Carnegie-Mellon University (where Kass chairs the Statistics Department) arguing that atomic particle decay, which appears random, may not be.

In his own words:

> Once we set aside coincidences having apparent causes, four principles account for large numbers of remaining coincidences: hidden cause; psychology, including memory and perception; multiplicity of end-

---

*In the specific sense that their occurrence is not statistically beyond what may be expected by mere chance.

points, including the counting of "close" or nearly alike events as if they were identical; and the law of truly large numbers, which says that when enormous numbers of events and people and their interactions accumulate over time, almost any outrageous event is bound to occur. These sources account for much of the force of synchronicity.[16]

In short, it would be hard to find someone more fiercely disposed to discover an error in the Bible Code than Diaconis. It was his extremely elegant and conservative suggestion to use the method of analysis that Witztum and his co-authors ultimately incorporated into their paper to produce the significance statistic; and in spite of his professed lack of interest, he has been providing fundamental advice (and offering strategies) to the group of critics now developing a series of further tests of the codes phenomenon.[17] We are sure to hear more from him before the saga is concluded.

At present, a number of world-class statisticians from universities around the world have combined their efforts to find the fatal flaw they are certain must be there—Harvard, Cornell, the Princeton Institute for Advanced Study, Australian National University (ANU), and universities in Israel are among the institutions represented by this group. To *Slate* reporter Benjamin Wittes, Brendan McKay of ANU gave a preliminary draft of a paper of his own that claims to have found this flaw (as reported in the article Wittes subsequently published[18]). In my view, and the view of a number of professional mathematicians and scientists, the flaw he claims to have found does not exist. But McKay is properly investigating, with Rips's cooperation, the two areas in the paper that need further exploration (the effect on the results of varying the compactness measure; the rules that determine the data set).

It is a measure of the frustration critics have come to feel in their inability to detect a serious flaw, that some members of this group (including academics in Israel) have begun to suggest that Witztum, Rips, and Rosenberg—as well as the historical scholars and librarians responsible for helping assemble the data for the "Great Sages" lists—have "conspired" to rig the data. Knowing the people involved, a conspiracy seems to me utterly impossible. If the work contains a flaw, it is most certainly not deliberate. Yet as the intensity and sophistication of the scrutiny rise, the results continue to hold their own, causing the polarization of opinion—and the stakes—to increase dramatically.

Part of the challenge is the fact that the subject itself comes far closer to the domain of cryptologists than that of academic statisticians. A number of prominent statisticians have themselves suggested that the best critic would be "a professional code-cracker." But in the words of one, "Unfortunately it's not so well established an academic field—I doubt if any of the referees were cryptologists—they're pretty hard to come by."

There's a reason for this.

Code Crackers

When World War II ended, you will recall, a committee was convened to assess the strategic value to the war of the cryptologic efforts organized under the Army Security Agency. The result was a dramatic and unequivocal reversal of the sentiment that these efforts could now be wound down. Late in 1951, President Harry Truman convened a top-level committee to make further recommendations. The result was

> a still-secret memorandum [that] established the National Security Agency. . . . During the 1950s and 1960s, *NSA became the world's leader in the development of computing equipment—pushing far beyond the publicly available technologies of the day.* [My emphasis][19]

How far beyond? Today's top-end desktop Intel processors have "clock" speeds of 300 MHz. Yet *forty years ago,*

> "lightning" was NSA's costly and far-flung effort to achieve faster clock speeds (1000 MHz) for its cryptanalytic attacks.
> . . . . Some years ago, *Electronic News* reported that NSA standards for its electronic components were demanding to a degree almost beyond belief. . . . Due to logic complexity, NSA needed a circuit board with about 15 layers . . . [and] more than 70,000 pin-sized holes drilled in them with tolerances of a thousandth of an inch. The interconnections between the layers was another nightmare.[20]

The current budget of the NSA is secret, of course, but is estimated at between $2 *billion* and $4 *billion* annually, with more than half of that for operations and research. It is now estimated to employ about twenty-thousand individuals in Maryland alone:

Scientists in colleges throughout the country refer promising gradu-
ates to NSA . . . their high professional caliber has been a major factor in the recruitment program's success. . . . [yet] so rigorous is [the
screening] that, despite the agency's urgent need for scientific talent,
five out of every six applicants are rejected.[21]

Nonetheless, the agency is the single largest employer of mathematicians
in the world.

The atmosphere of strictest security; the continuing possibility of dismissal without explanation or review; the fact that one's entire publishing
career, however brilliant, may remain completely unknown outside the con-
fines of the agency itself, are ever-present stresses. But to a certain caliber of
mind, there can also be little else so exciting as to be at the very cutting edge
of intellectual endeavors that the world outside the walls of the NSA may not
catch up to for decades. And, as David Kahn describes it:

The factors that outweigh all these, however, and that largely enable
NSA to retain its staff, are patriotism and the opportunity to serve.
These provide spiritual satisfaction that money cannot buy.[22]

This is the setting in which Harold Gans was working when he performed his replication of Witztum, Rips, and Rosenberg's paper described at
the very beginning of this book. He had attained the status of Senior
Cryptologic Mathematician and had authored over 180 papers—most of
them classified. He had won the coveted Meritorious Civilian Service Award
for heading up a team of mathematicians, cryptanalysts, programmers, and
engineers in solving a high-priority problem considered virtually uncrackable.
(The nature of the problem, and his solution, is, of course, classified.) But
because of what he learned from that replication, from his later personal
experience with the chief codes researchers, Doron Witztum in particular—
and from the work described below—Gans left the NSA after two decades of
fulfilling and highly accomplished commitment, to devote his full energies to
the codes in the Torah.

Gans, too, had examined the question of errors in the text :

Several experiments that I performed indicate that the error rate that is necessary to obliterate the statistical significance of the codes is about 1 deleted letter every 1,000 letters [78 letters].*[23]

But there is a far more significant experiment that he performed independently.

The Cities of the Great Sages

Gans has recently completed a paper entitled "Coincidence of Equidistant Letter Sequence Pairs in the Book of Genesis." In this paper, he repeats the original Witztum, Rips, and Rosenberg compactness measure, but assesses its statistical significance using a different technique. The results, he reports, are at a "significance level of 7×10^{-6} ($p < 0.000007 = 1/143,000$)."

Gans then took the names of *all* 66 Great Sages from both the first list of 34 individuals and the second list of 32. He paired all 66 names with their *cities* of birth and/or death, the spellings of those cities being searched out—as in the original Witztum, Rips, and Rosenberg experiment with their dates of death and/or birth—at minimum or near-minimum equidistant letter intervals. This kind of experiment could accomplish two things. First, Gans was de facto testing the reality of the phenomenon on the first list of Great Sages (which results were not reported in the *Statistical Science* article as protection against "tuning and snooping"). But, second, for this approach to validate the Bible Code—*it would have to work with a whole new set of historical pairings*: the cities as well. The results were startling: They were significant at a level of $p < 0.000005$; that is, less than $1/200,000$.

These results are especially striking when you consider that in the original experiment, the "internal" control was the elegant randomization procedure suggested by Dianconis: The rabbis' names were matched up with 999,999 different sets of wrong dates. Think of those dates as simply strings of letters. With these "wrong" strings the phenomenon was utterly erased. Surely if there was an underlying flaw in the procedure, or if the phenome-

---

*Though it is reasonable to presume that the codes imply a fairly intact text, it's not possible to extrapolate backward. Perhaps more than 1/1,000 letter errors have crept in, leaving the Bible Code only as robust as it now is and not much more so.

non was due to inadvertent tinkering over the years in which the compactness measure was "fitted" to *those* particular data (or vice versa, or both)—or if the codes themselves simply do not really exist—then matching the rabbis' names with a different set of letter strings (the cities) should have produced results nearly identical to the mismatched names and dates.

Gans has submitted his paper to a number of journals. He has been told that, on the one hand, the mathematics is perfectly in order, but on the other, "nobody is interested." Yet many expert critics have suggested that not only would a critique by a cryptologist be in order as a reasonable next step, but what would now be publishable were replications of the phenomenon, and extensions, using different data.

My guess is that replicating and extending studies on the codes will not be published until someone publishes a worthy critique of the original Witztum, Rips, and Rosenberg paper. With that, precisely because of the code of honor among scientists, the door will be open for the kind of free exchange of ideas that alone will reveal whether the Bible Code is a chimera—or the most astounding scientific research ever.

Postscript to "The Debate"

In the meantime, the reader should know that Doron Witztum and his colleagues have not been resting. In the little over two and a half years since their original publication, they have put together *seven* new controlled experiments, with highly significant results, all with very different data sets, all in light of the various criticism and challenges that have been raised. All use the rigorous methodology established by the initial refereeing process, or improvements suggested by yet other critics. One of these papers has already been submitted for publication, but so far has met with the same response as Gans's: insufficient interest. But the results of these experiments will soon be released to the world in the definitive book on the subject that Witztum is even now preparing for publication.

~

CHAPTER FOURTEEN

THE SIXTH MILLENNIUM

What are the roots that clutch, what branches grow
Out of this stony rubbish? Son of man,
You cannot say, or guess, for you know only
A heap of broken images, where the sun beats,
And the dead tree gives no shelter, the cricket no relief,
And the dry stone no sound of water. . . .

By the waters of Leman I sat down and wept . . .
—*T. S. Eliot, The Waste Land,*
Nobel Prize, Literature, 1948

It would be wonderful to find in the laws of nature a plan prepared by a concerned creator in which human beings played some special role. I find sadness in doubting that we will. There are some among my scientific colleagues who say that the contemplation of nature gives them all the spiritual satisfaction that others have found in a belief in an interested God. Some of them may even really feel that way. I do not. And it does not seem to me to be helpful to identify the laws of nature as Einstein did with some sort of remote and disinterested God. The more we refine our understanding of God to make the concept plausible, the more it seems pointless.
—*Steven Weinberg,*
Nobel Prize, Physics, 1979

Magic Mountain for a Refugee from the Sixties

About a quarter century ago I lived for a time along the rail line to Davos in a tiny Swiss village called Maria Montagna, the Mountain of Mary. Though I was studying psychology in Zurich, two and a half hours away, I couldn't resist the opportunity to live in the heart of the Swiss Alps.

From the window of my ancient three-story farmhouse I could look down to the valley far below and watch the train as it made its way up the ever steeper track to the end of the line among the snow-covered mountains that harbored Davos. There is something instantly, ineffably spiritual about the place and its distinctive kind of beauty. Even the train, struggling up toward the peaks, turns itself into a metaphor of our search for the higher things.

I was twenty-two then, callow and innocent and eager. I was certain that God was just around the corner. If only I reached my hand out. . . . I recall one day quite vividly when He seemed especially close. It was a glorious morning in May, during that season when the dandelions come out. A local farmer had left a pile of manure for me outside my garden gate, and I awoke early to pitchfork it into the rich soil of the garden itself. A mountain lake lay in the valley below, reflecting the snowy peaks; the sky was a brilliant blue with towering cumulus clouds here and there casting their moving shadows across the landscape; and the rolling foothills were thickly dusted with dandelions, giving the hills the appearance of undulating green and yellow velvet. All the cows from all the farms in the valley were out at pasture, every one wearing its cowbell.

This morning the air was filled with their bells: the low rounded clonk of my neighbor's cows close at hand, gazing at me with indolent, liquid eyes as I tossed their steaming manure over the fence; the faint tinkling of cows so far across the lake that I could not see them at all; and every tone in between. Those nearby were few; those far away many; and so the air was filled with a hemispheric tapestry of interwoven sound, I and "my" cows seemingly at the very pre-Copernican center of a never changing universe of nature and domesticity.

I stopped my work, overcome by the beauty. And in that moment, it was as though the sky itself opened up and I sensed the presence of heaven. The beauty all about me evoked and pointed with sudden, limpid conviction to a Reality beyond itself—but the beauty wasn't that reality, not quite. Reality was there, radiating splendor, but just out of reach. The veil had parted, just a fraction; at the end of a long corridor, as it were, I glimpsed the Ark of eternity. The thrum of wings beat the air, barely below the threshold of hearing.

The moment lasted perhaps five or ten minutes, then quietly faded. I've often wondered whether in that brief span something happened to me that was to shape my life ever since. Until that moment, I had always longed for but questioned the reality of a spiritual domain other and greater than the world of matter and molecules and mechanism. After, I was convinced of it beyond argument, though with no greater understanding of how to prove its reality. But that certainty was like a hand laid lightly upon my shoulder, intent on guiding me—if only I would listen.

But there was something else, something most significant, I knew, which I could not quite grasp: The moment was not perfect; it was bittersweet, filled with a profound sense of home yet at the same time, a sharp awareness of *exile*.

Two years later, I was invited to deliver the William James Lectures in Psychology and Religion at Harvard. Naturally, at such a tender age, I was thrilled and thoroughly pleased with myself at having been asked to address the august professors of so eminent an institution—on spiritual matters, no less. I didn't hesitate for a moment in seeing myself as worthy to follow in the footsteps of previous James Lecturers: the great psychoanalyst Erik Erikson, for example, or Wolfgang Köhler, the conceptualizer of the gestalt basis of perceptual psychology. Like them, I, too, would penetrate to the very heart of *meaning* itself.

Over the next year or so, I worked on my talk every day, making careful notes on grid-lined paper, outlining a theory of . . . well, everything. I felt like an intellectual and spiritual giant, my comprehension growing larger by the day. The next spring rolled around and I looked forward eagerly to the dandelions emerging once again, perhaps to revisit me with another glimpse of the world to come.

By the time I was due to leave for Harvard, I felt my lectures were in superb shape. I was optimistic and filled with enthusiasm. Three nights before my departure, I had the following dream:

> I am on a glorious field of dandelions, radiating beauty as on that mystical day a year before. But the dandelions are laid out in a perfect grid, much like the paper on which I had been making notes for my

lectures. And I am on my hands and knees, moving from one dande-lion to the next, eating each one in sequence down to the root. I am concentrating so intently on each dandelion immediately before me, that I have no awareness of where I'm heading. Suddenly my head bumps into something. I look up, and see a colossal object in front of me, so huge that at first I can't even tell what it is. Then I realize that I am looking at the front of the big toe of a giant so astoundingly enormous that I can barely make out the top of just this one toe. I crane my head up and up and up. There, towering above the Alps, in the clouds, I *think* I might be able to make out the edge of his toe-nail. In the dream, I start laughing so hard that I wake myself up.

The bubble burst. I looked at what I had written. It was absurd, and I was, at last, terrified. What did I have to say that was worth saying? I couldn't com-prehend so much as the tip of the toe of the subject I was attempting to describe.

I knew very little about William James, the lectureship's namesake, and casting about for a new, more modest point of entry, I began to read up on him. Once he was the dean of American psychology and philosophy; now he was no longer widely studied, except as a matter of history.

But I found his life fascinating, and in a funny way calming. He grew up in a household profoundly affected by his own father's spiritual quest, a quest that took place outside the boundaries of established religion. Though his brother Henry was renowned as a novelist, William was a superb writer whose style is widely considered superior to his brother's. Like his father, William was profoundly interested in religion, and was the first to study reli-gious experience from a "psychological" point of view. His most widely known and accessible work is *The Varieties of Religious Experience*.

This work, I learned, was born out of the following sequence of events. He had been invited to deliver the Gifford Lectures in Natural Religion at the University of Edinburgh. One day in 1898, while climbing in the Adirondack Mountains—his love of nature, and of the mountains in particu-lar, was lifelong—the veil parted. Upon his return to his cabin, he wrote his wife: "It seemed as if the gods of all the nature-mythologies were holding an indescribable meeting in my breast with the moral Gods of the inner life . . . Doubtless, in more ways than one, things in the Edinburgh lectures will be traceable to it."[1] I was struck by that phrase "with the moral Gods of the inner life." The gods of nature I had met, but what *were* the "moral Gods"?

This much was clear to me about his life as a whole: As a young man, his affliction—and mine—was simply that by the middle to late years of the nineteenth century, the greatest minds in the world seemed all to be converging upon a single inescapable conclusion—that all the world is nothing but a gigantic, mechanistic system, a huge machine. In any moment, the arrangement of every component in it—including us and all we hold dear—is determined entirely by the arrangement of everything in the moment before. It was a gigantic pinball game; once the ball was released, it could be influenced by nothing. The threat of the atomic bomb that pundits sagely concluded was to blame for the terrible angst and alienation of my generation was as nothing in comparison to the terrible power of such *meaninglessness*.

James had been too smart not to see the final implication of the "Enlightenment": that meaning, purpose, aspiration, spirit, choice, free will, morality, goodness—all would stand revealed as mirage. Searching for an answer to this quandary, in succession he studied art, chemistry, anatomy, and physiology; he accompanied the great Harvard naturalist Louis Agassiz on his expedition to the Amazon; in 1869, he obtained a medical degree from Harvard, but never practiced, and seems never to have intended to.

This early crisis in his life resolved itself in a telling way: upon reading the works of the great French mathematician and philosopher, Charles Bernard Renouvier. Renouvier was one of the contributors to the modern system of mathematics upon which science is built. But as a philosopher, Renouvier saw that the mystery of human freedom, of the mind's seeming ability to consider options freely and then select a course of action, was not a mere philosophic speculation: It was the sine qua non of the moral life. Consciousness, will, freedom—all had profound implications for the very notion of "goodness" itself.

For James, this idea meant liberation. "My first act of free will," he declared, "shall be to believe in free will." The rigor of James's intellect set him off on what was, in essence, a lifelong religious quest. Nor did he ever abandon it. But, paradoxically, James was convinced that to understand more accurately the action of the divine in the universe, it was necessary to set aside subjective preferences and adopt the discipline of science.

As I uncovered the details of James's quest, I began to appreciate the enormity of the project I had tackled so blithely. I spent the next twenty-five years of my own life retracing an updated version of James's footsteps. The most recent of those have brought me, on the one hand, to the Bible Code, and the possibility that it might be genuine, and on the other hand, to modern physics, for the reasons outlined below.

The Wasteland

Ever since the scientific revolution, the world has looked more and more like a giant machine—truly a spiritual "wasteland." Science urges us to put away our childish longings for "spirit" and "meaning," and we are hard pressed to do otherwise. So much of our daily lives depend upon the machine point of view—cars, food production and distribution, telecommunications, energy sources, medical care, the list is almost endless. Even if we articulate an opposing philosophy, our very brains cannot help but be shaped by the dominating idea that makes all these benefits possible. And so we are split. We long for meaning and spirit, but fear there is nothing there.

In the portion of *The Waste Land* cited earlier, the great poet T. S. Eliot describes the chill that has settled upon the Judeo-Christian dynamic that for so long was the beating heart of the West. The helix of time comes around again and again: The spiritual desert in which we have been wandering is yet also the "Galut," the Great Exile.[1] "By the waters of Babylon we wept," cried the Jews after being cast out of Eretz Yisroel by the heathen conquerors. The lament has continued ever since, carried on the wind to every man, woman, and child, Jew or gentile, who has ever yearned for that eternal land the heart knows so well, and longs to return to, but which the head has learned to deny.

Don't we live in a world that has a purpose, we cry? And ourselves: Surely *we* are not mechanical and predictable. Doesn't our impression that we choose—and choose purposefully—have a basis in reality?

The new, scientific broom of world-as-machine swept into near-oblivion domain after domain of human knowledge and experience, accumulated over millennia. Witch doctors and spiritists and priests and rabbis were bundled together in one great ball of detritus and flung into the trash compactor of history. In less than a century, the pursuit of religious truth went from being queen of the disciplines at the major universities to scullery maid at best; taught as a kind of propaganda adjunct to social faddism—or not at all. "There is a supposition, very common among thinkers from many disciplines," writes Michael Kellman, professor of chemical physics at the Institute of Theoretical Science at the University of Oregon, "of a radical incompatibility between the notions of free agency of will and the operation of physical law."[2]

Jacques Monod, discover of messenger RNA (hence of cell as automated factory), and winner of the 1965 Nobel Prize in Biology, put it precisely thus:

> Anything can be reduced to simple, obvious, mechanical interactions. The cell is a machine. The animal is a machine. Man is a machine.[3]

> Man lives on the boundary of an alien . . . world that is deaf to his music, just as [it is] indifferent to his sufferings or his crimes.[4]

Steven Weinberg, winner of the 1979 Nobel Prize in Physics, captures the feeling of these facts in an earlier variant of the epigraph cited above: "The more the universe seems comprehensible, the more it seems pointless."[5]

To which his colleague, Harvard astronomer Margaret Geller, responds: "Why should it have a point? What point? It's just a physical system, what point is there?"[6]

And physicist Gerald Feinberg draws the inevitable philosophical conclusion: "Life [is] . . . a disease of matter."[7]

The Way Out?

Is there no exit from the wasteland? The Bible Code suggests that there may be. Surprisingly, it is one of the most ancient and hallowed: the claim of the Torah that it is the "instruction manual" from mankind's Creator and guide. But how could such an "archaic" set of propositions as those contained in the Torah be as true at the same time as those of modern science?

Here, too, the Bible Code itself may give us a hint. For what its own peculiar nature seems to imply about time and destiny turns out to be strikingly similar to what the most modern of sciences has discovered as well. As we have seen, ancient kabbalistic mysticism gave birth to cryptology; cryptology to mathematical statistics; and these two joined during the Holocaust to produce the computer and the "age of information." All of these converge in quantum mechanics, whose first applications are in the domain of cryptology, precisely because its fundamental theory points to a hidden layer of knowledge mysteriously coordinating everything in the universe.

And thus—like the ancient encryption wheels that spiral the letters of the alphabet back on themselves, we return to kabbalah. ("In its end is its beginning," said the kabbalists about their cryptologic devices. But perhaps they were speaking of more than that, too, as in Eliot's words, "In *my* end is my beginning . . ."). The Zohar put it as follows, in a passage cited earlier: "In the sixth part of the sixth millennium, the gates of supernal knowledge will open above along with the wellsprings of secular wisdom below. This will begin the process whereby the world will prepare to enter the seventh, Sabbath, millennium."

It is to the last of the wellsprings of secular wisdom that we now turn, for yet another peculiar interweaving of the spiritual and the scientific. The best point of entry turns out to be some of the long-forgotten ideas of William James.

Necessity and Sufficient Reason

The entire "Enlightenment," the scientific revolution, and the inevitable "death of God" that followed were contained in the elegantly simple proposition of the German philosopher and mathematician Gottfried Leibniz, who lived and died in the century following Pascal: "Nothing takes place without a sufficient reason; that is to say, if one has sufficient knowledge, one may always explain why anything happens as it does."

This is the essence of determinism. Whatever "happens," whether it be the simple motions of two balls upon a pool table, or the complex interactions of two men in a pool hall, is determined *wholly* by their prior positions and motions. Whatever happens does because it must: No other result is possible.

Consider what it would mean were this not so—if the motion of a billiard ball, for instance, were only partially determined by "reasons." Then after accounting for all the influences that act on the ball—the cue, the felt, other balls, any tilt or imperfection in the table—there would still remain open the possibility that the ball would go somewhere else *against* these influences (which we call "forces"). But that would mean that the ball was somehow exerting its own force—or that there were yet other unaccounted-for forces acting on the ball. But we've already said that we've accounted for all the influences acting on it. So there can't be such a thing.

Yet while we fully expect this law of determinism to hold true for billiard balls, we recoil at the prospect that the same principle holds true for our own actions as well. According to John Searle, psychiatrist and philosopher, "Our conception of physical reality simply does not allow for radical freedom . . . [but] neither this discussion nor any other will ever convince us that our behavior is unfree."[8]

Still, the conclusion seems inescapable: It only feels to us that we "choose" and direct our actions. Actually, we do what we are obliged to, *and then tell ourselves after the fact that we chose it.* In such a world there is no meaning, no higher order, no conscience, no morality. There is only the inevitability of triumph and dominance for some, failure and destruction for others. "Right" is determined by the prevailing force: "might."

But James saw something subtler: If the mind were to have any genuine effect at all, that could only occur *if Leibniz was wrong.* It is a testament both to James's genius and to his intellectual courage that, in the swelling blare of prominent voices arrayed about him, he quietly insisted that Leibniz *was* wrong. While all events are largely influenced by prior reasons—perhaps mostly so—prior reasons are not sufficient, James maintained. After everything is added up, the trajectories of the elements of the physical world *must still be open to alternatives.*

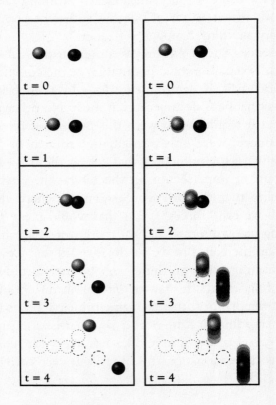

The above pictures illustrate James's idea. The left and right columns show two versions of the same sequence of events, the first wholly deterministic, the second only partially so: A stationary ball (dark gray) is struck by a moving ball (light gray) and the trajectories of each (position, speed, and direction of motion) are laid out over time according to the basic rules of physics. Five different snapshots are shown of equally spaced moments starting at t (time) = 0. (Each snapshot is formally called a "*state* of the system" as "the system evolves over time.")

Looking at the chart on the left, you see that the position of each ball is well defined and directly related to the prior state of both balls—and to nothing else.* Both balls move precisely as they do after the collision *and in no other way* because there's nothing to deflect them. That comports with our commonsense understanding of reality. The first ball continues on its path prior to the collision without changing its direction or speed because there's nothing to cause such a change.

But the diagrams on the right depict how James concluded that a system must actually evolve—presuming the reality of human consciousness, free will, and moral choice. After all possible influences have made their contributions, it is still possible for the system to evolve *in more than one way*. The paler gray disks symbolize places the balls could still go, *even though there are no forces of any kind causing them to go there*. (For if there were only one possible configuration of, say, the molecules that compose the nervous system, then all human action would be mechanically determined.)

This picture does not in any way comport with common sense. At the time James insisted this must be so, there was a growing mountain of evidence that just the opposite was true. But James insisted that, no, the truth must be as on the right, because otherwise the mind was not real and our "experience" would be no more than an illusion.

James was not claiming that there were no deterministic influences, but that after all of them were accounted for, there remained a mysterious residue of absolute freedom. The mind must exert its effect, James argued, by freely choosing before the act from among a *range of possible outcomes*, thereby affecting the *single actual outcome*. Further than this James could not go. His

---

*In this simplified model, we are going to assume that either all other influences that could possibly act on the balls are taken into account and produce just this one sequence; or else there are no other forces except those that set the first ball into motion, and the collision itself.

ideas seemed to him a psychological, philosophical—even spiritual—necessity. But they also seemed to most people either too difficult to understand, or too absurd to take seriously. After all, what James was really saying was *that nothing whatever in the physical universe* was causing these trajectories to be altered. They just did it for no apparent physical reason.

Interestingly, these same ideas had been anticipated a century and a half earlier by a brilliant Italian Talmudist and kabbalist from Padua, Rabbi Moshe Chayim Luzzatto—called the Ramchal. In a book he wrote to lay out the ancient fundamental principles of the Jewish worldview, he wrote:

> The world . . . contains two opposite general influences. The first is that of natural determinism, while the second is indeterministic. . . . The indeterministic influence . . . is the result of man's free will here in the physical world. Since both man and his actions are physical, the only direct influence that he can have is on physical things.[9]

The Dawn of Quantum Mechanics

As the nineteenth century wound down, scientists were in a jubilant mood. After two hundred years of pitched battle, the religious worldview was in full retreat. Everywhere that mechanical determinism decided to fight, it triumphed.

Among the scientists, the undisputed mandarins were the physicists, for it was upon their theories and researches that everything else built. In the words of Sir Ernest Rutherford, the Nobel Prize–winning discoverer of the atomic nucleus: "In science, there is only physics. Everything else is stamp collecting." What he meant was that people behaved they way they did because of the mechanical operation of collections of organs, tissues, and cells; cells, because of collections of molecules; molecules, because of collections of atoms; atoms, because of collections of subatomic particles, waves of "electromagnetic radiation," and forces such as magnetism and gravity that could be transmitted over a distance. Once the atomic rules were laid down and put into play, outcomes were fixed and inevitable, without "wiggle room."

So swift and far-reaching had been the advancing front of physics that as the new century dawned, it was widely held that the absolute end was in sight. Soon, the only obstacles to total understanding would be technical. There were perhaps three fundamental phenomena that had not yet yielded to mechanistic analysis. These, it was predicted, would be cracked shortly and the game would be over.

The three holdouts were (1) the fact that the relative speed of light did not seem to change whether one was rushing toward its source or away from it; (2) the fact that the equations governing radiation allowed ultraviolet rays to have far more energy than they measurably did; and (3) the fact that atomic radiation seemed to be absolutely random: There was no known mechanism that "ticked off the time" inside an atom and then "triggered" it to decay just at *that* moment and no other.

William James died in 1910, four years after Albert Einstein published his paper on the theory of special relativity and solved the first of the three remaining physical quandaries. Two years later, a physicist in Germany, Max Planck, conceived an extraordinarily strange solution to the second problem in physics, which he had been attempting to crack for years without success. His answer would prove to offer an explanation for the third problem as well, one completely consistent with James's philosophical deductions.

Planck himself found his solution almost laughable and states that he never could figure out exactly *why* he thought such a thing, since it made no sense whatsoever. His idea was both discontinuous with everything that preceded it, in physics and anywhere in science, and inconsistent with both common sense and with everyday experience. He had not even the advantage of previous philosophical inquiries along the line of James's. The idea simply appeared in his mind one night.

Boiled down considerably, the idea was this: Perhaps particles of matter don't move from here to there continuously—as it would seem all physical items must. Perhaps they just . . . jumped (as in science-fiction versions of "teleportation").[10]

Planck reduced his strange "what if" notion to mathematics. To his surprise, his intuition must have been correct. For these odd equations yielded precisely the results found in the laboratory with radiating black bodies (objects that radiate in all wavelengths without preference). Thus was born *quantum* mechanics.

Later, it would become evident that even such quotidian matters as household electricity depend critically upon this same phenomenon. Consider simple electrical wires made of copper. Copper oxide—verdigris—

is a superb electrical insulator. The only reason that two copper wires twisted together continue to conduct after even a few seconds of exposure to air is that electrons "jump," or "teleport," themselves past the verdigris.

But there was more to the idea, implications that only revealed themselves slowly as physicists reluctantly began to grapple with quantum mechanics and take it seriously. It became clear that although we can use the equations of quantum theory to determine *statistically* what proportion of electrons will actually jump and where they'll distribute themselves on average, we can't say anything about whether *a particular electron* will in fact jump, or when, or where—*because there is nothing that determines these outcomes.*

In other words, William James was exactly correct about what the physical world must be like—if consciousness was not an illusion. There was, as he foresaw, a determined part of events *and* a nondetermined part. The determined part was the weighted distribution of likely outcomes: a 50 percent chance that the ball will go here; a 40 percent chance that it will go there; a 5 percent chance over here; a 3 percent chance over there, and so on. The nondetermined part was the actual result. James, of course, was not thinking so much of billiard balls colliding in empty space, but of the very atoms and molecules that make up our brains. Somehow, he was convinced, the mind exercises a genuine agency in the world by influencing events in the brain.

The "worst" part of the emerging quantum equations was in a sense the most understated. Consider our example above, on the right, of "fuzzily" colliding billiard balls. Quantum mechanics does not merely say that *we don't yet know what causes the actual outcome.* Nor does it say that *we can never know, even though there is some such determining influence.* It says, rather, that *there is absolutely nothing causing the actual events*—more precisely, *nothing in the physical universe.*[11]

In an attempt to avoid such irreducible mysteriousness, some serious physicists have proposed that alternate universes, one embodying each *possible* outcome, spring into existence at every single "choice point."[12] The number of such universes since the "big bang" can hardly be imagined. Others have proposed that the world is filled with waves of "active knowledge" that not only determine the outcomes as a pilot steers an aircraft in accord with instructions from the tower, but coordinates traffic instantaneously across the entire universe. (How atomic particles—the aircraft—have pilots, and the identity of the controller, not to mention the controller's qualifications, is left unstated.)[13]

The strange phenomenon of jumping particles is often called "tunneling," but that word doesn't accurately describe the phenomenon. It is as though upon approach to an impassable mountain wall, cars simply reappeared on the far side, instantaneously, unpredictably, yet with amazing usefulness. It is no wonder that quantum mechanics has been a burr under the saddle of anyone who is fixed in his conviction that the world is a machine and God at most an absentee caretaker.

Einstein, for example, was very much irritated by quantum mechanics, viewing it as at best incomplete. He died in a futile quest to find (among other things) something better. Oddly, though, he won his own Nobel Prize not for relativity, but for "solving" the last great problem in physics: atomic decay. To his own great dismay, he did it by applying the very theory he loathed: quantum mechanics.

Indeed, it was his application of the new theory to certain kinds of radiation that made him most keenly aware of that feature of quantum mechanics he found most implausible: precisely *that there is absolutely nothing in the universe that "causes" an atom to decay; it just does*—whenever it pleases, as it were. It was his own repellent discovery that led him to insist, "the Lord does not play dice." Unfortunately, all the evidence has lined up in refutation to this most famous of all physicists' bons mots.

Eighty years of experiments in quantum mechanics have yielded a track record of success unmatched in scientific history. Quantum mechanics has proven itself—in all its bizarreness—more rigorously than has any prior theory. Even the most absurd implications have been substantiated by experiments that are published on a regular basis in major journals.

Here are some examples:

- The decision of an experimenter influences the outcome of an *earlier* part of the experiment. The particles seemingly "anticipate" the experimenter's future action and alter their trajectories ("teleport") accordingly, though still statistically—that is, among a range of weighted probable outcomes.
- When (some) particles in one place "decide" to change course, that is associated with (some of) a set of other particles "deciding" to change course elsewhere in coordination with the first group. We can't say that the one "causes" the other because (a) the changes happen at the same time and (b) the two clusters of particles are so far apart that light

wouldn't have time to reach the other with a signal by the time the second "responds," and (c) the "influence" is only probable—there will be slight but measurable differences in the outcome every time the experiment is performed.

Another way to put it is to say that there seems to be an instantaneous "adjustment" process at work in the universe. Depending on an action that takes place *here*, "it"[14] instantly—or even in anticipation—adjusts everything else *there*, in some measure. Moreover, what seems to be adjusted is not the precise final outcome of what happens *there*, but rather the *probabilities* of what can occur.

So, if I decide to do A here, instead of B, then the probability of C occurring there goes up by, say, 10 percent while the probability of D occurring goes down by 10 percent. And this is in spite of the fact that A and B *are completely unrelated causally* to C and D.

- The relationship of quantum tunneling to teleportation has recently become more than an analogy. In 1993, a group of research scientists came together at IBM, led by IBM Fellow Charles H. Bennett, to create an initial design for methods of perfect teleportation. Experiments are under way to demonstrate teleportation in microscopic objects, such as individual or small clusters of atoms. The obstacles to teleportation of complex macroscopic objects (for example, people) are of course enormous, but as Bennett notes, they are purely a matter of engineering. Practical teleportation would not violate any fundamental laws—as these have now come to be understood.[15]

In fact, quantum theory allows for, and experiments have validated, the following astounding principle: *Any* aggregate of matter may *spontaneously* "teleport" from its present location to any other place in the universe for reasons unknowable from any information in the physical universe and via "influences" not part of the physical universe. The probability of any given such event may be very small, but it is often finite (not zero).* For very complex events, the probabilities are so small that they *probably* won't happen. Very much less complex events happen ubiquitously throughout the universe. Events of intermediate complexity are rare, but likely to happen from

---

*Some actions are in fact precluded (zero probability), including many that commonsense tells us should be frequent. The point is that many of the most bizarre such actions are *not* precluded.

time to time. To put it in slightly different language: Miracles are not only possible, they are ubiquitous. Miracles of the sort that we are apt to take notice of, the biblical kind, for instance, are neither impossible nor do they violate the "laws of nature." On the contrary, they are "probable," in the sense of having statistical likelihoods that can be roughly calculated. But while the odds can be calculated, which miracles actually do occur are not only unpredictable, they occur for reasons that are not part of the physical system itself, the system we call the "universe."

For example, there is a genuine probability that the entire earth will suddenly jump from its current orbit around the sun to another star.

> When one computes the corresponding probability according to elementary quantum mechanics, it is found to be very small, on the order of 10^{-84} [1 in 10 with 84 following zeroes] . . . However small this probability may be, it is not strictly 0. One can therefore agree with common sense in saying that the sun will rise tomorrow, but one should allow for the possibility of such crazy events.[16]

All the biblical miracles are enormously *more* probable than this example, though we may expect them to be rare. The only "laws of nature" they would violate are the mechanistic ones. But these have proven to be no more than approximations of the vastly more accurate quantum laws.

In short, quantum mechanics has demonstrated that it is *not* true that everything happens with sufficient cause. Indeed, everything happens *without sufficient cause*—at least, there are insufficient causes within the universe. This is so within the human brain, as James concluded, and has given rise to a resurgence of interest in "consciousness" itself as an object of inquiry by serious physicists and mathematicians (Roger Penrose, the Rouse-Ball Professor of Mathematics at Oxford; Henry Stapp, professor of physics at the Berkeley Radiation Laboratory at the University of California; Michael Kellman, professor at the Institute of Theoretical Science and Chemical Physics at the University of Oregon; and many others). According to Kellman:

> The theory of quantum mechanics, by virtue of its fundamental principles, . . . is consistent with a role for mind as agent in determining some activities of purely material portions of biological systems.[17]

But a similar agency appears at work within the universe as a whole, giving rise to serious speculations as to an overarching consciousness not part "of" the universe, but nonetheless at work "in" it. A recent issue of *Nature*, probably the world's most prestigious scientific publication, offered its readers the following editorial speculation, only partly tongue-in-cheek:

> If [Einstein] is correct, the Universe . . . is a completely defined structure, and everything in it is already determined, future as well as past.* God may have declared it good, but there is nothing He or we can do about it now.
>
> The quantum view is quite different. The Universe is steadily emerging from innumerable quantum uncertainties, "dice thrown by God," as Einstein saw it. Newton himself thought that God must intervene now and then in His creation to keep it on track; and the uncertainty principle [the range of possible outcomes beyond what classical mechanistic influences determine] provides the ideal mechanism. By tweaking certain parameters by less than their . . . uncertainty, He could affect distant outcomes without breaking any physical law.[18]

Note, too, that a truly random (causeless) action *is utterly indistinguishable from an action that is "freely willed."* This is precisely what Alan Turing had glimpsed in quantum mechanics, and why the subject took on for him spiritual connotation: "The apparent non-predestination of physics is almost a combination of chances."[19]

"Time and Chance Happeneth to All Men"

One of the striking features of the Bible Code is that it presents a picture of "chance" and "predestination" that is eerily parallel to what has emerged in quantum mechanics. These ideas are completely at odds with the mechanistic presumptions of the Enlightenment, yet they are not identical to common theological assumptions, either. They have striking similarities, however, with certain conceptions found in the ancient Jewish tradition, especially in its less familiar, more "mystical" dimensions.

---

*Einstein specifically concluded that free will is an illusion. See "My Credo," in M. White and J. Gribbin, *Einstein: A Life in Science* (New York: Dutton, 1994), cited in Kellman, p. 19.

First, quantum mechanics placed *probability and statistics* at the very heart of reality. Pure chance—indistinguishable from "free will"—is everywhere and always reshaping the universe anew. The Bible Code, too, seems intrinsically probabilistic, a "language" that seems to offer no *specific* message about what will happen in the universe, but whose *statistical* orderliness belies intention and will, arranged in such a way as to allow for multiple outcomes (as we saw in the arrays of dates for the Scud missile attack in Chapter Eleven—each possible date being similar to the possible positions of the "fuzzy" billiard balls).

Second, in the quantum view, only the broad probabilities are determined; the selection of actual events occurs on a universal scale through some astounding and unimaginable coordination and readjustment of all future probabilities in the light of what actually happens in the present. Man, on his own small scale, similarly weighs and chooses, a tiny simulacrum—an image—of the larger "intention" that selects events throughout the universe. Man's choices, too, are taken into account, and the universe is adjusted accordingly.*

Something quite similar appears in the Bible Code as well: It does not present the portrait of a wholly determined world known in advance, but one in which many paths are possible, and in which our own choices are crucial. Recall again the hypothetical events surrounding the Gulf War codes, when three likely dates were supposedly found encoded in a tight cluster near other Gulf-related events and people. Even if the events did not occur as rumored, the description highlights a subtlety of the codes (assuming, of course, that they are real): that many different dates of an event, for instance, are likely to be "extractable" from any region of text. If you know the name of someone, but not when he died, you couldn't search for his date of death to learn (that is, predict) it. You could search for all the dates within a certain compactness, and presume that his actual date may be one of these—but only probably. It is only *likely* that an actual name-date pair will be compact, not assured. Thus does the intrinsically statistical nature of the codes prevent them from being

---

*This notion raises the thorny question as to the "boundary" between man's mind and will, and God's. The topic is a famous subject of theological dispute—and an infamous seedbed of heresy. Now even the physicists are joining the fray. See, for example, Alan Harkavy's "Speculations Concerning Will and a Local God," in which he offers a quantum-mechanical argument for localized deities. (In *Human Will: The Search for Its Physical Basis*, vol. 22 of *Revisioning Philosophy*, ed. David Appelbaum [New York: Peter Lang, 1995], pp. 93–98)

used as an oracle. This finding also suggests something else: that there are many possible dates on which someone might actually die, even though only one on which he does. If the analogy to the quantum nature of time is correct, then we would expect those dates to be spread out in a "probability" curve, with some outcomes more likely than others. Perhaps, then, the most highly probable dates before the fact are those closest to the name (in the Great Sages experiment), and those most highly improbable—but not impossible—are those far from the name.

But again, many dates *might* actually occur, and in a large enough sample of various events, many low-probability dates (and therefore many noncompact pairings) *will* occur. Only in the aggregate can an orderly "pairing"—a *tendency* toward compactness—be confirmed. For this reason, we cannot distinguish in any single pairing whether it occurred "just by chance," or meaningfully. And we therefore bump up against yet another "fence" that seems to have been placed with exquisite precision about the Bible Code, circumscribing our potential to misuse it: We cannot use even startling individual findings to verify a matter. The Code points to one thing and one thing only: the Authorship of the document in which it is found.

Nonetheless, we may ask, Why does one event happen and not another? As in quantum mechanics—and in certain related theories of brain action similar to James's—the actual event is selected[20] from among the various possibilities by the action of those entities that embody free will: by man himself within a limited domain—and by "something else" everywhere. In my own words: God lays out the broad patterns of history, acts in the world alongside us, willingly "contracts" some proportion of his omnipotence so that we may be granted the gift of genuine freedom, but in the fashion of a concerned and kindly father, adjusts matters to take into account our endlessly foolish use of His gift.

Within these parameters, the "impossible" becomes real: Two atoms may in fact coexist in the same place, forming a single seamless entity called a Bose-Einstein condensate. (Condensates of up to 16 million merged beryllium atoms have been formed in the laboratory just this past year. The entity is large enough to see with the naked eye and has been photographed.) Conversely, one atom may be forced to exist simultaneously in two places at once, a so-called quantum superposition (this, too, has been accomplished in the past year)—and a first step in actual "quantum teleportation" of visible objects.

There are some locations and states that are absolutely forbidden. An electron may "jump" from here to there; may exist at the same time in more than one place; yet may be absolutely precluded from ever being in a set of immediately adjacent spots. Many probability curves in quantum mechanics are thus sharply dichotomous: either A or B (in varying degree of likelihood), but nothing in between. (That is the very meaning of the word "quantum.")

The ancient Jewish view of time and prophecy is not unlike this: "The Messiah will come either in a generation that is completely virtuous or in one that is completely corrupt," states one famous aphorism. Specific events that are predestined may yet be averted by proper human action: ". . . but prayer, charity and good deeds avert the stern decree," in the words of the prayer book. God may adjust his actions to compensate for ours, but the freedom He has granted us is ours to affect history for better or for ill. Though all allowable outcomes may be distributed in the Bible Code, what those are we cannot know. We can only discover the ones that have occurred after the fact.

How Can Such a Thing Be?

There is one obvious question concerning the Bible Code that we have not yet asked: How could such a thing be possible? Those who are already convinced beyond a doubt of the Code and its reality will simply answer, To God, nothing is impossible. But one of the effects of quantum mechanics has been to get people thinking about the specific avenues that divine influence might use to penetrate our physical world *without* suspending the rules. The irreducible reality of *chance* is one such avenue.

But as quantum mechanics and other advanced domains in science have focused their attention on the human brain and mind, more specific pathways of influence have begun to suggest themselves. These provide what we might call an initial "plausibility argument" for the Bible Code, enabling us to hypothesize how it came into existence, without violating the rules. The argument is complex because it synthesizes findings and hypotheses from a great many domains. Only a sketch of it will be given here.

How the Codes Came into Existence: A Speculation

We can begin by noting that quantum mechanics is itself a "boundary."[21] In other words, the very law that guides the world simultaneously ensures that its own consequences are partially the result of "something" outside that law—something not part of the physical universe itself. If quantum mechanics is correct (and so far it is the most rigorously tested physical theory ever), then no matter what we can deduce from the physical features of the universe, we can never know *anything* about the nature or form of this "something" else that stands "outside" the universe "influencing" it.

The "effects" of this "something" will inevitably appear to us as absolute, irreducible randomness, even though in large ensembles of events, they balance each other out statistically to form orderly distributions. (Recall Turing, again: "The apparent non-predestination of physics is almost a combination of chances."[22])

Therefore, the only way we would ever be able to know anything about this "something," would be if "it" were capable of communicating with us in some fashion, and interested in doing so.

Is it "plausible" that the laws of the physical universe would allow such communication? In the mechanical, Enlightenment view, the answer would have been an unequivocal no. Under determinism, the Creator himself would be powerless to influence the course of His creation once it was set into motion. Shout as He might, hearing Him would be absolutely impossible.

But now the answer—only since quantum mechanics—is a surprising yes. In the quantum understanding, such outside-the-universe effect is *required* to make sense of even the most trivial aspects of reality. Our own "influence," which we label our "consciousness" or "will," subtly alters trajectories and outcomes within the ensemble of particles that constitute our brains, in one view at least. If that is so, there is nothing to exclude the possibility that a larger, universal "will" can do likewise—*also within the ensemble of particles that constitute our brains.* This, then, would be its "mechanism" for communicating.

But how would we know that it was "He" communicating to us in this way and not merely the imaginings of our own minds? We wouldn't, not with any certainty. So how could such a communication be validated? Surely it could not depend upon the word of one or more witnesses, however respected. It would need to be an essentially permanent communiqué, whose very content would bear irrefragable testimony. Its seal could only consist of something the Author alone could know. (Recall our spy example in Chapter Nine—identifying the "real" message involved finding encrypted meanings known only to control *and* to our spy.)

Could any individual be the suitable recipient of such a momentous message? Could everyone? Given human nature, that seems to me more implausible than the Bible Code itself. I think, rather, it would need to be someone who—if we call him the "receiver"—would have tuned himself *just so,* so as uniquely to be able to "hear."

What would be the qualifications of such an individual? What would constitute the necessary "tuning"? Would it be of a "technical" nature where skill, determination, cleverness, persistence, and practice would be sufficient to yield results? For example, might one think of the Bible Code's origins in kabbalah in this way, treating kabbalah (as is too commonly done) as a "spiritual" if not "magical" technique for gaining some kind of "psychic power"? Given the Torah's own prohibition concerning such things, I suspect not. There is a better way to answer these questions.

Robert Haralick is an independent researcher into the Bible Code who has assisted a prominent rabbi in writing a book concerning it, and has presented various findings using somewhat different techniques than those outlined above.[23] Haralick is the Boeing Professor of Electrical Engineering at the University of Washington in Seattle who has published over four hundred scientific papers. He is presently organizing an international symposium on the codes to be held at and sponsored in conjunction with the Technion in Haifa. Presentations will be exclusively scientific and will have to meet the rigorous standards of the International Association for Pattern Recognition of which he is a fellow. His observations about kabbalah are especially astute and sensitive. They relate directly to the question who would be able to receive and pass on such a thing.[24]

For while the Bible Code as a cryptologic phenomenon is rooted deeply in kabbalah, as we've seen, kabbalah itself is something far more. To a group of codes enthusiasts unfamiliar with kabbalah, some pro, some con, but all distorting it, he writes:

> Kabbalah has to do with receiving . . . the will of G-d. In this language one could say that we receive the will of G-d when we so align our will with G-d's will that we become totally servants of G-d. This means transforming the mind and body so that our physical resistance to receiving G-d's will is nullified. This physical resistance is what [Christians] refer . . . to as "carnal nature." The parallel Christian language of receiving the will of G-d can be understood from the language in the "Lord's prayer": *thy will be done* . . . As we become better able to receive the will of G-d in our living we will also begin to rec-

ognize the ways in which G-d is present in our lives. And we will be conscious of this presence to a greater and greater degree. There is only delight in being able to carry out G-d's will as a humble servant of G-d and being conscious of the presence of G-d. The only doing [that is required] is the kind of spiritual growth undertaken by a person who is desirous of becoming closer to G-d. *The changing can be recognized by way the person is living life.* [My emphasis][25]

One of the greatest of the later kabbalists was Rabbi Luzzatto, the Ramchal, whose comments about nondeterministic influences were cited earlier. Describing the act of "receiving," he comments:

> "Bestowed enlightenment" consists of an influence granted by God through various particular means especially prepared for this purpose. When this influence reaches a person's mind, certain information becomes fixed in it. . . . In this manner one can gain knowledge . . . that could not be otherwise gained through logic alone. . . . The main concept of true prophecy is . . . that a living person achieves such an attachment and bond with God. . . . The revelation of God's Glory is what initiates everything transmitted in a prophetic vision. This is then transmitted to the power of imagination in the prophet's soul, which in turn forms images of the concepts forced upon it by the power of the highest revelation.
>
> All Israel comprehended two important truths. First they had to realize that God's true essence is not included in any image whatsoever, and that He is totally divorced from any possible visualization. Once they realized this, certain prophetic depictions were revealed to them. . . . the mysteries of God's divinity, as well as of His creation and direction of the universe.*

---

*Luzzatto is here explicating one of the most important kabbalistic understandings of the reason for the commandment not to make any graven images of God—for to do so is subtly to train oneself to be unable to "see" something of His genuine nature and effect in the world. Physicists are now likewise realizing that the "nonvisualizability" of the most fundamental features of quantum mechanics is not a defect in the theory, but a powerful hint as to the true nature of reality. In the words of physicist Menos Kefatos at George Mason University: "Classical physics presents us with a picture of physical reality that is visualizable. . . . A more complete description of physical reality . . . is unvisualizable. (Menos Kefatos and Robert Nadeau, *The Conscious Universe: Part and Whole in Modern Physical Theory* [Berlin: Springer Verlag, 1990], p.14)

Thus, the "prophet" is the individual who, by the manner of his life, progressively binds himself to God. As a consequence, he becomes transformed into a suitable recipient for what God says. But note that it is his *character* that takes clear priority: his godliness.

The transmission of information occurs via particular images stimulated in the human imagination by the nonvisualizable dimension of reality. The results in this instance are more or less suitable "allegories" and "metaphors," the "more or less" reflecting the "level" of the recipient, hence the "level" of his *inspiration*.

But "of all the prophets, none was so great as Moses." Rabbi Luzzatto explains that while the speech of God is transformed in the minds of all other prophets into visualizable *imagery*, this was not so with Moses. God says, "With him do I speak mouth to mouth . . . not in dark speeches" (Numbers 12:8). It is this direct speech, the letters of the creation itself, that Moses then committed to writing, with a precision that would have been unattainable by anyone else before or since.[26] Why was Moses vouchsafed so singular and precious a missive? Was it because of his accomplishments and spiritual technique? According to the Torah, it was chiefly because "he was the most humble of men."

What Next?

The level of attention given the Bible Code has never been higher, from skeptics, enthusiasts, professionals, and amateurs. We do not know yet whether the phenomenon will continue to resist refutation, or will prove itself yet another in a long line of insubstantial religious enthusiasms. Most of the studies that are currently under way fall into the following categories:

Replications and detailed critiques. These studies are carefully examining the Great Sages experiment. This experiment with its fixed data set has been replicated, as noted. But further variations are being tested to see how "robust" the findings are under the influence of alternate spellings, compactness measures, and techniques for measuring significance.

Extensions. The primary researchers themselves are attempting to extend their findings via wholly new experiments on different data sets (as mentioned above).

Research on the Torah as a whole. New research examines not only Genesis but all Five Books of Moses. Preliminary reports indicate that the Bible Code is indeed found throughout the Torah. Most of the new research focuses on ELS clusters in the Torah *as a whole*, with all five books treated as a single string of text. The question is now being raised as to whether different kinds of information is encoded on a book-by-book basis, and in the Torah taken as a whole.

The search for codes in other texts. There is no evidence for codes within any of the other books of the Bible. However, there are those who believe or hope that similar codes will be found there. So long as these studies are done in a properly controlled fashion, their results will be useful.

There is also the question of the strange "Ezekiel Tablets" in raised lettering mentioned in Chapter Four. Along with the opening chapters of Genesis, certain passages in Ezekiel were foundational in kabbalistic studies. As noted, the "Ezekiel Tablets" were discovered in Iraq (Ezekiel lived in ancient Babylon) and brought to Israel during the War for Independence. One must ask, Why would anyone bother to carve out the entire text in *raised* lettering on sixty-eight stone tablets (an enormous undertaking) in perfectly uniform *scripta continua* arrays?

The search for "parameters." If the world at large is to take it seriously, the scientific world especially, the Bible Code cannot remain something that only one or two people are able to uncover. The "rules" that allow genuine, statistically verifiable codes to be found must eventually be reduced to writing, however complex and nuanced they may prove to be. Without such "param-eterization," the suspicion will continually arise that positive findings are merely the result of inadvertent "tuning and snooping"—or worse: deliberate fraud.

The testing of different encoding rules and classes of information. Ancient tradition holds that there are "seventy gates" of wisdom: seventy different methods of interpreting the text of the Torah. Of these, "skipping letters" is one (according to the Zohar, the fiftieth).* But if the Vilna Gaon's claim that *all* the details of history are contained in the Torah—a text of only 300,000-plus letters—is correct, then the Bible Code must use many different encryption schemes to accommodate them, that is, not only *equidistant* skips; not only minimal spacing, and so on. But if there are many different coding rules, there must also be rules that define which class of information is encrypted according to which rule.

Once you consider the complexities involved in simultaneously uncovering both a class of data and a rule that matches it, something else suddenly becomes apparent. Because the rule can only be "verified" on a class of data,

---

*Rabbi Eliezer (Rokeach), a teacher of the Ramban (Nachmanides), enumerates "73 ways to comprehend and interpret the letters of the Torah." He lists number 54 as "the way of skipping."

and because a class of data can only be verified as a genuine class by appearing under a rule, *it is astounding that anyone could have found even one such correspondence in the first place.* That is why Eliyahu Rips has spoken of Doron Witztum as a scientist on a par with Ernest Rutherford.

The Seventh Millennium

Long ago, in the first century after the destruction of the second Temple by the Romans, at the beginning of the great exile, the ancient kabbalists foretold a better time: when knowledge of the mundane material world below and understanding of the sublime spiritual world above would together burst forth in a twin fountain—as when the "fountains of the great deep were broken up" and "the windows of heaven were opened" in the days of Noah—but to mankind's betterment, not destruction.

The first hints of those days would appear, it was said, at the "six hundredth year of the sixth millennium"—roughly the mid-nineteenth century. Their actual arrival—when science and knowledge of God would no longer destroy each other but embrace as long estranged brothers, the seventh millennium—would be heralded by the end of the Jews' exile, sometime before the sixth millennium concluded. (The State of Israel was established in 1948; the sixth millennium ends less than 250 years from now.)

Are we at the threshold of such an era? Or are such notions merely sentimental "tuning and snooping"—reading what one wants into passages selected from the unimaginably vast "data set" of human speculation? Perhaps the Bible Code will prove to be yet another chimera—vastly more sophisticated and befuddling, perhaps, than any that has come before. If so, I will continue my search, for the portrait of a world in which all is mechanical is a frightening one indeed: Who can be sanguine about mere humanism when surveying what we humans most often do with our illusion of absolute freedom? Indeed, nothing strikes me as more self-deluded and sentimental than the notion that we are perfectly capable of conducting our lives without God. In the words of the Ramchal—as though foreseeing our own age:

> The opposite of [an] optimum world exists when man becomes overwhelmed by the pursuit of his physical desires. . . . It is a world of false values, where good qualities are eclipsed and evil ones prevail. As a result of this, tranquility ceases . . . there is no security, and there is

much suffering and injury. God hides his Glory from the world, and it goes on *as if left to chance, abandoned to the laws of nature*. . . . In such a world, the wicked become strong, and the good are deprived of all status. [My emphasis][27]

In response, there are many who would immediately—and properly—point to the huge injustices committed in the name of God: not least against the Jews. No wonder that so many moderns, Jews preeminent among them, have developed a profound distrust of *all* religious notions, their own ancestors' included.

This is precisely the point where, in my view, a proper, hard-nosed union of science and religion is a necessity, not a sentiment: For the scientific standard of truth—controlled experimentation, restrained assertion, quantitated probability of error, dispassionate acceptance of evidence, the ability to say "I don't know" for very long stretches of time, the willingness to abandon cherished ideas that lack substantiation—is the only counterbalance I know to the human tendency to turn partial religious understandings into dogmatic absolutes. That there is *some* absolute truth to most matters seems to me inescapably obvious; but that we may often do no better than approximate it—getting closer, perhaps, but never quite *there*—seems equally evident. Science is merely the mathematical formalization of humility.

But if the Bible Code indeed turns out to be the first genuine instance of that union of the waters above with the waters below foretold by the kabbalists, here is what I think it promises:

The Bible Code could signal the start of an age of combined scientific and spiritual exploration such as has not been seen since the great sea journeys that ushered in the global society of the modern world. (Columbus was convinced that the earth was round because of mystical interpretations of Scripture; he was also convinced that by setting sail in 1492, he was fulfilling prophecy and initiating the end of the Jewish exile.[28])

The scientist will be driven to seek more than mere proof of the Bible Code's reality and the validity of the Torah. He will want to understand the peculiar probabilistic, holographic, and multidimensional structure of the Code.*An investigation into these features will inevitably raise analogies to both quantum mechanics and to ancient kabbalistic understandings. And as it happens, quantum mechanics is just now beginning to develop—with a

---

*Presuming there is not an actual message-bearing plaintext to be uncovered.

speed that has surprised skeptics—a subdiscipline that is eerily congruent with the codes. This is the emerging field of *quantum cryptology* (noted briefly in Chapter Seven). In a replay of the historical process we studied in Chapter Seven, researchers have already noted that the "potential use of quantum mechanics for code-breaking purposes raises an obvious question— *what about building a quantum computer?*" (My emphasis)[29]

Second, from a religious perspective, the Bible Code raises the question, If the Torah is truly "from heaven," what does heaven expect of us? Because Judaism has been the most ancient repository of the Torah—and because the Bible Code itself emerged from Jewish tradition—greater value than ever before will inevitably be placed on that tradition's ancient interpretations of the Torah. That is not to say that everything Judaism has ever had to say about the Torah is or will be accepted as correct, but I believe it inevitable that a spirit of open inquiry and curiosity about the treasures hidden deep within traditional Judaism, and long ignored or rejected, will quickly replace adversarial contentions over theology.

The Bible Code is itself congruent with this theological restraint. The codes concerning Hanukkah, for example, cannot "prove" that the Hasmonean dynasty was founded by the Maccabees, or that the Hanukkah miracle actually occurred. It could equally well reflect the importance of the historical belief in this miracle among Jews. The belief is an undisputed fact; the miracle the belief refers to is disbelieved by many who accept that "Hanukkah exists." In short, when it comes to theological dispute, the Bible Code offers but limited assistance. Neither can it be used to validate, or invalidate, such major beliefs as that of Jesus' Messiahship. "Positive" codes on *any* subject address the question of authorship alone; they therefore point us to the Torah: nothing more, nothing less.

But I also believe that the scientific advances that lie before us, and which the Code heralds, will require—more than ever before in our checkered history—that we indeed set aside our squabbles and listen to the central message of the Torah. For the risks of living in an "atomic" era pale by comparison to the risks of living in the era that lies before us. If we do not take to heart and live by what the Code points to in the Torah, then we may well die from having grasped—and put to bad use—the principles that made it possible. Here is what I see coming:

The Tree of Life

One of the amazing features of the Bible Code discovered even before its "prophetic" nature, is its sheer complexity. The amount of information encoded into a finite text by using the same configuration of letters to embody multiple meanings is self-evidently beyond the capacity of any human being (or group) with whatever computing resources.

Quantum cryptology *can* solve such a problem. It does so in the following way. We previously discussed how in quantum mechanics an object does not follow a fixed, predetermined trajectory. But not only can an object (say one of our tiny billiard balls) *potentially be* in two or more possible future positions, there are circumstances where *in the present* an object actually is in two or more positions at the same time. (That effect has been accomplished and photographed.) These simultaneous states are called "superpositions." It turns out that those superpositions can be taken advantage of in computing, causing on-off logic gates to generate many more "bits" of information than they "logically" ought to be capable of.

If a standard computer could process one billion steps per second (about the level of current chip technology), it would process roughly 3×10^{16} steps in one year of continuous operation. But a (still-idealized, 100-bit)[30] quantum version of the same computer would process more than 10^{30} steps *at once*, yielding *more than 10^{39}* steps in one second. To accomplish what the quantum computer accomplishes in one second, a standard computer would require more than 10^{22} years. The universe is only 1.5×10^9 years old. Could this open the door to quantum computers capable of solving problems that otherwise are utterly "noncomputable," because they require an infinite number of steps?

With quantum computers, combinatorics problems such as are raised by the Bible Code become imaginable. At present, however, the only known place in the physical universe where there is any suggestion at all (albeit debatable) of an already existing "information processing system" that incorporates quantum effects is within the human brain. Under normal circumstances, of course, it cannot process information at this accelerated rate.

Such ideas would have been thought absolutely impossible just a few years ago; yet at least some of them now seem on the verge of realization by teams of scientists at Stanford University, the Weizmann Institute in Israel, Oxford, the University of Rochester, Duke University, the University of Montreal, and elsewhere. Such feats not only suggest, once again, a possible link between quantum mechanics and the mysterious features of the human mind; they raise the distinct possibility that *artificially constructed devices that incorporate quantum computation might also thereby genuinely embody mind—and therefore consciousness itself.* Do we stand ready to eat, truly, for the first time, of the Tree of Life? In the eloquent, restrained speculation of physical chemist Michael Kellman:

> I believe, in accord with Penrose and Lockwood that the mind must have capabilities in thinking beyond . . . purely computational processes. . . . this kind of mental agency could also be used rapidly and flexibly to "reprogram" purely mechanistic computational processes in the brain, as a result of higher-level cognition of some sort operating within the mind.[31] In addition, the idea of quantum computers . . . may be suggestive. If the mind has properties of a quantum observer as proposed here, this might have powerful uses in perception and cognition if linked with some kind of quantum computation in the brain.[32]

Or outside the brain.

The Golem

An ancient Jewish legend (one that influenced Mary Shelley in her writing of *Frankenstein*) is of a thinking creature invented by a kabbalist to assist him in his mysterious tasks. But ultimately, the creature overpowered and destroyed him. I have a friend who is a prominent scientist at a major university. He, too, is keenly interested in the emerging study of the mind's relation to quantum mechanics. But he is also genuinely frightened. He believes that we are indeed on the verge of cracking the greatest secret of all—producing, in effect, genuine Golems: creatures that at our doing incorporate the same divine spark of mind by which God formed us, and which we ourselves contain. As he surveys the wreck that mankind has so often made of our great gifts and good fortune, he is not at all sanguine about how such immense power will be used. The United States Department of Defense has already initiated a seed-grant of $5 million to begin an Institute for Quantum Information and Computing (QUIC) at the NSA: necessary and predictable—but ominous.

When Robert Oppenheimer witnessed the terrible power he unleashed in his creation of the hydrogen bomb, he uttered a passage from the Bhagavad

Gita: "Now I am become the destroyer of worlds." My friend understands that just as electronic tube computers of the 1940s made the hydrogen bomb possible, so too will the emerging creation of a genuine Golem make possible destruction on a scale that could shrink the H-bomb into triviality. And, alas, when mankind becomes capable of some new form of destruction, sooner or later we seem to employ it. It is for this reason in particular that I not only see a possible convergence between the Bible Code and quantum information processing—I hope and pray for it. For in my view only something as astonishing and humbling as the Code—and the Torah to which it points—will be capable of restraining us once we have grasped hold of the fruit of the Tree of Life.

The Final Choice

The peculiar limits of the Bible Code reflect something distinctive about Judaism, the peculiar kind of "bounded latitude" expressed in the Torah. As the original monotheistic religion, Judaism proclaims that there is only one God, and that He is the God not only of the Jews, but of all mankind. In this, there is no latitude. It also proclaims that, under the authority of this one God, there is but a single moral code to which all mankind is accountable, not only the Jews. It does not proclaim that Judaism is a requirement for everyone; nor does it exclude from the world to come those of other faiths. It allows tremendous room for disagreement even on major points of theology—a prime cause of bloodshed and war and persecution, as the Jews know only too well.

The point is this: Judaism makes no bones about the necessity for living a moral life, the parameters of which are outlined in the Torah (with additional details in the oral tradition). Those parameters place specific limitations on action, and a subset of the Ten Commandments (the so-called Noahide commandments) are considered universally binding. But the limitations these place on worldview are far less stringent than upon *action*—depending, of course, upon the kind of action a given worldview leads to. Idolatry is out of bounds, because it inevitably leads to immorality (how and why is another, fascinating, study), but otherwise the Torah leaves quite open the forms of worship acceptable to God.

Jews are commanded to eschew any visualizable conception of God, and we've seen that the kabbalists understood this guideline to have special consequences in the domain of understanding—but the command is not universal. Judaism has therefore never developed an interest in disproving the tenets of other faiths, especially when those tenets shape character in accord with morality.* Some of the prominent righteous gentiles in the Hebrew Scriptures are even referred to as "anointed ones"—literally, "messiahs," the same term used for David himself, and for the promised Messiah to come. The object lessons taught in the Torah may have been first given to one people, but they are for the world. They require no statement of faith to cling to and to live by. I believe that anyone who submits himself to the Torah's generous spirit will learn the following:

We live in a world that is driven both by impersonal mechanical forces and by a vast, unfathomable Spirit that is yet also keenly concerned with each of us as individuals. But He seems less concerned with our simple material well-being than with the state of our souls. And for Him, the state of our souls boils down to something quite straightforward—shockingly so, even: *goodness*. Upon this primary principle the cosmos itself is ordered.

An electron in an unimaginably distant galaxy adopts a spin $+\frac{1}{2}$ state, and not a $-\frac{1}{2}$ state, though each state may be equally likely, because something makes it happen *just so*. But why? A leaf falls *just so* in a forest somewhere in the Carpathian Mountains, in largest part because of "sufficient reason"—the wind, the season, the autumn raindrops that happen to strike it—but also because God wills it. So claimed the Baal Shem Tov—the "Master of the Name"—the founder of Hasidic Judaism; so claimed the ancient kabbalists; so, too, for that matter, did Jesus of Nazareth and many others of his time.

God wills these events because in the mysterious interconnectedness of all things great and small now known to prevail throughout His creation, there is introduced thereby a *moral* effect, tiny and indirect though it may be in such cases. Goodness, in other words, is not the desiccated philosophical concept we have made of it: Goodness is the very substance of God's presence in the universe, as real and efficacious as light itself—as *mind*. And if He is concerned to take action for an electron or a leaf, how much more so is He concerned with *us*, bearers of an awesome capacity much like His, however much smaller, to choose freely either good or evil, to repair an entire world with our smallest actions, or open a breach thereby that an omnipotent, omnipresent God alone has the ability to heal—even then, perhaps only over long stretches of time. In the words of Maimonides, "One thought, one utterance, one deed may tip the scale of the individual—and of the whole universe—to the side of merit."

---

*When Jewish scholars take up the question of the *general* acceptability or unacceptability of a religious form, which is rare, it is almost always from the point of view of the query, Is it idolatry?

But there is a dire implication to all this: For in such a world, it is God, not we, who determines what is good and what is evil. By appealing to our pride, the serpent of autonomous intellect told us to decide the matter for ourselves—regardless of what God says; to eat of the Tree of Knowledge of Good and Evil. To the Gnostics, therefore, and the occultists, and the alchemists, and eventually, too, the humanists and materialists (though they eschew the symbols), the serpent is not himself the embodiment of evil, but rather of "illumination," of "enlightenment," of a Nietzschean "higher" wisdom "six-thousand miles beyond good and evil." The vision of the Torah directly opposes such notions of total self-sufficiency.

Most of what Judaism has taken from the Torah is enormously expansive, tolerant, filled with compassion toward human frailty and variability—but not endlessly so: The land is large and welcoming, but certain boundary stones may be moved only at peril. The Torah has no interest in changing people's religious beliefs or way of life—except insofar as these directly conflict or lead to what the Torah defines as "evil." Then it is stern and unyielding; there is mercy, but in the form of patience, not latitude: "It may take you a long time to change in the ways I wish," the Lord seems to say, "and you may hold pretty much whatever theological notions you find easiest to assimilate—but do not mistake my patience for acceptance; when it comes to how you behave, change you must—for you will not be able to survive otherwise, but will destroy yourselves with your cleverness." In a world where the Bible Code is real, trying to understand what God expects of us with as little self-delusion as possible—what, as a matter of our own self-preservation and happiness He allows and what He forbids—would become a matter of high importance. Who would want to risk misunderstanding *what* He was telling us, once we were certain *that* it was He telling us? There will surely be disagreement, but the world will no longer be a welcoming place for sophists.

What about theological debate? Would there be none? The careful observer of Torah and of Judaism will soon learn the following. There are many key concepts—for example, on the nature of the Messiah and when he will come; on points of Jewish Law—that have two or more directly contradictory explanations. Sometimes whole schools have sprung up around hotly contested divergent opinions and no resolution is ever reached. In those cases, it is said—with a certain age-old shrug—"When the Messiah arrives, he will tell us which is correct." Or, in other cases, "When the Messiah comes, he will explain to us how both are true." Theology in such matters is a fairly restrained discipline: "We don't know."

But: How did you treat your wife today? Your husband? Child? Friend? Neighbor? These are theological inquiries of vastly greater import. Indeed, very little in the way of formal theology is discussed in the Torah—arguably none at all. But upon matters of practical living, it expounds ceaselessly, in the voice of a Father desperately concerned for His children. Upon the enacted response to these kinds of inquiries, God will alter the very fabric of the universe, compounding right action with His blessings; compensating for, though not effacing, our errors. THINK LOCALLY, ACT BIBICALLY , reads the bumper sticker on the Divine Chariot. I'LL TAKE CARE OF THE BIG PICTURE. The entire storehouse of human knowledge and understanding, all the stories and lessons embodied in the Torah, all the attentions of an inconceivably gigantic Creator and Operator of a universe, will be seen to be concentrated upon the small daily choices of our individual lives. And we will learn to concentrate our own attention there likewise.

Eventually, perhaps, it will be understood as vain to hope that wars will end if only we develop a better "program," or because one faith will have triumphed over others; or if only mankind will grow out of religious belief altogether into some mechanico-Freudian-Marxist void, or because all come to accept that there *is* no truth beyond the unending deconstruction of all truths. If the Messianic Era ever does come when mankind "shall neither hurt nor destroy in all My holy mountain," as the prophet Isaiah proclaimed, it will be also as he says, "for the earth shall be full of the knowledge of the LORD, as the waters cover the sea" (Isaiah 11:9).

But what is that "knowledge"? What is it that the "seventy gates" of wisdom reveal and lead to? Perhaps in the current flurry of publicity over sensationalized accounts of the Bible Code, we would be tempted to conclude with the ancient gnostics and alchemists that there is little difference between true wisdom and magic; between knowledge of the heart and foretelling the future. The Vilna Gaon, who stated that all of existence was written in the Torah, also offered this caution:

> First learn the laws and commandments of the Torah, and fulfil them. For this alone is the bread of life which satisfies man's hunger. Only afterwards should you occupy yourself with the study of secrets—the wine and oil into which you dip your bread. But he who reverses this order shall not succeed. Indeed, he will lose everything: wine, oil and bread.[33]

" 'Depart from evil and do good,' " wrote Rabbi Luzzatto. "*This is all that God desires of man, and it is the entire purpose of His Creation.*"
And the end of exile.

האל צפן אלהים אמת
= HaEL TziPeN AeLoHYM EMeT
= "God encoded; God is Truth"
הכר נא למי החתמת
= HiKeR NA LiMiY HaChoTeMeT
= "Discern, I pray thee, whose sign this is."
(Genesis 38:25)[1]

~

REPORT FROM THE FRONT LINES

June 1997
Connecticut Cyberspace

Just eleven days ago, another book on the codes was published to great fan-fare, written by the man who had been rumored to be seeking a meeting with Israeli Prime Minister Benjamin Netanyahu around the same time I was in Israel (see Chapter One).[1] His book presents the Bible Code in a most unfor-tunate light—portraying it as able to be used to predict the future almost as a matter of routine. It has the potential to discredit the serious research with-out a hearing.

On the same day this book was placed on sale, a careful critique of the genuine research was also made public by two scientists (and two nonscientist collaborators), not in a peer-reviewed venue, but rather on the Internet. Brendan McKay is a world-class probabilist at Australia National University (some of his critiques of the Code were mentioned in Chapter Thirteen), and Dror Bar-Natan is a similarly renowned quantum-field theorist at Hebrew University. Persi Diaconis was acknowledged to have helped devise portions of the challenge. With critics prepared by the claims made in the popular book to treat the entire subject as nonsense, a serious attack from academically qual-ified critics could easily deliver the coup de grâce, whether deserved or not.

Furthermore, Harold Gans's extension of the research was also under serious attack. McKay and others claimed to have found fatal errors in the way that Gans had assembled the names of the cities, with spelling errors that would completely invalidate the results. In response, Gans submitted his list to an outside expert whose job it would be to come up with a corrected list of cities on which Gans would have to rerun his experiment.

The paper McKay and Bar-Natan have posted on the Internet is well thought out, aimed at flushing into the open the presence of "data snooping" discussed in Chapter Thirteen. They perform a set of experiments identical to that of Witztum, Rips, and Rosenberg, using the same list of rabbis but with a new set of variations in the form of the dates of birth and/or death, devised according to different criteria than in the original. They also perform a second series of experiments in the same format but using the titles of each rabbi's "most notable written works" (not unlike the example in Chapter Ten of Rabbi Abraham HaMalach's book), instead of birth or death dates.* Their conclusion is as follows: "In each case, the result was unambiguously negative. No indication of any extraordinary phenomenon was found."

Though work of this kind inevitably demands long and careful scrutiny, Doron Zeilberger, an accomplished mathematician at Temple University, promptly weighed in on McKay and Bar-Natan's paper: "a poignant and watertight rebuttal of the 'Bible Code nonsense.' " Some of his words seemed directed at the codes researchers themselves:

> . . . we mathematicians are also human. As humans we have to sur-
> vive in this seemingly meaningless, cold and hostile world. There is
> nothing wrong in having some mystical and religious warmth to keep
> us going. Newton did it, Kepler did it, and lots of mathematicians and
> scientists are deeply religious. The logical contradiction is only appar-
> ent, since after all, modern science is just another religion, and the
> apparent contradictions and "paradoxes" will hopefully all be resolved
> . . . when the Messiah comes.
>
> Besides, a little dose of embarrassment may be good for our col-
> lective psyche. We deserve our own Cold Fusion. . . . [2]

But this was not the end of the story. One day later, I got an e-mail through the grapevine: Harold Gans had received the corrected list of cities and

---

*They also ran the same set of experiments using a different method of aggregate relative compactness, suggested to them by Persi Diaconis, aimed at "tuning." But as they acknowledge was severely protested by Rips, this method would tend to wash out the apparent tendency, claimed to be distinctive of the Bible Code, for the shorter related ELSs to tend toward immediate proximity (zero distance).

rerun his experiment: the p-value actually *improved*. Witztum reviewed the corrected material and reran Gans's experiment himself. His run generated a $p < 1/1,000,000$. And with regard to the McKay/Bar-Natan refutation, according to Rabbi Mechanic, Witztum and Rips promptly found at least fourteen errors of fact and spelling in the new data set compiled by McKay and Bar-Natan. When the errors were corrected, even this (in Rips and Witztum's view) flawed "refutation" produced significant results. Furthermore, when Witztum reran his own original experiment eliminating what the critics claimed were biases that alone made it successful, the results actually *improved;* from $p < 1/62,500$ to $p < 1/5,000,000$.* If accurate, these would constitute the first truly "outside" validations of the phenomenon, by openly hostile critics no less.

At present, Robert Haralick is coordinating an extremely careful re-do of a "Great Sages" experiment from the ground up, using independent criteria for the selection of data, stringent checks against bias, and even more rigorous measures of "closeness" and of statistical significance than have been previously applied by either critics or proponents. Each step of his experiment is open to comment, discussion, and, when needed, revision. When the results are in, they will provide the best evidence to date either for or against the reality of the code.

The critics, of course, have reason to disagree. Whichever side one is on, one may be certain the matter will not rest here, nor should it. The happy news is that the debate is now fully engaged. Will the higher things once again recede, just beyond our reach, or are we on the verge of an unprecedented opening of "the gates of supernal knowledge above"? In the end, the truth will out.

---

*Announced just this winter in a response to critics: "The Seal of God Is Truth," by Doron Witztum, *Jewish Action,* February 1998, p. 25.

DETAILS OF
THE NEW MOON

There are many features of traditional Judaism that seem archaic to the modern sensibility of Jews and gentiles alike. Many find its most hallowed rituals—the monthly celebration of the new moon is a prime example—passé, vestiges of an era when the misunderstood mechanisms of nature overwhelmed primitive man with superstitious awe.

So arcane have these ancient traditions come to seem that they have long been dropped from the major branches of modernized Judaism. Yet the traditional Jewish position accords profound respect to the ability to calculate the seasons and the months, to detect and quantify with precision relations between the ebb and flow of the moon and the cycles of the sun (the "times" and the "seasons") for "the nations reckon by the sun, but Israel reckons by the moon."[1] This reckoning—rational, not magical—was the key that released the mind into true contemplation of the divine:

> he who learns a single thing from a magian[2] is worthy of death; and he
> who is able to calculate the times and the seasons but does not, one
> may hold no conversation with him.

Why should such calculations be afforded such importance? There are a number of answers, but the one suggested above is of particular relevance to the modern world.

Human spiritual frailty is such that most people invariably require experiences that renew their faith. People crave miracles, to put it bluntly. That is especially so given that in the biblical view one is being asked to dramatically change one's "natural" way of life on the say-so of a completely invisible and intangible being.

But there is a curious thing about miracles: They lose their effect, surprisingly quickly. And secondhand reports of miracles are of even thinner substance. How, then, does a critical mind retain faith in the transcendent and invisible? Only by evidence of a distinctive sort; evidence that is in some sense always there to be contemplated directly, yet which never becomes so familiar as to lose its power to inspire.

The *power* of natural forces has long served this purpose—until those forces began to be understood as merely mechanical. Their size alone ceases to amaze us anymore. A more recent variant of this theme contemplates the sheer *complexity* of nature, and suggests that this complexity and interdependence of function is the true evidence for divine guidance: subtlety, in other words, not size. But recent research into "complexity" suggests that this, too, is the result of merely mechanical processes.

The genuinely inspirational "contemplation" long ago envisioned by the Jewish sages was not the contemplation of nature in isolation; *it was the contemplation of nature and her patterns in the light of written descriptions of those processes—descriptions that by all rights shouldn't exist.* The Jewish approach to the question of whether there is a higher meaning to the world is, "Come, let us search out the hidden *depths of the Torah* and then you will see for yourself evidence of *a divine hand in the world.*"

The length of the "synodical" lunar cycle—from one sun-moon conjunction to the next—is extremely difficult to measure or to calculate. That is because every monthlong revolution of the moon about the earth differs slightly from the one before. (As the Talmud puts it, "The sun knows the time of its going down, but the moon does not."[3]) Lunar variability has long vexed astronomers and has to be taken into account in space flight—the first landing on the moon would have been impossible, for example, without the new, highly accurate data obtainable only by satellite.

Even an *average* value for the lunar cycle is almost impossible to calculate. Since the moon returns to the exact same position vis-à-vis the sun only once every 689,282 years,[4] there are never enough monthly measurements to know where in this "supercycle" an average lies. (Is it near a peak? In a trough? On the upslope? The downslope?) Even if accurate measurements could be taken once a month without fail for 10,000 years, the sample would amount to less than 1.5 percent of the complete supercycle.

Knowledge of the moon's variability is not itself remarkable; it was known to the Babylonians, too, for example, and they spent much time trying to solve the problem by detailed measurements and statistical calculations. After centuries of effort, they found that 235 lunar months have about the same number of days as 19 solar years. And since there has never been a solution to the so-called three-body problem, there has never been an equation for the moon's orbit, either. (An equation would allow you to predict the cycle on theoretical grounds. With the development of advanced numerical approximation techniques that require high-speed computers, one can now generate a "good-enough" orbital equation. As recently as 1923—before the advent of machine computation—hand-calculated equations used 1,500 terms to arrive at an approximation. Current approximations use over 6,000 terms.) Because of these complications, scientific estimates for the mean lunar month have inevitably varied, as the handful of samples in the book suggests.[5]

Nonetheless, through a series of complex calculations, the oral tradition maintained that the average length of a lunar cycle was 29.53059 days—the number that corresponds to the Rambam's figure in the table (given small rounding errors: the final digit is shown expanded in parentheses to one more digit based on the 1/100 seconds in the table).[6] In his text on the subject, Maimonides (the Rambam) took pains to emphasize that the method produces an *average* for the lunar cycle.[7] Rabbi Weissmandl would do likewise in his first publication, *Hilchot HaChodesh* (*The Laws for Fixing the New Moon*), written in 1931, before the Holocaust. This average is of special interest.

In the Beginning

Unlike the other figures shown, both old and new, these ancient Jewish calculations do not seem to be based on the observations of astronomers or on any of the various theories of celestial mechanics that have been refined over the centuries by many cultures. (Observational astronomy in Judaism was limited to identifying the moment of religiously significant events; it was not oriented toward developing methods of prediction or models of planetary motion.)

If not from planetary theory and observation, where does this number—29.53059 days to the lunar month—come from? This exact value is known without doubt to date back to (at the latest) the first century B.C. (and evidence suggests it is far older than that). Over the years, scholars have suggested that it must simply have been adopted from others in the Mediterranean Basin.

The suggestion is certainly plausible. Both the Babylonians and Greeks of that era had sophisticated calendar systems that share many features of the Jewish calendar. (The Babylonian development of both astronomy and astrology was especially advanced.) And for more than a millennium following the destruction of Solomon's Temple, the Jewish exile community in Babylonia remained the most important center of Jewish scholarship—even after the exile officially ended. There would have been plenty of time for cross-fertilization. Likewise with respect to Greeks: They conquered Judea and dominated it for many years and much of Jewish culture became profoundly Hellenized. (The overthrow of the Greeks is celebrated at Hanukkah.)

The problem with these suggestions is that although close, neither the Greek nor the Babylonian value is precisely the same as that used without fail by the Jews. (While the differences seem slight on paper, significant discrepancies accumulate over time.) The "Metonic" month calculated by the famous Athenian astronomer Meton in 432 B.C. was 29.52969 days long—roughly one and a quarter minutes shorter than the Jewish value; this was later improved on by Hipparchus in the second century B.C. to 29.53051 days—seven seconds shorter. The Babylonians were better astronomers than the Greeks by far. In 379 B.C., Kidinnu, head of the famed astronomical school at Sippar, reckoned the lunar month at 29.53061 days—less than one second longer than the Jewish value.

The best modern estimates set an ever more accurate and precise standard, and we therefore now know how far off each of these earlier estimates was. But at the time, there was no such standard. Each culture (or group within a culture) could believe only that its value was the right one. The astronomers who produced the numbers had decent scientific explanations for their day—the numbers were not simply pulled out of thin air. But the Jews had no such astronomical tradition. No Stonehengelike observatories have ever been discovered under tells in Israel; the Bible mentions little such activity; there is no record of anything like it in the literature. Historians have simply assumed that the Jews must have adopted what they considered the best astronomical calculations from one of the many societies in which they lived, once their many dispersions began.

If the Jews indeed took their number from the Greeks or Babylonians, why did they alter it (and by such seemingly slight amounts)? If they *did* alter it, how did they decide to what it should be altered? And if they were once willing to accept guidance in this matter from outsiders—in spite of its religious, not scientific or agrarian, significance to them—why did they later cling to an older number so tenaciously? This they did even during Maimonides' era, when wide knowledge of the secular sciences was encouraged among Jews, and sophisticated gentile astronomers were backing different values. Indeed, Maimonides himself *was* a sophisticated astronomer. In his most broadly read "manual" of Jewish spiritual direction, *The Guide of the Perplexed*, he counseled all Jews, "If you wish to grasp the relationship between the physical world and God's governance of it, you must carefully study physics and astronomy." On what grounds then, with regard to the precise value of the synodical month, did Maimonides stick with the value handed down by tradition?

The ancient answer to all these questions is simply that the Jews did not obtain the length of the lunar month from anyone. Rather, it is said, when God gave Moses the letter-sequence of the Torah, He gave him as well all the necessary explanations as to what was in it and how it was to be used. This included certain "raw data" (not the number itself) from which the value of the lunar month could be derived. Peculiar as it must seem, this piece of information was of utmost practical significance in the religious life of the new nation, since the identification of the precise times and seasons was chronologically "the first commandment given to all Israel," in that it was established for the coming nation *before* the transmission of the Torah, on the eve of the Exodus. (See Exodus 11:9–12:13. Note that this command is formally codified as such by Maimonides in his greatest work, the *Mishne Torah,* which firmly established the 613 commands that define Jewish observance to this day.[8]) Furthermore, in line with the ancient principle that "everything contained in the oral tradition is alluded to in the Torah itself"—the divinely ordained value of the lunar month would be expected to have some kind of additional, "hidden" confirmation in the written text of the Torah. It was this confirmation that Weissmandl learned from Bachya.

The Mystery of the New Moon

The critical data, and how to use it, was contained in the *Midrash Sod HaIbbur* (*Mystery of the New Moon*)—and was long kept secret: from the Babylonians, the

Greeks and the Romans, all of whom suspected that it might be uncannily accurate. But when the Church Council under the Emperor Constantine made Christianity the official religion of the Roman Empire in A.D. 325, it recalculated the Julian calendar both to correct accumulated errors and to ensure that Easter would never coincide with Passover. As a result, the many close linkages between the ancient Hebrew timekeeping system and the ascending Christian culture were broken. Outside interest in the Jewish "mysteries of the moon" began to fade.

By 1582, a second set of calendar reforms was once again needed to erase ten extra days that had accumulated since the prior reform. Pope Gregory XIII directed that these ten days should simply be abolished—and they were. Once again, however, care was taken with the new Gregorian calendar to ensure that Easter should never occur on Passover. Inevitably, these theological concerns threw sand into the timekeeping gears. Though this fact was widely recognized, keeping Easter wholly independent of Passover took priority: "Better wrong with the moon than right with Jews," went a popular refrain as the Gregorian reforms were instituted. Here is what was being alluded to:

Sod HaIbbur identifies certain critical moments in the unfolding biblical account of the creation, especially to that moment—according to the oral tradition—when God *created time* by setting everything into motion. Documented references to this moment—and to the calculations based upon it—can be found as far back as the writings of Rabban Gamliel the Elder who died in about A.D. 50 (who states that he is only writing down what was told him by his grandfather). The largest body of Gamliel's teachings concern the precise details for calculating the "times and the seasons," and for dealing with those who err in this regard—leniently, since mistakes are so easy to make. (Incidentally, the New Testament Book of Acts states that Paul was a student of Rabban Gamliel for a time, before becoming convinced that Jesus was the prophesied Messiah. The New Testament likewise contains many allusions to the "times and seasons"—especially in its prophetic passages—but says nothing about the methods.)

If there is such a thing as an original "starting date," it would be very useful. With it, the correct long-term average for the lunar cycle could be added month after month to *predict* the moment of each successive new moon. Since the lunar cycle varies, there would be a certain error in the prediction—sometimes it would be short, sometimes long—but over time the errors wouldn't accumulate, they'd cancel out. The same wouldn't be true by starting to count with just any new moon. If you did that, your long-term average would be late or early by the same (unknown) amount as your arbitrarily selected first one.

But where could one find such a date—the year, month, day of the week, hour, minute, and second of the "first" new moon ever? From the scientific point of view the question itself is absurd.

Nonetheless, the oral tradition maintains that there is such a date. As expected, it looks to the biblical creation account as an explanation. But its particular angle is bound to seem peculiar to anyone not steeped in its methods. The tradition states—

counterintuitively—that the first-ever new moon occurred at a specific moment on the *sixth* morning of creation, when man was created, *not* when the sun and moon were suspended in the heavens on the fourth day. And it states when this was: exactly at the end of the second hour on the morning of the sixth day of creation (fourteen hours after sunset of the fifth day). This is written in Hebrew as ו׳יד, which stands for "6/14."

This precise moment when the lunar clock started ticking has been passed down from sage to sage throughout the millennia, and was recorded in innumerable locations. From that point forward, the time of any subsequent new moon may be calculated by taking the total number of elapsed months (by now roughly 70,000) and multiplying it by 29.53059.*

But it's also possible to work backward. Given an exact date and time for the first new moon—*and assuming that the current calendar date is accurate and that any corrections have been properly accounted for*—then one may divide the total elapsed time by the number of months (to fractional accuracy) and obtain the average length of one month: 29.53059. But one must know at least one of these numbers to calculate the other. The oral tradition claims that Moses was given the date and time of the first new moon and that's why the Jews persisted in using 29.53059 for the length of the lunar month, whether surrounding cultures considered it astronomically correct or not.

The Hint

But where is the indication in the Torah itself that this traditional date and time for the first new moon is correct? It may be found by retracing the links that Rabbi Weissmandl followed as a youth.

First, there is an ancient understanding that God was mysteriously active for a period of time *before* the creation itself—and that of this activity we have been given certain glimpses. (Anybody who has ever wondered, "But what was there before there was anything?" has begun to knock at the door of these mysteries; such states of mind are quite conducive to meditation and one may find the world over directives to contemplate exactly such paradoxes as a way to initiate deep contemplation.)

Second, the kabbalists claim that God's 42-lettered name alludes specifically to this precreation activity. So, even though the world did not yet exist physically (it was still *tohu v'bohu*, formless and void) there came into being, as it were, a concept — "in the mind of God"—of what the ideal year ought to be. This was the "Platonic" prototype (using Hellenic language), or "archetype" (using scholastic or Jungian language) for all actual years to follow. In the Jewish tradition, it is simply called the "primordial" or "formless" year—and it is directly linked to God's 42-lettered name.

---

*There are other adjustments needed to line up the result with the solar year, but these do not affect the basic principle.

But this primordial year must have begun twelve lunar months previously—that is, twelve ideal new moons before the first actual new moon. When must that have been? 12×29.50359 days previously.

We therefore have the following calculation. If 29.50359 is the correct number of days in the long-term average for the lunar month; and if 6/14 (sixth day, fourteenth hour) is the correct timing of the "first" new moon after the creation, then the first "primordial" new moon occurred (hypothetically, in the mind of God) 354.04308 days before. What date and time is that? The Rambam explains:

> The very first conjunction with which you begin, however, is the conjunction of the first "primordial" year of creation, which occurred in the fifth hour and two hundred and fourth part of an hour of the night of Monday—in numerals, 2d 5h 204p (orig. Hebrew: בהר״ד = D"RHB; or reading left to right in English, BHR"D); this is the starting point of the calculation.*

Since the Jewish calendar treats the sixth day of creation (when God made man) as day one of the beginning of the world, this calculation has the practical advantage of making subsequent lunar calculations line up evenly with years and twelfths of years (otherwise they'd be shifted forward by five days). But that's a mere convenience. What struck Weissmandl was Bachya's assertion (regarding a yet earlier observation by Rabbenu Tam) that encoded into the opening passages of the creation account in Genesis *is* the 42-letter name of God, and that this encoding identified the location of the confirming "hint"—the information needed to calculate precisely the unfolding of the "times and seasons." (Tam had also noted, you'll recall, that this 42-letter name refers explicitly to the "work of creation"; he was referencing information known as long ago as the days of Nechunya, in the first century.)

Bachya wrote:

> The primordial new moon of Tishri from which we calculate is the hypothetical בהר״ד [BHR"D—2-5-204] had the luminaries actually been created then. But since they were not created until the fourth day of creation, we know that בהר״ד never really occurred [since there were not yet any "days" as we know them]. It is, however, the true starting point for all the calculations of the astronomers.

---

*In Hebrew, numbers may be written with letter equivalents. A mark (here a quotation mark) is usually inserted between the last and next-to-last letters being used as digits. Here, ב = 2, ה = 5, ר = 200, ד = 4. Thus בהר״ד (BHR"D) means 2-5-204. Since Saturday is the original Jewish Sabbath, Sunday is the first day (d1) and Monday is the second day (d2).

In other words, the accurate timing of events in the present requires that one project backward beyond the beginning to a hypothetical, earlier beginning that in physical reality never occurred. That is because God decided—for reasons only He knows; perhaps as a signal of His involvement for those who could detect it—that when the cosmic clock snapped into existence, it should show a certain amount of elapsed time; more time, in fact, than the world had yet existed. Bachya continued:

> And you may also know that we have a kabbalah that has been passed down to us that beginning from the verse "In the beginning . . ." the 42-lettered name that hints at God's activities before the creation emerges up to the letter ב (Bet) of Bohu but only by means of "many permutations."

Bachya was citing Rabbenu Tam who noted that the first 42 letters of Genesis can be transformed into the 42-lettered name of God. The correspondence between the first twenty letters is as follows:*

... י מ ש ה ת א מ י ה ל א א ר ב ת י ש א ר ב *Genesis*
... Y M S H T E M Y H L E A R B T Y S A R B

... ט ב ש כ י ד נ נ ט ש ע ר ק צ ת י נ ג ב א *Name*
... T B S K Y D G N N T S E R Q C T Y G B A

Taking for granted his readers' understanding of the allusion to "many permutations," Bachya went on to draw their attention to something else that dovetailed strikingly with the precreation significance of the 42-lettered name:

> And if the eyes of your heart will be illumined, you will find here precisely the code number בהר"ד that I mentioned above. It is encoded into the text in such a way that between each of its four letters lie 42 intervening letters. He who is wise will discern that this is not by chance, but rather a clear sign of Him who created the world.[9]

Bachya provided no diagrams, so as a boy, Weissmandl created his own arrays. The very first would have what Bachya claimed, the number, בהר"ד: 2-5-204, at the

---

*With S representing "Sh" and C representing "Tz"; the silent letters א and ע are transliterated from Genesis as they would in context; no pronunciation of the "Name" is here specified.

very beginning of Genesis. The first 42 letters were the encoded 42-lettered name; at 42 letter intervals was the date and time of the primordial new moon. Only one piece of the puzzle remained.

The exact time of the first *actual* new moon following creation was handed down by the oral tradition—fourteen-plus hours into the sixth day of creation. The exact time of the *hypothetical* new moon one year prior was encoded in the Torah. The two dates gave the length of an ideal year, and one twelfth of this ideal year generated the length of an ideal lunar month. That is, 29.53059 days, the number recorded by Rabban Gamliel as having been passed down from antiquity.

Of course, the skeptic would claim that which pieces of the puzzle were presumed and which deduced was something no one could know. Perhaps the encoding of BHRD in so perfect a place in Genesis was merely a coincidence. With any one of the three pieces and a few clever assumptions the other two could be constructed. The real mystery—for the scientist—boils down to this: Just how accurate is the value of 29.53059 days?

With the advent of modern scientific techniques—and eventually satellites—the length of the mean synodical month has been measured and calculated with ever greater accuracy. The top-value in the following chart shows NASA's most recent satellite-based figure. In the middle is a somewhat older scientific figure from before space travel. At the bottom is the traditional Jewish figure:

Synodical Month: Method	Length of One Month (Days)	Difference in Days from NASA Figure
Satellite (as of 1996)	29.530588	—
Numerical pre-Satellite (as of 1968)	29.53059	0.000000–0.000002
Jewish Month based on בהרד"ו (50 A.D. latest)	29.53059	0.000000–0.000002

How this uncanny accuracy came to be in the hands of the ancient Jews no one knows. There is certainly no way of proving that it was anything more than luck; the encoding of בהרד a coincidence. In any event, the oral tradition insisted that the date and time of the first new moon was specifically told to Moses; and that the date and time of the "primordial new moon" that never really happened was placed *precisely there*, in just that portion of Genesis, at just that interval, in the midst of the name of the God who existed before the creation itself, for a purpose: so that frail humankind would know that there *is* a purpose.

The Age of the Universe

Does this imply, then, that the account of the creation in Genesis—six twenty-four hour days, 5,757 years ago—is *literally* correct, as so-called creation science has it? It does not.

Recall that the Jewish understanding of the Bible has *always* been complex and subtle; that while these accounts surely point to or suggest something *real* —they are by no means myths or fables or psychological projections—not all of them are meant to be taken as simple, literal history (except by those who can assimilate their moral lessons in no other way). In the words of Maimonides, "The creation account [in Genesis] is natural science, but so recondite that it is cloaked in parable. . . . Discrepancies between science and religion arise out of misinterpretations of the Bible."

Not even the Bible's apparent placement of mankind at the center of the creation epic implied to the ancient Jews what literalists nowadays take it to mean. For example, a number of commentators as early as the eighth century A.D. accepted the possibility of life on other planets. If it existed, then it, too, was subject to the same divine moral law as are we.[10]

What *is* the literal age of the world according to this ancient, unexpectedly rational, version of the biblical view? To prepare an answer, let's first consider the "gold standard"—what modern science has concluded. Current scientific consensus (not universal, however) has arrived at the following points:

1. For reasons unknown the universe sprang into existence *ex nihilo*—out of nothing.

2. It first appeared as an almost unimaginably tiny "micropellet."

3. It was initially composed of a tiny proportion of matter admixed with an enormous quantity of "compressed" energy.

4. The "micropellet" then exploded outward at nearly the speed of light—the "big bang." In the first *second* of its existence it went from being a speck smaller than a single atom to being globular mass more than 270,000 miles across, with a volume 5,000 times that of the earth. Its expansion caused much of the energy to convert, by stages, into matter. It has been expanding at a similar rate ever since.

5. The micropellet started out with *ten* dimensions, six of which quickly "collapsed down" to size scales so small they are inaccessible to us now, leaving the familiar four dimensions: three of space and one of time (which, according to relativity, are interconvertible directions of a four-dimensional space-time). The initial substance within the pellet took the form of a ten-dimensional "string" of almost pure energy. The strings that now fill the universe remain almost unimaginably thin and insubstantial—10^{-27} centimeters in diameter—but since they extend entirely across the universe, each one is estimated to have a mass equivalent to 10^{17} suns. This is the so-called superstring theory, or TOE: "theory of everything."[11]

Given (a) the above considerations, (b) the density of the residual light from the initial explosion (the so-called 2.7K cosmic background radiation), and (c) estimates of the current size of the universe, cosmologists can calculate that the age of the universe is about 15 billion years.[12]

The notion that the universe is *this* old is a conclusion that took a very long time to reach. It was first suspected only in the twentieth century, in light of certain features of Einstein's general theory of relativity. Before that, the universe was assumed either to have no age at all (having existed forever with neither beginning nor end) or to be relatively young: a few thousand years old or so. The boldest scientific thinkers—and kooks—occasionally proposed larger numbers—but only slightly: tens or hundreds of thousands of years at most. But here, too, the ancient Jews seemed to have struck out on their own.

First, let's compare the general conditions at the creation which the oral tradition insisted may be understood directly from the account in Genesis—properly interpreted. Note that the latest commentators referenced below lived and died in the Middle Ages:

1. Both Maimonides (Rambam) and Nachmanides (Ramban) state that neither space nor time existed prior to the creation; hence it came into existence *ex nihilo*.

2. The kabbalists of that same era explain further that prior to the creation God filled all of eternity perfectly and uniformly. At the instant of creation, however, He "withdrew" Himself from a spherical region at the very center of eternity to create a "hollow" or "vacuum." Into this he placed a portion of His own essence in the form of a minutely thin line of "Upper Light," which was to evolve into the physical universe. According to Nachmanides (Ramban) in his commentary on the creation account, at the moment it appeared the universe was "no larger than a mustard seed." To the ancients, the mustard seed was the smallest unit of life capable of expanding and growing into something huge.[13]

3. Nachmanides' characterization of the size of this "seed" is as follows, in Gerald Schroeder's summary translation:

> The matter at this time was so thin, so intangible, that it did not have real substance. It did have, however, the potential to gain substance and form and to become tangible matter.[14]

4. Nachmanides then describes what occurs with this tiny "seed"-size universe:

> From the initial concentration of this intangible substance in its minute location, the substance expanded, expanding the universe as it did so. As the expansion progressed, a change in the substance occurred. This initially thin, non-corporeal substance took on the tangible aspects of matter as we know it. From this initial act of creation, from this ethereally thin pseudosubstance, everything that has existed, or will ever exist, was, is and will be formed.

5. The pencil-beam of "Upper Light" that formed the universe in its "seed" state was composed of ten aspects or dimensions.[15] During the six days of creation, six of these ten aspects became so small that we are capable only of detecting four—the four dimensions of physical existence.[16]

With this striking parallelism in mind, let us now answer our question concerning the age of the universe according to (at least certain representatives of) the oral tradition.

The kabbalist whose studies of the creation account in Genesis are the most precise and authoritative was Nechunya ben HaKanah. Among other matters in which he was expert, Nechunya specifically asserted that the 42-lettered name allowed one to deduce from the creation account the correct age of the universe. Because in his day this kind of information was considered religiously sensitive (as it is today), Nechunya's own explanation of the numbers involved was somewhat sketchy. But another kabbalist who followed closely in Nechunya's footsteps—Rabbi Yitzhak deMin Acco—laid out the calculations precisely. These make it doubly clear that the calculations of the synodical "starting date" for the first new moon and of the "primordial year" (which values both Nechunya and deMin Acco used) were to be understood *literally* only insofar as the numbers produce accurate results. They were not meant to be taken literally as indicating the age of the world.

Thus, Nechunya claimed that if you properly understand how to use the 42-lettered name, Genesis provides for a period of time between the origin of the universe and the creation of man, namely 42,000 "Divine Years." But a "Divine Year" isn't 365¼ of our days; it's 365,250 of our years. So, between the origin of the universe and the creation of man there transpired 42,000 × 365,250 years. In other words, says Nechunya, Genesis tells us that the universe came into existence *15.3 billion years ago*.

Did Nechunya (or deMin Acco) obtain this number from some other source and then retrofit the information into complicated "permutations" of Genesis? It's hard to imagine how: DeMin Acco lived in the thirteenth century A.D.; Nechunya himself in the first century A.D.

~

TRANSFORMATIONS OF
SPACE AND TIME

Raffiniert is der Herr Gott, aber boschaft is Er nicht.
Subtle is the Lord, but malicious He is not.

—*Albert Einstein*

The rigorous statistical analysis of huge quantities of data could only happen with the development of the computer. This quantitative advance not only made possible the testing of heretofore untestable hypotheses; it bred a qualitative expansion in insight. Principles that would seem ridiculous if applied to small numbers or sizes (and which therefore could hardly even be thought of) could prove possible and important when dealing with large quantities. For example, it was in this way that new kinds of patterns were discovered called "chaotic." Even though no rule can be deduced from them, and they are quite fuzzy, when you have enough samples to examine, you can see that an order is there. Computer-based visualization of large data sets makes this phenomenon especially striking—like squinting at a million little dots and seeing that it forms a portrait—and has led to quite amazing advances.

For example, the first several prime numbers seem to fall into no particular pattern. They look perfectly random. (Primes are whole numbers that are the product of no two other whole numbers besides 1 and themselves. Thus, 2, 3, 5, 7, . . . are primes; 6 is not since it is the product of 2×3.) And indeed, no one has ever been able to write out a formula that will generate every prime number. Yet strange patterns emerge once you begin looking at enough of them.

One of the strangest is the following. It incidentally illustrates two other principles suggested by the codes research, but only begun to be realized by Doron Witztum and Eliyahu Rips: (1) that the "space" within which the codes seemed embedded was fundamentally *not* a linear string of text wrapped for convenience at various line lengths, but was actually two-dimensional in principle. (2) This "space" was stretchable, in that different possible line-lengths played a critical role in shaping the "space" and revealing the codes.

But we should note that these ideas are strikingly analogous to foundational principles in modern physics, especially in relativity theory. It, too, views "space" as having higher, mutually interconvertible, dimensions than the familiar three; and it, too, considers this space "stretchable." (In fact, it required Einstein's theory of relativity for us to realize that the space we live in is four-dimensional, as the kabbalists learned from Genesis, not three—see Technical Appendix A.) Many solutions to difficult problems in physics, and many basic patterns of the universe, only show themselves when analyzed in a four-dimensional "space-time continuum"[1] that has been "stretched" (mathematically) just so. Otherwise, there seems to be no pattern—or at least, it's too difficult to prove there is. With respect to primes, the analogy is as follows:

First, look at the list of primes between 1 and 100 laid out, for convenience, in a 10-by-10 grid:

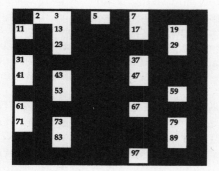

A couple of possible patterns can be seen, some of them curious, others trivial. For instance, out of the 25 primes, 15 are in pairs two numbers apart (called "twins" in number theory). This phenomenon occurs as high as primes have been calculated. But nobody knows why, nobody can predict where they will occur (they appear often, but not predictably), and nobody can even prove that at some incredibly high number they won't stop.

But there is one further phenomenon that, though on the face of it seems obvious, turns out to contain a startling feature. Notice that even in this short list, the *number* of primes contained in a fixed interval seems to diminish, though only statistically, not according to a fixed rule. The next chart shows how many primes there are in each row; this number seems to meander downward:

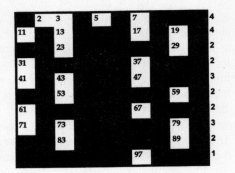

This phenomenon persists no matter how large the number, and reflects the fact that as you go higher and higher, you "pass" more and more primes that can be factors for still larger numbers. Hence, the primes fall farther and farther apart—*on average*.

The question may be asked, Is there some kind of structured pattern to the "rate" at which they fall farther and farther apart? In fact, this average distance, though always increasing, increases ever more slowly. The average distance between primes gets ever closer to an absolute maximum distance which it appears never to reach.* We know that there is not a precise formula from which a pattern might necessarily emerge (since there's apparently no formula for primes), but perhaps there's a fuzzy boundary rule that we can describe, related to the way the distance between them increases.

The fact that the average distance between primes gets larger and larger suggests that one might search for a "transformation" of the "one-dimensional" line of numbers ("a linear space") that would make this evident. (Note: Even though we've shown the primes in a 10-by-10 grid, this is a mere convenience. It is really just a string. Or, if we were to think of it as an elementary transformation, then it's one that highlights the twinning phenomenon, since the twins appear in vertical columns for certain line lengths.) One way would be to write every number in sequence on a straight line, but making them closer and closer as the numbers got larger and larger:

1   2   3   4   5   6 7 8910...

This would also decrease the distance on paper between primes and compensate for them getting spread out. If you shrunk the paper distance according to a rule, you might then end up with a statistical (approximate, fuzzy) order that governed the average distance between primes. (This has been done.)

But there is a more clever transformation that "maps" this principle of "increasing distance" in "one-dimensional space" directly onto a space with *one added*

---

*It approaches this value "asymptotically."

dimension: a genuinely two-dimensional space of numbers that need *not* be contracted. That can be accomplished by coiling the string of whole numbers around itself:

73	74	75	76	77	78	79	80	81	82
72	43	44	45	46	47	48	49	50	83
71	42	21	22	23	24	25	26	51	84
70	41	20	7	8	9	10	27	52	85
69	40	19	6	1	2	11	28	53	86
68	39	18	5	4	3	12	29	54	87
67	38	17	16	15	14	13	30	55	88
66	37	36	35	34	33	32	31	56	89
65	64	63	62	61	60	59	58	57	90
00	99	98	97	96	95	94	93	92	91

This transformation preserves the linear distance between numbers but (roughly speaking) increases every line length and rotates it 90 degrees through the second dimension. The primes then lay out as follows, in what is called "the Ulam spiral":*

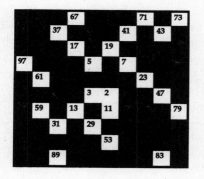

Something else curious shows up—perhaps: There seems to be a large number of continuous diagonal "strings." But there aren't enough for us to be certain this hasn't happened just by chance. We might hypothesize that it's so, but for it to be convincing, we'd need to look at more data. Here is the same kind of spiral array between 1 and 1,000 (952, to be precise):

---

*Ulam was a mathematician who worked with John von Neumann to develop the Monte Carlo simulation method during World War II.

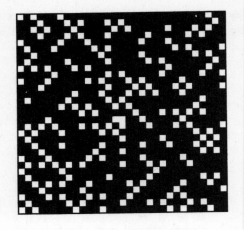

The tendency of primes to form diagonal strings seems considerably stronger when we stand back like this and "squint" (to sharpen up the fuzziness). If you wanted to, you could try mathematically to quantitate the phenomenon by counting how many primes belong to diagonal strings and how many do not. Of course, this would require that you decide what counts as a "string": two in a row? Three? Ten? Obviously, the more stringent your criterion, the more the phenomenon will have to "declare itself" to pass the bar. Intuitively, however—which is to say, visually—we can be pretty certain that this is indeed a pattern. (The human brain's capacity to detect patterns, even when we can't prove they're there, is quite phenomenal.) Whether this will continue or not as the numbers get larger we don't yet know. (Just as we don't know why primes twin and whether the twinning will stop at some point.) But it would make sense, just based on what we see in the numbers 1 to 1,000, to suppose that the phenomenon continues, to check it, and, if possible, to produce a statistic that tells us what the odds are that what we find has happened just by chance.

It turns out that as you spiral higher and higher, the tendency to form diagonal strings persists and therefore grows ever more obvious. And yet, the phenomenon never settles down into some kind of routine order: It remains fuzzy and unpredictable except as a general trend.

Here are all the primes between 1 and 40,000:

Here are all the primes between 1 and 160,000:

If you look carefully, you can see some other strange features. However imprecise or fuzzy, not only are there diagonal strings (in both orientations), but these seem to be spaced rather equally—though not perfectly so. If you look more closely, you'll see that although strings break at unpredictable intervals, the "same" string gets picked up again later. Also, there are vertical and horizontal strings, including an especially sharp one forming a "+" dead center. Even more difficult to detect—fuzzier still, yet apparently there—are lines that run at +20 degrees and −20 degrees off the horizontal. There are also areas where the primes form partial circles and other small, tight clusters. All these require a great many more primes than do the diagonals before you can begin to detect them. And remember, all these patterns are being formed in *two-dimensional space*, with "nearby" parts of the same pattern being formed by primes that linearly are very far apart. (Imagine how difficult it would be to design a two-dimensional rug pattern if you had to predict the different points of color as a sequence on an unbroken string of yarn. Rug patterns are only possible because the designer "sees" the string as a two-dimensional unity.)

What is perhaps most startling about this pattern is *that no one can explain how or why it's there*. However fuzzy, this structure is statistically unequivocal and points to some underlying order whose nature is, at least at present, utterly mysterious. Will it continue indefinitely? As with twinning, no one knows for certain. We do know that the patterning persists up to the highest prime yet discovered (as of November 1996): the number $2^{1398269}-1$ (that's $2 \times 2 \times 2 \times \ldots \times 2$ for a total of 1,398,269 times, minus 1).*

Finally, the degree of structure is actually greater and more complex than the human eye can detect. You may apply sets of fixed rules to each point that will further transform the picture mathematically, thereby bringing out even subtler levels of order. (Placing the primes in a spiral is one transformation—or "mapping" as it's sometimes called; establishing the rule, "prime = white square, nonprime = black square" is another. Such rules cannot create order if it isn't already there, but can magnify and enhance the order, and reduce the fuzziness: extract signal from noise.)

Thus, the Ulam spiral can be transformed to produce the following picture, which reveals an incredibly beautiful structure (from all the primes between 1 and 262,144):[2]

---

*This number, the so-called 35th Mersenne Prime, required the cooperative efforts of more than 700 people working together over the Internet to discover and confirm as prime. Even the truly industrious would have a difficult time using this number, however. With roughly half a million *digits*, just to write it down would require a 250-page book.

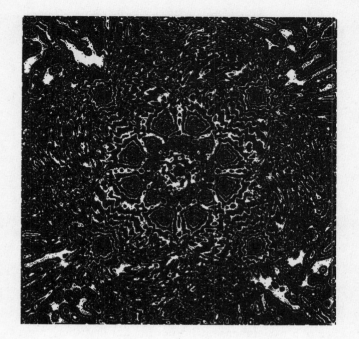

The following points emerge that were not visible in the simple Ulam spiral (or at best suspected):

1. Not only is there a tendency for the primes to cluster on 45 degree and −45 degree parallel diagonals, they are more highly (or at least differently) structured along the four corners of the array. (The same phenomenon occurs if the spiral is circular, rather than square.) Why these four directions are favored, instead of three equally spaced rays, or five, is utterly mysterious.

2. The varying density of primes in the Ulam spiral form complex structures with many axes of symmetry. Some of these are local (circles and other symmetrical shapes), which then form part of larger "supersymmetries."

3. The entire structure appears "fractal," with recursive, yet fuzzy symmetries at ever larger levels. This is consistent with some of the most recent discoveries in quantum mechanics, where it now appears that the structure of energy levels follows a roughly primelike distribution, yet can be shown to be "chaotic." (Chaotic patterns and fractal patterns are closely related.) Nonetheless, why this is so is unknown.

One additional transformation brings out more sharply the diagonal symmetries in particular, while downplaying some of the others. It also confirms the presence of radial symmetries at angles other than the vertical, horizontal, or diagonal:

The presence of a two-dimensional order implies that there must be something ordered to the location of primes along the one-dimensional sequence of real numbers. For many years, it was presumed that the spacing of primes was random since no linear order could be detected. Recently, however, an underlying second- and third-degree order to the spacings—spacing of the spacings, and spacing of the spacings of the spacings—has been demonstrated by a physicist who noticed a similarity to the spacing of energy quanta in large atoms. In sum, the quantization levels of energy and the distribution of primes follow the same rules for mysterious reasons and both show "chaotic" ordering.[3]

About the time that Eliyahu Rips was pushing into more sophisticated decryptions of the Torah, Doron Witztum completed master's level studies in general relativity and turned his attention to the codes. Like other scientists before him, he had the necessary critical skills to see that there was quite possibly something extraordinary here. Building on the work of the researchers who came before him, he pushed the investigation to a higher level of sophistication and complexity. This he did by treating the text of the Torah not simply as a cryptographic string, but as an inherently two-dimensional structure whose "axes" (vertical measure = number of rows, horizontal measure = line length) were interconvertible. In physics, any measurement consists of three spatial extensions and one temporal duration. But by changing one's "frame of reference" (e.g., by increasing one's velocity), extension in space (in the direction of travel) will wane a bit and temporal duration will wax by the same amount. (Picture a cardboard box that is slowly flattened: As its height diminishes, its width increases; as space contracts, time dilates.)

Following in Einstein's footsteps, Witztum would later entitle his first book on the codes *The Added Dimension*. His insight was a keen, but subtle one. It incorporated, unified, distilled into essential form—and most important, quantified—a large number of the hints about the Torah's hidden layers that had already emerged. It would produce results that were not only more impressive, but of a sort that could be assessed statistically. And Witztum would produce not just one, or a handful of results, but hundreds. His method not only incorporates the three principles of (1) relationships between different words, (2) minimal or near-minimal skip distances between the letters of decoded words, and (3) minimal or near-minimal amount of text within which words cluster, but a fourth principle as well, similar to the example of primes: (4) transformation of the linear text into a reshapable "two-dimensional space," certain configurations of which reveal the hidden structure. (Of course, Rabbi Weissmandl had already worked out a preliminary version of this idea in his own arrays, which he deliberately chose to be 10 by 10.) The "minimal or near-minimal amount of text" mentioned in (3) therefore takes on a more general form: *it is not the amount of text in a linear string that counts, but the smallest amount of text in a deformable two-dimensional array that accommodates the decrypted words.*

Furthermore, the essence of the theory of relativity is the discovery that even if things *appear* different to us in different frames of reference, "the underlying laws of physics [the rules that govern relationships between elements of the universe] remain the same in *all* frames." The codes researchers had uncovered the following analogy to relativity: Words in the Torah seem to be encrypted in a genuinely two-dimensional, deformable space such that the rules that govern the relationship between any two words is the same regardless of how the text is deformed: that is, wrapped with varying line lengths.

Proximity and Compactness

There is no reason to expect that any word extracted from a text will be more likely to occur at one location along the string (say, near an end) than any other location. The same is true with respect to its location in any array (say, near a corner). Likewise, there's no reason to think that the appearance of a word at its *minimum* skip interval will have some preferred location either in a string or in an array.

If we were to take the entire text of Genesis, pick a word at random, look for all its equidistant interval appearances, and locate its three most minimal occurrences, we would be as likely to find any of them at one spot as in any other. If we did the same with any other text, selected at random, we'd find the same thing. If we took three hundred words and did likewise, there would be no general "preference" at all to where minimum or other skip locations appear: The results would be as random as if we were throwing darts blindfolded—both in Genesis or anywhere else. This is because text is laid out solely with attention to its linear sequence. No relationships are established based on how the text will look when it's wrapped. A schematic picture of extracted words on a grid (viewed from far away) would look something like this (imagine that each figure represents a short word with relatively small intervals between letters; to simplify, only three are shown). Assume the square is the word at its 100 percent minimum skip; the circle is the same word but at a 75 percent skip; and the triangle the same word at a 25 percent skip:

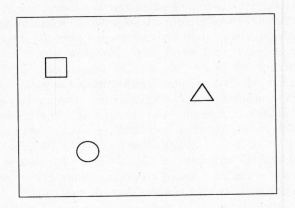

Now, we take another word related to the first (e.g., for "HAT," we choose, "HEAD." We search for these embedded in the same text at its three shortest equidistant skips. There is no reason to expect any kind of pattern to where these may be found, either. They will be scattered all over randomly, just like the first set. And of course, there will be no reason for the locations of the second word to bear any relation to the locations of the first, just because their meanings seem to be related. If we depict the first and second sets together, it should look something like this:

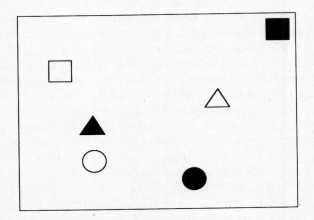

In other words, if we were to search for "HEAD" in our snippet of text above, we might find it. But where it happened to be at its minimum equidistant skip would be completely unrelated to where "HAT" happened to be. If we measured enough word pairs, we'd find that the average distance between words in pairs was just "middling." In fact, it would be the same average as between *any* two words, related or not, and that average would turn out to be half the length of the text, measured as a string (or one over the square root of the diagonal of a rectangular array). That's because on average there'd be an equal number "far away" and "close together," for every degree of "far" and "close."

But in Genesis, here's what seemed to be happening instead (exaggerating its precision for clarity):*

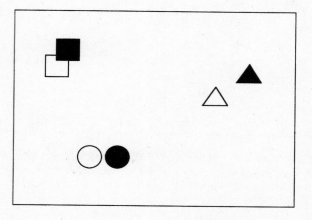

Notice that matched pairs of words at their respective minima are found "close" to one another. But "close" is not a defined distance; it refers to the statistical fact that matched pairs are closer *on the whole* than unmatched pairs; pairs at minimal skips are closer than pairs at nonminimal skips. Some—perhaps most—matched pairs could be far apart (and unmatched ones close together) and the aggregate closeness of matched pairs could still be too close to be likely to have happened just by chance. The analysis used by the researchers quantifies this aggregate proximity, and determines the odds of its "just having happened." *But individual examples cannot be assessed statistically.*

A less schematic representation of "proximity" is shown on page 288.

---

*Also, squares need not always line up with squares and so on; the pairing need not be perfect.

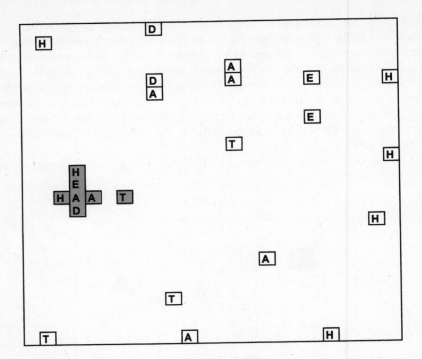

Various locations of "HAT" and "HEAD" embedded in a text, showing close intrapair proximity of both words where embedded at their respective minimal equidistant skip intervals

Note that by showing the individual letters of the words we can surmise something else: Depending on how the array is wrapped (what line length), the relationships between the word pairs will change. *By "deforming" the two-dimensional array into just the correct dimensions, a previously invisible "proximity" may leap out.* (If the Ulam spiral is laid out in rectangular grids that are not square, the pattern is altered, degraded, and eventually destroyed altogether.)

Furthermore, more salient than the simple proximity of two words is the overall "compactness" of their configuration in an optimally chosen array. (Compactness is determined both by the proximity of the words and the closeness of the letters within the words. The letters in a word with a skip distance of 100 will appear closest—directly on top of one another—when the array is wrapped with a line length of 100.)

This method of embedding words at equidistant letter skip intervals, and relating them by "compactness," is extraordinarily elegant, once its subtleties are grasped. There is yet another feature to it, not so much a further complexity, as an elegant way of "transforming" the space within which compactness is defined so as to reveal a certain natural simplicity.

The process of "wrapping the text" can most easily be displayed in *three* dimensions, then converted back to two, using a three-dimensional cylindrical helix. Take the amount of text encompassing both terms in a pair and lay it out in a string. Spiral the string of letters up (or down). The (circular) row length is now defined by the circumference of the cylinder.

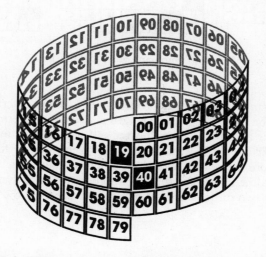

3D spiral of 80 text positions (00–79) with row length $h = 20$

Then "slice" the three-dimensional cylinder between two columns and flatten it out to create a two-dimensional array:

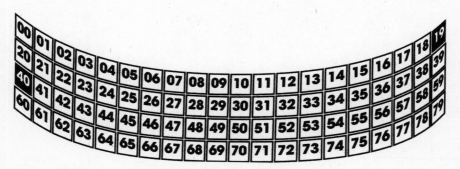

3D spiral flattened to form 2D array

Note that between any two letters in the array, there are at most two possible straight-line (simple, physical) distances,* depending on where the cylinder is cut, as in the simplified example below:

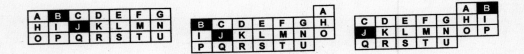

Three different cuts of a 7-column array

Finally, at the same time that the proper "cut" is being determined, the optimal line length has to be found. If the line length is altered, one letter at a time, so that the array gets taller and slimmer (or shorter and wider), any display of two tightly compact words will slowly loosen, as though "going out of focus" (see example above).† With more than two words, the matter becomes more complicated. Although the best line length for three or more words is likely to be *near* the best line length for any two of the words, it may not be precisely the same.

---

*This is more technically referred to as the "Euclidean" distance.
†Whenever the line length is a factor, or close to a factor, of the original length, the array may still be relatively compact.

~

THE "GREAT SAGES" EXPERIMENT

This appendix has four purposes:

1. To raise certain general considerations that affect the ongoing attempt to validate the Bible Code, and that make such validation (or refutation) challenging.

2. To provide a summary of the approach developed by Rips and then Witztum, published in their paper in *Statistical Science,* which is at most no more technical than theirs. This is for readers who are curious as to the science and math behind the best research to date. Certain details have been left out, however, and the reader who wishes to examine every aspect of the process is encouraged to go directly to their original paper. This Technical Appendix is not intended as a substitute for the original paper published in *Statistical Science* by Witztum, Rips, and Rosenberg, nor is it intended to supplant the original paper in any way.

3. To expand on selected topics in place of details left out. Based on four years of conversations about the Bible Code with many people, I've noticed that certain subtleties remain confusing even to fairly sophisticated readers. Some of these pertain to the Code itself, and some to the method of their investigation as developed by Witztum, Rips, and Rosenberg. The "global" nature of the Code is one such area having to do with the Code itself; the use of "perturbed ELSs" as a proxy for "expected compactness" is another area having more to do with analytic technique. Where it seems helpful, I have also provided diagrams.

4. To highlight aspects of the research that are incomplete or problematic or where alternative approaches might be used.*

A full exposition of all the complexities involved in this research is beyond the scope of any book meant for a general readership. Some of these complexities include: how the data set was selected and structured, its strengths and weaknesses, the pros and cons of possible alternative selection methods and formats, and the debate as to whether the data are inadvertently skewed so as to ensure noteworthy results. Another area of investigation is the compactness measure itself and how the results it gives compare with plausible alternatives. Probably the most important topic, however, is what directions further research should take and how it should be structured in order to improve upon the work already done to carry the process forward toward a convincing conclusion. All this is likely to take quite a few years of increasingly sophisticated back-and-forth.

General Considerations

There are a number of related methods that can be used to uncover the Bible Code. Most of these produce tantalizing results—but ELSs in principle are very difficult either to confirm as genuine decryptions or disconfirm as mere chance concatenations. Take special note of the caution raised by Professors Bernstein, Kazhdan, Furstenberg, and Piatetski-Shapiro cited before:

> Rather than noting the occurrence of individual words along arithmetic progressions [ELSs], a sounder basis for the measurement of the phenomenon is provided by looking for occurrences of related words and measuring their proximity.

Since *individual* ELSs (equidistant letter sequences) can rarely serve as evidence, and since the phenomenon in question seems so far only to appear genuine when considering combinations of ELSs, all of the scientifically rigorous codes investigation to date has come to focus only on the latter. The mass of "pop" religious publication on the subject focuses instead almost exclusively on individual ELSs and therefore lacks a solid basis for statistical assessment. In the days prior to computers, one might have been able to argue that only a genuine phenomenon could have been detectable just by "eyeballing" the text. But with computers it is not only possible to show how ubiquitous are ELSs that spell words; generating individual ELSs in almost any way one wishes has become trivial.

---

*The reader should note, however, that neither this Appendix nor *Cracking the Bible Code* as a whole, officially represents Witztum, Rips, or anyone else. I have attempted to present their work as accurately as possible, from an obviously sympathetic, but still open-minded point of view. But the presentations, explanations, and arguments—pro and con—are strictly my own understandings in response to what they have written and otherwise communicated.

Difficulties in testing the even more rigorous ELS-combination phenomenon for validity arise for the following reasons:

1. "Amazing" ELS combinations will arise by chance from time to time, just not very often—or so it seems. Part of the problem is assessing exactly how unlikely "amazing" combinations really are. If any one, or a few, can be shown to be truly unlikely, that fact is only a *piece* of evidence at best, and must be combined with sufficiently many other pieces of like evidence. And it may not even be that, because:

2. In order for an unlikely ELS combination to have evidentiary value at all, it cannot have been picked out from a string of unimpressive ELS combinations, then presented in isolation. Both its content and location (within quantifiable parameters) must have been committed to *before* the searching process begins (hypothesized a priori).

3. Finally, and most important, the Bible Code may prove to be utterly unlike the codes and ciphers used by human spies and cryptologists. The latter are not inherently statistical, even though the means used to detect them are. When a typical, man-made code is correctly deciphered, the result is a well-defined string of letters with a fixed meaning, not a fuzzy, statistical "tendency" toward order, with lots of exceptions, that seems based on meaning in general. At least as it has been "decoded" so far, the Bible Code seems to have no content at all—it is only a watermark, a faintly visible seal of authenticity that must be looked at just-so to be seen at all. (What makes it important nonetheless is the implication as to whose watermark it is.) Perhaps this "watermark" may prove to be the first indication of a truly languagelike structure with a distinct "message," as Witztum and Rips hypothesize. As noted in Chapter Fourteen, however, I suspect that this is not the case, and that the Bible Code is rather similar in its linear expression to the unfolding, only limited determinism of quantum mechanics: that is, intrinsically probabilistic. That the Code uses a reshapable two-dimensional space to create proximity relations certainly argues against any kind of "language" of the form with which we are familiar. Meaning in any other language—even pictographic ones such as Chinese—is critically dependent upon a linear sequence, and proximity as measured in the Bible Code directly cuts across such sequencing. Of course, the idea of an inherently probabilistic code is likely to be as unsatisfying to many scientists as was quantum mechanics to Einstein, who termed the latter "incomplete." As with quantum mechanics, only time and further investigation will tell.

In any event, to date, the ELS combinations found in the Torah do not seem to be arranged according to a rigid rule, but rather according to general guidelines. And, as will be evident when we discuss the nuances behind the compactness measure developed by Witztum, Rips, and Rosenberg, the compactness of any single related pair of words found as ELSs seems to be a global characteristic of the text as a whole—or of portions of the text, in rather "holographic" fashion—perhaps of *all* the appearances of those words as ELSs, and not just of a single, best, instance of their combination. (There is a hint of this in the fact that *two* minimal appearances each of the name, date of death, and city of birth of Rabbi Abraham "the Angel," discussed in Chapter Ten, were found in close proximity.)

To use an analogy other than holography, the phenomenon seems somewhat like the storing of images and memories in the brain: not in local, labeled pigeonholes, but globally, across whole sheets of tissue, as a pattern of connection strengths between neurons; millions of such images and memories stored one blended into the other, as it were, like interpenetrating palimpsests. If the letters of the Torah really do form a "blueprint" or "map," it is not the one-to-one mapping of an architect's drawing to a house; it is more like the map of a lifetime contained in the thoughts of a mind.

With regard to the Bible Code, this means that it may be exceedingly difficult to show that any individual ELS combination is unlikely. In fact, if it is the global *tendency* that reveals the phenomenon, then there will be many instances where a given ELS combination is quite likely to happen by chance, without invalidating the phenomenon.* ("Men are taller than women" is true, if imprecisely stated. Its truth is not contradicted by the statement, also true, that "a very large proportion of men are shorter than most women.") Such broad trends require long, arduous, and scrupulous investigation either to confirm or refute convincingly. The evidence so far suggests that if the Bible Code exists, it is precisely of that sort. Serious investigation is really therefore just in its infancy. In fact, from the point of view of science, the "argument" at present amounts to: "Is there sufficient evidence of adequate quality, to date, to warrant further investigation?" Kazhdan, Bernstein, Furstenberg, and Piatetski-Shapiro, who, though writing in 1988, were examining essentially the same material as in the 1994 *Statistical Science* paper, say, yes, but not more than that. Critics say, no.

Let's summarize these three points ordered as a single concept. *Evidence for the Bible Code will be valid only if it comes in the form of rigorously controlled tests that allow us to examine a large enough number of properly selected, representative, and sufficiently similar ELS combinations. These combinations, in the aggregate, must then occur in "close proximity" (which has to be defined) more often than would be likely to happen merely by chance.*

Outline of the Test Developed by Witztum, Rips, and Rosenberg

One of the accomplishments of Witztum and the group around him is their devising of a method of analysis of the Bible Code that meets these criteria (though as in all complex scientific debates, there are thoughtful critics who argue that one or

---

*If a sample is not normally distributed (bell curve), it may even be true that most ELS combinations will fall within the range of likely by chance alone. If the phenomenon is genuine, and this is the case, it will be even more difficult to verify.

more criteria only *seem* to have been met, but haven't been). In their 1994 paper in *Statistical Science,* they provide a concise, well-written description of their approach, which has enabled others to duplicate and extend or criticize their findings. Its technical level is rather modest as research papers in mathematics and statistics go, but requires a solid grounding in basic college mathematics, statistics, and research design to be understood properly.

The concept behind the method for finding ELS pairs and assessing their statistical significance is presented here first in oversimplified form. Following this list is a precise description of how the concept was implemented:

> Identify beforehand a set of potential ELS-pairs (for example, a list of names each matched to some appropriate date).
>
> Look for every name and every date in the set of pairs by searching the text until each is found as an ELS at (its) minimum equidistant letter interval, called its "skip"—assuming it is found as an ELS at all; some may not be.
>
> Measure the distance between the locations of both terms in a pair.
>
> Calculate the actual "average distance"* between all related pairs of terms (Name A to Date A, Name B to Date B . . .).
>
> Compare this "average" with the "average distance" produced by mere chance.
>
> Repeat the process on other texts.
>
> Perform a statistical analysis on the results to see whether the averages obtained show a significant difference between related pairs of terms in Genesis and unrelated pairs of terms in Genesis, and pairs of terms anywhere else whether related or not.

Implementation of the Concept

The actual methods are complex variants of the above ideas. Point by point, these are:

Identify beforehand a set of potential ELS-pairs (for example, a list of names each matched to some appropriate date). There may be common spelling variants of the name and/or date (e.g., birth and death). Rules must be drawn up and standardized ahead of time for creating name-date pairs and there must also be a method for deciding upon the source for historical data. Witztum, Rips, and Rosenberg created more than one name-date pair for each of the personalities they included in their data set by pairing each name variant with each date variant for every individual. Variations could be caused by such things as availability of the date of birth or death or both, honorific names, use or lack of titles, presence or absence of silent letters in names translated from non-Hebrew sources. In general, Witztum, Rips, and

---

*In quotations here and below because the measure is not a genuine average but a weighted composite of a more complex set of aggregated measurements. The precise details follow.

Rosenberg created name-date pairs by making informed guesses as to which variations were plausible, or likely, within certain guidelines. These are detailed in their paper.

The names they used were selected from a standardized reference of Jewish biography (not unlike *Who's Who*) entitled *Encyclopedia of Great Men in Israel*.[1] This dictionary contained some known date errors, however, and when these were identified, they were corrected.

The selection criteria for inclusion in the data set were:

1. The individual must be referenced in the *Encyclopedia of Great Men in Israel*.

2. His entry must have at least three columns of text (for the first sample); between 1.5 and three columns (for the second).

3. The resulting terms must contain no less than five and no more than eight letters.

4. The individual must also be represented in a second list of prominent sages, the "Responsa" database.

The third criterion arose because of the "perturbation" method the authors used to assess the degree of "unlikeliness" for the compactness measure of each name-date pairing (explained below). This method could not be applied exactly to ELSs with fewer than five letters and would yield too little data to be useful when applied to words with more than eight letters. There are other methods, however, that should allow one to extend the experiment so as to include both longer and shorter ELSs.

These criteria resulted in a final list of 32 individuals for the second sample, upon which the analysis was conducted: (see chart on pages 298–299)

The first list was not analyzed for the *Statistical Science* paper to ensure that the data set had been created only after the selection criteria and analytic methods had been fixed. The 34 individuals together yielded 91 name terms and 74 date-terms. By pairing every name term for an individual with every date term for that individual, a total of 298 name-date pairs was created. This formed the raw data set ("set of pairs") upon which the analysis was then performed.

Look for every name and every date in the set of pairs by searching the text until each is found as an ELS at (its) minimum equidistant letter interval, called its "skip." An "equidistant letter sequence (ELS)," e, is defined as a sequence of letters in a given text with positions n, $n + d$, $n + 2d$, ..., $n + (k-1)d$, where Witztum, Rips, and Rosenberg let:

d = "equidistant letter interval," or more simply, the "skip" of the ELS
n = "start" of the ELS
k = "length" of the ELS (i.e., number of letters in the word)

Search the text over a range of equidistant letter intervals, or "skips," adjusted so as to expect to capture within that range no more than the ten ELSs with the shortest skips for both terms in every pair in the data set. (Do not simply look for the minimal skip.) This adjustment of the range of skips to search is based upon the number of letters in the term being searched for as an ELS, and the frequencies in Genesis of the letters that compose the term. For every term, take each of the ten or so ELSs actually found in this way and calculate its "domain of minimality." This domain is simply the fraction of text considered as a linear string (i.e., the percentage of letters) that contains the ELS in question and no other ELS for the same term with a smaller skip. The "domain of minimality" will therefore be a number between 0 and 1 (0 percent and 100 percent) attached to every ELS obtained according to these restrictions for every term in the data set.

Measure the distance between the locations of both terms in a pair. This must be done in a number of steps.

Step 1: Create a measure of two-dimensional distance δ between any two ELSs, e_1 and e_2. Call this distance $\delta(e_1, e_2)$. There are many reasonable measures of two-dimensional distance between ELSs, and no one can be sure which one would optimize the results in general (which would imply that the phenomenon is genuine) or for just this data set (which would skew the results and invalidate them). The measure devised by Witztum, Rips, and Rosenberg is as follows.

• Defining "Distance" Between Letters and between ELSs

It is necessary to define the "distance" δ between any two ELSs in such a way as to give the notion of "closeness" and "compactness" an unambiguous and quantifiable meaning.

Between Letters
The text containing two terms in a pair (the letters of which have been located at their respective ELSs) is laid out in a string. The string of letters is then spiraled up (or down) in a cylindrical array or helix. The "compactness" of the ELS pair will change, of course, as the helix is wound or unwound. For any single ELS, note that there will be a certain winding where the letters of the ELS sit vertically one on top of the next. This is because the number of letters forming the circumference of the cylinder is exactly equal to the skip, d, for that ELS. At that point, the cylinder of text will have a *row length h*, equal to the number of vertical columns of text. At any point in the winding process, the cylinder may be sliced vertically to create a flattened two-dimensional array.

Now, consider two letters in any two locations on such a flat two-dimensional array. Depending on where the vertical slice was made, there are only two possible straight-line distances between these letters. *The smaller of the two possible distances is always used to define the distance between letters.*

English Name	Hebrew Appellations		Date(s)	Variations of Hebrew Date(s)			
Rabbi Avraham Av-Beit Din of Narbonne	הראב"ד הראב"ד	אברהם האברהם	d 20 Heshvan	כ' חשון	כ' מרחשון	כ"ו חשון	כ'
Rabbi Avraham Yizhaki	זקן אברהם	אברהם	d 13 Sivan	י"ג סיון	מולד	י"ג סיון	י"ג
Rabbi Avraham Ha-Malach	המלאך	אברהם	d 12 Tishrei	י"ב תשרי	י"ב תשרי	י"ב תשרי	י"ב
Rabbi Avraham Saba	צרור המור	אברהם סבא	No Dates Available[1]				
Rabbi Aaron of Karlin		אהרן	d 19 Nisan	י"ט ניסן	י"ט ניסן	י"ט ניסן	י"ט
Rabbi Eliezer Ashkenazi		אליעזר	d 22 Kislev	כ"ב כסלו	כ"ב כסלו	כ"ב כסלו	כ"ב
Rabbi David Oppenheim	אופנהיים	דוד	d 7 Tishrei	ז' תשרי	ז' תשרי	ז'	ז'
Rabbi David Ha-Nagid	הנגיד	דוד	No Dates Available[2]				
Rabbi David Nieto	ניטו	דוד	d 28 Teveth[3]	כ"ח טבת	כ"ח טבת	כ"ח טבת	כ"ח
Rabbi Haim Abulafia	אבולעפיא	חיים	d 6 Nisan[4]	ו' ניסן	ו' ניסן	ו' אלול	ו'
Rabbi Haim Benbenest	בנבנשתי	חיים	d 19 Elul	י"ט אלול	י"ט אלול	י"ט אלול	י"ט
Rabbi Haim Capusi	כ' אלעז	חיים קאפוסי	d 12 Shevat	י"ב שבט	י"ב שבט	י"ב שבט	י"ב
Rabbi Haim Shabetai	שבתי	חיים	d 13 Nisan	י"ג ניסן	י"ג ניסן	י"ג ניסן	י"ג
Rabbi Yair Haim Bacharach	חוות יאיר	יאיר חיים	d 1 Teveth	א' טבת	א' טבת	א' טבת	א'
Rabbi Yehuda Hasid	החסיד	יהודה	d 5 Heshvan[6]	ה' חשון	ה' חשון	ה' חשון	ה'
Rabbi Yehuda Ayash	לחם יהודה	יהודה עיאש	d 1 Tishrei	א' תשרי	א' תשרי	א' תשרי	א'
Rabbi Yehosef Ha-Nagid	הנגיד	יהוסף	d 9 Teveth	ט' טבת	ט' טבת	ט'	ט'
Rabbi Yehoshua of Cracow	מגיני שלמה	יהושע	d 27 Av	כ"ז אב	כ"ז אב	כ"ז אב	כ"ז
The Maharit	מהרי"ט יוסף טראני	המהרי"ט	d 14 Tammuz	י"ד תמוז	י"ד תמוז	י"ד תמוז	י"ד
Rabbi Yosef Teomim	פרי מגדים	יוסף תאומים	d 14 Iyar	י"ד אייר	י"ד אייר		

Rabbi Yakov Beirav	d 30 Nisan
Rabbi Israel Yaakov Hagiz	b 28 Shevat
The Maharil	d 22 Elul[3]
The Yaabez	d 30 Nisan
Rabbi Yizhak Ha-Levi Horowitz	d 6 Iyyar[7]
Rabbi Menachem Mendel Krochmal	d 2 Shevat
Rabbi Moshe Zacuto	d 16 Tishrei
Rabbi Moshe Margalith	d 12 Teveth
Rabbi Azariah Figo	d 1 Adar I
Rabbi Immanuel Hai Ricchi	d 1 Adar
Rabbi Shalom Sharabi	d 10 Shevat
Rabbi Shelomo of Chelm	21 Tammuz[2]

[1] Legendary
[2] Uncertain
[3] Source in error; date corrected by authors in consultation with historical scholars
[4] Source in error; date corrected by authors in consultation with historical scholars
[5] Source in error; date corrected by authors in consultation with historical scholars
[6] Source in error; date corrected by authors in consultation with historical scholars
[7] Source in error; date corrected by authors in consultation with historical scholars
[8] Source in error; date corrected by authors in consultation with historical scholars

Between ELSs

The "distance" between any two ELSs actually found in the text, e_1 and e_2, and after the string has been "wound" and "sliced" to create a specific two-dimensional array with row length h, is now defined by Witztum, Rips, and Rosenberg as follows:

1. Let f_1 = the distance between consecutive letters in the word e_1
2. Let f_2 = the distance between consecutive letters in the word e_2
3. Let m = the minimal possible distance between any letter in e^1 and any letter in e_2

Then the distance δ (e_1, e_2) between any two words is:

$\delta(e_1, e_2) = f_1^2 + f_2^2 + m^2$.

Compact array of two words with excess text excised

Note that this "distance" is more like the square of a distance. There is nothing intrinsically strange about this fact. The "metric" for the two-dimensional "space" of ELSs need not be Euclidean. Physicists are familiar with many non-Euclidean metrics. The probability space in quantum mechanics, for example, is a square. In any event, a squared distance of this kind correlates somewhat with the more intuitive idea of "area," as pertaining to two-dimensional compactness. (It is not actually an "area," however.) But simple areas could arguably be a poorer measure of "closeness" if one of the two terms happens to have a somewhat large skip that is still less than h.

In the above example:

e_1 = "HAT" and e_2 = "HEAD"

f_1 (the distance between consecutive letters in e_1) = 2

f_2 (the distance between consecutive letters in e_2) = $\sqrt{(1+1)} = \sqrt{(2)} = 1.41$

Since the distance between letters is not necessarily the same as the skip, d, the distance between letters is not affected by how much text is left out of the illustrations. The distance *is* affected, however, by the "wrapping" of the spiral of text, hence the row length h, especially for words with large skips. In looking for the most *compact* configuration, the wrapping may or may not stop when the letters of a word are at their minimal spacing, since the measure of compactness (as will be defined precisely below) balances the distances between letters in both *words* and the distance *between* words, as well as their orientation to one another.

• Determining the "Compactness" of a Pair of ELSs

Continuing the above example: m, the distance between the "T" of "HAT" and the "H" of "HEAD" = $\sqrt{(1^2 + 2^2)} = \sqrt{(5)} = 2.23$.

Putting together what we have formalized so far: the "distance" between words in a pair is δ, and for this example, $\delta (e_2, e_2) = (2^2 + \sqrt{2}^2 + \sqrt{5}^2) = (4 + 2 + 5) = 11$.

Now, as a string of text is wrapped in a tightening helix, the number of possible rows in the resulting flattened array will increase, and the number of possible columns will decrease. For any pair of terms found encoded in the text in the form of ELSs, there will be a different δ (as defined above) depending upon the number of letters in any row, h.* Let $\delta_h(e_1, e_2)$ represent *a specific* δ (e_1, e_2) for a given row length h. Then define μ_h as the inverse of δ_h, that is, let $\delta_h=1/\mu_h$. Thus the larger is μ_h, the more compact is the configuration (e_1, e_2).

Note that for those ELSs (with skip d) that *do* wrap around the edge of an array, certain row lengths will tend strongly to favor compactness, that is, they will tend to cause large values of μ_h. These are row lengths h (= number of columns) that cause successive letters in e_1 or e_2 (whichever one wraps, assuming both do not), to line up vertically, on top of one another in successive rows, or perhaps skipping a small number of rows; or that cause successive letters to line up at a diagonal, skipping a small number of rows and no (or a few) columns, as in a knight's move on a chessboard.

Three different "wrappings" of 26 letters (00–25) with the words "UP"
at $d = +2$ and "DOWN" at $d = +6$ embedded. Each wrapping has a different "row length" h. From left to right, $h = 5$, 6, and 7 respectively.
Each has a somewhat different overall compactness. By inspection, the
most compact appears to be the middle one, but the others do not differ
by much. Had the text been much longer, and the skip d for "DOWN"
also much longer, it would still be possible to find similarly compact
arrangements. But in that case the vast majority of wrappings would produce noncompact arrangements of words. (This is what actually occurs
using real texts.) In most arrays with large row lengths, the letters in
"DOWN" would be far apart, as would the two words themselves.

---

*The number of columns is the same as the length of the row.

The tightest vertical configurations of a word will occur when the row length h, is evenly divisible by the skip, d. More formally, these are row lengths $h_i = h_1$, h_2, $h_3 \ldots$, where h_i is the integer whose value $= |d|/i$. (By convention, ½ is always rounded up.) Thus, if the row length in the array equals 10 and the skip $d = 10$ as well (or -10, hence the use of the absolute value $|d|$) then $h_i = h_1$ and two successive letters will appear on top of one another. If the skip were 20, $h_i = h_2$ and two letters would appear vertically, but skipping one row; if 40, $h_i = h_3$ and skipping two rows, and so on. If the skip equals 11, then $h_i = h_1$ (again, since 1 is the nearest integer) and two successive letters will appear catty-corner, one row down and one letter over. If $d = 21$, then $h_i = h_2$ and letters will appear two rows down and one over, and so on.

In general, therefore, those arrays will tend to be most compact in which the index i in h_i is a relatively small number, so terms that lay out vertically have few skipped letters between them. However, this need not be the case in every instance, since the overall compactness is a function of other factors—the compactness of the other word, the distance between words, the weighted composite of other ELS pairs for the same set of terms. "Compactness" is a global measure that includes these. When the index i in h_i is large, the likelihood is small that the configuration is compact, and vice versa. A better method than trying to define this inverse relation exactly so as to identify one single maximally compact configuration from among many arguably comparable ones (and where there may occur odd exceptions) is to measure the compactness from a *set* of row lengths h_i with small i. This will capture the tendency of configurations to be compact as a function of the many factors contributing to it. (This method is analogous to assigning a certain total amount of space of a certain shape to every person on an airplane and allowing each one to fill it with whatever shape objects he wishes.)

Witztum, Rips, and Rosenberg chose to calculate the compactness μ_{h_i} (the inverse of δ_{h_i}) for the first ten configurations ($i=1,2,3,4,5,6,7,8,9,10$) that "clustered" around the absolute maximal compactness for the first term in the pair, add them all together, and then add these to the first ten such configurations for the second term in the pair. In other words, the final measure of compactness of a pair consists of twenty separate compactness numbers. Each number in both groups of ten is the inverse of the distance between the two words (as defined above) in a slightly different configuration, the first set of ten configurations based on the first term in the pair, the second set on the second term. More formally:

$$\sigma\,(e_1 + e_2) = \sum_{i=1}^{10} \mu_{h(e_1)i}(e_1, e_2) + \sum_{i=1}^{10} = \mu_{h(e_2)i}(e_1, e_2)$$

where $\mu_h(e_1)_i$ represents the inverse of the distance between e_1 and e_2 as measured for the ith configuration with respect to e_1; and $\mu_h(e_2)_i$ represents the inverse of the distance between e_1 and e_2 as measured for the ith configuration with respect to e_2. σ is the measure of compactness used throughout for all actual name-date pairs, for all control pairs (mismatched name-date pairs) both in Genesis and in all control texts.

Step 2: For every pair of terms in the data set, create every possible pairing between the first term as an ELS and the second term as an ELS, each term having about 10 such ELS appearances. (Each pair of terms in the data set will therefore generate about 100 pairings.) For every such pairing of ELSs, calculate a "domain of *simultaneous* minimality." This is the fraction of text for which the domain of minimality for the first term overlaps with the domain of minimality for the second term:

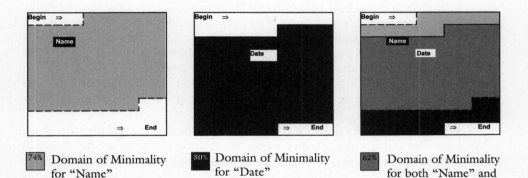

74% Domain of Minimality for "Name"   80% Domain of Minimality for "Date"   62% Domain of Minimality for both "Name" and "Date"

Assign the value of the domain of minimality to each pair as a "weight" for that pair: ω_1 = weight of pair 1; ω_2 = weight of pair 2, . . . ω_n = weight of pair *n*.

Then multiply the compactness σ of each pairing of ELSs by the weight ω of that pairing (its domain of simultaneous minimality). Add the 100 or so products together to obtain a single measure, call it Ω, of the maximum degree of compactness for each pair in the data set:

$$\Omega = \sum \omega\sigma = \omega_1 \sigma_1 + \omega_2 \sigma_2 + \ldots + \omega_n \sigma_n,$$ where *n* = the number of pairings formed for each name-date pair.

The larger is Ω, the more compact is the pair of terms. Note that this measure of compactness for a single pair of terms (name of a person, date of his death) is itself an aggregate, taking into account and weighting the contributions of many ELSs for the same word and many different possible array configurations for each word. It measures a pervasive *tendency* throughout the text to create compactness between related terms in pairs; it does not "detect" a fixed, mechanical rule that every such pair is "compact."

Calculate the actual "average distance" between all related pairs of terms (Name A to Date A, Name B to Date B and, . . .)

Compare this "average" with the "average distance" produced by mere chance. Once the measure of compactness for each individual name-date pair has been determined, a measure of the overall compactness of all the pairs in the data set must be calculated and contrasted with what is produced by mere chance. This was not done by first obtaining an aggregate, absolute measure of compactness for related pairs of terms and then comparing it with an aggregate, absolute measure of compactness for words in general (as is the simplest approach conceptually). Rather, a measure of *relative* compactness was obtained in one step in the following way:

First, note that the basic hypothesis is that there is something unique about words identified in the text at *equidistant* skips. By contrast, there should be nothing special about words identified in the text at *random* skips—words pulled out in that way certainly ought to be pure chance phenomena. Hence, any individual term (in a pair, in the data set) found as an ELS (more precisely: found as about 10 ELSs at minimal skips), could be contrasted with that same word found not exactly as an equidistant letter sequence, but as a *non*-equidistant letter sequence in which the skip distance between letters in a word has been "jiggled" and randomized—"perturbed."*

Rips had previously developed this approach (a derivative of Monte Carlo simulation methods) and it was implemented for the *Statistical Science* article. For each name or date in the data set, the identical process of searching for an expected 10 most minimal skips was repeated, but with each of 124 different patterns of non-equidistant skips between letters, plus the one equidistant skip. This produced a total of 125 compactness measures for each pairing, only one of which was the "genuine" ELS. These 125 measures were ranked and the place of the genuine ELS pair noted. The average rank for a genuine ELS pairing over all the data set was then calculated. If there is something special about ELSs, the genuine ELS compactness measures (in the aggregate) should rank somewhere significantly above the halfway mark in the competition.

The perturbations were arrived at as follows:

Call the various non-equidistant letter sequences for a word its "perturbed ELSs." Let $x, y, z \in \{-2, -1, 0, 1, 2\}$; i.e., x, y, and z may each take on the value of any of the 5 integers between -2 and $+2$, including zero. Consider all possible combinations of x, y, z, of which there will be $5 \times 5 \times 5 = 125$, one of which (no. 63) will have x, y, z all = 0.

---

*This does not exclude the possibility that there might be something special as well about letter sequences at *orderly* (nonrandom, rule-determined) but still nonequidistant skips. The perturbation method developed by Rips could be used equally well to test whether information is encoded in this way as well.

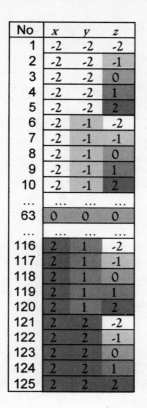

No	x	y	z
1	-2	-2	-2
2	-2	-2	-1
3	-2	-2	0
4	-2	-2	1
5	-2	-2	2
6	-2	-1	-2
7	-2	-1	-1
8	-2	-1	0
9	-2	-1	1
10	-2	-1	2
...	...	...	...
63	0	0	0
...	...	...	...
116	2	1	-2
117	2	1	-1
118	2	1	0
119	2	1	1
120	2	1	2
121	2	2	-2
122	2	2	-1
123	2	2	0
124	2	2	1
125	2	2	2

These 125 "triples" $(x, y, z)_1, (x, y, z)_2, \ldots (x, y, z)_{124}, (x, y, z)_{125}$ will be used to create 125 perturbed ELSs by using the values of x, y, and z to alter the last three skips in the searches for a term. (Actually, the various combinations of x, y, and z are used to affect directly the letter position in the search, not the skip; but the end result is variation in the interval.) The positions of the last three letters are shifted away—"perturbed"—from what their genuine ELS positions would be by anywhere from −6 to +6 letters, by adding the value $x + y + z$ to the position of the last letter; $x + y$ to the position of the second-to-last letter; and x to the position of the third to last letter.

For example, assume we are searching for the six-letter word "JOSHUA" appearing as an ELS at a skip of 3. (Assume it starts at position 2 in the string of text.) In other words, we will need to find it at positions 4, 7, 10, 13, 16, and 19. For the remaining 124 perturbed ELSs, however, only the first three positions are the same; the remaining three are shifted by using the above rule.

The sole genuine ELS with no perturbation corresponds to the "perturbed" ELS with $(x, y, z) = (0, 0, 0)$. Of the 125 possible perturbation patterns listed in the sequence above, this pattern is number 63. It is shown first on the table below, with a few of the remaining 124 below it. A "perturbed" ELS will of course show up at a different location in the text than the genuine ELS (if it does at all). Thus, each line on the chart below would map onto different sections of text which have the letters of JOSHUA at various distances.

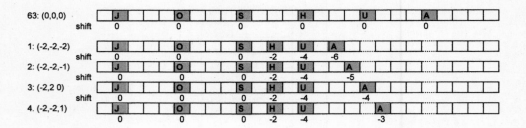

The identical procedure for measuring compactness for the genuine ELS pair is now done for all the pairs (and pairings) derived from 124 perturbed ELSs for every term in the data set. The closeness rank for the genuine ELS pair provides a measure of how compact it is in the aggregate compared with what may be expected by chance. Its relative rank is then rescaled (normalized) so that the maximum distance is 1 and the minimum 0.

Repeat the process on other texts. Strictly speaking, the perturbation method of obtaining a compactness measure is internally "self-controlling" precisely because it is not a simple number, but a rank among randomized competitors. Nonetheless, additional controls and checks were performed. The results were outlined in Chapter Twelve. Thus the same phenomenon using the same data set was looked for in a number of other texts of comparable length, including the Book of Isaiah, a section from the Hebrew translation of Tolstoy's *War and Peace*, and (in an earlier study not published as part of the *Statistical Science* piece and using the first list of rabbis) the Samaritan text of Genesis. The phenomenon appeared in none of these control texts, only in Genesis itself. Nor did it appear in the text of Genesis when its words were randomized over the whole text or within verses.

Perform a statistical analysis on the results to see whether the "averages" obtained show a significant difference between related pairs of terms in Genesis and unrelated pairs of terms in Genesis, and pairs of terms anywhere else whether related or not. The final concern was the development of an accurate measure of how significant the overall findings were: how likely it is that any of these results could have occurred merely as a coincidence. There are a great many ways of approaching this and other problems of statistical analysis. Early in their researches, Witztum, Rips, and others used methods that were criticized as inapplicable and that yielded probabilities (p-values) that were far too low. In their response to Bartholomew in the *Journal of the Royal Statistical Society* in which they reported initial results (presumably for the first set of rabbis, though they do not say so directly there), they offered a p of 1.8×10^{-17}. One of the referees of the paper eventually published in *Statistical Science* suggested the elegant alternate method eventually used. That method, too, uses a Monte Carlo type randomization procedure that, strictly speaking, is another kind of internal control. With that method applied to the second set of rabbis, a $p < 0.000016$ was obtained.

The Significance Test[2]

The method for obtaining a significance value—the likelihood the results were just by chance—also served as an additional, highly rigorous, set of controls. In addition to running the experiment on the correct name-date pairings, the researchers were requested to run an additional 999,999 experiments using incorrect pairings. In other words:

Correct name & date		Mismatch 1		Mismatch 2		...	Mismatch 4,389,331		...
1	1	1	32	1	31	...	1	22	...
2	2	2	1	2	32	...	2	16	...
3	3	3	2	3	1	...	3	7	...
4	4	4	3	4	2	...	4	10	...
5	5	5	4	5	3	...	5	3	...
6	6	6	5	6	4	...	6	31	...
7	7	7	6	7	5	...	7	15	...
8	8	8	7	8	6	...	8	4	...
...	...	...	...	...	...	...	...	...	...

Thirty-two names and 32 dates can be mismatched 32! (32 factorial) different ways ("one from column A, one from column B"). This equals $1 \times 2 \times 3 \times \ldots \times 31 \times 32 = 2.6 \times 10^{35}$ different sets (that's about 3 with 55 zeroes after it). Of these, 999,999 mismatched name-date pairs were selected at random.

With nearly a million possibilities, a certain (small) number of these pseudopair sets should generate what appears to be a significant result when they are tested in Genesis—merely by chance. (If you invent a large enough number of data sets, eventually you'll get ones that seem to work—much like the well-known "million monkeys at work on typewriters for a million years": one of them is eventually bound to reproduce Hamlet's soliloquy.) Most of course will perform poorly, some will do moderately well, a very few will seem to do extremely well—again, all by chance. An elegant way to check the significance of the correct set is to rank its results against the 999,999 mismatches. It should fall well within the middle of the million, doing neither significantly better nor worse than the vast majority. (The thought process behind this method is the heart of Von Neumann's Monte Carlo simulation method for calculating probabilities. In effect, it requires no deep knowledge of the underlying principles, just a lot of patience—or very fast computers. It's a "brute force" method that has the potential to trump sophisticated analyses.)

But in fact, the correct set of name-date pairs ranked near the very top of the competition.

The fact that so much of the design includes internal controls suggests strongly that the effect claimed by Witztum, Rips, and Rosenberg does indeed exist within that data set. Critics' concerns have therefore been focused chiefly on the question whether the data set is somehow skewed or inadvertently preselected to generate results that would vanish in other comparable data sets; or whether the particular "metric"—the measure of distance—is keyed to that data set and is not generally applicable. Debate over precisely these concerns is now heated. A very strong supportive study is the one by Harold Gans showing comparably robust p-values when the dates of the individuals' birth and/or death are replaced with their cities of birth and/or death, for all 66 rabbis (both first and second lists). Even more powerfully than a completely new data set, these results tend to confirm the lack of either "tuning" or "snooping" in creating the list of individuals.

CHAPTER ONE: THE ANCIENT LEGEND

1. Introduction to the *Sifra Ditzniut*.
2. This tale shows evidence of having been constructed in the aftermath of the conversion to Christianity of one Rabbi Abner of Burgos under the influence of a messianic movement in Spain. The Ramban was influential in opposing this movement and paid dearly for it. Because of the mortal danger associated with openly attacking Jews who had converted to Christianity, especially in Spain, many such tales were constructed in semidisguised form. In reality, Abner rose to a high position within the Spanish ecclesiastical hierarchy.
3. Y. Rambsel, *Yeshua, the Hebrew Factor* (Toronto: Frontier Research, 1996).
4. G. Jeffrey, *The Signature of God* (Toronto: Frontier Research, 1996).

CHAPTER THREE: PIERCING THE VEIL

1. Weissmandl, *Toras Chemed*, p. 12
2. Quoted in Kahn, p. 740.
3. Daniel Michaelson, "Codes in the Torah: Reading with Equal Intervals." *B'Or HaTorah*, No. 6 (1987), pp. 7–39. Jerusalem: Shamir.
4. Personal communication.

CHAPTER FOUR: BLUEPRINT FROM HEAVEN

1. *Anchor Bible Dictionary*, Vol. 6, pp. 396, 408.
2. Babylonian Talmud, *Berachoth* 61b.
3. Babylonian Talmud, *Avodah Zerah* 18a.

4. Rav Hoshaiah.

5. Babylonian Talmud, *Pesachim* 54a.

6. Franz Rosenzweig, "The Builders," in *On Jewish Learning,* ed. Nathan Glatzer (1955), p. 78.

7. Zohar II, 204a.

8. Zohar IV, 151b.

9. Babylonian Talmud, *Erubin* 21a.

10. Ibid. 13b.

11. In fact, when in the Book of Revelation in the Christian Scriptures the writer violently attacks the "Jews who are not Jews," he is not criticizing the majority of Jews of his time, who did not accept that Jesus of Nazareth was the prophesied Messiah (as modern interpreters have taken him to mean, thereby adding to the burden of anti-Semitism); rather, he is specifically attacking the Samaritan "Jews who are not Jews," because of their Babylonian, magic-based distortion of Judaism. It is no surprise that the same author (John) spends the better part of his letters attacking the newly emerging Christian Gnostics as well. Recent archaeological digs in Israel have unearthed numerous Samaritan "synagogues." The symbolism used in these structures points to what both traditional Christians and Jews would have considered pagan "demon worship"—that is, treating the (astrological) "starry hosts" to be "gods"—playing a large role alongside traditional Jewish forms of worship. This strange combination is similar to the mixture of Christian symbolism and African animism that makes up Caribbean voodoo and Santeria. These houses of Samaritan worship were also the "synagogues of Satan" that John elsewhere refers to, not the synagogues of the Jews, as has unfortunately long been taught.

12. Aryeh Kaplan, *Handbook of Jewish Thought* (Brooklyn, N.Y.: Maznaim, 1979), pp. 128–148 passim.

13. Sacred writings with variant word-breaks would not be considered "kosher," but rather errors, since the correct word-break is traditionally held to have been given Moses by God.

14. In 1985, archaeologists found a twenty-two-line long inscription near the city of Sidon written in *scripta continua*, dating to the biblical era. Five sixths of the text can be readily separated into words with singular or unambiguous meanings. Even so, more than 50 percent of the inscription remains ambiguous with innumerable possible meanings.

CHAPTER FIVE: THE BLACK FIRE OF HOLOCAUST

1. Kranzler, *Thy Brother's Blood*, p. 275.

2. Personal communication from relatives of Rabbi Weissmandl reporting his own

account, and firsthand from friends and students who were with him in Europe during this time, now living in America and in England.

3. Personal communication.

4. Personal communication.

5. Numerous accounts of this event exist among Weissmandl's students and family. See, for example, Fuchs, *The Unheeded Cry*, p. 34.

6. Weissmandl, *Out of the Depths*, pp. 42–43; referenced in ibid., p. 228. (Available in Hebrew only)

7. Some of this information may be found in Fuchs; as much as is known was confirmed by Rabbi Weissmandl's family and friends from that era who survived the Holocaust and now live in the United States and in England.

8. Fuchs, p. 214.

9. Ibid., p. 212.

CHAPTER SIX: THE WHITE FIRE OF DESTINY

1. Fuchs, p. 19.

2. Ibid.

3. In the Jewish tradition, God has a number of names each of which reflects some distinctive aspect of His nature. The best-known of these is the so-called tetragrammaton, the four-letter name transliterated in lay English as "Jehovah" and in the scholarly literature as "YHWH." Other names of special interest to the kabbalist contain twelve, forty-two, or seventy-two letters. These names were obliged to be pronounced, with strict attention to accuracy and clarity, on certain solemn occasions, and only then.

4. *Midrash Rabbah* on Ecclesiastes.

5. Zohar, *Yitro* 87a and *Mishpatim* 124.

6. Babylonian Talmud, *Berachot* 55a.

Rabbi Weissmandl's method of writing out the Torah on 10-by-10 grids, with spaces removed

The first 200 letters of Genesis are shown here, starting with בראשיתבראאלהימ = B'RAShYTBaRAAeLoHYM = "InthebeginningcreatedGod . . ." (בראשית ברא אלהימ = B'RAShYT BaRA AeLoHYM = "In the beginning created God . . ."). Hebrew reads from right to left.

Because many readers will be unfamiliar either with Hebrew or with the various scholarly transliteration schemes for converting Hebrew letters into Latin equivalents, I am using a roughly phonetic (non-standard) scheme throughout the book:

- Upper-case Latin letters correspond to an actual Hebrew letter, all of which are consonants, except for two silent letters. Thus B = ב (the letter "beyt"), R = ר (the letter "reysh").

- The silent letters in Hebrew are א ("aleph") and ע ("ayin"), which can take on *any* vowel sound. Many words may be spelled either with them or without them. (Such a letter is called a *mater lexionis*.)
- The vowel sounds in Hebrew are represented by lower-case Latin letters. (Vowelizations, as they're called, do not actually appear in the earliest Hebrew texts, but were passed down in the oral tradition. About two thousand years ago, this traditional knowledge was formalized as a set of written vowel symbols consisting of dots and dashes that were attached to copies of the text that were not being used for worship.)

Thus, the word "created" is spelled ברא in Hebrew (reading right-to-left), which I have transliterated as BaRA (reading left-to-right). The lower-case "a" in BaRA does not appear in the text. It is simply the vowelization attached to "B," giving it approximately the sound "ba." The last "A" is capitalized, however, because the sound "ah" appears by itself in the text as one of the *matres lexioni* (א) rather than as a vowelization attached to a consonant.

- Some individual letters in Hebrew have what in English is a compound spelling: ש (the letter "Shin") is pronounced "Sh" (though other times it is "Sin"). When letters such as this appear, with compound sounds, the "modifying" sound, as in the case of a vowel, does not appear in the text, and is therefore written in lower-case.
  In the word for "In the beginning" = בראשית = B'RAShYT, there is such a ש, which is written in the transliteration as "Sh."

This scheme is not perfect (and that's why different ones are used by scholars, where for example, the letter "shin" may be replaced by $). But in general, upper-case letters will have a one-to-one correspondence with the letters in the actual Hebrew text; lower-case letters are serving as "helpers" to give the reader an idea of the pronunciation.

For example: in modern Hebrew there exists the following actual word: מיסיסיפי = MYSYSYPY = "Mississippi." But the second-to-last letter could equally be an F instead of a P: MYSYSYFY (a dot in the center of it would tell us it's a P). Furthermore, modern Hebrew goes out of its way to create spellings that, even without the dots and dashes, come close to reproducing the intended sounds. But had the Bible written about the Mississippi, it might well have spelled it מססיפי, which we could read as MSSFY. It would be almost impossible to know that this should be pronounced "mee-see-see-pee" (which is how Israelis pronounce "Mississippi"). It could equally well be "moses-fee" or a great many other possibilities.

8. For a modern, scientific, yet thoroughly Orthodox Jewish attempt at precisely this kind of correspondence, see Gerald Schroeder, *Genesis and the Big Bang.*

9. Similar ideas made their way into Renaissance speculations via the influence of the Florentine philosopher and (gentile) Hebraist, Pico della Mirandola (1463–1494). He is most often referred to as a neo-*Platonist,* reflecting a routine presumption that his ideas were based primarily on the Gnosticism of Greek antiquity. In fact, most of his ideas closely reflect those of the kabbalists of the time under whom he studied intensively. He claimed, however, that kabbalah was really Christian in spirit, whereas the Talmud was a deliberate attempt to avoid the Christian truths that kabbalah reflected. The Jews also perceived the ways in which Christianity reflected Jewish mysticism in (as they understood it) distorted form. Thus a tale is told of Rabbi Akiba from the second century who alone of four sages returned intact from his immersion in the "garden" of mysticism. Not so the other three: One died, one went crazy, and the last became (in one version of the tale) a Gnostic, or (in another version) a Christian.

10. The anthropomorphism is only a metaphor, of course. In the Jewish understanding, God's nature is both ineffable and perfectly "one," as in the Shema: "Hear O Israel, the LORD our God, the LORD is one." Since He has no "parts," He cannot literally be spoken of as "having" anything, including a mind. But in His relating to us, it is *as if* He does.

11. Fuchs, p. 22.

12. *Encyclopedia Judaica*, Vol. 2, p. 186.

13. Flannery, pp. 114–115. Father Flannery's book is a comprehensive, scholarly, and dispassionate treatment of the history of anti-Semitism from pagan to modern times. He is but rarely sparing of the role of his own Church.

14. Fuchs, p. 145.

15. Ibid., p. 147; Weissmandl, pp. 25–27.

16. *Encyclopedia Judaica*, Vol. 12, p. 782.

17. Ibid., p. 778.

18. Flannery, p. 129.

19. Personal communication.
20. Fuchs, p. 216.
21. All lunar months referred to are "synodical" months: the time between two successive conjunctions of sun and moon as seen from the earth.
22. Because in his day this kind of information was considered religiously sensitive (as it is today), Nechunya's own explanation of the numbers involved was somewhat sketchy. But another medieval kabbalist who followed closely in Nechunya's footsteps—Rabbi Yitzhak deMin Acco—laid out the calculations precisely.
23. Yisroel Stern, personal communication.
24. Personal recollection of Siegmund Forst.
25. Of course, Christians are not celebrating the giving of the Torah at Pentecost, but the "giving" of the Holy Spirit.

CHAPTER SEVEN: FROM ENIGMA TO ATBASH AND BACK

1. *The Origin and Development of the Army Security Agency, 1917–1947*, p. 2.
2. Kahn, p. 613.
3 However, under congressional pressure, the NSA has recently been forced to alter its employment standards to consider factors other than sheer ability.
4. Kahn, p. 79.
5. Most modern, secular scholars maintain that the Zohar was actually composed in the fourteenth century by Rabbi Moses de Leon who pseudonymously attributed its contents to Rabbi Simon bar Yochai. DeLeon's contemporary, Rabbi Yitzhak deMin Acco, took it upon himself to investigate the Zohar's true authorship, since rumors of a false attribution arose even at the time. The story of Acco's investigation (given in *Sefer HaYuchasin*) breaks off just before he reaches his conclusion. Scholars have long maintained that deMin Acco's conclusion is unknown, and they have formed their own opinion based on far later sources. But in 1976, Rabbi Aryeh Kaplan was given a photocopy of the only complete manuscript of the work of deMin Acco, *Otzar HaChaim*, located in the Günzberg Judaica Collection of the Lenin Library in Moscow. It was written in deMin Acco's own hand twenty years after he completed his investigation of Rabbi de Leon. Acco states unequivocally that the Zohar was written by Rabbi Simon bar Yochai. (A. Kaplan, *Kaballah and the Age of the Universe*, keynote address to the Midwinter Conference of the Association of Orthodox Jewish Scientists, February 19, 1976, privately circulated.)
6. Kahn, p. 127.
7. Quoted in ibid. p. 128.
8. Ibid., p. 133.

9. Ibid., p. 144.

10. Blaise Vigenère, "Tractatus de Igne et Sale," *Theatricum Chemicum Britannicum*, VI, 1661, p. 3, referenced in C. G. Jung, *The Archetypes of the Collective Unconscious*, (Princeton, N.J.: Princeton University Press, 1968), p. 4.

11. Abraham ben Jechiel Michal HaKohen, *Ve-Shav HaKohen* (Leghorn, 1788).

12. The modern scholarly consensus holds that Jewish mysticism emerged only during the late second Temple period, along with the seeds of what would develop into Christianity. But once it is understood how central to Jewish mysticism is cryptology, pointers to a far earlier origin may be read directly out of the Bible itself.

13. The Greek mathematician Apollonius of Perga (now part of modern Turkey) is best known for his eight-volume *Treatise on Conic Sections,* of which four volumes survive. He, too, wrote on statistics, a subject discovered over the centuries to be of ever more appreciated foundational significance, as will emerge in our own discussion. Conic sections are a family of curves that result when you intersect, at various angles, a hollow cone (or two cones, placed point to point) with a single plane: i.e., circles, ellipses, parabolas, and hyperbolas. This simple relationship between three-dimensional geometry and two-dimensional algebraic functions is unexpected and elegant. It has exerted considerable fascination on mathematical minds for centuries and continues to do so today, especially as extended to higher-dimensional space—and space-time.

14. A race is now under way among most of the major pharmaceutical companies to develop just such drugs.

15. Kahn, p. 204.

16. Haldane, p. 23.

17. Ibid., pp. 99–100.

18. Ibid., p. 102.

19. Kahn, p. 573.

20. Haldane, p. 123.

21. Kahn, pp. 392–393.

22. Ibid., pp. 383–384.

23. Paul D. Townsend, "Quantum Cryptography on Multi-user Optical Fibre Networks," *Nature,* No. 385 (1997), pp. 47–49.

24. Richard J. Hughes, "Quantum Security Is Spookily Certain," *Nature*, No. 385 (1997), pp. 17–18.

25. Hodges, p. 383.

26. See the books of the mathematical physicist Roger Penrose for a fascinating tour of these ideas. Also in his mid-nineteen-eighties lectures on computation, Richard Feynman gives a superb outline of Turing's ideas. These lectures are widely recognized as having laid the foundation for the development of quantum computation. (R. Reynman, *Feynman Lectures on Computation*, edited by

J. G. Hey and R. W. Allen. Reading, Mass.: Addison-Wesley, 1996. See especially pp. 52–93.)

27. Quoted in Hodges, p. 63.
28. Quoted in ibid., p. 513.
29. See John Keegan, "What the Allies Knew: The 'Ultra' Scandal That Wasn't," *The New York Times*, November 25, 1996, p. A15.
30. Arthur R. Butz, *The Hoax of the Twentieth Century: The Case Against the Presumed Extermination of European Jewry* (Newport Beach, Calif.: The Historical Review Press, 1992; first published in England, 1975).

CHAPTER EIGHT: THE BIBLE CODE EMERGES

1. Michaelson, pp. 7–39.

CHAPTER NINE: THE ARCHITECTURE OF THE GARDEN

1. Susan Gabar, "Eating the Bread of Affliction: Judaism and Feminist Criticism," in *People of the Book: Thirty Scholars Reflect on Their Jewish Identity* (Madison: University of Wisconsin, 1996).
2. Paul Lauter, in ibid.
3. Bonnie Zimmerman, in ibid.
4. Elaine Marks, in ibid.
5. We are following the line of thought laid out by the researchers in Israel:

> The approach we have taken in this research can be illustrated by the following example. Suppose we have a text written in a foreign language that we do not understand. We are asked whether the text is meaningful (in that foreign language) or meaningless. Of course it is very difficult to decide between these possibilities, since we do not understand the language. [Doron Witztum, Eliyahu Rips, and Yoav Rosenberg, "Equidistant Letter Sequences in the Book of Genesis," *Statistical Science*, Vol. 9, No. 3 (1994), pp. 429–438; p. 429.]

They, in turn, were following the principles recently laid down by the great Russian linguist N.D. Andreyev of the Leningrad Academy of Sciences, and being used to develop techniques for translating ("decrypting") extraterrestrial messages, should the SETI radio-telescope project ever receive them:

> Andreyev . . . has recently proposed a method that he believes will enable men to decipher any language. Using what he calls "statistical-combinatory" analysis, he measures six different parameters in a text, such as the distance of one word from another in a sentence, to arrive

at a semantic relationship between words. Testing this on human languages, he has ascertained the meaning of verbal symbols. "The data are uneven," he wrote. "For several words their exact meanings are obtained; other words group themselves into clearly delimited and semantically homogeneous sets with a definite meaning in common . . . ; some words reveal only their broad semantic class." [Kahn, p. 953.]

This approach suggests that the orderliness of the Bible Code is a mere consequence of its being a message-bearing "plaintext," whose precise meaning we are as yet unable to decipher. However, that need not be the case. Andreyev's rules require (and therefore "filter out" or detect) statistical orderliness alone. Strictly speaking, there need be no more, even though such a notion departs from our everyday experience of meaning and language.

6. Michaelson, p. 33.

CHAPTER TEN: THE HELIX OF TIME

1. Menachem Gerlitz, *The Heavenly City: Retold from the Hebrew by Sheindel Weinbach* (Jerusalem: Feldheim, 1979), p. 210.
2. Ibid., p. 218.
3. A "skip" of 1 implies a sequence of letters in the surface, "ciphertext," with *no* intervening letters. Such an ELS will be either a word (or words) in the text itself, or a different word (or words) caused by breaking the *scripta continua* in a different way. Treating the word as an ELS can be confusing—especially if it occurs frequently, as with "Joseph." Furthermore, a word that is found both in the text itself (skip = 1) and as an ELS with some skip > 1 would have a minimal skip = 1 for 100 percent of the text. For this reason, careful statistical analyses of the phenomenon often eliminate ELSs of skip = 1, whether they are words found in the text or not.
4. Witztum, *HaMaimod HaNosaf*, Chapter 10.

CHAPTER ELEVEN: THE FLAMES OF AMALEK

1. *Yisrael Kedoshim*, pp. 94–95. I have added the details about Amalek's ancestry and progeny in order to place the statement in context that would be familiar to many Jewish readers.
2. As noted before, Yoav Rosenberg (of Witztum, Rips, and Rosenberg) is completing a doctoral dissertation on advanced signal detection techniques with just these kind of pattern-recognition capabilities. Perhaps this is a coincidence; per

haps not. In any event, it certainly reflects how much of Israel's intellectual effort must be devoted to military defense.

3. Moshe Katz, *Computorah*, p. 153.

4. The last time in antiquity that Babylon attacked the nation of Israel, it was under the leadership of Nebuchadnezzar. His original name in its proper spelling and pronunciation is a compound: "O Nebu!" he cries to the god of Babylon. "Guard my border!" (נבו קדרצר = NeBU KaDReTzeR) In Genesis, an array of width 29 shows the sole 100 percent minimal appearance of his name in close proximity to the word for "missile." (טיל = TYL) and the sole minimal appearance of the year of Saddam's attack, 5751 (תשנא). The date of the destruction of the first Temple by Nebuchadnezzar's army is commemorated on the ninth of Ab. In the same compact array found by Witztum that shows "Saddam" and "in Bagdad" at their 100 percent minimal skips, one may also find the 100 percent minimal appearance of the date, "the ninth of Ab."

The captain of Nebuchadnezzar's army, the man who actually destroyed Jerusalem and the Temple, prohibited Jewish worship, and directed the slaughter of its inhabitants and the exile of the remnant was Nebu*zaradan*: "the seed of Nebu." His sobriquet in Jewish tradition was taken from the story of Joseph. There the term "captain of the guard" (שר הטבחים = SaR HaTaVaChYM) was interpreted as "chief [lit: *prince*] of the butchers." (Doron Witztum found the minimal ELS of Eichmann's name in close proximity in Genesis to just that phrase, suggesting the linkage between ancient and modern attacks on the Jews.)

An array of line length 5,785 also displays the perfect juxtaposition of the phrase "captain of the guard"/"chief of the butchers" (שר הטבחים = SaR HaTaVaChYM) and the 100 percent minimal appearance of "the guard"/"the butchers," with a common letter ח (Ch) (the biblical word in Hebrew literally means "stewards," but has been interpreted down through the ages as "butcher"):

(JS)

But also sharing a letter of one of only six appearances of "missile" in the text itself (טיל = TYL), and one of only two appearances of "the missile" (הטיל = HaTYL). At a line length of 826, the name of the "chief of the butchers"—

"Zaradan" (זראדן = ZaRADaN)—emerges at its 100 percent minimal skip as an ELS in Genesis. (In combined form as a single word, Nebu + Chadnezzar, + Chadrezzar and + Zaradan do not appear in Genesis at all as ELSs. The common prefix "Nebu," by contrast, is ubiquitous. Only the distinctives appear as noted.) At a line length of 1,157, the year of the missile attack appears at its 100 percent minimum (נתשא = 5751).

Finally, above the compact juxtaposition found by Doron Witztum of "Saddam" (צדאמ = TzaDAM) and "in Bagdad" (בבגדד = B'BaGDaD) one may also find the 100 percent minimal occurrence in Genesis of "the ninth of Ab," the date of Nebuzarradan's destruction of ancient Israel. Saddam, incidentally, nicknamed the commander of his armies "Nebuzaradan" just as he portrayed himself as Nebuchadnezzar; Saddam himself is known in Israel as "the butcher of Bagdad."

5. Theodore Postol, a physicist and former classmate of mine at MIT, published a sharp and highly controversial critique arguing that the Patriot was not anywhere near so effective as news reports made it seem.

6. *Kol Israel* (*Voice of Israel*) radio broadcast, cited in Katz, *Computorah*.

7. Cited in Katz, *Computorah*, p. 201.

8. General Moshe Bar Kochba, *Kfar Chabad*, February 6, 1991, pp. 34–36.

9. Cited in Katz, p. 203.

10. Witztum, pp. 182 passim.

11. Babylonian Talmud, *Pesachim* 94a–b.

12. Zohar, *Vayikra* (Leviticus) 31b.

13. Even the correct millennium is hinted at. The letter "vav" (ו), in the name that contains the third number for the year, is uniquely *enlarged*. The Zohar (on Genesis, 117a), devoting much time to the creative powers of the letters of the Torah, makes the following cryptic comment: "And when the *sixth* millennium [the current one], represented by the final 'vav' (ו) of God's name, is about to begin, then the final Hay of the Name [ה, that which was added to Abram to make him the father of the Jewish people] *will be lifted up from the dust of exile*" (my emphasis). Of course, the Holocaust and the defeat of the Nazis paved the way for the refounding of the nation of Israel.

CHAPTER TWELVE: THE GREAT SAGES

1. Quoted in Susan Orenstein, "Breakthrough: Back to the Future" *Lifestyles*, Vol. 18, No. 107 (Summer 1990), p.35.

2. Harold Gans, personal communication.

3. Witztum, p. 85 passim.

4. Bernard Sussman, letter to *Bible Review*, February 1996. Mr. Sussman is a Bible scholar and librarian at the Library of Congress.

5. Witztum, Rips, and Rosenberg, response to D. J. Bartholomew, pp. 137–178.

6. "Words may be related by meanings that are geographic, chemical, physical, medical, and so on. It would miss the point to try to come up with a universal definition of such relatedness. For each topic in question, the conceptual connection between words is intuitively obvious." Witztum, *The Added Dimension,* p. 58. The book is available only in Hebrew. This passage is my own amplified translation. A book by Witztum detailing his methods in depth and providing many hundreds of examples of great beauty is being prepared.

7. M. Margolioth, ed. (Tel Aviv: Chachik 1961). This information was coordinated with data from the so-called "Responsa" database. Critics unfamiliar with Judaism have complained that some of the most famous entries in the encyclopedia seem to have been excuded arbitrarily from the data set. They are unaware that this is because they are not found in the Responsa database: though famous, they did not happen to write Responsa (clarifications of points of Jewish law). It is genuinely not clear, however, that the selection rules were adequately fixed.

8. These limitations are explained in the Technical Appendix C. Briefly, words could not be shorter than five letters because internal controls consisted of perturbations of the interletter interval by −2, −1, 0, +1, +2 letters for each of five letters in a word. They could not be longer than eight letters because two many eight-letter (or longer) words simply do not appear at all in Genesis at equidistant intervals.

9. Actually, because of the computing burden of such simulation, an abbreviation of this method was used.

10. The referees suggested the additional data set as a precaution against the possibility that the authors had inadvertently shaped the first data set over years of working with it so as to maximize the results. Since they used a different (and as it turns out, inaccurate) method to arrive at a p-value for the first data set, they refrained altogether from using the referees' suggested method on the first data set at all, until after the results of the second set had been published. The results on the first set turn out to be as good or better than on the second.

CHAPTER THIRTEEN: ARE THEY REAL? THE DEBATE IGNITES

1. Marty Kaplan, "Maybe Reason Isn't Enough," *The New York Times,* March 31, 1997, p. A15.

2. J. Satinover, responses to "Divine Authorship?" pp. 10, 11 ff.

3. Doron Witztum says as much in his book; this was confirmed as well by Eliyahu Rips.

4. The BHS Genesis differs from the Koren Genesis as follows (1 word break difference, 5 substitutions, 4 deletions, and 13 additions for a net +9 frameshift over the whole text):

4:13	7:11	8:20	8:20	9:29	13:8	14:17	14:22	19:16	19:20	25:3	26:7	27:31	35:5	35:23	40:10	41:35	45:15	46:9	46:12	46:13	46:14	49:13	NET
+1	+1	+1	-1	+1	+1	0b	+1	-1	0s	+1	0s	+1	-1	0s	0s	-1	+1	+1	+1	+1	0s	+1	+9

5. Personal communication.

6. Professor Persi Diaconis, phone conversation.

7. Edward J. Larson and Larry Witham, "Scientists Are Still Keeping the Faith," *Nature*, No. 386 (1997), pp. 435–436.

8. Referenced in George P. Hansen, "CSICOP and the Skeptics: An Overview (1)," unpublished article.

9. Ibid.

10. Papers on the subject authored by Diaconis include, "The Mathematics of Perfect Shuffles," *Advances in Applied Mathematics*, No. 4 (1983), pp. 175–196; "Shuffling Cards and Stopping Times," *American Mathematical Monthly*, No. 93 (1986), pp. 333–348; with David Bayer, "Tracking the Dovetail Shuffle to Its Lair," *Annals of Applied Probability*, No. 2 (1992), pp. 294–313; with Jim Fill and Jim Pitman, "Analysis of Top to Random Shuffles," *Combinatorics, Probability Computing*, No. 1 (1992), pp. 135–155; with M. McGrath and Jim Pitman, "Riffle Shuffles, Cycles and Descents," *Combinatorica*, No. 15, pp. 11–29. See also Gina Kolata, "In Shuffling Cards, 7 Is Winning Number," *The New York Times*, January 11, 1990, Section C, pp. 1 and 12.

11. P. Diaconis, "Statistical Problems in ESP Research," *Science*, No. 201, pp. 131–136; No. 202, pp. 1145–1146.

12. P. Diaconis and D. Freedman, "The Persistence of Cognitive Illusions: A Rejoinder to L. J. Cohen, *Behavioral and Brain Science*, No. 4 (1981), pp. 333–334.

13. Diaconis and Engel, pp. 171–174.

14. Diaconis and Mosteller, pp. 853–861.

15. Referencing Diaconis, the director of Chance, Professor J. Laurie Snell, writes:

> The goal of this unit . . . is to debunk the outrageously high odds that are commonly reported in news reports when a surprising event occurs. Also, since statistical tests of significance are based on calculating how unlikely certain observations would be based on chance alone, discussion of coincidences can provide a useful vocabulary framework and

help to sharpen intuitive notions. . . . Coincidences and patterns of events that are predictable—*and in large samples nearly guaranteed* [my emphasis]—by the laws of probability seem to be too implausible to be attributed to mere chance. This gives rise to the tendency to seek explanation in terms of predestination, ESP, etc. (Posted at http://www.geom.umn.edu/doc.)

16. Diaconis and Mosteller, pp. 853–861.
17. In an Internet "Announcement of New ELS Tests for Genesis," dated April 17, 1997, Dror Bar-Natan, Alec Gindis, Aryeh Levitan, and Brendan McKay describe two new methods for testing new lists of word pairs drawn up from the first and second lists of Great Sages. "The second method," they write, was "suggested by Persi Diaconis." It is described briefly in Technical Appendix C.
18. Http://www.slate.com/Features/codes/codes.asp.
19. Deavours and Kruh, p. 28.
20. Ibid., pp. 28–30.
21. Kahn, p. 706.
22. Ibid., p. 707.
23. Private communication to Rabbi Moshe Zeldman of Aish HaTorah in response to a query concerning the codes and the integrity of the Koren text of the Torah.

CHAPTER 14: THE SIXTH MILLENNIUM

1. William James, *The Principles of Psychology*, Vol. 53. *Great Books of the Western World*, ed. Robert Maynard Hutchins (Chicago: Encyclopaedia Britannica and the University of Chicago Press, 1952), note, p. vi.
2. Michael E. Kellman, "A Model of Free Will Exercised by Mind Acting as Quantum Observer," University of Oregon preprint, p. 1.
3. Jacques Monod, *Beyond Chance and Necessity*, ed. J. Lewis (London: Cornerstone Press, 1974).
4. Jacques Monod, cited in Ilya Prigogine and Isabelle Stengers, *Order Out of Chaos* (New York: Bantam Books, 1984), p. 187.
5. Steven Weinberg, *Dreams of a Final Theory: The Search for the Fundamental Laws of Nature* (New York: Pantheon, 1992), p. 255; citing himself in an earlier book, *The First Three Minutes* (1977).
6. Cited in ibid.
7. Gerald Feinberg, cited in Heinz Pagels, *The Cosmic Code* (New York: Bantam Books, 1983), p. 187.
8. John Searle, *Minds, Brains and Science* (Cambridge: Harvard University Press,

1984); cited in Kellman, p. 3. James framed the dilemma as follows: "There is . . . reason for denying causal efficacy to our feelings. We can form no positive image of the modus operandi of a volition or other thought affecting the cerebral molecules."

9. Luzzatto, *The Way of God* p. 81.

10. Actually, Planck's idea came in the form of an equation that produced a certain curve. This curve of his looked far more like one that physicists measured in real life than the one that all of physical theory until then predicted should be found. Planck's out-of-the-blue equation produced results that have proven to be in as close agreement with actual measurements as is physically possible to detect. Every generation since, new experiments have validated it with even greater precision.

11. There has been a lengthy debate over whether this interpretation of quantum mechanics, partially due to Niels Bohr, is precisely true. The most effective alternative states that the universe "as a whole" instantaneously determines each of the constituent events, a model attributable largely to David Bohm. This "superdetermination," however, is only seemingly deterministic. It merely shifts the mystery of cause from the part to the whole, as there is no sufficient reason for the whole to be in one state and not another.

12. H. Everett, " 'Relative State' Formulation of Quantum Mechanics," *Review of Modern Physics*, Vol. 29 (1957), p. 454.

13. David Bohm and Basil Hiley, *The Undivided Universe* (London: Routledge, 1993).

14. What is this "it"? Physical scientists need constrain themselves to analyses that depend upon, and therefore to speaking only of, items that have some form of material existence, i.e., are a part of the physical universe. Thus, various "interpretations" of quantum mechanics have sprung up that try to identify this "it" with something or things *in* the universe, or with the universe as a whole, since to do otherwise would violate the premise (usually unstated) that there "is" nothing else. So, some speak as if the locus of "action" is within the particle; others as if the locus of action is within an ensemble of particles that makeup a mysterious coordinated "whole" (however widely separated its constituents); others as if the "whole" is a unity that embraces future actions as well as past, and is capable of altering the latter in response to the former; others that the entire universe is such a whole, past and present, possessing consciousness, will, and instrumentality. Without realizing it, physicists are thus now recapitulating the theological disputes of earlier eras, as to what is the nature (and boundaries) of nonphysical agencies. (See Jeffrey Satinover, "Interpretations of Quantum Mechanics and Their Theological Analogs," *Consciousness Research Abstracts, Journal of Consciousness Studies,* from "Toward a Science of Consciousness 1996," conference proceedings, *Physics and Mathematics,* pp. 116–117.)

15. C. H. Bennett et al., "Teleporting an Unknown Quantum State via Dual Classical and EPR Channels," *Physical Review Letters*, Vol. 70 (1993), pp. 1895–1899.

16. Roland Omnés, *The Interpretation of Quantum Mechanics* (Princeton: Princeton University Press, 1994), p. 159.

17. Kellman, op. cit., p. 1.

18. David Jones, "Daedalus: God Plays Dice," *Nature*, January 9, 1997, p. 122.

19. Quoted in Hodges, p. 63.

20. This selection is often referred to as the "collapse of the wave function." Kellman does "not believe that the question of free will [in relation to quantum mechanics] hinges on controversial issues of whether there is a collapse, inasmuch as the postulates of working quantum mechanics invoked here [in his paper, "A Model of Free Will Exercised by Mind Acting as Quantum Observer,"] do not rely upon any orthodoxy regarding collapse, or necessarily preclude other, 'non-orthodox' interpretations."

21. In the words of Roland Omnés, a physicist at the University of Paris, XI:

    > Quantum mechanics has crossed an ultimate threshold in the history of our knowledge of the basic laws of physics, beyond which a mathematical theory must acknowledge its ultimate inability to account for all the aspects of reality . . . That quantum mechanics has reached such an ultimate frontier in the field of knowledge means that what one is contemplating at its most extreme point of contact with reality is a witness to its feats and not at all to its failure, as quite a few people believed. [Omnés, op. cit., p. 327]

22. Quoted in Hodges, p. 63.

23. Haralick and Glazerson, *Torah Codes and Israel Today*. There is substantial disagreement between him and other code researchers about his methodology. But it would be fair to say that he is a qualified disputant, and there will necessarily emerge a wide range of opinions and approaches as the phenomenon becomes more widely known.

24. There is an intermediate step I have left out of this argument for brevity's sake. That is the question how such small-scale fluctuations as those on the quantum scale can be "amplified" into large-scale (brain-size) influences. Much of the "hard" research into consciousness is examining precisely this link between "microcosm" and "macrocosm." A number of plausible linkages have been proposed, some with experimental support, but all still highly theoretical. For my own small contribution to this discussion, see Jeffrey Satinover, "A Neural Network Model of Archetypal Structures and of the Relationship Between Nature and Nurture in Brain-Mind Development," *Consciousness Research Abstracts, Journal of Consciousness Studies,* from "Toward a Science of

Consciousness 1996," conference proceedings, *Physics and Mathematics*, pp. 102–103.

25. Posting to tcode express.ior.com, February 5, 1997, message to ID 9702052225.AA03000@ptah.ptah.ee

26. Luzzatto, pp. 213–235.

27. Ibid., p. 169.

28. "It is a fact that Columbus discovered America by prophecy rather than by astronomy. 'In the carrying out of this enterprise to the Indies,' he wrote to King Ferdinand and Queen Isabella in 1502, 'neither reason nor mathematics nor maps were any use to me: fully accomplished were the words of Isaiah 11:10-12' " (*Encyclopaedia Britannica*, Vol. 6 [1968], p. 111). The words from Isaiah are:

> "And it shall come to pass in that day, that the LORD will set His hand again the second time to recover the remnant of His people . . . and will assemble the dispersed of Israel, and gather together the scattered of Judah from the four corners of the earth."

Columbus's favorite book of prophecy, however, appears to have been the apocryphal First Book of Esdras, dating from about the second century B.C. It clearly echoes—and amplifies—the allusion to Isaiah he sent his royal patrons. Chiefly, it tells the story of how a Jew at the court of a foreign king (Darius = Ferdinand), in a land to which his people have been exiled (Persia = Spain and Portugal), is awarded the right to lead his people out of exile and to restore them to their homeland. This right he has earned because he argues that of all things in the world, nothing is stronger than truth. In mystical circles, both Jewish and Christian, this "truth" was understood as the secret wisdom hidden within Scripture. Indeed, Columbus specifically claimed that he learned the truth of the globe's shape, and adduced the locations of its land masses, via his reading of the Book of Esdras. Columbus seems to have believed that a final, cataclysmic expulsion would necessarily precede any "gather[ing] together [of] the scattered of Judah from the four corners of the earth." Recall that he set sail one-half hour before the deadline for all Jews to be out of Spain.

29. A. Sanpera and C. Machiavello, "Un Saut d'echelle pour les calculateurs," *La Recherche*, November 1996.

30. Writes Marc J. Feldman, professor and senior scientist at the Electrical Engineering Department of the University of Rochester:

> But there is also the question of technological scalability. If an n bit computer is technologically feasible, is a 100-n bit computer techno-

logically feasible? Could one build a glass-vacuum-tube computer 100 times as big as ENIAC? I don't know. But surely a quantum computer built with ion traps or NMR spins will be difficult or impossible to scale by 100x. On the other hand, integrated circuit technology [has] proven to be technologically scalable. It would seem to be the only way to enter the Moore's law regime for quantum computation [Moore's law pertains to the power/scale relationship in computation]. [Personal communication]

31. This is a "by your bootstraps" process that is necessarily nondeterministic and not *completely* describable by any symbolic logic, according to the proof adduced by Gödel. Mathematicians, physicists, and neuroscientists have all begun to scrutinize carefully the long-puzzling feature of mind—first described by mystics and philosophers—that it seems irreducibly self-referential. It is this above all that points toward quantum mechanics. Writes neuropsychiatrist Donald Mender, M.D.: "As [pointed out] by Dr. Piet Hut of the Institute for Advanced Studies [at Princeton], the mind exhibits a peculiar kind of self-reference, whereby content subsumes its own structure. Among physical constructs, only quantum mechanics . . . exhibits similarly self-referent features" (*The New York Times*, May 5, 1997, p. A14). Similarly, "Prominent interpretations of quantum mechanics, especially as these play themselves out in the attempt to understand consciousness, . . . depend upon circularity of some sort . . . in their argumentation (non-computable knowledge, for example, can be so characterized . . .)." (J. Satinover, "Interpretations of Quantum Theory and Their Theological Analogs," *Consciousness Research Abstracts*, Tucson II, 1996, p. 116)

32. Kellman, p. 16.

33. Vilna Gaon, *Commentary* Mishlei 21:17.

END PLATE

1. From Doron Witztum; printed in Michaelson, "Codes in the Torah." The passage refers to a signet that indicates who is the true father of an otherwise illegitimate child. (King James Version)

EPILOGUE: REPORT FROM THE FRONT LINES

1. Michael Drosnin, *The Bible Code* (New York: Simon & Schuster, 1997).

2 Doron Zeilberger, "Opinion 16: Apropos the BIBLE CODE and Its Alleged Refutations: Ramsey Theory Has Already Proven That Harmony (May I Say God) Exists." At website http://www.math.temple.edu/~zeilberg/opinion16.html. Posted June 3, 1997.

TECHNICAL APPENDIX A: DETAILS OF THE NEW MOON

1. Babylonian Talmud, *Sukkah*.
2. Babylonian Talmud, *Shabbath* 75a. The "magians," or "magi," are specifically Persian astrologers, whose *magical* approach (whence the term) involved fortune-telling ("sorcery"); they were considered blasphemers. The conflict between Judaism and the pagan religious traditions of "the nations" is not between naturalism and supernaturalism as it often seems today. It is rather a conflict between two distinct forms of spirituality that in the ancient biblical view must never be confused. Clear examples of his conflict may be found in Moses' "battle" with the Egyptian court magicians (who had a few tricks of their own, we recall) (Exodus); in Joseph's contest with the official court dream interpreters (Genesis); in Daniel's similar contest with the Persian interpreters (Daniel).
3. Babylonian Talmud, *Rosh HaShanna* 25a.
4. Hugo Mandelbaum, "The Problem of *Molad Tohu*," *Proceedings of the Association of Orthodox Jewish Scientists*, III–IV (1976), p. 30. Cited in *Discovery*, Aleynu (R. Ari Kahn, Educational Director), 1992, p. 136. Jerusalem: Aish HaTorah.
5. Bernstein, loc. cit.
6. Rabban Gamaliel notes: "I have it on the authority of the house of my father's father that the renewal of the moon takes place after not less than twenty-nine days and a half and two-thirds of an hour and seventy-three 'parts' (73/1080) of an hour" (Babylonian Talmud, *Rosh HaShanna* 25a). In this traditional reckoning, the hour was not divided into 3,600 of our seconds, but 1,080 *halakin*.

    Maimonides (Rambam), in his own book, *Laws of Sanctifying the New Moon*, comments: "By these figures, the interval between two conjunctions of moon and sun according to their mean motion is 29 days and 12 hours of the 30th day, beginning with the night of this day, and 793 parts of the 13th hour. That is the time that elapses between one mean conjunction and the other, and that is the duration of the lunar month" (Chapter 6, pp. 2–3).

    In other words: 793 ÷ 1,080 = 0.734529 hours; 0.734529 hours ÷ 24 hours per day = 0.03059 days; 29 days + 0.5 days + 0.03059 days = 29.53059 days.
7. "We have allowed that shortage intentionally; as against this another result . . . yields a surplus that will balance the shortage, so that the final result will contain the correct figure" (Maimonides, *Laws of Sanctifying the New Moon*, Vol. 11, pp. 5–6).
8. Rabbi Yitzhak commenting on Exodus 12:1–2: "This month shall be to you the first of the months."
9. *Midrash Rabbenu Bachya*, Genesis 1. I am most grateful to Mr. Jack Freedman who honored me with a copy of Bachya's two-volume commentary.
10. In "Deborah's Song" in Judges 5:23, the poet commands, "Cursed be Meroz,

cursed be its inhabitants." Jewish tradition holds that Meroz refers either to an unknown town somewhere in ancient Israel or to a certain star that is a planet. Which explanation is correct is held to be unknown; Christian commentaries presume and provide only the first interpretation (Babylonian Talmud, *Megillah* 18a). The *Sefer Bris* (*Book of the Covenant*) specifically notes in its amplification of *Megillah* 18a, "If Meroz is a star [planet], the verse explicitly speaks of its 'inhabitants' " (quotation from Rabbi Aryeh Kaplan, Keynote Address, Midwinter Conference, Association of Orthodox Jewish Scientists, February 19, 1979; unpublished).

11. M. Green, J. Schwarz, and E. Witten, *Superstring Theory*, 2 vols. (Cambridge: Cambridge University Press, 1987).

12. A short, only somewhat technical summary of these calculations may be found in Halliday, Resnick, and Krane, *Physics*, Vol. 2, extended, 4th ed. (New York: Wiley, 1992), pp. 1189–1216.

13. See Schroeder, *Genesis and the Big Bang*, for a general overview of this description. Additional details may be found in Rabbi Isaac Luria, *Ten Luminous Emanations*.

14. Nachmanides, *Commentary on the Torah*, Genesis 1:1, in Schroeder, p. 65.

15. Luria, op. cit.

16. Schroeder, p. 59.

TECHNICAL APPENDIX B: TRANSFORMATIONS OF SPACE AND TIME

1. Struck by the profound grandeur of what Einstein discovered, and seeing in some ways even more deeply into its implications than Einstein himself, one of Einstein's former teachers, Herman Minkowski, wrote in 1908: "Henceforth space by itself, and time by itself, are doomed to fade away into mere shadows, and only a kind of union of the two will preserve an independent reality."

2. This black and white structure is a further transformation and simplification of a multicolored Ulam spiral transformation created by Jean-François Colonna, ©1996, CNET and the École Polytechnique, Paris, France. Starting from the origin, follow a square spirallike path and number each integer point encountered (1, 2, 3, . . .). Display the N-th point with the false color $f(d(N))$ where $d(N)$ = number of divisors of N, thus $d(N) = 2$ if N is a prime number (including N=1 for the sake of simplicity), and : $f(x)$ = an arbitrary function, for example, $f(x) = x$. The first important structure-revealing picture consists of points of the same color. For example, when choosing : $f(2)$ = white and $f(d)$ = black, the picture displays all the prime numbers: the Ulam spiral. Then transform the picture P1 into the picture P2 using the following conformal mapping : $1 z \rightarrow -z$, the picture plane being the Complex Plane. A Fourier filtering of picture P2 gives a colored structure (not shown). A simple threshold function transforms

the colored picture into this one (P3). P4 (following) is created by identifying boundaries and nonboundaries and remapping black as boundary and white as nonboundary.

3. S. J. Miller and F. W. Firk, "Symmetries of Higher-Order Spacing Distributions in Number-Theoretic Systems," Yale University preprint, in submission to *Mathematics and Computation*. The authors note: "1st-, 2nd- and 3rd-order spacing distributions of 5×105 prime-22 pairs beginning at 2×108, are consistent with a 1st order Poisson distribution." But only fuzzily so! I speculate that these symmetries reflect the symmetries in the Ulam spiral.

TECHNICAL APPENDIX C: THE "GREAT SAGES" EXPERIMENT

1. M. Margolioth, ed., *Encyclopedia of Great Men in Israel; a Bibliographical Dictionary of Jewish Sages and Scholars from the Ninth to the End of the Eighteenth Century,* Vols 1–4 (Tel Aviv: Joshua Chachik, 1961).

2. For a later test of the method conducted by critics Dror Bar-Natan, Alec Gindis, Aryeh Levitan, and Brendan McKay (mentioned in Chapter Two), Persi Diaconis suggested the following variation of the above method (also devised by him): "For each pair of persons p,p', compute one distance t(p,p') by averaging the defined values c(w,w') where w is in the first word-set of o and w' is in the second word-set of p'. If there are no such values defined, t(p,p') is undefined. For a permutation pi of the persons, define T(pi) to be the average over all p of the defined values t[p,p(pi)]. If there are no such defined values, T(pi) is undefined. The result will be the rank position of T(id) amongst all defined T(pi) for a large set of random permutations pi." Internet posting dated April 17, 1997.

BIBLIOGRAPHY

BOOKS

Anonymous. *The Origin and Development of the Army Security Agency, 1917–1947.* Laguna Hills, Calif.: Aegean Park Press, 1978.

Deavors, C. A., and L. Kruh. *Machine Cryptography and Modern Cryptanalysis.* Dedham, Mass.: Artech House, 1985.

Flannery, E. H. *The Anguish of the Jews: Twenty-three Centuries of Anti-Semitism.* New York: Paulist Press, 1985.

Fuchs, A. *The Unheeded Cry.* Brooklyn, N.Y.: Mesorah, 1986.

Glazerson, M., and R. Haralick. *Torah Codes and Israel Today.* Jerusalem: Lev Eliyahu, 1996.

Haldane, R. A. *The Hidden World.* London: Robert Hale & Company, 1976.

Hodges, A. *Alan Turing: The Enigma.* New York: Simon & Schuster, 1983.

Kahn, D. *The Codebreakers: The Story of Secret Writing.* New York: Macmillan, 1967.

Katz, M. *B'Otiyoteiha Nitna Torah* (Hebrew). Jerusalem: Tel-Co, 1991.

———. *Computorah: On Hidden Codes in the Torah.* Jerusalem: Achdut, 1996.

Kranzler, D. *Thy Brother's Blood: The Orthodox Jewish Response During the Holocaust.* Brooklyn, N.Y.: Mesorah Publications, 1987.

Luzzatto, M. C. *The Way of God.* Jerusalem: Feldheim, 1988.

Nash, S. G., ed. *A History of Scientific Computing*. New York: ACM Press, 1990.

Norman, B. *Secret Warfare: The Battle of Codes and Ciphers*. Newton Abbot, England: David & Charles, 1973.

Novick, N. A. *Fascinating Torah Prophecies Currently Unfolding*. Jerusalem: Netzach Yisrael Publications, 1997. Distributed by Judaica Press, New York.

Schroeder, G. *Genesis and the Big Bang*. New York: Bantam, 1990.

Weissmandl, H.M.D. *Toras Chemed* (*Torah of Delight*) (Hebrew). Mount Kisco, N.Y.: Yeshivath Mount Kisco, 1958.

Witztum, D. *HaMaimod HaNosaf* (*The Added Dimension*) (Hebrew). Jerusalem: Agudah L'Machkor Torani, 1989.

ARTICLES

Diaconis, P., and E. Engel. "A Subjective Guide to Objective Chance." *Statistical Science: A Review Journal of the Institute of Mathematical Statistics*, Vol. 1, No. 4 (November 1986), pp. 171–174.

Diaconis, P., and F. Mosteller. "Methods for Studying Coincidences." *Journal of the American Statistical Association*, Vol. 84 (1989), pp. 853–861.

Eidelberg, F., et al. "Codes in the Torah: A Discussion." *B'Or HaTorah*, No. 9 (1995) Jerusalem: Shamir.

HaSofer, A.M. "Codes in the Torah." *B'Or HaTorah*, No. 8E (1990). Jerusalem: Shamir.

Michaelson, D. "Codes in the Torah" *B'Or HaTorah*, No. 6 (1987), pp. 7–39. Jerusalem: Shamir.

Satinover, J. "Divine Authorship? Computer Reveals Startling Word Patterns." *Bible Review*, October 1995.

———. Responses to "Divine Authorship? Computer Reveals Startling Word Patterns," and Rejoinders. *Bible Review*, February 1996.

Witztum, D., E. Rips, and Y. Rosenberg. *Journal of the Royal Statistical Society*, Sect. A, 151, Pt. 1 (1988), pp.137–178. Response to D. J. Bartholomew, "Probability Statistics and Theology."

———. "Equidistant Letter Sequences in the Book of Genesis." *Statistical Science: A Review Journal of the Institute of Mathematical Statistics*, Vol. 9, No. 3 (August 1994), pp.429–438.

FOR FURTHER STUDY

Aish HaTorah/Discovery Seminars. 805 Kings Highway, Brooklyn, N.Y. 11223; 718-376-2775; E-mail: AishNY@aol.com.

Aish HaTorah, Jerusalem. 1 Rehov Shvut, Post Office Box 14149, Old City, Jerusalem, Israel; 02-894-441.

I have found the Aish HaTorah Discovery Seminar to be the single most reliable source of general information concerning the codes in the Torah. However, the reader should keep in mind that presentations on codes comprise only a small fraction of the material offered by Aish HaTorah. Discovery is chiefly an educational program that aims at demonstrating the rational basis for Jewish belief. Discovery is at present the most well-attended and fastest-growing educational outreach program of its kind and has been featured broadly in the media. Its seminars have been guest-hosted by such well-known individuals as *Seinfeld*'s Jason Alexander, Kirk Douglas, and Elliot Gould. Its programs are presented to well over 20,000 people annually throughout the world. Over 65,000 people have seen it since its inception.

Aish HaTorah was founded in 1974 by Rabbi Noah Weinberg. Its major emphasis is on providing Jews from all backgrounds with a keener appreciation for their heritage. It aims neither to urge non-Orthodox Jews toward Orthodoxy, nor to encourage people of other faiths—or of none—in the direction of conversion. It aims to provide Jews of every persuasion with good reasons to be more committed to their Judaism, and to provide all people of goodwill, whatever their religious point of view, with an understanding of why such Jewish commitment is a good thing.

The codes material in the United States is organized, presented, and continually refined by Aish HaTorah/Discovery. Rabbi Daniel Mechanic, a senior codes lecturer for the Discovery seminar, maintains what is easily the most comprehensive archive on codes-related information in the world—indeed, one might well say that he is such an archive himself. All scientific material is reviewed and updated as rapidly as possible by expert consultants, chief among them being Harold Gans, formerly Senior Cryptologic Mathematician, and Meritorious Civilian Service honoree, at the National Security Agency of the United States Department of Defense.